THE GOLDEN BOUGH

A STUDY IN MAGIC AND RELIGION

THIRD EDITION

PART V

SPIRITS OF THE CORN
AND OF THE WILD

VOL. II

SPIRITS OF THE CORN

AND OF THE WILD

BY

SIR JAMES GEORGE FRAZER

O.M., F.R.S., F.B.A.

IN TWO VOLUMES

VOL. II

LONDON

MACMILLAN & CO LTD

NEW YORK · ST MARTIN'S PRESS

1955

MACMILLAN AND COMPANY LIMITED
London Bombay Calcutta Madras Melbourne

THE MACMILLAN COMPANY OF CANADA LIMITED
Toronto

ST MARTIN'S PRESS INC
New York

PRINTED IN GREAT BRITAIN

CONTENTS

v

Chapter X.—Eating the God . . Pp. 48-108

Chapter XII.—Homoeopathic Magic
of a Flesh Diet . . . . Pp. 138-168

Chapter XIII.—Killing the Divine
Animal . . . . . . Pp. 169-203

CHAPTER XIV.—THE PROPITIATION OF

WILD ANIMALS BY HUNTERS . Pp. 204-273

CHAPTER XV.—THE PROPITIATION OF
VERMIN BY FARMERS . . . Pp. 274-284

CHAPTER IX

ANCIENT DEITIES OF VEGETATION AS ANIMALS

§ 1. *Dionysus, the Goat and the Bull*

HOWEVER we may explain it, the fact remains that in peasant folk-lore the corn-spirit is very commonly conceived and represented in animal form. May not this fact explain the relation in which certain animals stood to the ancient deities of vegetation, Dionysus, Demeter, Adonis, Attis, and Osiris?

To begin with Dionysus. We have seen that he was represented sometimes as a goat and sometimes as a bull.[1] As a goat he can hardly be separated from the minor divinities, the Pans, Satyrs, and Silenuses, all of whom are closely associated with him and are represented more or less completely in the form of goats. Thus, Pan was regularly portrayed in sculpture and painting with the face and legs of a goat.[2] The Satyrs were depicted with pointed goat-ears, and sometimes with sprouting horns and short tails.[3] They were sometimes spoken of simply as goats;[4] and in the drama their parts were played by men dressed in goatskins.[5] Silenus is represented in art clad in a goatskin.[6] Further, the Fauns, the Italian counterpart of the Greek Pans and Satyrs, are described as being half goats, with goat-feet and goat-horns.[7] Again, all these minor

Marginal notes: Ancient deities of vegetation as animals.

Dionysus as a goat: his association with the Pans, Satyrs, and Silenuses, who have been interpreted as semi-goat-shaped deities of the woods.

---

[1] See above, vol. i. pp. 16 *sqq.*
[2] Herodotus, ii. 46; L. Preller, *Griechische Mythologie,*⁴ i. (Berlin, 1894), pp. 745 *sq.*; K. Wernicke, in W. H. Roscher's *Lexikon der griech. und röm. Mythologie,* iii. 1407 *sqq.*
[3] L. Preller, *Griechische Mythologie,*³

i. 600; W. Mannhardt, *Antike Wald- und Feldkulte,* p. 138.
[4] W. Mannhardt, *op. cit.* p. 139.
[5] Julius Pollux, iv. 118.
[6] W. Mannhardt, *op. cit.* pp. 142 *sq.*
[7] Ovid, *Fasti,* ii. 361, iii. 312, v 101; *id., Heroides,* iv. 49.

goat-formed divinities partake more or less clearly of the
character of woodland deities. Thus, Pan was called by the
Arcadians the Lord of the Wood.[1] The Silenuses associated
with the tree-nymphs.[2] The Fauns are expressly designated
as woodland deities ;[3] and their character as such is still
further brought out by their association, or even identification, with Silvanus and the Silvanuses, who, as their name
of itself indicates, are spirits of the woods.[4] Lastly, the
association of the Satyrs with the Silenuses, Fauns, and
Silvanuses,[5] proves that the Satyrs also were woodland
deities. These goat-formed spirits of the woods have their
counterparts in the folk-lore of Northern Europe. Thus,
the Russian wood-spirits, called *Ljeschie* (from *ljes*, " wood ")
are believed to appear partly in human shape, but with the
horns, ears, and legs of goats. The *Ljeschi* can alter his
stature at pleasure ; when he walks in the wood he is as tall
as the trees ; when he walks in the meadows he is no higher
than the grass. Some of the *Ljeschie* are spirits of the corn
as well as of the wood ; before harvest they are as tall as
the corn-stalks, but after it they shrink to the height of
the stubble.[6] This brings out—what we have remarked
before—the close connexion between tree-spirits and corn-
spirits, and shews how easily the former may melt into the
latter. Similarly the Fauns, though wood-spirits, were believed to foster the growth of the crops.[7] We have already
seen how often the corn-spirit is represented in folk-custom
as a goat.[8] On the whole, then, as Mannhardt argues,[9]

---

[1] Macrobius, *Sat.* i. 22. 3.

[2] Homer, *Hymn to Aphrodite*, 262
sqq.

[3] Pliny, *Nat. Hist.* xii. 3 ; Ovid,
Metam. vi. 392 ; *id.*, *Fasti*, iii. 303,
309 ; Gloss. Isid. Mart. Cap. ii. 167,
cited by W. Mannhardt, *Antike Wald-
und Feldkulte*, p. 113.

[4] Pliny, *Nat. Hist.* xii. 3 ; Martianus
Capella, ii. 167 ; Augustine, *De civitate
Dei*, xv. 23 ; Aurelius Victor, *Origo
gentis Romanae*, iv. 6.

[5] Servius on Virgil, *Ecl.* vi. 14 ;
Ovid, *Metam.* vi. 392 *sq.* ; Martianus
Capella, ii. 167.

[6] W. Mannhardt, *Baumkultus*, pp.
138 *sq.* ; *id.*, *Antike Wald- und Feldkulte*, p. 145.

[7] Servius on Virgil, *Georg.* i. 10.

[8] Above, vol. i. pp. 281 *sqq.*

[9] *Antike Wald- und Feldkulte*, ch.
iii. pp. 113-211. In the text I have
allowed my former exposition of Mannhardt's theory as to ancient semi-goat-
shaped spirits of vegetation to stand as
before, but I have done so with hesitation, because the evidence adduced in
its favour appears to me insufficient to
permit us to speak with any confidence
on the subject. Pan may have been,
as W. H. Roscher and L. R. Farnell
think, nothing more than a herdsman's
god, the semi-human, semi-bestial representative of goats in particular. See W.
H. Roscher's *Lexikon der griech. und
röm. Mythologie*, iii. 1405 *sq.* ; L. R.

the Pans, Satyrs, and Fauns perhaps belong to a widely diffused class of wood-spirits conceived in goat-form. The fondness of goats for straying in woods and nibbling the bark of trees, to which indeed they are most destructive, is an obvious and perhaps sufficient reason why wood-spirits should so often be supposed to take the form of goats. The inconsistency of a god of vegetation subsisting upon the vegetation which he personifies is not one to strike the primitive mind. Such inconsistencies arise when the deity, ceasing to be immanent in the vegetation, comes to be regarded as its owner or lord ; for the idea of owning the vegetation naturally leads to that of subsisting on it. We have already seen that the corn-spirit, originally conceived as immanent in the corn, afterwards comes to be regarded as its owner, who lives on it and is reduced to poverty and want by being deprived of it.[1]

Thus the representation of wood-spirits in the form of goats appears to be both widespread and, to the primitive mind, natural. Therefore when we find, as we have done, that Dionysus—a tree-god—is sometimes represented in goat-form,[2] we can hardly avoid concluding that this representation is simply a part of his proper character as a tree-god and is not to be explained by the fusion of two distinct and independent worships, in one of which he originally appeared as a tree-god and in the other as a goat. If such a fusion took place in the case of Dionysus, it must equally have taken place in the case of the Pans and Satyrs of Greece, the Fauns of Italy, and the *Ljeschie* of Russia. That such a fusion of two wholly disconnected worships should have occurred once is possible ; that it should have occurred twice independently is improbable ; that it should have occurred thrice independently is so unlikely as to be practically incredible. *Wood-spirits in the form of goats.*

Dionysus was also figured, as we have seen,[3] in the shape of a bull. After what has gone before we are naturally led to expect that his bull form must have been only another *The bull as an embodiment of Dionysus*

Farnell, *The Cults of the Greek States,* v. (Oxford, 1909) pp. 431 *sqq.* And the Satyrs and Silenuses seem to have more affinity with horses than with goats. See W. H. Roscher's *Lexikon*

der *griech. und röm. Mythologie,* iv. 444 *sqq.*

[1] Above, vol. i. pp. 231 *sqq.*
[2] Above, vol. i. pp. 17 *sq.*
[3] Above, vol. i. pp. 16 *sq.*

seems to be
another ex-
pression of
his charac-
ter as a god
of vegeta-
tion.
expression for his character as a deity of vegetation, especially
as the bull is a common embodiment of the corn-spirit in
Northern Europe;[1] and the close association of Dionysus
with Demeter and Persephone in the mysteries of Eleusis
shews that he had at least strong agricultural affinities.
The other possible explanation of the bull-shaped Dionysus
would be that the conception of him as a bull was originally
entirely distinct from the conception of him as a deity of
vegetation, and that the fusion of the two conceptions was
due to some such circumstance as the union of two tribes,
one of which had previously worshipped a bull-god and the
other a tree-god.   This appears to be the view taken by
Mr. Andrew Lang, who suggests that the bull-formed
Dionysus "had either been developed out of, or had succeeded to, the worship of a bull-totem."[2]   Of course this is
possible.   But it is not yet certain that the Aryans ever had
totemism.[3]   On the other hand, it is quite certain that many
Aryan peoples have conceived deities of vegetation as
embodied in animal forms.   Therefore when we find
amongst an Aryan people like the Greeks a deity of
vegetation represented as an animal, the presumption must
be in favour of explaining this by a principle which is
certainly known to have influenced the Aryan race rather
than by one which is not certainly known to have done so.
In the present state of our knowledge, therefore, it is safer
to regard the bull form of Dionysus as being, like his goat
form, an expression of his proper character as a deity of
vegetation.

The *bou-
phonia*, an
Athenian
sacrifice of
an ox to
Zeus
Polieus.
The probability of this view will be somewhat increased
if it can be shewn that in other rites than those of Dionysus
the ancients slew an ox as a representative of the spirit of
vegetation.   This they appear to have done in the Athenian
sacrifice known as "the murder of the ox" (*bouphonia*).   It
took place about the end of June or beginning of July, that
is, about the time when the threshing is nearly over in
Attica.   According to tradition the sacrifice was instituted
to procure a cessation of drought and dearth which had

---

[1] Above, vol. i. pp. 288 *sqq.*

[2] A. Lang, *Myth*, *Ritual*, *and*

Religion,[2] ii. 252.

[3] Compare *Totemism and Exogamy*, iv. 12 *sqq.*

afflicted the land. The ritual was as follows. Barley mixed with wheat, or cakes made of them, were laid upon the bronze altar of Zeus Polieus on the Acropolis. Oxen were driven round the altar, and the ox which went up to the altar and ate the offering on it was sacrificed. The axe and knife with which the beast was slain had been previously wetted with water brought by maidens called "water-carriers." The weapons were then sharpened and handed to the butchers, one of whom felled the ox with the axe and another cut its throat with the knife. As soon as he had felled the ox, the former threw the axe from him and fled ; and the man who cut the beast's throat apparently imitated his example. Meantime the ox was skinned and all present partook of its flesh. Then the hide was stuffed with straw and sewed up ; next the stuffed animal was set on its feet and yoked to a plough as if it were ploughing. A trial then took place in an ancient law-court presided over by the King (as he was called) to determine who had murdered the ox. The maidens who had brought the water accused the men who had sharpened the axe and knife ; the men who had sharpened the axe and knife blamed the men who had handed these implements to the butchers ; the men who had handed the implements to the butchers blamed the butchers ; and the butchers laid the blame on the axe and knife, which were accordingly found guilty, condemned and cast into the sea.[1] The name of this sacrifice,—"the *murder* of the ox," [2]—

---

[1] Pausanias, i. 24. 4 ; *id.*, i. 28. 10 ; Porphyry, *De abstinentia*, ii. 29 *sq.* ; Aelian, *Var. Hist.* viii. 3 ; Scholia on Aristophanes, *Peace*, 419, and *Clouds*, 985; Hesychius, Suidas, and *Etymologicum Magnum, s.v.* βούφονια ; Suidas, *s.v.* Θαύλων ; Im. Bekker's *Anecdota Graeca* (Berlin, 1814-1821), p. 238, *s.v.* Διπόλια. The date of the sacrifice (14th Scirophorion) is given by the Scholiast on Aristophanes and the *Etymologicum Magnum* ; and this date corresponds, according to W. Mannhardt (*Mythologische Forschungen*, p. 68), with the close of the threshing in Attica. No writer mentions the trial of both the axe and the knife. Pausanias speaks of the trial of the axe, Porphyry and Aelian of the trial of the knife. But

from Porphyry's description it is clear that the slaughter was carried out by two men, one wielding an axe and the other a knife, and that the former laid the blame on the latter. Perhaps the knife alone was condemned. That the King (as to whom see *The Magic Art and the Evolution of Kings*, i. 44 *sq.*) presided at the trial of all lifeless objects, is mentioned by Aristotle (*Constitution of Athens*, 57) and Julius Pollux (viii. 90, compare viii. 120).

[2] The real import of the name *bouphonia* was first perceived by W. Robertson Smith. See his *Religion of the Semites*,[2] pp. 304 *sqq.* In Cos also an ox specially chosen was sacrificed to Zeus Polieus. See Dittenberger, *Sylloge Inscriptionum*

the pains taken by each person who had a hand in the slaughter to lay the blame on some one else, together with the formal trial and punishment of the axe or knife or both, prove that the ox was here regarded not merely as a victim offered to a god, but as itself a sacred creature, the slaughter of which was sacrilege or murder. This is borne out by a statement of Varro that to kill an ox was formerly a capital crime in Attica.[1] The mode of selecting the victim suggests that the ox which tasted the corn was viewed as the corn-deity taking possession of his own. This interpretation is supported by the following custom. In Beauce, in the district of Orleans, on the twenty-fourth or twenty-fifth of April they make a straw-man called " the great *mondard.*" For they say that the old *mondard* is now dead and it is necessary to make a new one. The straw-man is carried in solemn procession up and down the village and at last is placed upon the oldest apple-tree. There he remains till the apples are gathered, when he is taken down and thrown into the water, or he is burned and his ashes cast into water. But the person who plucks the first fruit from the tree succeeds to the title of " the great *mondard.*"[2] Here the straw figure, called " the great *mondard*" and placed on the oldest apple-tree in spring, represents the spirit of the tree, who, dead in winter, revives when the apple-blossoms appear on the boughs. Thus the person who plucks the first fruit from the tree and thereby receives the name of " the great *mondard*" must be regarded as a representative of the tree - spirit. Primitive peoples are usually reluctant to taste the annual first-fruits of any crop, until some ceremony has been performed which makes it safe and pious for them to do so.

Graecarum,[2] No. 616; Ch. Michel, *Recueil d'Inscriptions Grecques,* No. 716; H. Collitz und F. Bechtel, *Sammlung der griechischen Dialekt-Inschriften,* iii. pp. 357 *sqq.,* No. 3636; J. de Prott et L. Ziehen, *Leges Graecorum Sacrae e Titulis collectae,* Fasciculus i. (Leipsic, 1896) pp. 19 *sqq.,* No. 5; M. P. Nilsson, *Griechische Feste* (Leipsic, 1906), pp. 17-21. A month Bouphonion, corresponding to the Attic Boedromion (September), occurred in the calendars of Delos and

Tenos. See E. Bischoff, " De fastis Graecorum antiquioribus," in *Leipziger Studien für classische Philologie,* vii. (Leipsic, 1884) p. 414.

[1] Varro, *De re rustica,* ii. 5. 4. Compare Columella, *De re rustica,* vi. praef. § 7. Perhaps, however, Varro's statement may be merely an inference drawn from the ritual of the *bouphonia* and the legend told to explain it.

[2] W. Mannhardt, *Baumkultus,* p. 409.

The reason of this reluctance appears to be a belief that the
first-fruits either belong to or actually contain a divinity.
Therefore when a man or animal is seen boldly to appropriate the sacred first-fruits, he or it is naturally regarded
as the divinity himself in human or animal form taking
possession of his own.   The time of the Athenian sacrifice,
which fell about the close of the threshing, suggests that the
wheat and barley laid upon the altar were a harvest offering ; and the sacramental character of the subsequent repast
—all partaking of the flesh of the divine animal—would
make it parallel to the harvest-suppers of modern Europe,
in which, as we have seen, the flesh of the animal who stands
for the corn-spirit is eaten by the harvesters.   Again, the
tradition that the sacrifice was instituted in order to put an
end to drought and famine is in favour of taking it as a
harvest festival.   The resurrection of the corn-spirit, enacted
by setting up the stuffed ox and yoking it to the plough,
may be compared with the resurrection of the tree-spirit in
the person of his representative, the Wild Man.[1]

    Still more clearly, perhaps, does the identification of the Sacrifice of
corn-spirit with an ox come out in the sacrificial ritual which an ox to
the Greeks of Magnesia on the Maeander observed in honour polis at
of Zeus Sosipolis, a god whose title of Sosipolis (" Saviour Magnesia
of the City ") marks him as the equivalent of Zeus Polieus Maeander.
(" Zeus of the City ").   The details of the ritual are happily
preserved in an inscription, which records a decree of the
council and of the people for the regulation of the whole
proceedings.   Every year at a festival in the month of
Heraeon the magistrates bought the finest bull that could
be had for money, and at the new moon of the month of
Cronion, at the time when the sowing was about to begin,
they and the priests dedicated the animal to Zeus Sosipolis,
while solemn prayers were offered by the voice of a sacred
herald for the welfare of the city, of the land, and of the
people, for peace and wealth, for the corn-crops and all
other fruits, and for the cattle.   Thereafter the sacred
animal was kept throughout the winter, its keep being
undertaken by a contractor, who was bound by law to drive
the bull to the market and there collect contributions for its

[1] See *The Dying God*, p. 208.

maintenance from all the hucksters and in particular from the corn-chandlers ; and a prospect was held out to such as contributed that it would go well with them.   Finally, after having been thus maintained at the public cost for some months, the bull was led forth with great pomp and sacrificed in the market-place on the twelfth day of the month Artemision, which is believed to have been equivalent to the Attic month of Thargelion and to the English month of May, the season when the corn is reaped in the Greek lowlands. In the procession which attended the animal to the place of sacrifice the senators, the priests, the magistrates, the young people, and the victors in the games all bore a part, and at the head of the procession were borne the images of the Twelve Gods attired in festal array, while a fluteplayer, a piper, and a harper discoursed solemn music.[1]   Now in the bull, which was thus dedicated at the time of sowing and kept at the cost of the pious, and especially of corn-chandlers, to be finally sacrificed at harvest, it is reasonable to see an embodiment of the corn-spirit.   Regarded as such the animal was consecrated when the seed was committed to the earth ; it was fed and kept all the time the corn was growing in order that by its beneficent energies it might foster that growth ; and at last, to complete the parallel, when the corn was reaped the animal was slain, the cutting of the stalks being regarded as the death of the corn-spirit.[2] Similarly we have seen that in the harvest-fields and on the threshing-floors of modern Europe the corn-spirit is often conceived in the form of a bull, an ox, or a calf, which is supposed to be killed at reaping or threshing ; and,

The bull so sacrificed seems to have been regarded as an embodiment of the corn-spirit.

---

[1] Dittenberger, *Sylloge Inscriptionum Graecarum* [2] (Leipsic, 1898-1901), vol. ii. pp. 246-248, No. 553. As to the identification of the Magnesian month Artemision with the Attic month Thargelion (May), see Dittenberger, *op. cit.* ii. p. 242, No. 552 note [4]. It is interesting to observe that at Magnesia the sowing took place in Cronion, the month of Cronus, a god whom the ancients regularly identified with Saturn, the Italian god of sowing.   In Samos, Perinthus, and Patmos, however, the month Cronion seems to have been equivalent to the

Attic Scirophorion, a month corresponding to June or July, which could never have been a season of sowing in the hot rainless summers of Greece. See E. Bischoff, "De fastis Graecorum antiquioribus," in *Leipziger Studien für classische Philologie*, vii. (1884) p. 400 ; Dittenberger, *Sylloge Inscriptionum Graecarum*,[2] No. 645 note [14], vol. ii. p. 449.

[2] In thus interpreting the sacrifice of the bull at Magnesia I follow the excellent exposition of Professor M. P. Nilsson, *Griechische Feste* (Leipsic, 1906), pp. 23-27.

further, we saw that the conception is sometimes carried out in practice by slaughtering a real ox or a real calf on the harvest-field. Thus the parallelism between the ancient Greek and the modern European idea of the corn-spirit embodied in the form of a bull appears to be very close.

On the interpretation which I have adopted of the sacrifices offered to Zeus Polieus and Zeus Sosipolis the corn-spirit is conceived as a male, not as a female, as Zeus, not as Demeter or Persephone. In this there is no inconsistency. At the stage of thought which the Greeks had reached long before the dawn of history they supposed the processes of reproduction in nature to be carried on by a male and a female principle in conjunction ; they did not believe, like some backward savages, that the female principle alone suffices for that purpose, and that the aid of the male principle is superfluous. Hence, as we have seen, they imagined that the goddesses of the corn, the mother Demeter and the daughter Persephone, had each her male partner with whom she united for the production of the crops. The partner of Demeter was Zeus, the partner of Persephone was his brother Pluto, the Subterranean Zeus, as he was called ; and reasons have been shewn for thinking that the marriage of one or other of these divine pairs was solemnised at Eleusis as part of the Great Mysteries in order to promote the growth of the corn.[1]

> *The Greek conception of the corn-spirit as both male and female*

The ox appears as a representative of the corn-spirit in other parts of the world. At Great Bassam, in Guinea, two oxen are slain annually to procure a good harvest. If the sacrifice is to be effectual, it is necessary that the oxen should weep. So all the women of the village sit in front of the beasts, chanting, " The ox will weep ; yes, he will weep ! " From time to time one of the women walks round the beasts, throwing manioc meal or palm wine upon them, especially into their eyes. When tears roll down from the eyes of the oxen, the people dance, singing, " The ox weeps ! the ox weeps ! " Then two men seize the tails of the beasts and cut them off at one blow. It is believed that a great misfortune will happen in the course of the year if the tails are not severed at one blow. The oxen are after-

> *The ox as a representative of the corn-spirit at Great Bassam in Guinea.*

---

[1] See above, vol. i. pp. 36 *sq.*, 65 *sqq.*

wards killed, and their flesh is eaten by the chiefs.[1] Here
the tears of the oxen, like those of the human victims
amongst the Khonds and the Aztecs,[2] are probably a rain-
charm.   We have already seen that the virtue of the corn-
spirit, embodied in animal form, is sometimes supposed to
reside in the tail, and that the last handful of corn is sometimes conceived as the tail of the corn spirit.[8]   In the
Mithraic religion this conception is graphically set forth in
some of the numerous sculptures which represent Mithras
kneeling on the back of a bull and plunging a knife into its
flank ; for on certain of these monuments the tail of the
bull ends in three stalks of corn, and in one of them corn-
stalks instead of blood are seen issuing from the wound
inflicted by the knife.[4]   Such representations certainly
suggest that the bull, whose sacrifice appears to have
formed a leading feature in the Mithraic ritual, was conceived, in one at least of its aspects, as an incarnation of
the corn-spirit.

The ox as a personi-
fication of the corn-
spirit in China.

Still more clearly does the ox appear as a personification
of the corn-spirit in a ceremony which is observed in all the
provinces and districts of China to welcome the approach of
spring.   On the first day of spring, usually on the third or
fourth of February, which is also the beginning of the Chinese
New Year, the governor or prefect of the city goes in procession to the east gate of the city, and sacrifices to the Divine
Husbandman, who is represented with a bull's head on the
body of a man.   A large effigy of an ox, cow, or buffalo has
been prepared for the occasion, and stands outside of the
east gate, with agricultural implements beside it.   The
figure is made of differently-coloured pieces of paper pasted
on a framework either by a blind man or according to the
directions of a necromancer.   The colours of the paper
prognosticate the character of the coming year ; if red
prevails, there will be many fires ; if white, there will be
floods and rain ; and so with the other colours.   The

[1] H. Hecquard, *Reise an die Küste
und in das Innere von West-Afrika*
(Leipsic, 1854), pp. 41-43.
    [2] See above, vol. i. p. 248.
    [8] Above, vol. i. pp. 268, 272.
    [4] Franz Cumont, *Textes et Monu-*

*ments figurés relatifs aux Mystères de
Mithra* (Brussels, 1896-1899), ii.
figures 18, 19, 20, 59 (p. 228, corn-
stalks issuing from wound), 67, 70, 78,
87, 105, 143, 168, 215, also plates v
and vi.

mandarins walk slowly round the ox, beating it severely at each step with rods of various hues. It is filled with five kinds of grain, which pour forth when the effigy is broken by the blows of the rods. The paper fragments are then set on fire, and a scramble takes place for the burning fragments, because the people believe that whoever gets one of them is sure to be fortunate throughout the year. A live buffalo is next killed, and its flesh is divided among the mandarins. According to one account, the effigy of the ox is made of clay, and, after being beaten by the governor, is stoned by the people till they break it in pieces, "from which they expect an abundant year." [1]   But the ceremony varies somewhat in the different provinces. According to another account the effigy of the cow, made of earthenware, with gilded horns, is borne in procession, and is of such colossal dimensions that forty or fifty men can hardly carry it. Behind this monstrous cow walks a boy with one foot shod and the other bare, personifying the Genius of Industry. He beats the effigy with a rod, as if to drive it forward. A great many little clay cows are afterwards taken out of the large one and distributed among the people. Both the big cow and the little ones are then broken in pieces, and the people take the sherds home with them in order to grind them to powder and strew the powder on their fields, for they think thus to secure a plentiful harvest.[2]   In the cities nearest to Weihaiwei, in northern China, the ceremony of "the Beginning of Spring" is a moveable feast, which falls usually in the first moon. The local magistrate and his attendants go in procession to the eastern suburbs of the city to "meet the Spring." A great pasteboard effigy of an ox is carried in the procession, together with another pasteboard image of a man called Mang-Shen, "who represents either the

[1] *China Review*, i. (July 1872 to June 1873, Hongkong), pp. 62, 154, 162, 203 *sq.* ; Rev. J. Doolittle, *Social Life of the Chinese*, ed. Paxton Hood (London, 1868), pp. 375 *sq.* ; Rev. J. H. Gray, *China* (London, 1878), ii. 115 *sq.*

[2] *Ostasiatischer Lloyd*, March 14, 1890, quoted by J. D. E. Schmeltz, " Das Pflugfest in China," *Internationales Archiv für Ethnographie*, xi. (1898) p. 79. With this account the one given by S. W. Williams (*The Middle Kingdom* (New York and London, 1848, ii. 109) substantially agrees. In many districts, according to the *Ostasiatischer Lloyd*, the Genius of Spring is represented at this festival by a boy of blameless character, clad in green. As to the custom of going with one foot bare and the other shod, see *Taboo and the Perils of the Soul*, pp. 311-313.

typical ox-driver or ploughman or the god of Agriculture."
On the return of the procession to the magistrate's court,
that dignitary himself and his principal colleagues beat and
prod the pasteboard ox with wands, after which the effigy
is burned along with the image of its attendant. The
colours and apparel of the two effigies correspond with the
forecasts of the Chinese almanack. Thus if the head of the
ox is yellow, the summer will be very hot ; if it is green,
the spring will be sickly ; if it is red, there will be a
drought ; if it is black, there will be much rain; if it is
white, there will be high winds. If Mang-Shen wears a hat,
the year will be dry ; if he is bareheaded, it will be rainy ;
and so on with the other articles of his apparel. Besides
the pasteboard ox a miniature ox made of clay is also
supposed to be provided.[1] In Chinese the ceremony is
called indifferently " beating the ox " and " beating the
spring," which seems to prove that the ox is identified with
the vernal energies of nature. We may suppose that originally the ox which figures in the rite was a living animal, but
ever since the beginning of our era, when the custom first
appears in history, it has been an effigy of terra-cotta or
pasteboard. To this day the Chinese calendar devotes a
page to a picture of " the ox of spring " with Mang, the
tutelary genius of spring, standing beside it and grasping a
willow-bough, with which he is about to beat the animal for
the purpose of stimulating its reproductive virtue.[2] In one
form of this Chinese custom the corn-spirit appears to be
plainly represented by the corn-filled ox, whose fragments
may therefore be supposed to bring fertility with them. We
may compare the Silesian custom of burning the effigy of
Death, scrambling for the burning fragments, and burying
them in the fields to secure a good crop, and the Florentine
custom of sawing the Old Woman and scrambling for the
dried fruits with which she was filled.[3] Both these customs,
like their Chinese counterpart, are observed in spring.

The practice of beating an earthenware or pasteboard

[1] R. F. Johnston, *Lion and Dragon in Northern China* (London, 1910), pp. 180-182.

[2] Ed. Chavannes, *Le T'ai Chan, Essai de Monographie d'un Culte*

Chinois (Paris, 1910), p. 500 (*Annales du Musée Guimet, Bibliothèque d'Études*, vol. xxi.).

[3] See *The Dying God*, pp. 240 *sq.*, 250.

image of an ox in spring is not confined to China proper, The ox as
but seems to be widely spread in the east of Asia; for ex- a personifi
ample, it has been recorded at Kashgar and in Annam. the corn-
Thus a French traveller has described how at Kashgar, spirit in
on the third of February 1892, a mandarin, clad in his and
finest robes and borne in a magnificent palanquin, conducted
solemnly through the streets the pasteboard image of an ox,
"a sacred animal devoted to the deity of spring who gives
life to the fields. It is thus carried to some distance outside
of the town on the eastern side. The official who acts as
pontiff ceremoniously offers food and libations to it in order
to obtain a fruitful year, and next day it is demolished by
the lashes of a whip." [1]   Again, in Annam, every year at
the approach of spring the Department of Rites publishes
instructions to the provincial governors as to the manner in
which the festival of the inauguration of spring is to be celebrated. Among the indispensable features of the festival
are the figures of an ox and its warder made of terra-cotta.
The attitudes of the two and the colours to be applied to
them are carefully prescribed every year in the Chinese
calendar. Popular opinion attributes to the colour of the ox
and the accoutrement of its warder, who is called Mang
Than, a certain influence on the crops of the year: a green,
yellow, and black buffalo prognosticates an abundant harvest:
a red or white buffalo foretells wretched crops and great
droughts or hurricanes. If Mang Than is represented wearing a large hat, the year will be rainy; if on the other hand

---

1 J. L. Dutreuil de Rhins, *Mission Scientifique dans la Haute Asie, 1890–1895*, i. (Paris, 1897) pp. 95 *sq.* After describing the ceremony as he witnessed it at Kashgar, the writer adds : " Probably the ox was at first a living animal which they sacrificed and dis- tributed the flesh to the bystanders. At the present day the official who acts as pontiff has a number of small pasteboard oxen made, which he sends to the notables in order that they may participate intimately in the sacrifice, which is more than symbolical. The reason for carrying the ox a long distance is that as much as possible of the territory may be sanctified by the passage of the sacred animal, and that as many people as possible may share in the sacrifice, at least with their eyes and good wishes. The procession, which begins very early in the morn- ing, moves eastward, that is, toward the quarter where, the winter being now over, the first sun of spring may be expected to appear, whose divinity the ceremony is intended to render propitious. It is needless to insist on the analogy between this Chinese fes- tival and our Carnival, at which, about the same season, a fat ox is led about. Both festivals have their origin in the same conceptions of ancient natural religion."

he is bareheaded, long barren droughts are to be feared. Nay, the public credulity goes so far as to draw good or evil omens from the cheerfulness or ill humour which may be detected on the features of the Warder of the Ox. Having been duly prepared in accordance with the directions of the almanack, the ox and its warder are carried in procession, followed by the mandarins and the people, to the altar of Spring, which is usually to be found in every provincial capital. There the provincial governor offers fruits, flowers, and incense to the Genius of Spring (*Xuan Quan*), and gold and silver paper money are burnt on the altar in profusion. Lastly the ox and his warder are buried in a spot which has been indicated by a geomancer.[1] It is interesting to observe that the three colours of the ox which are taken to prognosticate good crops, to wit, green, yellow, and black, are precisely the colours which the ancients attributed to Demeter, the goddess of the corn.[2]

Annual inauguration of ploughing by the Chinese emperor.

The great importance which the Chinese attach to the performance of rites for the fertility of the ground is proved by an ancient custom which is, or was till lately, observed every year in spring. On an appointed day the emperor himself, attended by the highest dignitaries of the state, guides with his own hand the ox-drawn plough down several furrows and scatters the seed in a sacred field, or "field of God," as it is called, the produce of which is afterwards examined from time to time with anxious care by the Governor of Peking, who draws omens from the appearance of the ears ; it is a very happy omen if he should chance to find thirteen ears growing on one stalk. To prepare himself for the celebration of this solemn rite the emperor is expected to fast and remain continent for three days previously, and the princes and mandarins who accompany him to the field are bound to observe similar restrictions. The corn grown on the holy field which has thus been ploughed by the imperial hands is collected in yellow sacks and stored in a special granary to be used by the emperor in certain solemn sacrifices which he offers to the god

---

[1] Colonel E. Diguet, *Les Annamites, Société, Coutumes, Religions* (Paris, 1906), pp. 250-253.

[2] See above, vol. i. pp. 41 *sq.*, and below, pp. 21 *sq.*

Chan Ti and to his own ancestors. In the provinces of China the season of ploughing is similarly inaugurated by the provincial governors as representatives of the emperor.[1]

The sacred field, or "field of God," in which the emperor of China thus ceremonially opens the ploughing for the year, and of which the produce is employed in sacrifice, reminds us of the Rarian plain at Eleusis, in which a sacred ploughing similarly took place every year, and of which the produce was in like manner devoted to sacrifice.[2] Further, it recalls the little sacred rice-fields on which the Kayans of central Borneo inaugurate the various operations of the agricultural year by performing them in miniature.[3] As I have already pointed out, all such consecrated enclosures were probably in origin what we may call spiritual preserves, that is, patches of ground which men set apart for the exclusive use of the corn-spirit to console him for the depredations they committed on all the rest of his domains. Again, the rule of fasting and continence observed by the Emperor of China and his august colleagues before they put their hands to the plough resembles the similar customs of abstinence practised by many savages as a preparation for engaging in the various labours of the field.[4]

Analogy of the Chinese custom to the agricultural rites at Eleusis and elsewhere.'

[1] Du Halde, *The General History of China*, Third Edition (London, 1741), ii. 120-122 ; Huc, *L'Empire Chinois* (Paris, 1879), ii. 338-343 ; Rev. J. H. Gray, *China* (London, 1878), ii. 116-118. Compare *The Sacred Books of China*, translated by James Legge, Part iii., *The Lî Kî* (*Sacred Books of the East*, vol. xxvii., Oxford, 1885), pp. 254 *sq.* : "In this month [the first month of spring] the son of Heaven on the first day prays to God for a good year ; and afterwards, the day of the first conjunction of the sun and moon having been chosen, with the handle and share of the plough in the carriage, placed between the man-at-arms who is its third occupant and the driver, he conducts his three ducal ministers, his nine high ministers, the feudal princes and his Great officers, all with their own hands to plough the field of God. The son of Heaven turns up three furrows, each of the

ducal ministers five, and the other ministers and feudal princes nine. When they return, he takes in his hand a cup in the great chamber, all the others being in attendance on him and the Great officers, and says, 'Drink this cup of comfort after your toil.' In this month the vapours of heaven descend and those of the earth ascend. Heaven and earth are in harmonious co-operation. All plants bud and grow." Here the selection of a day in spring when sun and moon are in conjunction is significant. Such conjunctions are regarded as marriages of the great luminaries and therefore as the proper seasons for the celebration of rites designed to promote fertility. See *The Dying God*, p. 73.

[2] See above, pp. 74, 108.

[3] See above, p. 93.

[4] See above, pp. 94, 109; *The Magic Art and the Evolution of Kings*, ii. 105 *sqq.*

The rend-
ing of live
animals in
the rites of
Dionysus. On the whole we may perhaps conclude that both as a goat and as a bull Dionysus was essentially a god of vegetation. The Chinese and European customs which I have cited[1] may perhaps shed light on the custom of rending a live bull or goat at the rites of Dionysus. The animal was torn in fragments, as the Khond victim was cut in pieces, in order that the worshippers might each secure a portion of the life-giving and fertilising influence of the god. The flesh was eaten raw as a sacrament, and we may conjecture that some of it was taken home to be buried in the fields, or otherwise employed so as to convey to the fruits of the earth the quickening influence of the god of vegetation. The resurrection of Dionysus, related in his myth, may have been enacted in his rites by stuffing and setting up the slain ox, as was done at the Athenian *bouphonia*.

§ 2. Demeter, the Pig and the Horse

Association
of the pig
with
Demeter. Passing next to the corn-goddess Demeter, and remembering that in European folk-lore the pig is a common embodiment of the corn-spirit,[2] we may now ask whether the pig, which was so closely associated with Demeter, may not have been originally the goddess herself in animal form? The pig was sacred to her;[3] in art she was portrayed carrying or accompanied by a pig;[4] and the pig was regularly sacrificed in her mysteries, the reason assigned being that the pig injures the corn and is therefore an enemy of the goddess.[5] But after an animal has been conceived as a god, or a god as an animal, it sometimes happens, as we have seen, that the god sloughs off his animal form and becomes purely anthropomorphic; and that then the animal, which at first had been slain in the character of the god, comes to be viewed as a victim offered

---

[1] As to the European customs, see above, p. 12.

[2] See above, vol. i. pp. 298 *sqq*.

[3] Scholiast on Aristophanes, *Acharn.* 747.

[4] J. Overbeck, *Griechische Kunstmythologie*, Besonderer Theil, ii. (Leipsic, 1873-1878), p. 493; Müller-

Wieseler, *Denkmäler der alten Kunst,* ii. pl. viii. 94.

[5] Hyginus, *Fab.* 277; Cornutus, *Theologiae Graecae Compendium*, 28; Macrobius, *Saturn.* i. 12. 23; Scholiast on Aristophanes, *Acharn.* 747; *id.*, on *Frogs,* 338; *id.*, on *Peace,* 374; Servius on Virgil, *Georg.* ii. 380; Aelian, *Nat. Anim.* x. 16.

to the god on the ground of its hostility to the deity; in short, the god is sacrificed to himself on the ground that he is his own enemy. This happened to Dionysus,[1] and it may have happened to Demeter also. And in fact the rites of one of her festivals, the Thesmophoria, bear out the view that originally the pig was an embodiment of the corn-goddess herself, either Demeter or her daughter and double Persephone. The Attic Thesmophoria was an autumn festival, celebrated by women alone in October,[2] and appears to have represented with mourning rites the descent of Persephone (or Demeter)[3] into the lower world, and with joy her return from the dead.[4] Hence the name Descent or Ascent variously applied to the first, and the name *Kalligeneia* (fair-born) applied to the third day of the festival. Now from an old scholium on Lucian[5] we learn some details about the mode of celebrating the Thesmophoria, which shed important light on the part of the festival called the Descent or the Ascent. The scholiast tells us that it was customary at the Thesmophoria to throw pigs, cakes of dough, and branches of pine-trees into "the chasms of Demeter and Persephone," which appear to have been sacred caverns or vaults.[6] In these caverns or vaults

Pigs in the ritual of the Thesmophoria.

[1] See above, vol. i. pp. 22 *sq.*

[2] As to the Thesmophoria see my article "Thesmophoria" in the *Encyclopaedia Britannica*, Ninth Edition, vol. xxiii. 295 *sqq.*; August Mommsen, *Feste der Stadt Athen im Altertum* (Leipsic, 1898), pp. 308 *sqq.*; Miss J. E. Harrison, *Prolegomena to the Study of Greek Religion*[2] (Cambridge, 1908), pp. 120 *sqq.*; M. P. Nilsson, *Griechische Feste* (Leipsic, 1906), pp. 313 *sqq.*; L. R. Farnell, *The Cults of the Greek States*, iii. (Oxford, 1907) pp. 75 *sqq.* At Thebes and in Delos the Thesmophoria was held in summer, in the month of Metageitnion (August). See Xenophon, *Hellenica*, v. 2. 29; M. P. Nilsson, *Griechische Feste*, pp. 316 *sq.*

[3] Photius, *Lexicon*, s.v. στήνια, speaks of the ascent of *Demeter* from the lower world; and Clement of Alexandria speaks of both Demeter and Persephone as having been engulfed in the chasm (*Protrept.* ii. 17). The original equivalence of Demeter and Persephone

must be borne steadily in mind.

[4] Plutarch, *Isis et Osiris*, 69; Photius, *Lexicon, s.v.* στήνια.

[5] E. Rohde, "Unedirte Lucians-scholien, die attischen Thesmophorien und Haloen betreffend," *Rheinisches Museum*, N.F., xxv. (1870) p. 548; *Scholia in Lucianum*, ed. H. Rabe (Leipsic, 1906), pp. 275 *sq.* Two passages of classical writers (Clement of Alexandria, *Protrept.* ii. 17, and Pausanias, ix. 8. 1) refer to the rites described by the scholiast on Lucian, and had been rightly interpreted by Chr. A. Lobeck (*Aglaophamus*, pp. 827 *sqq.*) before the discovery of the scholia.

[6] The scholiast speaks of them as *megara* and *adyta*. The name *megara* is thought to be derived from a Phoenician word meaning "cavern," "subterranean chasm," the Hebrew מערה. See F. C. Movers, *Die Phoenizier* (Bonn, 1841), i. 220. In Greek usage the *megara* were properly sub-

there were said to be serpents, which guarded the caverns and consumed most of the flesh of the pigs and dough-cakes which were thrown in. Afterwards—apparently at the next annual festival [1]—the decayed remains of the pigs, the cakes, and the pine - branches were fetched by women called "drawers," who, after observing rules of ceremonial purity for three days, descended into the caverns, and, frightening away the serpents by clapping their hands, brought up the remains and placed them on the altar. Whoever got a piece of the decayed flesh and cakes, and sowed it with the seed-corn in his field, was believed to be sure of a good crop. With the feeding of the serpents in the vaults by the women we may compare an ancient Italian ritual. At Lanuvium a serpent lived in a sacred cave within a grove of Juno. On certain appointed days a number of holy maidens, with their eyes bandaged, entered the grove carrying cakes of barley in their hands. Led, as it was believed, by the divine spirit, they walked straight to the serpent's den and offered him the cakes. If they were chaste, the serpent ate the cakes, the parents of the girls rejoiced, and farmers prognosticated an abundant harvest. But if the girls were unchaste, the serpent left the cakes untasted, and ants came and crumbled the rejected viands and so removed them bit by bit from the sacred grove, thereby purifying the hallowed spot from the stain it had contracted by the presence of a defiled maiden.[2]

To explain the rude and ancient ritual of the Thesmo-

The sacred serpent at Lanuvium.

---

terranean vaults or chasms sacred to the gods. See Hesychius, quoted by Movers, *l.c.* (the passage does not appear in M. Schmidt's minor edition of Hesychius); Porphyry, *De antro nympharum*, 6; and my note on Pausanias, ii. 2. 1.

[1] We infer this from Pausanias, ix. 8. 1, though the passage is incomplete and apparently corrupt. For ἐν Δωδώνῃ Lobeck (*Aglaophamus*, pp. 829 *sq.*) proposed to read ἀναδῦναι or ἀναδοθῆαι. At the spring and autumn festivals of Isis at Tithorea geese and goats were thrown into the *adyton* and left there till the following festival, when the remains were removed and buried at a

certain spot a little way from the temple. See Pausanias, x. 32. 14. This analogy supports the view that the pigs thrown into the caverns at the Thesmophoria were left there till the next festival.

[2] Aelian, *De natura animalium*, xi. 16; Propertius, v. 8. 3-14. The feeding of the serpent is represented on a Roman coin of about 64 B.C.; on the obverse of the coin appears the head of Juno Caprotina. See E. Babelon, *Monnaies de la République Romaine* (Paris, 1886), ii. 402. A common type of Greek art represents a woman feeding a serpent out of a saucer. See *Adonis, Attis, Osiris*, Second Edition, p. 75.

phoria the following legend was told.   At the moment when Pluto carried off Persephone, a swineherd called Eubuleus chanced to be herding his swine on the spot, and his herd was engulfed in the chasm down which Pluto vanished with Persephone.   Accordingly at the Thesmophoria pigs were annually thrown into caverns to commemorate the disappearance of the swine of Eubuleus.[1]   It follows from this that the casting of the pigs into the vaults at the Thesmophoria formed part of the dramatic representation of Persephone's descent into the lower world ; and as no image of Persephone appears to have been thrown in, we may infer that the descent of the pigs was not so much an accompaniment of her descent as the descent itself, in short, that the pigs were Persephone.   Afterwards when Persephone or Demeter (for the two are equivalent) took on human form, a reason had to be found for the custom of throwing pigs into caverns at her festival ; and this was done by saying that when Pluto carried off Persephone, there happened to be some swine browsing near, which were swallowed up along with her.   The story is obviously a forced and awkward attempt to bridge over the gulf between the old conception of the corn-spirit as a pig and the new conception of her as an anthropomorphic goddess.   A trace of the older conception survived in the legend that when the sad mother was searching for traces of the vanished Persephone, the footprints of the lost one were obliterated by the footprints of a pig ;[2] originally, we may conjecture, the footprints of the pig were the footprints of Persephone and of Demeter herself.   A consciousness of the intimate connexion of the pig with the corn lurks in the legend that the swineherd Eubuleus was a brother of Triptolemus, to whom Demeter first imparted the secret of the corn.   Indeed, according to one version of the story, Eubuleus himself received, jointly with his brother Triptolemus, the gift of the corn from Demeter as a reward for revealing to her the fate of Persephone.[3]   Further, it is to be noted that at the Thesmophoria

---

[1] *Scholia in Lucianum*, ed. H. Rabe, pp. 275 *sq.*

[2] Ovid, *Fasti*, iv. 461-466, upon which Gierig remarks, " *Sues melius* *poeta omisisset in hac narratione.*" Such is the wisdom of the commentator.

[3] Pausanias, i. 14. 3.

the women appear to have eaten swine's flesh.[1]   The meal,
if I am right, must have been a solemn sacrament or communion, the worshippers partaking of the body of the god.

Analogy of the Thesmophoria to the folk-customs of Northern Europe.   As thus explained, the Thesmophoria has its analogies
in the folk-customs of Northern Europe which have been
already described.   Just as at the Thesmophoria—an autumn
festival in honour of the corn-goddess—swine's flesh was
partly eaten, partly kept in caverns till the following year,
when it was taken up to be sown with the seed-corn in the
fields for the purpose of securing a good crop; so in the
neighbourhood of Grenoble the goat killed on the harvest-
field is partly eaten at the harvest-supper, partly pickled
and kept till the next harvest;[2] so at Pouilly the ox killed
on the harvest-field is partly eaten by the harvesters, partly
pickled and kept till the first day of sowing in spring,[3]
probably to be then mixed with the seed, or eaten by the
ploughmen, or both; so at Udvarhely the feathers of the
cock which is killed in the last sheaf at harvest are kept
till spring, and then sown with the seed on the field;[4] so in
Hesse and Meiningen the flesh of pigs is eaten on Ash
Wednesday or Candlemas, and the bones are kept till
sowing-time, when they are put into the field sown or mixed
with the seed in the bag;[5] so, lastly, the corn from the last
sheaf is kept till Christmas, made into the Yule Boar, and
afterwards broken and mixed with the seed-corn at sowing
in spring.[6]   Thus, to put it generally, the corn-spirit is
killed in animal form in autumn; part of his flesh is eaten
as a sacrament by his worshippers; and part of it is kept
till next sowing-time or harvest as a pledge and security for
the continuance or renewal of the corn-spirit's energies.
Whether in the interval between autumn and spring he is
conceived as dead, or whether, like the ox in the *bouphonia*,
he is supposed to come to life again immediately after being
killed, is not clear.   At the Thesmophoria, according to
Clement and Pausanias, as emended by Lobeck,[7] the pigs

---

[1] Scholiast on Aristophanes, *Frogs*, 338.

[2] Above, vol. i. p. 285.

[3] Above, vol. i. p. 290.

[4] Above, vol. i. p. 278.

[5] Above, vol. i. p. 300.

[6] Above, vol. i. pp. 300 *sq.*

[7] In Clement of Alexandria, *Protrept.* ii. 17, for μεγαρίζοντες χοίρους ἐκβάλλουσι Lobeck (*Aglaophamus*, p. 831) would read μεγάροις ζῶντας χοίρους ἐμβάλλουσι.   For his emendation of Pausanias, see above, p. 18 note[1].

were thrown in alive, and were supposed to reappear at the festival of the following year. Here, therefore, if we accept Lobeck's emendations, the corn-spirit is conceived as alive throughout the year ; he lives and works under ground, but is brought up each autumn to be renewed and then replaced in his subterranean abode.[1]

If persons of fastidious taste should object that the Greeks never could have conceived Demeter and Persephone to be embodied in the form of pigs, it may be answered that in the cave of Phigalia in Arcadia the Black Demeter was portrayed with the head and mane of a horse on the body of a woman.[2] Between the portrait of a goddess as a pig, and the portrait of her as a woman with a horse's head, there is little to choose in respect of barbarism. The legend told of the Phigalian Demeter indicates that the horse was one of the animal forms assumed in ancient Greece, as in modern Europe,[3] by the corn-spirit. It was said that in her search for her daughter, Demeter assumed the form of a mare to escape the addresses of Poseidon, and that, offended at his importunity, she withdrew in dudgeon to a cave not far from Phigalia in the highlands of Western Arcadia. The very cavern, now turned into a little Christian chapel with its holy pictures, is still shewn to the curious traveller far down the side of that profound ravine through which the brawling Neda winds under overhanging woods to the sea. There, robed in black, she tarried so long that the fruits of the earth were perishing, and mankind would have died of famine if Pan had not soothed the angry goddess and persuaded her to quit the cave. In memory of this event, the Phigalians set up an image of the Black Demeter in the cave ; it represented a woman dressed in a long robe, with the head and mane of a horse.[4] The Black Demeter, in whose absence the fruits

The horse-headed Demeter of Phigalia.

---

[1] It is worth nothing that in Crete, which was an ancient seat of Demeter worship (see above, vol. i. p. 131), the pig was esteemed very sacred and was not eaten (Athenaeus, ix. 18, pp. 375 F-376 A). This would not exclude the possibility of its being eaten sacramentally, as at the Thesmophoria.

[2] Pausanias, viii. 42.

[3] Above, vol. i. pp. 292 *sqq.*

[4] Pausanias, viii. 25 and 42. At the sanctuary of the Mistress (that is, of Persephone) in Arcadia many terracotta statuettes have been found which represent draped women with the heads of cows or sheep. They are probably votive images of Demeter or Persephone, for the ritual of the sanctuary prescribed the offering of images (Dittenberger, *Sylloge Inscriptionum Graecarum,*[2] No.

of the earth perish, is plainly a mythical expression for the
bare wintry earth stripped of its summer mantle of green.

§ 3. *Attis, Adonis, and the Pig*

Attis and
the pig.

Passing now to Attis and Adonis, we may note a few
facts which seem to shew that these deities of vegetation
had also, like other deities of the same class, their animal
embodiments.   The worshippers of Attis abstained from
eating the flesh of swine.[1]   This appears to indicate that the
pig was regarded as an embodiment of Attis.   And the
legend that Attis was killed by a boar[2] points in the same
direction.   For after the examples of the goat Dionysus and
the pig Demeter it may almost be laid down as a rule that
an animal which is said to have injured a god was originally
the god himself.   Perhaps the cry of " Hyes Attes! Hyes
Attes!"[3] which was raised by the worshippers of Attis, may
be neither more nor less than " Pig Attis! Pig Attis!"—*hyes*
being possibly a Phrygian form of the Greek *hȳs*, "a pig."[4]

Adonis and
the boar.

In regard to Adonis, his connexion with the boar was
not always explained by the story that he had been killed by
the animal.[5]   According to another story, a boar rent with his
tusk the bark of the tree in which the infant Adonis was
born.[6]   According to yet another story, he perished at the

939, vol. ii. pp. 803 *sq.*).   See P.
Perdrizet, "Terres-cuites de Lycosoura,
et mythologie arcadienne," *Bulletin de
Correspondance Hellénique*, xxiii. (1899)
p. 635 ; M. P. Nilsson, *Griechische Feste*
(Leipsic, 1906), pp. 347 *sq.*   On the
Phigalian Demeter, see W. Mannhardt,
Mythologische Forschungen, pp. 244 *sqq.*
I well remember how on a summer
afternoon I sat at the mouth of the
shallow cave, watching the play of
sunshine on the lofty wooded sides of
the ravine and listening to the murmur
of the stream.

[1] See *Adonis, Attis, Osiris*, Second
Edition, p. 221.   On the position of
the pig in ancient Oriental and particularly Semitic religion, see F. C.
Movers, *Die Phoenizier*, i. (Bonn, 1841),
pp. 218 *sqq.*

[2] *Adonis, Attis, Osiris*, Second
Edition, p. 220.

[3] Demosthenes, *De corona*, p. 313.

[4] The suggestion was made to me in
conversation by my lamented friend, the
late R. A. Neil of Pembroke College,
Cambridge.

[5] See *Adonis, Attis, Osiris*, Second
Edition, p. 8 ; and to the authorities
there cited add Athenaeus, ii. 80, p.
69 B ; Cornutus, *Theologiae Graecae
Compendium*, 28 ; Plutarch, *Quaest.
Conviv.* iv. 5. 3, § 8 ; Aristides, *Apo-
logia*, 11, p. 107, ed. J. Rendel Harris
(Cambridge, 1891) ; Joannes Lydus,
De mensibus, iv. 44 ; Propertius,
iii. 4 (5). 53 *sq.*, ed. F. A. Paley ;
Lactantius, *Divin. Instit.* i. 17 ;
Augustine, *De civitate Dei*, vi. 7 ;
Firmicus Maternus, *De errore pro-
fanarum religionum*, 9 ; Macrobius,
Saturnal. i. 21. 4.   See further W. W.
Graf Baudissin, *Adonis und Esmun*
(Leipsic, 1911), pp. 142 *sqq.*

[6] See *Adonis, Attis, Osiris*, Second
Edition, p. 186.

hands of Hephaestus on Mount Lebanon while he was hunting wild boars.[1]   These variations in the legend serve to shew that, while the connexion of the boar with Adonis was certain, the reason of the connexion was not understood, and that consequently different stories were devised to explain it.   Certainly the pig ranked as a sacred animal among the Syrians.   At the great religious metropolis of Hierapolis on the Euphrates pigs were neither sacrificed nor eaten, and if a man touched a pig he was unclean for the rest of the day.   Some people said this was because the pigs were unclean ; others said it was because the pigs were sacred.[2] This difference of opinion points to a hazy state of religious thought in which the ideas of sanctity and uncleanness are not yet sharply distinguished, both being blent in a sort of vaporous solution to which we give the name of taboo.   It is quite consistent with this that the pig should have been held to be an embodiment of the divine Adonis, and the analogies of Dionysus and Demeter make it probable that the story of the hostility of the animal to the god was only a late misapprehension of the old view of the god as embodied in a pig.   The rule that pigs were not sacrificed or eaten by worshippers of Attis and presumably of Adonis, does not exclude the possibility that in these rituals the pig was slain on solemn occasions as a representative of the god and consumed sacramentally by the worshippers. Indeed, the sacramental killing and eating of an animal implies that the animal is sacred, and that, as a general rule, it is spared.[3]

The attitude of the Jews to the pig was as ambiguous as that of the heathen Syrians towards the same animal.   The Greeks could not decide whether the Jews worshipped swine or abominated them.[4]   On the one hand they might not eat swine ; but on the other hand they might not kill them. And if the former rule speaks for the uncleanness, the latter

Ambiguous position of pigs at Hierapolis.

Attitude of the Jews to the pig.

---

[1] W. Cureton, *Spicilegium Syriacum* (London, 1855), p. 44.

[2] Lucian, *De dea Syria*, 54.

[3] The heathen Harranians sacrificed swine once a year and ate the flesh (En-Nedîm, in D. Chwolsohn's *Die Ssabier und der Ssabismus*, St. Petersburg, 1856, ii. 42).   My friend W.

Robertson Smith conjectured that the wild boars annually sacrificed in Cyprus on 2nd April (Joannes Lydus, *De mensibus*, iv. 45) represented Adonis himself.   See his *Religion of the Semites,*[2] pp. 290 *sq.*, 411.

[4] Plutarch, *Quaest. Conviv.* iv. 5.

speaks still more strongly for the sanctity of the animal. For whereas both rules may, and one rule must, be explained on the supposition that the pig was sacred ; neither rule must, and one rule cannot, be explained on the supposition that the pig was unclean.   If, therefore, we prefer the former supposition, we must conclude that, originally at least, the pig was revered rather than abhorred by the Israelites.   We are confirmed in this opinion by observing that down to the time of Isaiah some of the Jews used to meet secretly in gardens to eat the flesh of swine and mice as a religious rite.[1]   Doubtless this was a very ancient ceremony, dating from a time when both the pig and the mouse were venerated as divine, and when their flesh was partaken of sacramentally on rare and solemn occasions as the body and blood of gods.   And in general it may be said that all so-called unclean animals were originally sacred ; the reason for not eating them was that they were divine.

§ 4. *Osiris, the Pig and the Bull*

Attitude of the ancient Egyptians to the pig.

In ancient Egypt, within historical times, the pig occupied the same dubious position as in Syria and Palestine, though at first sight its uncleanness is more prominent than its sanctity.   The Egyptians are generally said by Greek writers to have abhorred the pig as a foul and loathsome animal.[2]   If a man so much as touched a pig in passing, he stepped into the river with all his clothes on, to wash off the taint.[3]   To drink pig's milk was believed to cause leprosy to the drinker.[4]   Swineherds, though natives of Egypt, were forbidden to enter any temple, and they were the only men who were thus excluded.   No one would give his daughter in marriage to a swineherd, or marry a swineherd's daughter ; the swineherds married among themselves.[5]

[1] Isaiah lxv. 3, lxvi. 3, 17.   Compare R. H. Kennett, *The Composition of the Book of Isaiah in the Light of History and Archaeology* (London, 1910) p. 61, who suggests that the eating of the mouse as a sacrament may have been derived from the Greek worship of the Mouse Apollo (Apollo Smintheus).   As to the Mouse Apollo

see below, pp. 282 *sq.*
[2] Herodotus, ii. 47 ; Plutarch, *Isis et Osiris*, 8 ; Aelian, *Nat. Anim.* x. 16.   Josephus merely says that the Egyptian priests abstained from the flesh of swine (*Contra Apionem*, ii. 13).
[3] Herodotus, *l.c.*
[4] Plutarch and Aelian, *ll.cc.*
[5] Herodotus, *l.c.*   At Castabus in

Yet once a year the Egyptians sacrificed pigs to the moon Annual
sacrifice of
and to Osiris, and not only sacrificed them, but ate of their pigs to
flesh, though on any other day of the year they would Osiris and
neither sacrifice them nor taste of their flesh. Those who the moon.
were too poor to offer a pig on this day baked cakes of
dough, and offered them instead.[1]   This can hardly be
explained except by the supposition that the pig was a
sacred animal which was eaten sacramentally by his
worshippers once a year.

The view that in Egypt the pig was sacred is borne Belief that
out by the very facts which, to moderns, might seem to the eating
prove the contrary.   Thus the Egyptians thought, as animal
we have seen, that to drink pig's milk produced leprosy. causes skin-
But exactly analogous views are held by savages about especially
the animals and plants which they deem most sacred. leprosy.
Thus in the island of Wetar (between New Guinea and
Celebes) people believe themselves to be variously descended
from wild pigs, serpents, crocodiles, turtles, dogs, and eels ; a
man may not eat an animal of the kind from which he is
descended ; if he does so, he will become a leper, and go
mad.[2]   Amongst the Omaha Indians of North America men
whose totem is the elk, believe that if they ate the flesh
of the male elk they would break out in boils and white
spots in different parts of their bodies.[3]   In the same
tribe men whose totem is the red maize, think that if
they ate red maize they would have running sores all round

Chersonese there was a sacred precinct
of Hemithea, which no one might
approach who had touched or eaten of
a pig (Diodorus Siculus, v. 62. 5).

[1] Herodotus, ii. 47 *sq.* ; Aelian and
Plutarch, *ll.cc.* Herodotus distinguishes
the sacrifice to the moon from that to
Osiris.   According to him, at the
sacrifice to the moon, the extremity of
the pig's tail, together with the spleen
and the caul, was covered with fat
and burned ; the rest of the flesh was
eaten.   On the evening (not the eve,
see H. Stein's note on the passage) of
the festival the sacrifice to Osiris took
place.   Each man slew a pig before
his door, then gave it to the swineherd,
from whom he had bought it, to take
away.

[2] J. G. F. Riedel, *De sluik- en
kroesharige rassen tusschen Selebes en
Papua* (The Hague, 1886), pp. 432,
452.

[3] Rev. J. Owen Dorsey, "Omaha
Sociology," *Third Annual Report of
the Bureau of Ethnology* (Washington,
1884), p. 225 ; Miss A. C. Fletcher
and F. la Flesche, "The Omaha
Tribe," *Twenty-seventh Annual Report of the Bureau of American
Ethnology* (Washington, 1911), p. 144.
According to the latter writers, any
breach of a clan taboo among the
Omahas was supposed to be punished
either by the breaking out of sores
or white spots on the body of the
offender or by his hair turning white.

their mouths.[1]   The Bush negroes of Surinam, who practise totemism, believe that if they ate the *capiaï* (an animal like a pig) it would give them leprosy ;[2] perhaps the *capiaï* is one of their totems.   The Syrians, in antiquity, who esteemed fish sacred, thought that if they ate fish their bodies would break out in ulcers, and their feet and stomach would swell up.[3]   The Nyanja-speaking tribes of Central Angoniland, in British Central Africa, believe that if a person eats his totemic animal, his body will break out in spots.   The cure for this eruption of the skin is to bathe the body in a decoction made from the bone of the animal, the eating of which caused the malady.[4]   The Wagogo of German East Africa imagine that the sin of eating the totemic animal is visited not on the sinner himself but on his innocent kinsfolk.   Thus when they see a child with a scald head, they say at once that its father has been eating his totem and that is why the poor child has scabs on its pate.[5]   Among the Wahehe, another tribe of German East Africa, a man who suffers from scab or other skin disease will often set the trouble down to his having unwittingly partaken of his totemic animal.[6]   Similarly among the Waheia, another tribe of the same region, if a man kills or eats the totemic animal of his clan, he is supposed to suffer from an eruption of the skin.[7]   In like manner the Bantu tribes of Kavirondo, in Central Africa, hold that the eating of the totem produces a severe cutaneous eruption, which can however be cured by mixing an extract of certain herbs with the fat of a black ox and rubbing the body of the sufferer all over with the mixture.[8]   The Chasas of Orissa believe that if they were to injure their totemic animal, they

---

[1] Rev. J. Owen Dorsey, *op. cit.* p. 231.

[2] J. Crevaux, *Voyages dans l'Amérique du Sud* (Paris, 1883), p. 59.

[3] Plutarch, *De superstitione*, 10 ; Porphyry, *De abstinentia*, iv. 15.   As to the sanctity of fish among the Syrians, see also Ovid, *Fasti*, ii. 473 *sq.*; Diodorus Siculus, ii. 4.

[4] R. Sutherland Rattray, *Some Folklore Stories and Songs in Chinyanja* (London, 1907), pp. 174 *sq.*

[5] Rev. H. Cole, "Notes on the Wagogo of German East Africa," *Journal of the Anthropological Institute,* xxxii. (1902) p. 307, compare p. 317.

[6] E. Nigmann, *Die Wahehe* (Berlin, 1908), p. 42.

[7] J. Kohler, "Das Banturecht in Ostafrika," *Zeitschrift für vergleichende Rechtswissenschaft*, xv. (1902) pp. 2, 3.

[8] C. W. Hobley, "Anthropological Studies in Kavirondo and Nandi," *Journal of the Anthropological Institute,* xxxiii. (1903) p. 347.

would be attacked by leprosy and their line would die out.[1] These examples prove that the eating of a sacred animal is often believed to produce leprosy or other skin-diseases; so far, therefore, they support the view that the pig must have been sacred in Egypt, since the effect of drinking its milk was believed to be leprosy. Such fancies may perhaps have been sometimes suggested by the observation that the eating of semi-putrid flesh, to which some savages are addicted, is apt to be followed by eruptions on the skin. Indeed, many modern authorities attribute leprosy to this cause, particularly to the eating of half rotten fish.[2] It seems not impossible that the abhorrence which the Hebrews entertained of leprosy, and the pains which they took to seclude lepers from the community, may have been based on religious as well as on purely sanitary grounds; they may have imagined that the disfigurement of the sufferers was a penalty which they had incurred by some infraction of taboo. Certainly we read in the Old Testament of cases of leprosy which the historian regarded as the direct consequence of sin.[3]

Again, the rule that, after touching a pig, a man had to wash himself and his clothes, also favours the view of the sanctity of the pig. For it is a common belief that the effect of contact with a sacred object must be removed, by washing or otherwise, before a man is free to mingle with his fellows. Thus the Jews wash their hands after reading the sacred scriptures. Before coming forth from the tabernacle after the sin-offering, the high priest had to wash himself, and put off the garments which he had worn in the holy place.[4] It was a rule of Greek ritual that, in offering an expiatory sacrifice, the sacrificer should not touch the sacrifice, and that, after the offering was made, he must wash his body and his clothes in a river or spring before he could enter a city or his own house.[5] The Parjas, a small tribe of

Mere contact with a sacred object is deemed dangerous and calls for purification as a sort of disinfectant.

---

[1] *Central Provinces, Ethnographic Survey*, II. *Draft Articles on Uriya Castes* (Allahabad, 1907), p. 16.

[2] C. Creighton, *s.v.* "Leprosy," *Encyclopaedia Biblica*, iii. col. 2766.

[3] 2 Kings v. 27; 2 Chronicles xxvi. 16-21.

[4] Leviticus xvi. 23 *sq.*

[5] Porphyry, *De abstinentia*, ii. 44. For this and the Jewish examples I am indebted to my friend W. Robertson Smith. Compare his *Religion of the Semites*,[2] pp. 351, 426, 450 *sq.*

the Central Provinces in India, are divided into clans which have for their respective totems the tiger, the tortoise, the goat, a big lizard, a dove, and so on. If a man accidentally kills his totemic animal, "the earthen cooking-pots of his household are thrown away, the clothes are washed, and the house is purified with water in which the bark of the mango or *jamun* tree (*Eugenia jambolana*) has been steeped. This is in sign of mourning, as it is thought that such an act will bring misfortune."[1] If a Chadwar of the Central Provinces who has the pig for his totem should even see a pig killed by somebody else, he will throw away the household crockery and clean the house as if on the death of a member of his family.[2] The Polynesians felt strongly the need of ridding themselves of the sacred contagion, if it may be so called, which they caught by touching sacred objects. Various ceremonies were performed for the purpose of removing this contagion. We have seen, for example, how in Tonga a man who happened to touch a sacred chief, or anything personally belonging to him, had to perform a certain ceremony before he could feed himself with his hands ; otherwise it was believed that he would swell up and die, or at least be afflicted with scrofula or some other disease.[3] We have seen, too, what fatal effects are supposed to follow, and do actually follow, from contact with a sacred object in New Zealand.[4] In short, primitive man believes that what is sacred is dangerous ; it is pervaded by a sort of electrical sanctity which communicates a shock to, even if it does not kill, whatever comes in contact with it. Hence the savage is unwilling to touch or even to see that which he deems peculiarly holy. Thus Bechuanas, of the Crocodile clan, think it "hateful and unlucky" to meet or see a crocodile ; the sight is thought to cause inflammation of the eyes. Yet the crocodile is their most sacred object ; they call it their father, swear by it, and celebrate it in their festivals.[5] The goat is the sacred animal of the Madenassana

[1] *Central Provinces, Ethnographic Survey*, VII. *Draft Articles on Forest Tribes* (Allahabad, 1911), p. 97.

[2] *Central Provinces, Ethnographic Survey*, I. *Draft Articles on Hindustani Castes* (Allahabad, 1907), p. 32.

[3] See *Taboo and the Perils of the Soul*, pp. 133 *sq.*

[4] *Op. cit.* pp. 134-136.

[5] E. Casalis, *The Basutos* (London, 1861), p. 211 ; D. Livingstone, *Missionary Travels and Researches in South*

Bushmen; yet "to look upon it would be to render the man for the time impure, as well as to cause him undefined uneasiness."[1] The Elk clan, among the Omaha Indians, believe that even to touch the male elk would be followed by an eruption of boils and white spots on the body.[2] Members of the Reptile clan in the same tribe think that if one of them touches or smells a snake, it will make his hair white.[3] In Samoa people whose god was a butterfly believed that if they caught a butterfly it would strike them dead.[4] Again, in Samoa the reddish-seared leaves of the banana-tree were commonly used as plates for handing food; but if any member of the Wild Pigeon family had used banana leaves for this purpose, it was supposed that he would suffer from rheumatic swellings or an eruption all over the body like chicken-pox.[5] The Mori clan of the Bhils in Central India worship the peacock as their totem and make offerings of grain to it; yet members of the clan believe that were they even to set foot on the tracks of a peacock they would afterwards suffer from some disease, and if a woman sees a peacock she must veil her face and look away.[6] Thus the primitive mind seems to conceive of holiness as a sort of dangerous virus, which a prudent man will shun as far as possible, and of which, if he should chance to be infected by it, he will carefully disinfect himself by some form of ceremonial purification.

In the light of these parallels the beliefs and customs of the Egyptians touching the pig are probably to be explained as based upon an opinion of the extreme sanctity rather than of the extreme uncleanness of the animal; or rather, to put it more correctly, they imply that the animal was looked on, not simply as a filthy and disgusting creature, but as a being endowed with high supernatural powers, and that as

Thus the pig was probably at first a sacred animal with the Egyptians, and may have been re-

---

Africa (London, 1857), p. 255; John Mackenzie, *Ten Years north of the Orange River* (Edinburgh, 1871), p. 135 note. See further *Totemism and Exogamy*, ii. 372.

[1] J. Mackenzie, *l.c.*

[2] Rev. J. Owen Dorsey, "Omaha Sociology," *Third Annual Report of the Bureau of Ethnology* (Washington, 1884), p. 225.

[3] *Ibid.* p. 275.

[4] G. Turner, *Samoa* (London, 1884), p. 76.

[5] *Ibid.* p. 70.

[6] Captain C. Eckford Luard, in *Census of India, 1901*, vol. xix. *Central India*, Part i. (Lucknow, 1902) pp. 299 *sq.*; also *Census of India, 1901*, vol. i. *Ethnographic Appendices* (Calcutta, 1903), p. 163.

garded as an embodiment of the corn-god Osiris, though at a later time he was looked on as an embodiment of Typhon, the enemy of Osiris.

such it was regarded with that primitive sentiment of religious awe and fear in which the feelings of reverence and abhorrence are almost equally blended. The ancients themselves seem to have been aware that there was another side to the horror with which swine seemed to inspire the Egyptians. For the Greek astronomer and mathematician Eudoxus, who resided fourteen months in Egypt and conversed with the priests,[1] was of opinion that the Egyptians spared the pig, not out of abhorrence, but from a regard to its utility in agriculture ; for, according to him, when the Nile had subsided, herds of swine were turned loose over the fields to tread the seed down into the moist earth.[2] But when a being is thus the object of mixed and implicitly contradictory feelings, he may be said to occupy a position of unstable equilibrium. In course of time one of the contradictory feelings is likely to prevail over the other, and according as the feeling which finally predominates is that of reverence or abhorrence, the being who is the object of it will rise into a god or sink into a devil. The latter, on the whole, was the fate of the pig in Egypt. For in historical times the fear and horror of the pig seem certainly to have outweighed the reverence and worship of which he may once have been the object, and of which, even in his fallen state, he never quite lost trace. He came to be looked on as an embodiment of Set or Typhon, the Egyptian devil and enemy of Osiris. For it was in the shape of a black pig that Typhon injured the eye of the god Horus, who burned him and instituted the sacrifice of the pig, the sun-god Ra having declared the beast abominable.[3] Again, the story that Typhon was hunting a boar when he discovered and mangled the body of Osiris, and that this was the reason why pigs were sacrificed once a year,[4] is clearly a modernised version of an older story that Osiris, like Adonis and Attis, was slain

---

[1] Diogenes Laertius, *Vitae Philosophorum*, viii. 8.

[2] Aelian, *Nat. Anim.* x. 16. The story is repeated by Pliny, *Nat. Hist.* xviii. 168.

[3] E. Lefébure, *Le Mythe Osirien*, Première Partie, *Les yeux d'Horus* (Paris, 1874), p. 44 ; *The Book of the Dead*, English translation by E. A.

Wallis Budge (London, 1901), ii. 336 *sq.*, chapter cxii. ; E. A. Wallis Budge, *The Gods of the Egyptians* (London, 1904), i. 496 *sq.* ; *id.*, *Osiris and the Egyptian Resurrection* (London and New York, 1911), i. 62 *sq.*

[4] Plutarch, *Isis et Osiris*, 8. E. Lefébure (*op. cit.* p. 46) recognises that in this story the boar is Typhon himself.

or mangled by a boar, or by Typhon in the form of a boar. Thus, the annual sacrifice of a pig to Osiris might naturally be interpreted as vengeance inflicted on the hostile animal that had slain or mangled the god. But, in the first place, when an animal is thus killed as a solemn sacrifice once and once only in the year, it generally or always means that the animal is divine, that he is spared and respected the rest of the year as a god and slain, when he is slain, also in the character of a god.[1] In the second place, the examples of Dionysus and Demeter, if not of Attis and Adonis, have taught us that the animal which is sacrificed to a god on the ground that he is the god's enemy may have been, and probably was, originally the god himself. Therefore, the annual sacrifice of a pig to Osiris, coupled with the alleged hostility of the animal to the god, tends to shew, first, that originally the pig was a god, and, second, that he was Osiris. At a later age, when Osiris became anthropomorphic and his original relation to the pig had been forgotten, the animal was first distinguished from him, and afterwards opposed as an enemy to him by mythologists who could think of no reason for killing a beast in connexion with the worship of a god except that the beast was the god's enemy ; or, as Plutarch puts it, not that which is dear to the gods, but that which is the contrary, is fit to be sacrificed.[2] At this later stage the havoc which a wild boar notoriously makes amongst the corn would supply a plausible reason for regarding him as the foe of the corn-spirit, though originally, if I am right, the very freedom with which the boar ranged at will through the corn led people to identify him with the corn-spirit, to whom he was afterwards opposed as an enemy. *The havoc wrought by wild boars in the corn is a reason for regarding them as foes of the corn-god.*

As the depredations committed by wild swine on the growing crops in countries where these creatures abound are necessarily unfamiliar to most English readers, it may be well to illustrate them by examples. Thus, for instance, in Palestine the wild boar " is eagerly chased and destroyed on account of the frightful ravages it makes among the *Evidence of the depredations committed by wild boars on the crops.*

---

[1] This important principle was first recognised by W. Robertson Smith. See his article, " Sacrifice," *Encyclopaedia Britannica*, Ninth Edition, xxi. 137 *sq.* Compare his *Religion of the Semites*,[2] pp. 373, 410 *sq.*

[2] Plutarch, *Isis et Osiris*, 31.

crops. Not only does it devour any fruits within reach, but in a single night a party of wild boars will uproot a whole field, and destroy the husbandman's hopes for the year. The places they love to frequent are the reedy marshes and thickets by rivers and lakes, and they swarm in the thickets all along the banks of the Jordan from Jericho to the Lake of Gennesaret. From these fastnesses, whence neither dog nor man can dislodge them, they make nightly forays upon the corn-fields and root-crops of the villagers, returning at daybreak to their coverts. About Jericho they are especially destructive, and when the barley crop is ripening, the husbandmen have to keep nightly watch to drive them away. Their presence can always be detected by the crashing noise they make in forcing their way through the thickets, when the men fire, guided by the sound."[1] Wild pigs are the special enemies of the crops in South Africa ; the fences constructed by the Zulus round their gardens are mainly designed to guard against the devastating depredations of these brutes, though porcupines, baboons, hippopotamuses, and elephants also make havoc of the ripe grain. Sometimes small huts are erected on platforms in the gardens, and in these huts watchers are set to scare away the nocturnal invaders.[2] So in British Central Africa sentinels are posted day and night in huts raised on platforms to protect the maize fields from the inroads of baboons and of wild pigs, which are still more destructive than the baboons, for they grub up the plants as well as devour the grain ; and the watchers drum continually on any metal they have at hand to keep the marauders at bay.[3] In the island of Nias whole fields are sometimes trampled down by these pests between sunset and sunrise. Often the stillness of the serene equatorial night is broken by the strident cries of the watchers of the fields; the sound goes echoing through the wooded valleys for a long time, and here and there a dull grunting tells that the efforts of the sentinels have not been in vain.[4]

---

[1] H. B. Tristram, *The Natural History of the Bible*, Ninth Edition (London, 1898), pp. 54 *sq.*
[2] Rev. J. Shooter, *The Kafirs of Natal and the Zulu Country* (London, 1857), pp. 18-20.

[3] Miss A. Werner, *The Natives of British Central Africa* (London, 1906), pp. 182 *sq.*

[4] E. Modigliano, *Un Viaggio a Nías* (Milan, 1890), pp. 524 *sq.*, 601.

In Northern Luzon, of the Philippine Archipelago, the rice-
fields are similarly exposed to the depredations of wild
hogs, and watchers remain on guard day and night in out-
looks, sometimes in commodious structures of stone erected
for the purpose, who burn fires at night to frighten the
animals away.[1] At the beginning of their annual agricultural labours the Banars of Cambodia pray to Yang-Seri that
he would be pleased to give them plenty of rice and to prevent the wild boars from eating it up.[2] In Gayo-land, a
district of Sumatra, the worst enemies of the rice crops are
wild swine and field mice ; the whole of the harvest is sometimes destroyed by their inroads.[3] Among the Kai of
German New Guinea people who are engaged in the labour
of the fields will on no account eat pork. The reason is
that pigs, both wild and tame, are the most dangerous foes
of the crops ; therefore it seems clear to the mind of the
Kai that if a field labourer were to eat pork, the flesh of the
dead pig in his stomach would attract the living pigs into
the field.[4] Perhaps this superstition, based on the principle
of sympathetic magic, may explain the aversion to pork
which was entertained by some of the agricultural peoples
of the Eastern Mediterranean in antiquity.

To people thus familiarised with the ravages of wild boars
among the ripe crops the idea might naturally present itself
that the animal is either the enemy of the corn-god or perhaps the corn-god himself come in person to enjoy his own
despite all the efforts of mankind to keep him out of his
rights. Hence we can understand how an agricultural
people like the ancient Egyptians may have identified
the wild boar either with their corn-god Osiris or with his
enemy Typhon. The view which identifies the pig with
Osiris derives not a little support from the sacrifice of
pigs to him on the very day on which, according to
tradition, Osiris himself was killed ;[5] for thus the killing

The ravages of wild boars among the crops help us to under-stand the ambiguous attitude of the ancient Egyptians to swine.

---

[1] A. E. Jenks, *The Bontoc Igorot*, (Manilla, 1905), pp. 100, 102.

[2] A. Bastian, " Beiträge zur Kennt-niss der Gebirgs-stämme in Kambodia," *Zeitschrift der Gesellschaft für Erdkunde zu Berlin*, i. (1866) p. 44.

[3] G. Snouck Hurgronje, *Het Gajōland en zijne Bewoners* (Batavia, 1903), p.

348.

[4] Ch. Keysser, " Aus dem Leben der Kaileute," in R. Neuhauss, *Deutsch Neu-Guinea* (Berlin, 1911), p. 125.

[5] E. Lefébure, *Le Mythe Osirien*, Première Partie, *Les yeux d'Horus* (Paris, 1874), pp. 48 *sq.*

of the pig was the annual representation of the killing of
Osiris, just as the throwing of the pigs into the caverns at the
Thesmophoria was an annual representation of the descent of
Persephone into the lower world ; and both customs are
parallel to the European practice of killing a goat, cock, and
so forth, at harvest as a representative of the corn-spirit.

Egyptian
sacrifices of
red oxen
and red-
haired men.

Again, the theory that the pig, originally Osiris himself,
afterwards came to be regarded as an embodiment of his
enemy Typhon, is supported by the similar relation of red-
haired men and red oxen to Typhon. For in regard to the
red-haired men who were burned and whose ashes were
scattered with winnowing-fans, we have seen fair grounds for
believing that originally, like the red-haired puppies killed
at Rome in spring, they were representatives of the corn-
spirit himself, that is, of Osiris, and were slain for the express
purpose of making the corn turn red or golden.[1] Yet at
a later time these men were explained to be representatives,
not of Osiris, but of his enemy Typhon,[2] and the killing of
them was regarded as an act of vengeance inflicted on the
enemy of the god. Similarly, the red oxen sacrificed by the
Egyptians were said to be offered on the ground of their
resemblance to Typhon ;[3] though it is more likely that
originally they were slain on the ground of their resemblance
to the corn-spirit Osiris. We have seen that the ox is a
common representative of the corn-spirit and is slain as such
on the harvest-field.

Osiris iden-
tified with
the sacred
bulls Apis
and Mnevis.

Osiris was regularly identified with the bull Apis of
Memphis and the bull Mnevis of Heliopolis.[4] But it is hard

[1] See above, vol. i. pp. 261 *sq.* ;
Adonis, Attis, Osiris, Second Edition,
pp. 331, 338.

[2] Plutarch, *Isis et Osiris*, 33, 73 ;
Diodorus Siculus, i. 88.

[3] Plutarch, *Isis et Osiris*, 31 ; Diodorus Siculus, i. 88. Compare Herodotus, ii. 38.

[4] Plutarch, *Isis et Osiris*, 20, 29,
33, 43 ; Strabo, xvii. 1. 31 ; Diodorus
Siculus, i. 21, 85 ; Duncker, *Geschichte
des Alterthums*,[5] i. 55 *sqq.* On Apis
and Mnevis, see also Herodotus, ii. 153,
with A. Wiedemann's comment, iii. 27
sq. ; Ammianus Marcellinus, xxii. 14.
7 ; Pliny, *Nat. Hist.* viii. 184 *sqq.* ;

Solinus, xxxii. 17-21 ; Cicero, *De natura deorum*, i. 29 ; Augustine, *De civitate Dei*, xviii. 5 ; Aelian, *Nat. Anim.*
xi. 10 *sq.* ; Plutarch, *Quaest. Conviv.*
viii. 1. 3 ; *id.*, *Isis et Osiris*, 5, 35 ;
Eusebius, *Praeparatio Evangelii*, iii.
13. 1 *sq.* ; Pausanias, i. 18. 4, vii. 22.
3 *sq.* ; W. Dittenberger, *Orientis Graeci
Inscriptiones Selectae* (Leipsic, 1903-
1905), Nos. 56, 90 (vol. i. pp. 98, 106,
159). Both Apis and Mnevis were
black bulls, but Apis had certain white
spots. See A. Wiedemann, *Die Religion der alten Aegypter* (Münster i.
W., 1890), pp. 95, 99-101. When
Apis died, pious people used to put on

to say whether these bulls were embodiments of him as the corn-spirit, as the red oxen appear to have been, or whether they were not in origin entirely distinct deities who came to be fused with Osiris at a later time. The universality of the worship of these two bulls [1] seems to put them on a different footing from the ordinary sacred animals whose worships were purely local. Hence if the latter were evolved from totems, as they may have been, some other origin would have to be found for the worship of Apis and Mnevis. If these bulls were not originally embodiments of the corn-god Osiris, they may possibly be descendants of the sacred cattle worshipped by a pastoral people.[2]   If this were so, ancient Egypt would exhibit a stratification of three great types of religion or superstition corresponding to three great stages of society. Totemism, which may be roughly described as a species of superstitious respect paid to wild animals and plants by many tribes in the hunting stage of society, would be represented by the worship of the local sacred animals ; the worship of cattle, which belongs to society in the pastoral stage, would be represented by the cults of Apis and Mnevis ; and the worship of cultivated plants, which is peculiar to society in the agricultural stage, would be represented by the religion of Osiris and Isis.   The Egyptian reverence for cows, which were never killed,[3] might belong either to the second or the third of these stages.   The consecration of cows to Isis, who was portrayed with cow's horns [4] and may have been supposed to be incarnate in the animals, would indicate that they, like the red oxen, were embodiments of the corn-spirit.   However, this identification of Isis with the cow, like that of Osiris with the bulls Apis and Mnevis, may be only an effect of

Stratification of three great types of religion or superstition in ancient Egypt.

---

mourning and to fast, drinking only water and eating only vegetables, for seventy days till the burial.   See A. Erman, *Die ägyptische Religion* (Berlin, 1905), pp. 170 *sq.*
[1] Diodorus Siculus, i. 21.
[2] On the religious reverence of pastoral peoples for their cattle, and the possible derivation of the Apis and Isis-Hathor worship from the pastoral stage of society, see W. Robertson Smith, *Religion of the Semites*,[2] pp. 296 *sqq.*

[3] Herodotus, ii. 41.
[4] Herodotus, ii. 41, with A. Wiedemann's commentary ; Plutarch, *Isis et Osiris*, 19 ; E. A. Wallis Budge, *Osiris and the Egyptian Resurrection* (London and New York, 1911), i. 8.   In his commentary on the passage of Herodotus Prof. Wiedemann observes (p. 188) that "the Egyptian name of the Isis-cow is *ḥes-t* and is one of the few cases in which the name of the sacred animal coincides with that of the deity."

syncretism. But whatever the original relation of Apis to Osiris may have been, there is one fact about the former which ought not to be passed over in a disquisition on the custom of killing a god. Although the bull Apis was worshipped as a god with much pomp and profound reverence, he was not suffered to live beyond a certain length of time which was prescribed by the sacred books, and on the expiry of which he was drowned in a holy spring.[1] The limit, according to Plutarch, was twenty-five years;[2] but it cannot always have been enforced, for the tombs of the Apis bulls have been discovered in modern times, and from the inscriptions on them it appears that in the twenty-second dynasty two of the holy steers lived more than twenty-six years.[3]

On the stratification of religions corresponding to certain social types.

To prevent misunderstandings it may be well to add that what I have just said as to the stratification of three great types of religion or superstition corresponding to three great types of society is not meant to sketch, even in outline, the evolution of religion as a whole. I by no means wish to suggest that the reverence for wild animals and plants, the reverence for domestic cattle, and the reverence for cultivated plants are the only forms of religion or superstition which prevail at the corresponding stages of social development; all that I desire to convey is that they are characteristic of these stages respectively. The elements which make up any religious system are far too numerous and their interaction far too complex to be adequately summed up in a few simple formulas. To mention only a single factor of which I have taken no account in indicating roughly a certain correspondence between the strata of religion and of society, the fear of the spirits of the dead appears to have been one of the most powerful factors,

---

[1] Pliny, *Nat. Hist.* viii. 184; Solinus, xxxii. 18; Ammianus Marcellinus, xxii. 14. 7. The spring or well in which he was drowned was perhaps the one from which his drinking-water was procured; he might not drink the water of the Nile (Plutarch, *Isis et Osiris*, 5).

[2] Plutarch, *Isis et Osiris*, 56.

[3] G. Maspero, *Histoire ancienne*[4] (Paris, 1886), p. 31. Compare Duncker, *Geschichte des Alterthums*,[5] i. 56. It

has been conjectured that the period of twenty-five years was determined by astronomical considerations, that being a period which harmonises the phases of the moon with the days of the Egyptian year. See L. Ideler, *Handbuch der mathematischen und technischen Chronologie* (Berlin, 1825-1826), i. 182 *sq.*; F. K. Ginzel, *Handbuch der mathematischen und technischen Chronologie*, i. (Leipsic, 1906), pp. 180 *sq.*

perhaps, indeed, the most powerful of all, in shaping the course of religious evolution at every stage of social development from the lowest to the highest ; and for that very reason it is not specially characteristic of any one form of society. And the three types of religion or superstition which I have selected as characteristic of three stages of society are far from being strictly limited each to its corresponding step in the social ladder. For example, although totemism, or a particular species of reverence paid by groups of men to wild animals and plants, probably always originated in the hunting stage of society, it has by no means been confined to that primitive phase of human development but has often survived not only into the pastoral but into the agricultural stage, as we may see for example by the case of many tribes in Africa, India, and America ; and it seems likely that a similar overlapping of the various strata takes place in every instance. In short, we cannot really dissect the history of mankind as it were with a knife into a series of neat sections each sharply marked off from all the rest by a texture and colour of its own ; we may indeed do so theoretically for the convenience of exposition, but practically the textures interlace, the colours melt and run into each other by insensible gradations that defy the edge of the finest instrument of analysis which we can apply to them. It is a mere truism to say that the abstract generalisations of science can never adequately comprehend all the particulars of concrete reality. The facts of nature will always burst the narrow bonds of human theories.

Before quitting this part of our subject it may be well to illustrate by one or two examples the reverence which primitive pastoral tribes pay to their cattle, since, as I have just indicated, the worship of sacred bulls by the ancient Egyptians, like the modern Hindoo worship of cows, may very well have been directly derived from a similar respect paid by their remote ancestors to their cattle. A good instance is supplied by the Dinka, a large cattle-breeding tribe, or rather nation, of the White Nile. " Every idea and thought of the Dinka," says Schweinfurth, " is how to acquire and maintain cattle : a kind of reverence would

Reverence of the Dinka for their cattle

seem to be paid to them ; even their offal is considered of
high importance ; the dung, which is burnt to ashes for
sleeping in and for smearing their persons, and the urine,
which is used for washing and as a substitute for salt, are
their daily requisites.   It must be owned that it is hard
to reconcile this latter usage with our ideas of cleanliness.
A cow is never slaughtered, but when sick it is segregated
from the rest, and carefully tended in the large huts built for
the purpose.   Only those that die naturally or by an accident
are used as food.   All this, which exists among most of the
pastoral tribes of Africa, may perchance appear to be a
lingering remnant of an exploded cattle-worship ; but I may
draw attention to the fact that the Dinka are by no means
disinclined to partake of any feast of their flesh, provided
that the slaughtered animal was not their own property.   It
is thus more the delight of actual possession, than any superstitious estimate, that makes the cow to them an object
of reverence.   Indescribable is the grief when either death
or rapine has robbed a Dinka of his cattle.   He is prepared
to redeem their loss by the heaviest sacrifices, for they are
dearer to him than wife or child.   A dead cow is not,
however, wantonly buried ; the negro is not sentimental
enough for that ; such an occurrence is soon bruited abroad,
and the neighbours institute a carousal, which is quite an
epoch in their monotonous life.   The bereaved owner himself
is, however, too much afflicted at the loss to be able to
touch a morsel of the carcass of his departed beast.   Not
unfrequently in their sorrow the Dinka remain for days
silent and abstracted, as though their trouble were too heavy
for them to bear." [1]   A rich Dinka will sometimes keep a
favourite ox and treat it with such marks of respect that an
observer has compared the animal to the Apis of the
ancient Egyptians.   " Here and there," we are told, " beside
the hut of a wealthy negro is set up a great withered
tree.   From its boughs hang vessels containing food and
perhaps trophies of war ; to its trunk is fastened the
great drum (*Noqara*), which summons to war or to the
dance.   To this tree, separated from the rest of the cattle,

---

[1] G. Schweinfurth, *The Heart of Africa*, Third Edition (London, 1878),
i. 59 *sq.*

is tethered a great fat ox. It is of a white colour passing
into a slaty grey on the shoulders and legs : its long horns
are artificially bent to opposite sides and adorned with
bunches of hair : the tuft of the tail is cut off. This is the
makwi, the Apis of the negro. His master, who has singled
him out from his youth for his colour and certain marks, has
cherished and reared him in order that he may one day be
his pride in the eyes of the village. He has gelded him,
adorned him, trained him to walk at the head of the herd,
to dance, and to fight. His *makwi* is always an object of
his tenderest attention ; he never fails to bring him a bundle
of the finest herbs ; if he can procure a bell, he hangs it
round the animal's neck ; and at evening, if he has milk or
merisa enough for guests, the drum is beaten to summon the
youth to come and dance round the deified ox." [1]

Again, speaking of the Nuehr, another pastoral tribe of
the Upper Nile, a traveller tells us that " as among the Dinka,
so among the Nuehr-negroes the cattle enjoy a respect,
indeed we may say a veneration, which reminds us of the
animal worship of the ancient Egyptians, especially of that
of the holy steer Apis, though the respect may be grounded
on the simple fact that cattle are the only possession of these
negroes. The largest and handsomest bull is the leader of
the herd ; he is decked with bunches of hair and small bells,
marked out from the rest in every way, and regarded as the
guardian genius of the herd as well as of the family. His
loss is the greatest misfortune that can befall his owner. At
night his master drives the animal round the herd, couched
about the smoky fire, and sings of his beauty and courage,
while the bull signifies his contentment by a complacent
lowing. To him his master every morning commits the herd,
in order that he may guide them to the best pastures and
guard them from danger ; in him he reveres his ideal of all
that is beautiful and strong ; nay he designates him by the
same name which he applies to his own dim conception of a
Supreme Being, *Nyeledit*, and to the thunder." [2]

Reverence of the Nuehr for their cattle

---

[1] E. de Pruyssenaere, *Reisen und
Forschungen im Gebiete des Weissen und
Blauen Nil* (Gotha, 1877), pp. 22 *sq.*
(*Petermann's Mittheilungen, Ergän-
zungsheft*, No. 50).

[2] Ernst Marno, *Reisen im Gebiete
des Blauen und Weissen Nil* (Vienna,
1874), p. 343. The name *Nyeledit* is
explained by the writer to mean "very
great and mighty." It is probably

§ 5. *Virbius and the Horse*

The tradition that Virbius had been killed in the character of Hippolytus by horses, and the custom of excluding horses from the sacred Arician grove, may point to the conclusion that the horse was regarded as an embodiment of Virbius and was annually sacrificed in the grove.

We are now in a position to hazard a conjecture as to the meaning of the tradition that Virbius, the first of the divine Kings of the Wood at Aricia, had been killed in the character of Hippolytus by horses.[1] Having found, first, that spirits of the corn are not infrequently represented in the form of horses;[2] and, second, that the animal which in later legends is said to have injured the god was sometimes originally the god himself, we may conjecture that the horses by which Virbius or Hippolytus was said to have been slain were really embodiments of him as a deity of vegetation. The myth that he had been killed by horses was probably invented to explain certain features in his worship, amongst others the custom of excluding horses from his sacred grove. For myth changes while custom remains constant; men continue to do what their fathers did before them, though the reasons on which their fathers acted have been long forgotten. The history of religion is a long attempt to reconcile old custom with new reason, to find a sound theory for an absurd practice. In the case before us we may be sure that the myth is more modern than the custom and by no means represents the original reason for excluding horses from the grove. From their exclusion it might be inferred that horses could not be the sacred animals or embodiments of the god of the grove. But the inference would be rash.

Similarly at Athens the goat was usually The goat was at one time a sacred animal or embodiment of Athena, as may be inferred from the practice of representing the goddess clad in a goat-skin (*aegis*). Yet the goat was

equivalent to *Nyalich*, which Dr. C. G. Seligmann gives as a synonym for Dengdit, the high god of the Dinka. According to Dr. Seligmann, *Nyalich* is the locative of a word meaning "above" and, literally translated, signifies, "in the above." See C. G. Seligmann, *s.v.* "Dinka," in *Encyclopaedia of Religion and Ethics*, edited by J. Hastings, D.D., vol. iv. (Edinburgh, 1911), p. 707. The Sakalava of Ampasimene, in Madagascar, are said to worship a black bull which is kept in a sacred enclosure in the island of Nosy

Be. On the death of the sacred bull another is substituted for it. See A. van Gennep, *Tabou et Totémisme à Madagascar* (Paris, 1904), pp. 247 *sq.*, quoting J. Carol, *Chez les Hova* (Paris, 1898), pp. 418 *sq.* But as the Sakalava are not, so far as I know, mainly or exclusively a pastoral people, this example of bull-worship does not strictly belong to the class illustrated in the text.

[1] See *The Magic Art and the Evolution of Kings*, i. 19 *sqq.*

[2] See above, vol. i. pp. 292-294.

neither sacrificed to her as a rule, nor allowed to enter her excluded from the Acropolis but was admitted once a year for a necessary sacrifice.
great sanctuary, the Acropolis at Athens.   The reason
alleged for this was that the goat injured the olive, the
sacred tree of Athena.[1]   So far, therefore, the relation of
the goat of Athena is parallel to the relation of the horse
to Virbius, both animals being excluded from the sanctuary
on the ground of injury done by them to the god.   But
from Varro we learn that there was an exception to the
rule which excluded the goat from the Acropolis.   Once a
year, he says, the goat was driven on to the Acropolis for a
necessary sacrifice.[2]   Now, as has been remarked before,
when an animal is sacrificed once and once only in the year,
it is probably slain, not as a victim offered to the god, but
as a representative of the god himself.   Therefore we may
infer that if a goat was sacrificed on the Acropolis once a
year, it was sacrificed in the character of Athena herself ;[3]
and it may be conjectured that the skin of the sacrificed
animal was placed on the statue of the goddess and formed
the *aegis*, which would thus be renewed annually.   Similarly
at Thebes in Egypt rams were sacred and were not sacrificed.   But on one day in the year a ram was killed, and
its skin was placed on the statue of the god Ammon.[4]   Now,
if we knew the ritual of the Arician grove better, we might
find that the rule of excluding horses from it, like the rule
of excluding goats from the Acropolis at Athens, was
subject to an annual exception, a horse being once a year
taken into the grove and sacrificed as an embodiment of the
god Virbius.[5]   By the usual misunderstanding the horse

---

[1] Athenaeus, xiii. 51, p. 587 A; Pliny, *Nat. Hist.* viii. 204. Compare W. Robertson Smith, in *Encyclopaedia Britannica*, Ninth Edition, article "Sacrifice," vol. xxi. p. 135.

[2] Varro, *De agri cultura*, i. 2. 19 *sq.* : "*hoc nomine etiam Athenis in arcem non inigi, praeterquam semel ad necessarium sacrificium.*"   By *semel* Varro probably means once a year.

[3] The force of this inference is greatly weakened, if not destroyed, by a fact which I had overlooked when I wrote this book originally. A goat was sacrificed to Brauronian Artemis at her festival called the Brauronia (Hesychius,

s.v. Βραυρωνίοις ; compare Im. Bekker's *Anecdota Graeca*, p. 445, lines 6 *sqq.*). As the Brauronian Artemis had a sanctu- ary on the Acropolis of Athens (Pau- sanias, i. 23. 7), it seems probable that the goat sacrificed once a year on the Acropolis was sacrificed to her and not to Athena.   (Note to Second Edition of *The Golden Bough.*)

[4] Herodotus, ii. 42.

[5] It is worth noting that Hippolytus, with whom Virbius was identified, is said to have dedicated horses to Aescu- lapius, who had raised him from the dead (Pausanias, ii. 27. 4).

thus killed would come in time to be regarded as an enemy offered up in sacrifice to the god whom he had injured, like the pig which was sacrificed to Demeter and Osiris or the goat which was sacrificed to Dionysus, and possibly to Athena. It is so easy for a writer to record a rule without noticing an exception that we need not wonder at finding the rule of the Arician grove recorded without any mention of an exception such as I suppose. If we had had only the statements of Athenaeus and Pliny, we should have known only the rule which forbade the sacrifice of goats to Athena and excluded them from the Acropolis, without being aware of the important exception which the fortunate preservation of Varro's work has revealed to us.

The conjecture that once a year a horse may have been sacrificed in the Arician grove as a representative of the deity of the grove derives some support from the similar sacrifice of a horse which took place once a year at Rome. On the fifteenth of October in each year a chariot-race was run on the Field of Mars. Stabbed with a spear, the right-hand horse of the victorious team was then sacrificed to Mars for the purpose of ensuring good crops, and its head was cut off and adorned with a string of loaves. Thereupon the inhabitants of two wards—the Sacred Way and the Subura—contended with each other who should get the head. If the people of the Sacred Way got it, they fastened it to a wall of the king's house ; if the people of the Subura got it, they fastened it to the Mamilian tower. The horse's tail was cut off and carried to the king's house with such speed that the blood dripped on the hearth of the house.[1] Further, it appears that the blood of the horse was caught and preserved till the twenty-first of April, when the Vestal virgins mixed it with the blood of the unborn calves which had been sacrificed six days before. The mixture was then distributed to shepherds, and used by them for fumigating their flocks.[2]

---

[1] Festus, ed. C. O. Müller, pp. 178, 179, 220 ; Plutarch, *Quaestiones Romanae*, 97 ; Polybius, xii. 4 B. The sacrifice is referred to by Julian, *Orat.* v. p. 176 D (p. 228 ed. F. C. Hertlein). It is the subject of a valuable essay by W. Mannhardt, whose conclusions I summarise in the text. See W. Mannhardt, *Mythologische Forschungen* (Strasburg, 1884), pp. 156-201.

[2] Ovid, *Fasti*, iv. 731 *sqq.*, compare 629 *sqq.* ; Propertius, v. 1. 19 *sq.*

In this ceremony the decoration of the horse's head [1]
with a string of loaves, and the alleged object of the sacrifice,
namely, to procure a good harvest, seem to indicate that
the horse was killed as one of those animal representatives
of the corn-spirit of which we have found so many examples.
The custom of cutting off the horse's tail is like the African
custom of cutting off the tails of the oxen and sacrificing them
to obtain a good crop.[2]   In both the Roman and the African
custom the animal apparently stands for the corn-spirit, and
its fructifying power is supposed to reside especially in its
tail.   The latter idea occurs, as we have seen, in European
folk-lore.[3]   Again, the practice of fumigating the cattle in
spring with the blood of the horse may be compared with
the practice of giving the Old Wife, the Maiden, or the
clyack sheaf as fodder to the horses in spring or the cattle
at Christmas, and giving the Yule Boar to the ploughing
oxen or horses to eat in spring.[4]   All these usages aim at
ensuring the blessing of the corn-spirit on the homestead
and its inmates and storing it up for another year.

The horse so sacrificed seems to have embodied the corn-spirit.

The Roman sacrifice of the October horse, as it was
called, carries us back to the early days when the Subura,
afterwards a low and squalid quarter of the great metropolis,
was still a separate village, whose inhabitants engaged in a
friendly contest on the harvest-field with their neighbours
of Rome, then a little rural town.   The Field of Mars on
which the ceremony took place lay beside the Tiber, and
formed part of the king's domain down to the abolition
of the monarchy.   For tradition ran that at the time
when the last of the kings was driven from Rome, the
corn stood ripe for the sickle on the crown lands beside the
river ; but no one would eat the accursed grain and it was
flung into the river in such heaps that, the water being low
with the summer heat, it formed the nucleus of an island.[5]

Archaic character of the sacrifice and its analogies in the harvest customs of Northern Europe.

---

[1] The Huzuls of the Carpathians
attribute a special virtue to a horse's
head.   They think that fastened on a
pole and set up in a garden it protects
the cabbages from caterpillars.   See R.
F. Kaindl, *Die Huzulen* (Wienna, 1894),
p. 102.   At the close of the rice-harvest
the Garos of Assam celebrate a festival
in which the effigy of a horse plays an
important part.   When the festival is
over, the body of the horse is thrown
into a stream, but the head is preserved
for another year.   See Note at the end
of the volume.

[2] Above, pp. 9 *sq.*

[3] Above, vol. i. pp. 268, 272.

[4] Above, vol. i. pp. 141, 155, 156,
158, 160 *sq.*, 301.   [5] Livy, ii. 5.

The horse sacrifice was thus an old autumn custom observed upon the king's corn-fields at the end of the harvest. The tail and blood of the horse, as the chief parts of the corn-spirit's representative, were taken to the king's house and kept there ; just as in Germany the harvest-cock is nailed on the gable or over the door of the farmhouse ; and as the last sheaf, in the form of the Maiden, is carried home and kept over the fireplace in the Highlands of Scotland. Thus the blessing of the corn-spirit was brought to the king's house and hearth and, through them, to the community of which he was the head. Similarly in the spring and autumn customs of Northern Europe the Maypole is sometimes set up in front of the house of the mayor or burgomaster, and the last sheaf at harvest is brought to him as the head of the village. But while the tail and blood fell to the king, the neighbouring village of the Subura, which no doubt once had a similar ceremony of its own, was gratified by being allowed to compete for the prize of the horse's head. The Mamilian tower, to which the Suburans nailed the horse's head when they succeeded in carrying it off, appears to have been a peel-tower or keep of the old Mamilian family, the magnates of the village.[1] The ceremony thus performed on the king's fields and at his house on behalf of the whole town and of the neighbouring village presupposes a time when each township performed a similar ceremony on its own fields. In the rural districts of Latium the villages may have continued to observe the custom, each on its own land, long after the Roman hamlets had merged their separate harvest-homes in the common celebration on the king's lands. There is no intrinsic improbability in the supposition that the sacred grove of Aricia, like the Field of Mars at Rome, may have been the scene of a common harvest celebration, at which a horse was sacrificed with the same rude rites on behalf of the neighbouring villages. The horse would represent the fructifying spirit both of the tree and of the corn, for the two ideas melt into each other, as we see in customs like the Harvest-May.

However, it should be borne in mind that the evidence for thus interpreting the relation of horses to Virbius is

[1] Festus, ed. C. O. Müller, pp. 130, 131.

exceedingly slender, and that the custom of excluding
horses from the sacred Arician grove may have been
based on some other superstitious motive which entirely
escapes us.   At the city of Ialysus in Rhodes there was a
sanctuary of Alectrona, one of the daughters of the Sun,
into which no horse, ass, mule, or beast of burden of any
kind might enter.   Any person who broke the law by intro-
ducing one of these animals into the holy precinct, had to
purify the place by a sacrifice ; and the same atonement had
to be made by any man who brought shoes or any portion
of a pig within the sacred boundaries.   And whoever drove
or suffered his sheep to stray into the precinct was obliged
to pay a fine of one obol for every sheep that set foot
in it.[1]   The reasons for these prohibitions are quite unknown ; and the taboo on horses is particularly remarkable,
since the Rhodians were in the habit of offering a chariot
and horses every year to the Sun, the father of Alectrona,[2]
doubtless in order that he might ride on them through the sky.
Did they think that it was not for the daughter of the Sun
to meddle with horses, which were the peculiar property of
her father ?   The conjecture may perhaps be supported by
an analogy drawn from West Africa.   The Ewe negroes of the
Slave Coast conceive the Rain-god Nyikplä as a man who
rides a horse, and who may be seen galloping on it through
the sky in the form of a shooting star.   Hence in the town
of Angla, where he generally resides when he is at home, no
person may appear on horseback in the streets, that being
apparently regarded as an impious usurpation of the style of
the deity.   In former days even Europeans were forbidden
to ride on horseback in Angla ; and missionaries who
attempted to set the local prejudice at defiance have been
pelted with sticks and dirt by the outraged natives.[3]
Another deity who suffered not horses to enter his sacred

[1] Dittenberger, *Sylloge Inscriptionum Graecarum*,[2] No. 560 (vol. ii. pp. 259-261) ; Ch. Michel, *Recueil d'Inscriptions Grecques* (Brussels, 1900), No. 434, pp. 323 *sq.* ; P. Cauer, *Delectus Inscriptionum Graecarum propter dialectum memorabilium*[2] (Leipsic, 1883), No. 177, pp. 117 *sq.*   As to Alectrona or Alectryona, daughter of the Sun,

see Diodorus Siculus, v. 65. 5.
[2] Festus, *s.v.* "October equus," p. 181 ed. C. O. Müller.   See *The Magic Art and the Evolution of Kings*, i. 315.
[3] G. Zündel, "Land und Volk der Eweer auf der Sclavenküste in Westafrika," *Zeitschrift für Erdkunde zu Berlin*, xii. (1877) pp. 415 *sq.*

place was Rakelimalaza, a Malagasy god whose name signifies "renowned, although diminutive." His residence was a village situated on the top of a hill about seven miles east of Tananarivo. But horses were not the only animal or thing to which this fastidious being entertained a rooted aversion. "Within the limits of the ground which is considered sacred, and which embraces a wide circumference in the immediate vicinity of the idol's residence, it is strictly forbidden to bring, or to suffer to come, certain animals and certain objects, which are carefully specified by the keepers of the idol. Things thus forbidden are called *fady*; a term of similar import with the well-known tabu of the South Sea Islands. Every idol has its own particular *fady*. The things prohibited by Rakelimalaza are, guns, gunpowder, pigs, onions, sifotra (a shell-fish resembling a snail), sitry (a small animal resembling the young crocodile), striped or spotted robes, anything of a black colour, goats, horses, meat distributed at funerals or at the *tangena*, and cats and owls. Its keepers are forbidden to enter any house where there is a corpse ; and in crossing a river they are not permitted to say, ' Carry me,' otherwise they place themselves in danger of being seized by the crocodiles ; and in war they must not talk, or they are in danger of being shot." [1] To attempt to discover the particular reasons for all these numerous and varied taboos would obviously be futile ; many of them may be based on accidental circumstances which for us are lost past recovery. But it may be worth while to observe that a variety of taboos was enforced at other ancient Greek shrines besides the sanctuary of Alectrona at Ialysus. For example, no person was allowed to enter the sanctuary of the Mistress at Lycosura in Arcadia clad in black, purple, or flowered vestments, or wearing shoes or a ring, or with his or her hair plaited or covered, or carrying flowers in his hand ; [2] and no pomegranates might be brought into the sanctuary, though all other fruits of the orchard were free to enter.[3] These instances may warn us against the danger of

[1] Rev. W. Ellis, *History of Mada-gascar* (London, preface dated 1838), i. 402 *sq.*

[2] Dittenberger, *Sylloge Inscrip-tionum Graecarum*,[2] No. 939 (vol. ii. p. 803).

[3] Pausanias, viii. 37. 7.

arguing too confidently in favour of any one of the many possible reasons which may have moved the old Latins to exclude horses from the sacred Arician grove. The domain of primitive superstition, in spite of the encroachments of science, is indeed still to a great extent a trackless wilderness, a tangled maze, in the gloomy recesses of which the forlorn explorer may wander for ever without a light and without a clue.

Uncertainty as to the reason for excluding horses from the Arician grove.

CHAPTER X

EATING THE GOD

§ 1. *The Sacrament of First-Fruits*

Custom of eating the new corn sacramentally as the body of the corn-spirit. WE have now seen that the corn-spirit is represented sometimes in human, sometimes in animal form, and that in both cases he is killed in the person of his representative and eaten sacramentally. To find examples of actually killing the human representative of the corn-spirit we had naturally to go to savage races; but the harvest-suppers of our European peasants have furnished unmistakable examples of the sacramental eating of animals as representatives of the corn-spirit. But further, as might have been anticipated, the new corn is itself eaten sacramentally, that is, as the

Loaves baked of the new corn in human shape and eaten. body of the corn-spirit. In Wermland, Sweden, the farmer's wife uses the grain of the last sheaf to bake a loaf in the shape of a little girl; this loaf is divided amongst the whole household and eaten by them.[1] Here the loaf represents the corn-spirit conceived as a maiden; just as in Scotland the corn-spirit is similarly conceived and represented by the last sheaf made up in the form of a woman and bearing the name of the Maiden. As usual, the corn-spirit is believed to reside in the last sheaf; and to eat a loaf made from the last sheaf is, therefore, to eat the corn-spirit itself. Similarly at La Palisse, in France, a man made of dough is hung upon the fir-tree which is carried on the last harvest-waggon. The tree and the dough-man are taken to the mayor's house and kept there till the vintage is over. Then the close of the harvest is celebrated by a

---

[1] W. Mannhardt, *Mythologische Forschungen* (Strasburg, 1884), p. 179.

feast at which the mayor breaks the dough-man in pieces and gives the pieces to the people to eat.[1]

In these examples the corn-spirit is represented and eaten in human shape. In other cases, though the new corn is not baked in loaves of human shape, still the solemn ceremonies with which it is eaten suffice to indicate that it is partaken of sacramentally, that is, as the body of the corn-spirit. For example, the following ceremonies used to be observed by Lithuanian peasants at eating the new corn. About the time of the autumn sowing, when all the corn had been got in and the threshing had begun, each farmer held a festival called Sabarios, that is, " the mixing or throwing together." He took nine good handfuls of each kind of crop—wheat, barley, oats, flax, beans, lentils, and the rest ; and each handful he divided into three parts. The twenty-seven portions of each grain were then thrown on a heap and all mixed up together. The grain used had to be that which was first threshed and winnowed and which had been set aside and kept for this purpose. A part of the grain thus mixed was employed to bake little loaves, one for each of the household ; the rest was mixed with more barley or oats and made into beer. The first beer brewed from this mixture was for the drinking of the farmer, his wife, and children ; the second brew was for the servants. The beer being ready, the farmer chose an evening when no stranger was expected. Then he knelt down before the barrel of beer, drew a jugful of the liquor and poured it on the bung of the barrel, saying, " O fruitful earth, make rye and barley and all kinds of corn to flourish." Next he took the jug to the parlour, where his wife and children awaited him. On the floor of the parlour lay bound a black or white or speckled (not a red) cock and a hen of the same colour and of the same brood, which must have been hatched within the year. Then the farmer knelt down, with the jug in his hand, and thanked God for the harvest and prayed for a good crop next year. Next all lifted up their hands and said, " O God, and thou, O earth, we give you this cock and hen as

Old Lithuanian ritual at eating the new corn.

---

[1] W. Mannhardt, *Der Baumkultus der Germanen und ihrer Nachbarstämme* (Berlin, 1875), p. 205. It is not said that the dough-man is made of the new corn ; but probably this is, or once was, the case.

a free-will offering." With that the farmer killed the fowls with the blows of a wooden spoon, for he might not cut their heads off. After the first prayer and after killing each of the birds he poured out a third of the beer. Then his wife boiled the fowls in a new pot which had never been used before. After that, a bushel was set, bottom upwards, on the floor, and on it were placed the little loaves mentioned above and the boiled fowls. Next the new beer was fetched, together with a ladle and three mugs, none of which was used except on this occasion. When the farmer had ladled the beer into the mugs, the family knelt down round the bushel. The father then uttered a prayer and drank off the three mugs of beer. The rest followed his example. Then the loaves and the flesh of the fowls were eaten, after which the beer went round again, till every one had emptied each of the three mugs nine times. None of the food should remain over ; but if anything did happen to be left, it was consumed next morning with the same ceremonies. The bones were given to the dog to eat ; if he did not eat them all up, the remains were buried under the dung in the cattle-stall. This ceremony was observed at the beginning of December. On the day on which it took place no bad word might be spoken.[1]

Such was the custom about two hundred years or more ago. At the present day in Lithuania, when new potatoes or loaves made from the new corn are being eaten, all the people at table pull each other's hair.[2] The meaning of this last custom is obscure, but a similar custom was certainly observed by the heathen Lithuanians at their solemn sacri-

Modern European ceremonies at eating the new corn or new potatoes.

[1] M. Praetorius, *Deliciae Prussicae oder Preussische Schaubuhne, im wörtlichen Auszüge aus dem Manuscript herausgegeben* von Dr. William Pierson (Berlin, 1871), pp. 60-64 ; W. Mannhardt, *Antike Wald- und Feldkulte* (Berlin, 1877), pp. 249 *sqq.* Mathaeus Praetorius, the author to whom we owe the account in the text, compiled a detailed description of old Lithuanian manners and customs in the latter part of the seventeenth century at the village of Niebudzen, of which he was Protestant pastor.

The work, which seems to have occupied him for many years and to have been finished about 1698, exists in manuscript but has never been published in full. Only excerpts from it have been printed by Dr. W. Pierson. Praetorius was born at Memel about 1635 and died in 1707. In the later years of his life he incurred a good deal of odium by joining the Catholic Church.

[2] A. Bezzenberger, *Litauische Forschungen* (Göttingen, 1882), p. 89.

fices.[1] Many of the Esthonians of the island of Oesel will
not eat bread baked of the new corn till they have first
taken a bite at a piece of iron.[2] The iron is here plainly a
charm, intended to render harmless the spirit that is in the
corn.[3] In Sutherlandshire at the present day, when the
new potatoes are dug all the family must taste them, otherwise " the spirits in them [the potatoes] take offence, and the
potatoes would not keep." [4] In one part of Yorkshire it is
still customary for the clergyman to cut the first corn ; and
my informant believes that the corn so cut is used to make
the communion bread.[5] If the latter part of the custom is
correctly reported (and analogy is all in its favour), it shews
how the Christian communion has absorbed within itself a
sacrament which is doubtless far older than Christianity.

Among the heathen Cheremiss on the left bank of the
Volga, when the first bread baked from the new corn is to
be eaten, the villagers assemble in the house of the oldest
inhabitant, the eastern door is opened, and all pray with
their faces towards it. Then the sorcerer or priest gives to
each of them a mug of beer, which they drain ; next he cuts
and hands to every person a morsel of the loaf, which they
partake of. Finally, the young people go to the elders and
bowing down to the earth before them say, " We pray God
that you may live, and that God may let us pray next year
for new corn." The rest of the day is passed in mirth and
dancing. The whole ceremony, observes the writer who has
described it, looks almost like a caricature of the Eucharist.[6]
According to another account, each Cheremiss householder
on this occasion, after bathing, places some of each kind of
grain, together with malt, cakes, and drink, in a vessel, which
he holds up to the sun, at the same time thanking the gods
for the good things which they have bestowed upon him.[7]

Ceremony of the heathen Cheremiss at eating the new corn.

[1] Simon Grunau, *Preussischer Chronik*, herausgegeben von Dr. M. Perlbach, i. (Leipsic, 1876) p. 91.

[2] J. B. Holzmayer, "Osiliana," *Verhandlungen der gelehrten Estnischen Gesellschaft zu Dorpat*, vii. Heft 2 (Dorpat, 1872), p. 108.

[3] On iron as a charm against spirits, see *Taboo and the Perils of the Soul*, pp. 232 *sqq.*

[4] *Folk-lore Journal*, vii. (1889) p. 54.

[5] Communicated by the Rev. J. J. C. Yarborough, of Chislehurst, Kent. See *Folk-lore Journal*, vii. (1889) p. 50.

[6] Von Haxthausen, *Studien über die innern Zustände, das Volksleben und insbesondere die ländliche Einrichtungen Russlands*, i. 448 *sq.*

[7] J. G. Georgi, *Beschreibung aller Nationen des Russischen Reichs* (St. Petersburg, 1776), p. 37.

But this part of the ceremony is a sacrifice rather than a sacrament of the new corn.

The Aino or Ainu of Japan are said to distinguish various kinds of millet as male and female respectively, and these kinds, taken together, are called "the divine husband and wife cereal " (*Umurek haru kamui*). " Therefore before millet is pounded and made into cakes for general eating, the old men have a few made for themselves first to worship. When they are ready they pray to them very earnestly and say :— ' O thou cereal deity, we worship thee. Thou hast grown very well this year, and thy flavour will be sweet. Thou art good. The goddess of fire will be glad, and we also shall rejoice greatly. O thou god, O thou divine cereal, do thou nourish the people. I now partake of thee. I worship thee and give thee thanks.' After having thus prayed, they, the worshippers, take a cake and eat it, and from this time the people may all partake of the new millet. And so with many gestures of homage and words of prayer this kind of food is dedicated to the well-being of the Ainu. No doubt the cereal offering is regarded as a tribute paid to god, but that god is no other than the seed itself; and it is only a god in so far as it is beneficial to the human body." [1]

The natives of the Reef Islands in Melanesia describe as follows the ceremonies which they observe at eating new fruits : " When the fruit of trees that are eatable, such as bread-fruit, or *ninas* (nuts) is nearly ripe, about a month before the time that people eat it, they all go together into the bush. They must all go together for this ' holy eating,' and when they return they all assemble in one place, and no one will be absent ; they sit down and cook bread-fruit. While it is being cooked no one will eat beforehand, but they set it in order and cook it with reverence, and with the belief that the spirit has granted that food to them and they return thanks to him for it. When it is cooked a certain man takes a bread-fruit and climbs up a tree, and all the people stand on the ground and they all look up, and when he has reached the top they shout out, and when they have shouted they call out, ' This is the bread-fruit of the whole

[1] Rev. J. Batchelor, *The Ainu and their Folk-lore* (London, 1901), pp. 204, 206.

land '; then he throws down the bread-fruit and they pick it up and shout out again and give thanks, for they think that the spirit who protects the fruit will hear. Their thoughts are thus also with regard to the yam, there is no difference, it is all the same ; they think that a spirit gives them food, and the people assemble together and thank the spirit. In every island they think that there is a spirit presiding over food." [1]

At Bourail, in New Caledonia, the eating of the first yams of the season is a solemn ceremony. The women may take no part in it ; indeed for five days previously they may not even shew themselves on any pretext, and must hide in the forest. But the men of other tribes are invited to share in the festivity. On the day of the ceremony seven or eight yams are dug up with the greatest precaution, wrapt in leaves, and carried before the great wooden images, ten or twelve feet high, rudely carved in human form and painted black, red, and white, which represent the ancestors of the tribe. Special pots, only used on these occasions, are then disinterred by boys, who cook the new yams in them, eat them, and afterwards bury the pots in the places where they found them. Thereupon the chief or the oldest man mounts a ladder and addresses the crowd in a long and voluble harangue, telling them how their forefathers always respected the feast of the first yams, and exhorting the young men of the tribe to do the same in the time to come. After that, turning towards the ancestral images, he prays them to give a good crop of yams every year to the people and their descendants, adjuring them to remember how, while they were still on earth, they always ate to their heart's content, and beseeching them to reflect that their sons and grandsons naturally desire to do the same. When the orator has finished his discourse, and his hearers have signified their approval of his eloquence by a loud grunt, the new yams are dressed and eaten, each family cooking them in a pot of its own. [2]

Ceremony of the New Caledonians at eating the first yams.

[1] "Native Stories from Santa Cruz and Reef Islands," translated by the Rev. W. O'Ferrall, *Journal of the Anthropological Institute*, xxxiv. (1904) p. 230.

[2] Glaumont, "La culture de l'igname et du taro en Nouvelle-Calédonie," *L'Anthropologie*, viii. (1897) pp. 43-45.

Ceremonies
observed at
eating the
new rice in
Buru and
Celebes.

At the close of the rice harvest in the East Indian island of Buru, each clan (*fenna*) meets at a common sacramental meal, to which every member of the clan is bound to contribute a little of the new rice. This meal is called "eating the soul of the rice," a name which clearly indicates the sacramental character of the repast. Some of the rice is also set apart and offered to the spirits.[1] Amongst the Alfoors of Minahassa, in the north of Celebes, the priest sows the first rice-seed and plucks the first ripe rice in each field. This rice he roasts and grinds into meal, and gives some of it to each of the household.[2] Shortly before the rice-harvest in Bolang Mongondo, another district of Celebes, an offering is made of a small pig or a fowl. Then the priest plucks a little rice, first on his own field and next on those of his neighbours. All the rice thus plucked by him he dries along with his own, and then gives it back to the respective owners, who have it ground and boiled. When it is boiled the women take it back, with an egg, to the priest, who offers the egg in sacrifice and returns the rice to the women. Of this rice every member of the family, down to the youngest child, must partake. After this ceremony every one is free to get in his rice.[3]

Ceremonies
observed at
eating the
new rice in
Ceram and
Borneo.

On the north coast of Ceram every owner of a rice-field begins planting by making six holes in the middle of the field and depositing rice-seed in them. When the crop is ripe, the rice which has sprouted from these six holes must be the first to be reaped and the first to be eaten by the owner at the common harvest-feast of the village. When all the owners of the fields have thus partaken of the rice that was first planted and first reaped in their fields, the other villagers may help themselves to rice out of the pot. Not till this feast has been held may the owners of rice-fields sell their rice.[4] Among the Kayans of Central Borneo, who, as

[1] G. A. Wilken, "Bijdragen tot de kennis der Alfoeren van het eiland Boeroe," p. 26 (*Verhandelingen van het Bataviaasch Genootschap van Kunsten en Wetenschappen* vol. xxxviii., Batavia, 1875).

[2] P. N. Wilken, "Bijdragen tot de kennis van de zeden en gewoonten der Alfoeren in de Minahassa," *Mededeelin-*

gen van wege het Nederlandsche Zendelinggenootschap, vii. (1863) p. 127.

[3] N. P. Wilken en J. A. Schwarz, "Allerlei over het land en volk van Bolaang Mongondou," *Mededeelingen van wege het Nederlandsche Zendelinggenootschap,* xi. (1867) pp. 369 *sq.*

[4] J. Boot, "Korte schets der noordkust van Ceram," *Tijdschrift van het*

we have seen, believe rice to be animated by a soul,[1] before a family partakes of the new rice at harvest, a priestess must touch the face and breast of every person with a magical instrument (*kahe parei*) consisting of the husk of a certain fruit adorned with strings of beads. After this ceremony has been performed on every member of the family, he or she eats a few grains of the new rice and drinks a little water. When all have complied with this ritual, the feast begins.[2]

Amongst the Burghers or Badagas, a tribe of the Neilgherry Hills in Southern India, the first handful of seed is sown and the first sheaf reaped by a Curumbar—a man of a different tribe, the members of which the Burghers regard as sorcerers. The grain contained in the first sheaf "is that day reduced to meal, made into cakes, and, being offered as a first-fruit oblation, is, together with the remainder of the sacrificed animal, partaken of by the Burgher and the whole of his family, as the meat of a federal offering and sacrifice."[3] Amongst the Coorgs of Southern India the man who is to cut the first sheaf of rice at harvest is chosen by an astrologer. At sunset the whole household takes a hot bath and then goes to the rice-field, where the chosen reaper cuts an armful of rice with a new sickle, and distributes two or more stalks to all present. Then all return to the threshing-floor. A bundle of leaves is adorned with a stalk of rice and fastened to the post in the centre of the threshing-floor. Enough of the new rice is now threshed, cleaned, and ground to provide flour for the dough-cakes which each member of the household is to eat. Then they go to the door of the house, where the mistress washes the feet of the sheaf-cutter, and presents to him, and after him to all the rest, a brass vessel full of milk, honey, and sugar, from which each person takes a draught. Next the man who cut the sheaf kneads a cake of rice-meal, plantains, milk, honey, seven new rice corns, seven pieces

Ceremonies observed at eating the new rice in India.

Nederlandsch Aardrijkskundig Genootschap, Tweede Serie, x. (1893) pp. 671 *sq.*

[1] See above, vol. i. pp. 184 *sqq.*

[2] A. W. Nieuwenhuis, *In Centraal Borneo* (Leyden, 1900), i. 156; *id.*, *Quer durch Borneo* (Leyden, 1904-

1907), i. 117 *sq.* In the latter passage "*ist jeder*" is a misprint for "*isst jeder*"; the Dutch original is "*eet ieder.*"

[3] H. Harkness, *Description of a Singular Aboriginal Race inhabiting the Summit of the Neilgherry Hills* (London, 1832), pp. 56 *sq.*

of coco-nut, and so on. Every one receives a little of this cake on an Ashvatha leaf, and eats it. The ceremony is then over and the sheaf-cutter mixes with the company. When he was engaged in cutting the rice no one might touch him.[1] Among the Hindoos of Southern India the eating of the new rice is the occasion of a family festival called Pongol. The new rice is boiled in a new pot on a fire which is kindled at noon on the day when, according to Hindoo astrologers, the sun enters the tropic of Capricorn. The boiling of the pot is watched with great anxiety by the whole family, for as the milk boils, so will the coming year be. If the milk boils rapidly, the year will be prosperous; but it will be the reverse if the milk boils slowly. Some of the new boiled rice is offered to the image of Gaṇeṣa; then every one partakes of it.[2] In some parts of Northern India the festival of the new crop is known as *Navan*, that is, "new grain." When the crop is ripe, the owner takes the omens, goes to the field, plucks five or six ears of barley in the spring crop and one of the millets in the autumn harvest. This is brought home, parched, and mixed with coarse sugar, butter, and curds. Some of it is thrown on the fire in the name of the village gods and deceased ancestors; the rest is eaten by the family.[3] At Gilgit, in the Hindoo Koosh, before wheat-harvest begins, a member of every household gathers a handful of ears of corn secretly at dusk. A few of the ears are hung up over the door of the house, and the rest are roasted next morning, and eaten steeped in milk. The day is spent in rejoicings, and next morning the harvest begins.[4]

Ceremonies observed by the Chams at ploughing, sowing, reaping, and eating the new rice.

The Chams of Binh-Thuan, in Indo-China, may not reap the rice-harvest until they have offered the first-fruits to Po-Nagar, the goddess of agriculture, and have consumed them sacramentally. These first-fruits are gathered from certain sacred fields called *Hamou-Klêk-Laoa* or "fields of

[1] Ch. E. Gover, *The Folk-songs of Southern India* (London, 1872), pp. 105 *sqq.* ; "Coorg Folklore," *Folk-lore Journal*, vii. (1889) pp. 302 *sqq.*

[2] Gover, "The Pongol Festival in Southern India," *Journal of the Royal Asiatic Society*, N.S., v. (1871) pp. 91 *sqq.*

[3] From notes sent to me by my friend Mr. W. Crooke.

[4] Major J. Biddulph, *Tribes of the Hindoo Koosh* (Calcutta, 1880), p. 103.

secret tillage," which are both sown and reaped with
peculiar ceremonies. Apparently the tilling of the earth
is considered a crime which must be perpetrated secretly
and afterwards atoned for. On a lucky day in June, at
the first cock-crow, two men lead the buffaloes and the
plough to the sacred field, round which they draw three
furrows in profound silence and then retire. Afterwards at
dawn the owner of the land comes lounging by, as if by the
merest chance. At sight of the furrows he stops, pretends
to be much surprised, and cries out, " Who has been secretly
ploughing my field this night ? " Hastening home, he kills
a kid or some fowls, cooks the victuals, and prepares five
quids of betel, some candles, a flask of oil, and lustral
water of three different sorts. With these offerings and
the plough drawn by the buffaloes, he returns to the field,
where he lights the candles and spreading out the victuals
worships Po-Nagar and the other deities, saying : " I know
not who has secretly ploughed my field this night. Pardon,
ye gods, those who have done this wrong. Accept these
offerings. Bless us. Suffer us to proceed with this work."
Then, speaking in the name of the deities, he gives the
reassuring answer, " All right. Plough away ! " With
the lustral water he washes or sprinkles the buffaloes, the
yoke, and the plough. The oil serves to anoint the plough
and to pour libations on the ground. The five quids of
betel are buried in the field. Thereupon the owner sows a
handful of rice on the three furrows that have been traced,
and eats the victuals with his people. After all these rites
have been duly performed, he may plough and sow his
land as he likes. When the rice has grown high enough in
this " field of secret tillage " to hide pigeons, offerings of
ducks, eggs, and fowls are made to the deities ; and fresh
offerings, which generally consist of five plates of rice, two
boiled fowls, a bottle of spirits, and five quids of betel, are
made to Po-Nagar and the rest at the time when the rice
is in bloom. Finally, when the rice in " the field of secret
tillage " is ripe, it has to be reaped before any of the rest.
Offerings of food, such as boiled fowls, plates of rice, cakes,
and so forth, are spread out on the field ; a candle is lit,
and a priest or, in his absence, the owner prays to the

guardian deities to come and partake of the food set before them. After that the owner of the land cuts three stalks of rice with a sickle in the middle of the field, then he cuts three handfuls at the side, and places the whole in a napkin. These are the first-fruits offered to Po-Nagar, the goddess of agriculture. On being taken home the rice from the three handfuls is husked, pounded in a mortar, and presented to the goddess with these words : " Taste, O goddess, these first-fruits which have just been reaped." This rice is afterwards eaten, while the straw and husks are burned. Having eaten the first-fruits of the rice, the owner takes the three stalks cut in the middle of the field, passes them through the smoke of the precious eagle-wood, and hangs them up in his house, where they remain till the next sowing-time comes round. The grain from these three stalks will form the seed of the three furrows in " the field of secret tillage." Not till these ceremonies have been performed is the proprietor at liberty to reap the rest of that field and all the others.[1]

Ceremony at eating the new yams at Onitsha on the Niger. The ceremony of eating the new yams at Onitsha, on the Niger, is thus described : " Each headman brought out six yams, and cut down young branches of palm-leaves and placed them before his gate, roasted three of the yams, and got some kola-nuts and fish. After the yam is roasted, the *Libia*, or country doctor, takes the yam, scrapes it into a sort of meal, and divides it into halves ; he then takes one piece, and places it on the lips of the person who is going to eat the new yam. The eater then blows up the steam from the hot yam, and afterwards pokes the whole into his mouth, and says, ' I thank God for being permitted to eat the new yam ' ; he then begins to chew it heartily, with fish likewise." [2]

Ceremonies at eating the new yams among the Ewe negroes of Togoland. Among the Ewe negroes of West Africa the eating of the new yams is the greatest festival of the year ; it usually falls at the beginning of September, and its character is predominantly religious. We possess a native account of the festival

[1] E. Aymonier, " Les Tchames et leurs religions," *Revue de l'histoire des Religions*, xxiv. (1891) pp. 272-274.

[2] S. Crowther and J. C. Taylor, *The Gospel on the Banks of the Niger* (London, 1859), pp. 287 *sq.* Mr. Taylor's information is repeated in *West African Countries and Peoples*, by J. Africanus B. Horton (London, 1868), pp. 180 *sq.*

as it is celebrated by the tribe of the Hos in Togoland.
When the yams are ripe and ready to be dug up and brought
home, two days are devoted to cleansing the town of all ills,
whether spiritual or material, as a solemn preparation for the
ensuing celebration.   When these rites of purification, which
will be described in a later part of this work, have been
accomplished, then, in the words of the native account, "the
people make ready to eat the new yams.   And the manner
of making ready consists in going to the fields and digging
the yams.   However, they do not bring them home but lay
them down somewhere on the way.   The reason why they
do not bring them home is that the people have not yet been
on the place where they sacrifice to the deity.   When they
wish to go thither, the way to the sacrificial place of Agbasia
must first be cleared of grass.   Afterwards the people come
with their drums, which they beat loudly.   When they are
come to the place of sacrifice, they first raise two great
mounds of earth, and they bring to the place of sacrifice
palm wine, uncooked and cooked yams, and meal mixed
with oil.   First of all the uncooked yams are cut in two
through the middle, and then this prayer is offered : ' Agbasia,
thou art he who has given the yams ; therefore here is thine
own !   We thank thee sincerely.   May the eating of the
yams be a great joy, and may no quarrel intervene ! '   Thereupon they lay down on the ground yams mixed with oil and
not mixed with oil.   In doing so they say to Agbasia, ' He
who eats not the white yams, to him belong the yams mixed
with oil ; and he who eats not the yams mixed with oil, to
him belong the white yams.'   They do the same with the
meal that is mixed with oil and with the meal that is not
mixed with oil.   Thereby they say : ' Here we bring thee all
that thou hast given us.   Eat thereof what thou pleasest ! '
After that they pour palm wine into one pot and water into
another, and say, ' When one has eaten, one drinks water.'
Thereby the drums sound, songs are sung, and the priest says :
' Our father Agbasia, we pray thee, let us hear no more evil
but good only !   When women are with child, let them bear
twins and triplets, that we may increase and multiply !
When the time for sowing the yams comes again, make it to
rain upon them even more than hitherto, in order that we

Ceremonies
at eating
the new
yams
among
the Ewe
negroes of
Togoland.
may come again and thank thee more sincerely than hitherto!'
Thereupon the priest pours water on one of the mounds,
makes a paste with it, and calls the people thither.   Then
he dips his finger in the slime and smears it on their brows,
temples, and breasts, saying, ' This is the slime of Agbasia,
wherewith I smear you, that ye may remain in life.'   After
that they disperse and go home."   Further, the prayers and
offerings of the individual peasants on the occasion of the
yam festival are described as follows.   " In the evening, when
the town is swept clean, the people go to the fields to fetch
yams, which, however, they may not yet bring into the town
and therefore they hide them in the forest.   As soon as the
high priest quits the town next morning to go to the
sacrificial place of his god, the women set out to fetch the
yams which they had deposited.   Now they begin to cook.
Many people kill fowls or goats, and others buy fish for the
festival.   When the yams are sodden, a little is broken off,
mixed with oil, and laid, together with uncooked yams, on
the ground at the entrance to the homestead.   Thereby the
house-father says : ' That belongs to all those (gods) who
abide at the fence.'   He does the same under the door of
the house and says : ' That belongs to all those (gods) who
dwell with me.'   Then he goes to the loom, and brings it
its offering, and says : ' That belongs to all the " Artificers "
who have helped me in weaving.'   After that he lays all
his charms on a mat spread in the house, and brings them
also their offering, and speaks with them.

" Another account describes the priestly functions of the
house-father still more fully.   Every house-father takes a
raw piece of yam and goes with it to his loom (*agbati*) and
prays : ' May the Artificers take this yam and eat !   When
they practise their art, may it prosper !'   Again he takes
a raw yam and goes with it under the house-door and
prays : ' O my guardian-spirit (*aklama*) and all ye gods
who pay heed to this house, come and eat yams !   When I
also eat of them, may I remain healthy and nowhere feel
pain !   May my housemates all remain healthy !'   After
he has invoked their protection on his family, he takes a
cooked yam, crumbles it on a stone, and mixes it with red
oil.   With this mixture he goes again to the loom and prays

as before.   But even that is not the end of the worship of
the Artificers.   He again crumbles a cooked yam, but this
time he does not mix it with red oil ; he goes to the entrance
of the homestead and prays again to the loom : ' He among
the Artificers who does not relish yams mixed with oil, let
him come and take the white yam and eat it ! '   From
there he goes again under the house-door and prays : ' He
of my guardian gods and he of the watchers of the house
who likes not yams mixed with oil, let him come and take
the white yam from my hand and eat ! '   From the house-
door he steps into the midst of the chamber and says :
' He who relishes not the yams mixed with oil, may eat the
white ; he who relishes not the white may eat the red ; and
he who relishes not the red may eat the uncooked ! '   With
this prayer he has completed his duties as house-priest.
Just as the weaver prays to his loom, so the hunter prays
to his musket, the smith to his hammer and anvil, and the
carpenter to his plane and saw.

    " Now, while the free people begin to cook the yams so
soon as the priest has left the town, the slaves of the Earth
Gods, the *Trŏkluwo*, must first as children perform their duties
to the priest of their gods.   Each of these children receives
from his parents on the morning of the Yam Festival two
pieces of yam, which he brings to the priest of his god.   The
priest cuts off a small piece of the yam and divides the piece
again into four pieces.   The child kneels before him and
lolls out his tongue.   Holding two of these pieces of yam
in his hands, the priest utters a prayer over the child and
touches his tongue five times with the pieces of yam.   Then
the child stretches his hands out, each of which the priest
touches five times with the same pieces of yam and prays
as before.   Then he touches both feet of the child five times
and prays for the third time.   He takes half of the cowry-
shells which the child has brought, fastens them on a string,
and hangs it round the child's neck.   Thereby the child gets
leave to eat new yams.

    " After all these preparations the yams are pounded into
a mash, and every one calls his brother, that he may eat
with him.   When the meal is over, the people are called
together to amuse themselves and to drink palm wine.   In

the afternoon every one bathes, puts on a new garment, and girds himself with a new loin-cloth." [1]

Festival of the new yams among the Ashantees in September.

The Ashantees celebrate the festival of the new yams early in September; until it is over none of the people may taste of the new yams. "The Yam Custom," we are told, " is like the Saturnalia ; neither theft, intrigue, nor assault are punishable during the continuance, but the grossest liberty prevails, and each sex abandons itself to its passions." An eye-witness has described the scene at Coomassie, the capital : " The next morning the King ordered a large quantity of rum to be poured into brass pans, in various parts of the town ; the crowd pressing around, and drinking like hogs ; freemen and slaves, women and children, striking, kicking, and trampling each other under foot, pushed head foremost into the pans, and spilling much more than they drank. In less than an hour, excepting the principal men, not a sober person was to be seen, parties of four, reeling and rolling under the weight of another, whom they affected to be carrying home ; strings of women covered with red paint, hand in hand, falling down like rows of cards ; the commonest mechanics and slaves furiously declaiming on state palavers ; the most discordant music, the most obscene songs, children of both sexes prostrate in insensibility. All wore their handsomest cloths, which they trailed after them to a great length, in a drunken emulation of extravagance and dirtiness." About a hundred persons, mostly culprits reserved for the purpose, used to be sacrificed at this festival in Coomassie. All the chiefs killed several slaves that their blood might flow into the hole from which the new yam was taken. Such as could not afford to kill slaves took the head of a slave who had already been sacrificed and placed it in

---

[1] J. Spieth, *Die Ewe - Stämme* (Berlin, 1906), pp. 304-310, 340 ; compare *id.* pp. 435, 480, 768. The " slaves of the Earth-gods " are children whom women have obtained through prayers offered to Agbasia, the greatest of the Earth-gods. When such a child is born, it is regarded as the slave of Agbasia ; and the mother dedicates it to the service of the god, as in similar circumstances Hannah dedicated Samuel to the Lord (1 Samuel i.). If the child is a girl, she is married to the priest's son ; if it is a boy, he serves the priest until his mother has given birth to a girl whom she exchanges for the boy. See J. Spieth, *op. cit.* pp. 448-450. In all such cases the original idea probably was that the child has been begotten in the woman by the god and therefore belongs to him as to his father, in the literal sense of the word.

the hole. About ten days after these ceremonies the whole of the royal household ate new yams for the first time in the market-place, the King himself being in attendance. Next day he and his captains set off before sunrise to perform their annual ablutions in the river Dah ; almost all the inhabitants of the capital followed him, so that the streets appeared to be deserted. The following day the King, attended by his suite, washed in the marsh at the south-east end of the town and laved the water not only over himself but also over the chairs, stools, gold and silver plate, and the articles of furniture which were set aside for his special use.[1] From another account it appears that the King of Ashantee must eat the new yams before any of his subjects was at liberty to do so.[2] Similarly in the West African kingdom of Assinie, which forms part of the French possessions of Senegal, the king must eat the new yams eight full days before the people may taste them.[3]

A second festival of yams used to be celebrated at Coomassie in December, when the king or a fetish priest consecrated the new yams before they could be eaten by common folk. On one of the days of this December celebration all the laws were suspended, and every man might do what seemed good in his own eyes : he might even, contrary to custom, look at the king's wives, to the number of several hundreds, when they returned with the king and his suite from washing in the fetish water of Tana. All that day drinking went on, and the noise and uproar were prolonged far into the night. Early in the morning a human victim was sacrificed : the first man found near the gates of the palace was seized, butchered, and cut in pieces, and the executioners danced with the bleeding fragments of the victim in their hands or fastened round their necks. Before he ate of the new yams the king washed himself in fetish water brought from distant springs, and the chiefs performed similar ablutions.[4] In

Festival of the new yams at Coomassie and Benin

---

[1] T. E. Bowdich, *Mission from Cape Coast Castle to Ashantee*, New Edition (London, 1873), pp. 226-229.
[2] A. B. Ellis, *The Tshi-speaking Peoples of the Gold Coast* (London, 1887), pp. 229 *sq.*

[3] J. C. Reichenbach, "Etude sur le royaume d'Assinie," *Bulletin de la Société de Géographie* (Paris), vii.ème Série, xi. (1890) p. 349.
[4] Ramseyer and Kühne, *Four Years in Ashantee* (London, 1875), pp.

Benin the new yams might not be eaten until the king had performed certain ceremonies, among which one is said to have been a pretence of making a yam to grow in a pot. Dancing, merrymaking, and farces or plays formed part of the festival ; the city was crowded with people, and they indulged in a regular orgie.[1]

Ceremonies observed by the Nandi at eating the new eleusine grain.
Among the Nandi of British East Africa, when the eleusine grain is ripening in autumn, every woman who owns a cornfield goes out into it with her daughters, and they all pluck some of the ripe grain. Each of the women then fixes one grain in her necklace and chews another, which she rubs on her forehead, throat, and breast. No mark of joy escapes them ; sorrowfully they cut a basketful of the new corn, and carrying it home place it in the loft to dry. As the ceiling is of wickerwork, a good deal of the grain drops through the crevices and falls into the fire, where it explodes with a crackling noise. The people make no attempt to prevent this waste ; for they regard the crackling of the grain in the fire as a sign that the souls of the dead are partaking of it. A few days later porridge is made from the new grain and served up with milk at the evening meal. All the members of the family take some of the porridge and dab it on the walls and roofs of the huts ; also they put a little in their mouths and spit it out towards the east and on the outside of the huts. Then, holding up some of the grain in his hand, the head of the family prays to God for health and strength, and likewise for milk, and everybody present repeats the words of the prayer after him.[2] Amongst the Baganda, when the beans were ripe, a woman would call her eldest son to eat some of the first which she cooked ; if she neglected to do so, it was believed that she would incur the displeasure of the gods and fall ill. After the meal her husband jumped over her, and the beans might thereafter be eaten by all.[3]

Amongst the Caffres of Natal and Zululand, no one may eat of the new fruits till after a festival which marks

147-151; E. Perregaux, *Chez les Achanti* (Neuchatel, 1906), pp. 158-160.

[1] H. Ling Roth, *Great Benin* (Halifax, England, 1903), pp. 76 *sq.*

[2] A. C. Hollis, *The Nandi* (Oxford, 1909), pp. 46 *sq.*

[3] Rev. J. Roscoe, *The Baganda* (London, 1911), p. 428.

the beginning of the Caffre year and falls at the end of December or the beginning of January. All the people assemble at the king's kraal, where they feast and dance. Before they separate the "dedication of the people" takes place. Various fruits of the earth, as corn, mealies, and pumpkins, mixed with the flesh of a sacrificed animal and with "medicine," are boiled in great pots, and a little of this food is placed in each man's mouth by the king himself. After thus partaking of the sanctified fruits, a man is himself sanctified for the whole year, and may immediately get in his crops.[1] It is believed that if any man were to partake of the new fruits before the festival, he would die;[2] if he were detected, he would be put to death, or at least all his cattle would be taken from him.[3] The holiness of the new fruits is well marked by the rule that they must be cooked in a special pot which is used only for this purpose, and on a new fire kindled by a magician through the friction of two sticks which are called "husband and wife." These sticks are prepared by the sorcerers from the wood of the *Uzwati* tree and belong exclusively to the chief. The "wife" is the shorter of the two. When the magician has kindled the new fire on which the new fruits are to be cooked, he hands the fire-sticks back to the chief, for no other hand may touch them ; and they are then put away till they are required next season. The sticks are regarded as in a measure sacred, and no one, except the chief's personal servant, may go to the side of the hut where they are kept. No pot but the one used for the preparation of this feast may be set on a fire made by the friction of the "husband and wife." When the feast is over, the fire is carefully extinguished, and the pot is put away with the fire-sticks, where it remains untouched for another year.[4]

A remarkable feature of the festival, as it is observed at

---

[1] F. Speckmann, *Die Hermanns-burger Mission in Afrika* (Hermannsburg, 1876), pp. 150 *sq.*

[2] L. Grout, *Zulu-land* (Philadelphia, N.D.), p. 161.

[3] (*South African*) *Folk-lore Journal*, i. (1879) p. 135 ; Rev. H. Callaway,

Religious System of the Amazulu, Part iii. p. 389 note.

[4] Rev. J. Macdonald, *Light in Africa*, Second Edition (London, 1890), pp. 216 *sq.* On the conception of the two fire-sticks as husband and wife, see *The Magic Art and the Evolution of Kings*, ii. 208 *sqq.*

Dance of the Zulu king at the festival.

the court of the Zulu king, is a dance performed by the king himself in a mantle of grass or, according to another account, of herbs and corn-leaves. This mantle is afterwards burnt and its ashes are scattered and trodden into the ground by cattle.[1]

Licentious character of the festival.

Further, it is worthy of notice that the festival is described as a saturnalia, and we are told that " a great deal of noise and dancing goes on, and people are not supposed to be responsible for what they say or do."[2]

The festival as celebrated by the Pondos.

Thus, for example, among the Pondos the festival includes a period of license, during the continuance of which the chief abdicates his functions and any crime may be committed with impunity. The description of the Pondo festival comprises so many interesting features that I will reproduce it entire. "When a Pondo chief is to hold the feast of first-fruits, some of his people procure a ripe plant of the gourd family, pumpkin or calabash, from another tribe. This is cooked ; the inside cleaned out, and the rind made ready for use as a vessel. It is then presented to the chief with much ceremony. The first-fruits are now brought forward, and a sacrifice, generally a young bull, is offered, after which the feast commences. The chief issues certain orders for the conduct of the proceedings, tastes the fruits which are served in the gourd-dish with which he has been presented, and then abdicates

Bull-fights and games.

all his functions while the festival lasts. The cattle from all the neighbouring villages are collected in the vicinity, and now they are brought together, and the bulls incited to fight to determine which is to be king among them for the next year. The young people engage in games and dances, feats of strength and running. After these are over the whole community give themselves over to disorder, debauchery, and riot. In their bull-fights and games they but did honour to the powers of nature, and now, as they eat and drink, the same powers are honoured in another form and by other rites. There is no one in authority to keep order, and every man does what seems good in his

---

[1] J. Shooter, *The Kafirs of Natal* (London, 1857), p. 27 ; N. Isaacs, *Travels and Adventures in Eastern Africa* (London, 1836), ii. 293 ;　Dudley Kidd, *The Essential Kafir* (London, 1904), pp. 270, 271.

[2] J. Macdonald, *op. cit.* p. 189.

own eyes. Should a man stab his neighbour he escapes all punishment, and so too with all other crimes against the person, property, and morality. People are even permitted to abuse the chief to his face, an offence which at any other time would meet with summary vengeance and an uncere-monious dispatch to join the ancestors. While the feast continues, a deafening noise is kept up by drumming, shout-ing, hand-clapping, and every kind of instrument that can be made to emit sound. Men advance to the chief and ex-plain their origin, and also the object they hold sacred, by imitating the sounds and movements of their most sacred animal. This is the person's totem. Others imitate the gurgling made by an enemy when stabbed in the throat. Those who adopt this latter emblem are known as 'children of the spear.' When the ceremonies, revels, and mummeries are ended, the chief repairs to his accustomed place, and sitting down there, by that act resumes his kingly functions. He calls the bravest of his braves before him, who is immediately clothed and decorated with skins of animals suggestive of courage and strategy. He performs a dance amid the frenzied shouting of the multitude, after which the chief declares the festival at an end and harvest com-menced." [1] Another writer, speaking of the Zulu festival of first-fruits as it was celebrated in the time of the ferocious despot Chaka, says that "at this period the chiefs are allowed to converse unreservedly with the king, speaking with great freedom, and in some measure to be dictatorial." [2] Again, another traveller, who visited the Zulus in the reign of King Panda, tells us that "in spite of the practice of the most absolute despotism there are three days in the year when the nation in its turn has the right to call the king to a severe account for his acts. It is at the general assembly of the warriors, when the maize is ripe, that the lively discussions take place and the questions are put to which the king must answer at once in a manner satisfactory to the people. I have then seen

License ac-corded to chiefs and others at this festival among the Zulus.

[1] Rev. J. Macdonald, *Religion and Myth* (London, 1893), pp. 136-138, from manuscript notes furnished by J. Sutton. Mr. Macdonald has described the custom more briefly in his *Light in Africa*, Second Edition (London, 1890), p. 189.
[2] N. Isaacs, *Travels and Advent-ures in Eastern Africa* (London, 1836), ii. 292.

simple warriors come leaping from the ranks, assume the style of fluent and excessively energetic orators, and not only confront the fiery glare of Panda, but even attack him before everybody, blame his acts, call them infamous and base, compel him to vindicate his conduct, and then refute his vindication by dissecting it and exposing its falsehood, finally proceeding to haughty threats and winding up the harangue with a gesture of contempt." [1] Such liberties taken with the despotic Zulu kings seem to point to a time when they too, like the Pondo chiefs, abdicated or were deposed during the festival. Perhaps we may even go a step further. We have seen that on this occasion the Zulu king dances in a mantle of grass or of herbs and corn-leaves, which is afterwards burnt and the ashes scattered and trodden into the ground. This custom seems clearly intended to promote the fertility of the earth, and in earlier times the same end may have been compassed by burning the king himself and dispersing his ashes ; for we have seen that a Bechuana tribe, of the same Bantu stock as the Zulus, were wont to sacrifice a human victim for the good of the crops and to scatter his ashes over the ground.[2] In this connexion it should be borne in mind that we have found independent evidence of a custom of putting the Zulu king to death whenever his bodily strength began to fail.[3]

(marginal note:) Traces of an annual abdication of Zulu kings, perhaps of a custom of burning them and scattering their ashes.

---

[1] A. Delegorgue, *Voyage dans l'Afrique Australe* (Paris, 1847), ii. 237.

[2] Above, vol. i. p. 240.

[3] See *The Dying God*, pp. 36 *sq.* On the Zulu festival of first-fruits see also T. Arbousset et F. Daumas, *Voyage d'Exploration au Nord-Est de la Colonie du Cap de Bonne Espérance* (Paris, 1843), pp. 308 *sq.* ; G. Fritsch, *Die Eingeborenen Süd-Afrikas* (Breslau, 1872), p. 143. Fritsch mentions that after executing a grotesque dance in the presence of the assembled multitude the king gives formal permission to eat of the new fruits by dashing a gourd or calabash to the ground. This ceremony of breaking the calabash is mentioned also by J. Shooter (*Kafirs of Natal*, p. 27), L. Grout (*Zulu-land*, p. 162), and Mr. Dudley Kidd (*The Essential Kafir*, p. 271). According to this last writer the calabash is filled with boiled specimens of the new fruits, and the king sprinkles the people with the cooked food, frequently spitting it out on them. Mr. Grout tells us (*l.c.*) that at the ceremony a bull is killed and its gall drunk by the king and the people. In killing it the warriors must use nothing but their naked hands. The flesh of the bull is given to the boys to eat what they like and burn the rest ; the men may not taste it. See L. Grout, *op. cit.* p. 161. According to Shooter, two bulls are killed ; the first is black, the second of another colour. The boys who eat the beef of the black bull may not

Among the Bechuanas it is a rule that before they partake of the new crops they must purify themselves. The purification takes place at the commencement of the new year on a day in January which is fixed by the chief. It begins in the great kraal of the tribe, where all the adult males assemble. Each of them takes in his hand leaves of a gourd called by the natives *lerotse* (described as something between a pumpkin and a vegetable marrow); and having crushed the leaves he anoints with the expressed juice his big toes and his navel; many people indeed apply the juice to all the joints of their body, but the better-informed say that this is a vulgar departure from ancient custom. After this ceremony in the great kraal every man goes home to his own kraal, assembles all the members of his family, men, women, and children, and smears them all with the juice of the *lerotse* leaves. Some of the leaves are also pounded, mixed with milk in a large wooden dish, and given to the dogs to lap up. Then the porridge plate of each member of the family is rubbed with the *lerotse* leaves. When this purification has been completed, but not before, the people are free to eat of the new crops. On the night after the purification every man was bound, as a matter of ritual, to sleep with his chief wife. If she had been unfaithful to him during the past year, it was incumbent on her to confess her sin before she fulfilled her part of the ceremony. Having confessed she was purified by a medicine-man, who fumigated her with the smoke produced by burning a bean plant. Thereupon husband and wife cut each other slightly under the navel, and each of them rubbed his or her blood, mixed with " medicine," into the other's wound. That completed the purification of the woman, and the pair might now proceed with the rest of the rite. Should a married man be from home at the time when the annual purification

drink till the next morning, else the king would be defeated in war or visited with some personal misfortune. See Shooter, *op. cit.* pp. 26 *sq.* According to another account the sacrifice of the bull, performed by the warriors of a particular regiment with their bare hands, takes place several weeks before the festival of first-fruits, and

" the strength of the bull is supposed to enter into the king, thereby prolonging his health and strength." See D. Leslie, *Among the Zulus and Amatongas*[2] (Edinburgh, 1875), p. 91. For a general account of the Caffre festival of first-fruits, see Dudley Kidd, *The Essential Kafir* (London, 1904), pp. 270-272.

ceremony is performed, he is thought to be in a very sad
plight ; indeed his chances of surviving for another year are
supposed to be small.　On his return home, he dare not
enter his own house, for he would pollute it, and if even
his shadow were to fall on one of his children, the child
would die.　He must wait till his wife comes to him and
brings him a calabash of water to drink, which is a sign
that she has waited for his return to perform the rite of
purification together.　But if she does not bring the
water, he knows that in his absence she has performed the
rite with some other man, and it becomes necessary to
purge her by means of fumigation and blood-letting, as
described before.　But even when that purgation is completed, husband and wife may not indulge in connubial
intercourse for the rest of the year, that is, until the
next annual purification has taken place.　The Bechuanas
think that "any breach of this rule will be punished with
supernatural penalties—the husband, wife, or child will die." [1]

Ceremonies
observed
by the
Matabele
at eating
the new
fruits.
　　　　　Among the Matabele, another Bantu tribe of South
Africa, no one might partake of the new fruits till the king
had first tasted of them ; any one who was known to have
broken the law was instantly put to death.　On this
occasion the regiments assembled at Bulawayo, the capital,
and danced in a great semicircle before the king, who
occasionally joined in the dance.　When he did so, the
medicine-men and their satellites, armed with thorn-bushes,
rushed about among the dancers and incited them to fresh

[1] Rev. W. C. Willoughby, "Notes
on the Totemism of the Becwana,"
Journal of the Anthropological Institute,
xxxv. (1905) pp. 311-313.　It is very
remarkable that among several Bantu
tribes the cohabitation of husband and
wife is enjoined as a religious or magical
rite on a variety of solemn occasions,
such as after the death of a son or
daughter, the circumcision of a child,
the first menstruation of a daughter,
the occupation of a new house or of a
new village, etc.　For examples see
C. W. Hobley, *Ethnology of A-Kamba
and other East African Tribes* (Cambridge, 1910), pp. 58, 59, 60, 65, 67,
69, 74 ; H. A. Junod, " Les Conceptions physiologiques des Bantou

Sud-Africains et leurs tabous," *Revue
d'Ethnographie et de Sociologie*, i.
(1910) p. 148 ; Rev. J. Roscoe, *The
Baganda* (London, 1911), pp. 48, 144,
357, 363, 378, 428, etc. ; *id.*, "Further Notes on the Manners and
Customs of the Baganda," *Journal
of the Anthropological Institute*, xxxii.
(1902) pp. 59, 61.　Among the
Baganda the act of stepping or leaping
over a woman is regarded as equivalent to cohabitation with her, and is
accepted as a ritual substitute for it
(J. Roscoe, *The Baganda*, p. 357 note).
The ideas on which this custom of
ceremonial cohabitation is based are
by no means clear.

efforts by a vigorous application of the thorns to the bodies
of such as seemed to flag.   The king's wives also sang and
danced before him in long lines, holding the marriage ring in
their right hands and green boughs in their left.   On the
third day of the festival hundreds of oxen were sacrificed :
the flesh and blood of the black or sacred cattle were
converted into charms ; while the carcases of the rest were
cut up and distributed among the people, who feasted upon
them.   The fourth day was specially set apart for the
ceremony of the first-fruits.   In the morning all the people
went down to the river to wash, and on their return a witch-
doctor or medicine-man took a dish of the new vegetables
and corn, mixed with charms, and scattered the contents
by handfuls among the crowd, who seized and ate them.
After that the people were free to eat the new crops.
According to one account, this festival of first-fruits was
held at the first full moon which followed the summer
solstice (the twenty-first of December in the southern
hemisphere) ; according to another account, it took place a
few days after the full moon of February, which marked the
beginning of the Matabele year.[1]

The Ovambo or, as they call themselves, the Ovakuan- *Ceremony*
jama, of South-West Africa, may not partake of the new *observed by the*
fruits of the *omuongo* tree, which ripen in February and from *Ovambo*
which an intoxicating beverage is extracted, until certain *at eating the new*
ceremonies have been performed.   Among other things *fruits.*
husband and wife mutually offer each other one of the
fruits, make white strokes with chalk each on the brow,
cheeks, and nose of the other, and accompany the action
with the formal expression of good wishes.   If this ceremony,
which seems to mark the beginning of the New Year, were
omitted, they believe that they would be attacked by a
painful disease of the knee-joints which would cripple them.[2]

The Bororo Indians of Brazil think that it would be
certain death to eat the new maize before it has been blessed

---

[1] Ch. Croonenberghs, S.J., "La
fête de la Grande Danse dans le haut
Zambeze," *Les Missions Catholiques*,
xiv. (1882) pp. 230-234 ; L. Decle,
Three Years in Savage Africa (London, 1898), pp. 157 *sq.*   The two
accounts supplement each other.   I
have combined features from both in
the text.

[2] H. Tönjes, *Ovamboland, Land,
Leute, Mission* (Berlin, 1911), pp. 200
sq.

by the medicine-man. The ceremony of blessing it is as
follows. The half-ripe husk is washed and placed before
the medicine-man, who by dancing and singing for several
hours, and by incessant smoking, works himself up into a
state of ecstasy, whereupon he bites into the husk, trembling in every limb and uttering shrieks from time to
time. A similar ceremony is performed whenever a large
animal or a large fish is killed. The Bororo are firmly persuaded that were any man to touch unconsecrated maize or
meat, before the ceremony had been completed, he and his
whole tribe would perish.[1]

Amongst the Creek Indians of North America, the *busk*
or festival of first-fruits was the chief ceremony of the year.[2]
It was held in July or August, when the corn was ripe, and
marked the end of the old year and the beginning of the
new one. Before it took place, none of the Indians would
eat or even handle any part of the new harvest. Sometimes each town had its own busk; sometimes several towns
united to hold one in common. Before celebrating the
busk, the people provided themselves with new clothes and
new household utensils and furniture; they collected their
old clothes and rubbish, together with all the remaining
grain and other old provisions, cast them together in one

[1] V. Frič and P. Radin, "Contributions to the Study of the Bororo Indians,"
Journal of the Anthropological Institute,
xxxvi. (1906) p. 392.

[2] The ceremony is described independently by James Adair, *History of
the American Indians* (London, 1775),
pp. 96-111; W. Bartram, *Travels
through North and South Carolina,
Georgia, East and West Florida* (Lon-
don, 1792), pp. 507 *sq.*; A. Hodgson,
Letters from North America (London,
1824), i. 131 *sq.*; B. Hawkins,
"Sketch of the Creek Country," in
*Collections of the Georgia Historical
Society,* iii. (Savannah, 1848) pp. 75-
78; A. A. M'Gillivray, in H. R.
Schoolcraft's *Indian Tribes of the
United States* (Philadelphia, 1853-
1856), v. 267 *sq.*; F. G. Speck,
Ethnology of the Yuchi Indians
(Philadelphia, 1909), pp. 112-131.
The fullest descriptions are those

of Adair and Speck. In the text I
have chiefly followed Adair, our oldest
authority. A similar ceremony was
observed by the Cherokees. See the
description (from an unpublished MS.
of J. H. Payne, author of *Home, Sweet
Home*) in "Observations on the Creek
and Cherokee Indians, by William
Bartram, 1789, with prefatory and
supplementary notes by E. G. Squier,"
*Transactions of the American Ethno-
logical Society,* vol. iii. Part i. (1853)
p. 75. The Indians of Alabama also
held a great festival at their harvest
in July. They passed the day fasting, lit a new fire, purged themselves, and offered the first-fruits to
their *Manitoo*: the ceremony ended
with a religious dance. See Bossu,
*Nouveaux Voyages aux Indes occiden-
tales* (Paris, 1768), ii. 54. These
Indians of Alabama were probably
either the Creeks or the Cherokees.

common heap, and consumed them with fire.[1] As a preparation for the ceremony, all the fires in the village were extinguished, and the ashes swept clean away.   In particular,
the hearth or altar of the temple was dug up and the ashes
carried out.   Then the chief priest put some roots of the
button-snake plant, with some green tobacco leaves and a
little of the new fruits, at the bottom of the fireplace, which
he afterwards commanded to be covered up with white clay,
and wetted over with clean water.   A thick arbour of green
branches of young trees was then made over the altar.[2]
Meanwhile the women at home were cleaning out their
houses, renewing the old hearths, and scouring all the cooking vessels that they might be ready to receive the new fire
and the new fruits.[3]   The public or sacred square was carefully swept of even the smallest crumbs of previous feasts,
"for fear of polluting the first-fruit offerings."   Also every
vessel that had contained or had been used about any food
during the expiring year was removed from the temple
before sunset.   Then all the men who were not known to
have violated the law of the first-fruit offering and that of
marriage during the year were summoned by a crier to
enter the holy square and observe a solemn fast.   But the
women (except six old ones), the children, and all who had
not attained the rank of warriors were forbidden to enter
the square.   Sentinels were also posted at the corners of the
square to keep out all persons deemed impure and all
animals.   A strict fast was then observed for two nights Fast and
and a day, the devotees drinking a bitter decoction of purgation.
button-snake root "in order to vomit and purge their sinful
bodies."   That the people outside the square might also be
purified, one of the old men laid down a quantity of green
tobacco at a corner of the square ; this was carried off by
an old woman and distributed to the people without, who
chewed and swallowed it "in order to afflict their souls."
During this general fast, the women, children, and men of

---

[1] W. Bartram, *Travels*, p. 507.
[2] So amongst the Cherokees, according to J. H. Payne, an arbour of green
boughs was made in the sacred square ;
then "a beautiful bushy-topped shade-
tree was cut down close to the roots,
and planted in the very centre of the

sacred square.   Every man then provided himself with a green bough."

[3] So Adair.   Bartram, on the other
hand, as we have seen, says that the
people provided themselves with new
household utensils.

weak constitution were allowed to eat after mid-day, but not
before.   On the morning when the fast ended, the women
brought a quantity of the old year's food to the outside of
the sacred square.   These provisions were then fetched in
and set before the famished multitude, but all traces of them
New fire
made by
friction. had to be removed before noon.   When the sun was declin-
ing from the meridian, all the people were commanded by
the voice of a crier to stay within doors, to do no bad act,
and to be sure to extinguish and throw away every spark
of the old fire.   Universal silence now reigned.   Then the
high priest made the new fire by the friction of two pieces
of wood, and placed it on the altar under the green arbour.
This new fire was believed to atone for all past crimes
except murder.   Next a basket of new fruits was brought ;
the high priest took out a little of each sort of fruit, rubbed
it with bear's oil, and offered it, together with some flesh,
" to the bountiful holy spirit of fire, as a first-fruit offering,
and an annual oblation for sin."   He also consecrated the
sacred emetics (the button-snake root and the cassina or
black-drink) by pouring a little of them into the fire.   The
persons who had remained outside now approached, without
entering, the sacred square ; and the chief priest thereupon
made a speech, exhorting the people to observe their old
rites and customs, announcing that the new divine fire had
purged away the sins of the past year, and earnestly warning the women that, if any of them had not extinguished
the old fire, or had contracted any impurity, they must
forthwith depart, " lest the divine fire should spoil both them
and the people."   Some of the new fire was then set down
outside the holy square ; the women carried it home joy-
fully, and laid it on their unpolluted hearths.   When several
towns had united to celebrate the festival, the new fire
might thus be carried for several miles.   The new fruits
were then dressed on the new fires and eaten with bear's oil,
which was deemed indispensable.   At one point of the
festival the men rubbed the new corn between their hands,
then on their faces and breasts.[1]   During the festival which
followed, the warriors, dressed in their wild martial array,
their heads covered with white down and carrying white

[1] B. Hawkins, " Sketch," etc., p. 76.

feathers in their hands, danced round the sacred arbour, under which burned the new fire. The ceremonies lasted eight days, during which the strictest continence was practised. Towards the conclusion of the festival the warriors fought a mock battle ; then the men and women together, in three circles, danced round the sacred fire. Lastly, all the people smeared themselves with white clay and bathed in running water. They came out of the water believing that no evil could now befall them for what they had done amiss in the past. So they departed in joy and peace.

Ceremonies of the same general type are still annually observed by the Yuchi Indians of Oklahoma, who belong to the Creek nation but speak a different language. The rites are said to have been instituted by the Sun. They are solemnised in the public square, and are timed so as to coincide with the ripening of the corn, which usually takes place about the middle or early part of July. Continence and abstinence from salt are prescribed during their celebration, and all the men must fast for twelve hours before they take the emetic. A sacred new fire is kindled by striking two stones against each other, after which all the males are scarified or scratched by an official on the arm or breast, so as to let blood flow and drip on the ground of the public square. This bleeding of the men is said to be symbolical of the origin of the Yuchi people ; for the first Yuchi sprang from some drops of blood which the mother of the Sun let fall on earth at one of her monthly periods. Hence the Yuchi call themselves the Children of the Sun. The solemn rite of scratching is followed by the no less solemn rite of vomiting. This also was instituted by the Sun. He taught the Indians to steep the button-snake root and the red root in water and to drink the decoction, in order that they might vomit and so purify their bodies against sickness during the ensuing year. They think that if they did not thus purge themselves before eating the new corn, they would fall sick. The chief of the town is charged with the solemn duty of preparing the nauseous concoction, and he is assisted by four boys who have been initiated into the mysteries. The pots containing the stuff are decorated on the rim with a pattern representing the sun, and they stand east of the fire near

Festival of the new fruits among the Yuchi Indians.

the middle of the public square. The order of drinking is regulated by the rank of the drinkers. When the sun is about the zenith, the four noblest come forward, face eastward, and gulp down the vile but salutary potion ; then they retire to their places and await the usual results. When they feel the inward workings of the draught, they step out of the square and discharge the contents of their stomachs in a place set apart for the purpose. They are followed by another party of four, and that by another, and so on, till all the men have thus purged themselves. The rite is repeated several times. When it is over, they all go to water and wash off the paint with which they were adorned ; then returning to their places in the square they feast on the new corn. After a rest of some hours the men engage in ball play, not as a mere recreation but as a matter of ritual. Sides are chosen ; every player is equipped with two rackets, and the aim of each side is to drive the ball through their opponents' goal, which consists of two uprights and a crosspiece. The two goals stand east and west of each other. During the following night dancing is kept up, and a general laxity, degenerating into debauchery, prevails ; but parents and elders wink at the excesses of the young folk. Among the dances are some in which the dancers mimic the motions and cries of their totemic animals, such as ducks, buzzards, rabbits, fish, buffaloes, chickens, and owls.[1]

Game of ball.

Green Corn Dance among the Seminole Indians.

To this day, also, the remnant of the Seminole Indians of Florida, a people of the same stock as the Creeks,[2] hold an annual purification and festival called the Green Corn Dance, at which the new corn is eaten. On the evening of the first day of the festival they quaff a nauseous " Black Drink," as it is called, which acts both as an emetic and a purgative ; they believe that he who does not drink of this liquor cannot safely eat the new green corn, and besides that he will be sick at some time in the year. While the liquor is being drunk, the dancing begins, and the medicine-men join in it. Next day they eat of the green corn ; the following

[1] F. G. Speck, *Ethnology of the Yuchi Indians* (Philadelphia, 1909), pp. 86-89, 105-107, 112-131.

[2] Th. Waitz, *Anthropologie der Naturvölker*, iii. (Leipsic, 1862) p. 42 ; A. S. Gatschet, *A Migration Legend of the Creek Indians*, i. (Philadelphia, 1884) pp. 66 *sqq.* ; *Totemism and Exogamy*, iii. 167.

day they fast, probably from fear of polluting the sacred food in their stomachs by contact with common food ; but the third day they hold a great feast.[1]   Further, the Natchez Indians, another tribe of the same stock, who used to inhabit a district on the lower course and eastern bank of the Mississippi, ate the new corn sacramentally at a great festival which has been fully described by Du Pratz, the French historian of Louisiana.   As his work is probably not easily accessible to many of my readers, I shall perhaps consult their convenience by extracting his description entire.   The Natchez, he tells us, began their year in March and divided it into thirteen moons.   Their sixth moon, which answered to our August, was the Mulberry Moon, and the seventh was the moon of Maize or Great Corn.   " This feast is beyond dispute the most solemn of all.   It principally consists in eating in common, and in a religious manner, of new corn, which had been sown expressly with that design, with suitable ceremonies.   This corn is sown upon a spot of ground never before cultivated ; which ground is dressed and prepared by the warriors alone, who also are the only persons that sow the corn, weed it, reap it, and gather it.   When this corn is near ripe, the warriors fix on a place proper for the general feast, and close adjoining to that they form a round granary, the bottom and sides of which are of cane ; this they fill with the corn, and when they have finished the harvest, and covered the granary, they acquaint the Great Sun,[2] who appoints the day for the general feast.   Some days before the feast, they build huts for the Great Sun, and for all the other families, round the granary, that of the Great Sun being raised upon a mound of earth about two feet high.   On the feast-day the whole nation set out from their village at sun-rising, leaving behind only the aged and infirm that are not able to travel, and a few warriors, who are to carry the Great Sun on a litter upon their shoulders.

Festival of the new corn among the Natchez Indians.

---

[1] C. MacCauley, "Seminole Indians of Florida," *Fifth Annual Report of the Bureau of Ethnology* (Washington, 1887), pp. 522 *sq.*

[2] That is, the grand chief of the nation.   All the chiefs of the Natchez were called Suns and were connected with the head chief or Great Sun, who bore on his breast an image of the sun and claimed to be descended from the luminary.   See Bossu, *Nouveaux Voyages aux Indes occidentales* (Paris, 1768), i. 42.

The seat of this litter is covered with several deer-skins, and to its four sides are fastened four bars which cross each other, and are supported by eight men, who at every hundred paces transfer their burden to eight other men, and thus successively transport it to the place where the feast is celebrated, which may be near two miles from the village. About nine o'clock the Great Sun comes out of his hut dressed in the ornaments of his dignity, and being placed in his litter, which has a canopy at the head formed of flowers, he is carried in a few minutes to the sacred granary, shouts of joy re-echoing on all sides. Before he alights he makes the tour of the whole place deliberately, and when he comes before the corn, he salutes it thrice with the words *hoo, hoo, hoo*, lengthened and pronounced respectfully. The salutation is repeated by the whole nation, who pronounce the word *hoo* nine times distinctly, and at the ninth time he alights and places himself on his throne.

New fire made by friction.

"Immediately after they light a fire by rubbing two pieces of wood violently against each other, and when everything is prepared for dressing the corn, the chief of war, accompanied by the warriors belonging to each family, presents himself before the throne, and addresses the Sun in these words, 'Speak, for I hear thee.' The sovereign then rises up, bows towards the four quarters of the world, and advancing to the granary, lifts his eyes and hands to heaven, and says, 'Give us corn': upon which the great chief of war, the princes and princesses, and all the men, thank him separately by pronouncing the word *hoo*. The corn is then distributed, first to the female Suns, and then to all the women, who run with it to their huts, and dress it with the utmost dispatch. When the corn is dressed in all the huts, a plate of it is put into the hands of the Great Sun, who presents it to the four quarters of the world, and then says to the chief of war, 'Eat'; upon this signal the warriors begin to eat in all the huts; after them the boys of whatever age, excepting those who are on the breast; and last of all the women. When the warriors have finished their repast, they form themselves into two choirs before the huts, and sing war songs for half an hour; after which the chief of war, and all the warriors in succession, recount their brave exploits, and mention, in a boasting manner, the number of enemies they have slain. The youths are next allowed to harangue, and each tells in the best manner he can, not what he has done, but what he intends to do ; and if his discourse merits approbation, he is answered by a general *hoo* ; if not, the warriors hang down their heads and are silent.

" This great solemnity is concluded with a general dance by torch-light. Upwards of two hundred torches of dried canes, each of the thickness of a child, are lighted round the place, where the men and women often continue dancing till daylight ; and the following is the disposition of their dance. A man places himself on the ground with a pot covered with a deer-skin, in the manner of a drum, to beat time to the dancers ; round him the women form themselves into a circle, not joining hands, but at some distance from each other ; and they are inclosed by the men in another circle, who have in each hand a chichicois, or calabash, with a stick thrust through it to serve for a handle. When the dance begins, the women move round the men in the centre, from left to right, and the men contrariwise from right to left, and they sometimes narrow and sometimes widen their circles. In this manner the dance continues without intermission the whole night, new performers successively taking the place of those who are wearied and fatigued. *Torchlight dance.*

" Next morning no person is seen abroad before the Great Sun comes out of his hut, which is generally about nine o'clock, and then upon a signal made by the drum, the warriors make their appearance distinguished into two troops, by the feathers which they wear on their heads. One of these troops is headed by the Great Sun, and the other by the chief of war, who begin a new diversion by tossing a ball of deer-skin stuffed with Spanish beard from the one to the other. The warriors quickly take part in the sport, and a violent contest ensues which of the two parties shall drive the ball to the hut of the opposite chief. The diversion generally lasts two hours, and the victors are allowed to wear the feathers of superiority till the following year, or till the next time they play at the ball. After this the warriors perform the war dance ; and last of all they go and bathe ; *Game of ball.*

an exercise which they are very fond of when they are heated or fatigued.

" The rest of that day is employed as the preceding ; for the feast holds as long as any of the corn remains. When it is all eat up, the Great Sun is carried back in his litter, and they all return to the village, after which he sends the warriors to hunt both for themselves and him." [1]

Ceremonies observed by the Salish and Tinneh Indians before they eat the first wild berries or roots of the season.

Even tribes which do not till the ground sometimes observe analogous ceremonies when they gather the first wild fruits or dig the first roots of the season. Thus among the Salish and Tinneh Indians of North-West America, " before the young people eat the first berries or roots of the season, they always addressed the fruit or plant, and begged for its favour and aid. In some tribes regular First-fruit ceremonies were annually held at the time of picking the wild fruit or gathering the roots, and also among the salmon-eating tribes when the run of the ' sockeye ' salmon began. These ceremonies were not so much thanksgivings, as performances to ensure a plentiful crop or supply of the particular object desired, for if they were not properly and reverently carried out there was danger of giving offence to the ' spirits ' of the objects, and being deprived of them." For example, these Indians are fond of the young shoots or suckers of the wild raspberry, and they observe the following ceremony at gathering the first of them in season. " When the shoots are ready to pick, that is, when they are about six or eight inches above the ground, the chief, or directing elder of the community, instructs his wife or his

[1] Le Page Du Pratz, *History of Louisiana, or of the western parts of Virginia and Carolina*, translated from the French, New Edition (London, 1774), pp. 338-341. See also J. R. Swanton, *Indian Tribes of the Lower Mississippi Valley* (Washington, 1911), pp. 110 *sqq.*, where the passage of Du Pratz is translated in full from the original French. From Mr. Swanton's translation it appears that the English version of Du Pratz, which I have quoted in the text, is a good deal abridged. On the festival of first-fruits among the Natchez see also *Lettres édifiantes et curieuses*, Nouvelle Édi-

tion, vii. (Paris, 1781) p. 19 ; Charlevoix, *Histoire de la Nouvelle France* (Paris, 1744), vi. 183 ; De Tonti, " Relation de la Louisiane et du Mississippi," *Recueil de Voyages au Nord*, v. (Amsterdam, 1734) p. 122 ; Le Petit, " Relation des Natchez," *ibid.* ix. 13 *sq.* (reprint of the account in the *Lettres édifiantes* cited above) ; Bossu, *Nouveaux Voyages aux Indes occidentales* (Paris, 1768), i. 43. According to Charlevoix, Le Petit, and Bossu the festival fell in July. For Chateaubriand's description of the custom, see below, pp. 135 *sqq.*

daughters to pluck a small bundle of these and prepare them for eating. This they do, using a new pot or kettle for cooking them in. In the meantime all the settlement comes together to take part in the ceremony. They stand in a great circle, the presiding chief, elder, or medicine-man as the case may be, and his assistants being in their midst. Whoever is conducting the ceremony now silently invokes the spirit of the plants, the tenor of his prayer being that it will be propitious to them and grant them a good supply of the suckers. While the invocation is being made all in the circle must keep their eyes reverently closed, this being an essential part in all such ceremonies, the non-observance of which would anger the spirits and cause them to withhold the favours sought. To ensure this being strictly done, the assisting elders are armed with long wands with which they strike any person found opening his eyes during the prayer. After this part of the ceremony is over the cooked suckers are handed to the presiding officer in a newly carved dish, and a small portion is given to each person present, who reverently and decorously eats it. This brings the ceremony to a close. Later, when the berries of this plant are ripe, a second and similar ceremony takes place." [1]

The Thompson Indians of British Columbia cook and eat the sunflower root (*Balsamorrhiza sagittata*, Nutt.), but they used to regard it as a mysterious being, and observed a number of taboos in connexion with it ; for example, women who were engaged in digging or cooking the root must practise continence, and no man might come near the oven where the women were baking the root. When young people ate the first berries, roots, or other products of the season, they addressed a prayer to the Sunflower-Root as follows : " I inform thee that I intend to eat thee. Mayest thou always help me to ascend, so that I may always be able to reach the tops of mountains, and may I never be clumsy ! I ask this from thee, Sunflower-Root. Thou art the greatest of all in mystery." To omit this prayer would make the eater lazy and cause him to sleep long in the

Ceremonies observed by the Thompson Indians before they eat the first wild berries or roots of the season.

---

[1] C. Hill-Tout, *The Far West, the Home of the Salish and Déné* (London, 1907), pp. 168-170.

morning.   Again, when the first tobacco of the season was gathered and smoked for the first time, the inhabitants of each lodge among the Thompson Indians observed the following ceremony.   An elderly man assembled all the inmates, often outside the lodge and generally after sunset, and caused all the adult men and women, who were in the habit of smoking, to sit down in a circle, while he stood in the middle. Sometimes he made a long speech to the people, but as a rule he simply said, " Be it known to you that we will cut up the chief," meaning by the chief the tobacco.   So saying he cut up some of the tobacco, and after mixing it with bearberry leaves he filled a large pipe, lighted it, and handed it to each person, following the sun's course.   Everybody took one whiff, and holding up his or her hands, the palms close together, blew the smoke downwards between the fingers and over the breast ; and as the smoke descended, he crossed his hands on his breast, and rubbing his chest and shoulders with both hands, as if he were rubbing the smoke in, he prayed : " Lengthen my breath, chief, so that I may never be sick, and so that I may not die for a long time to come." By the chief he meant the tobacco.   When every one had had his whiff, the tobacco was cut up small and a piece given to each person.[1]

The ceremonies observed by savages at eating the first fruits of any crop seem to be based on the idea that the plant or tree is animated by a spirit, who must be propitiated before it is safe to partake of the fruit.   These customs of the Thompson and other Indian tribes of North-West America are instructive, because they clearly indicate the motive, or at least one of the motives, which underlies the ceremonies observed at eating the first fruits of the season.   That motive in the case of these Indians is simply a belief that the plant itself is animated by a conscious and more or less powerful spirit, who must be propitiated before the people can safely partake of the fruits or roots which are supposed to be part of his body.   Now if this is true of wild fruits and roots, we may infer with some probability that it is also true of cultivated fruits and roots, such as yams, and in particular that it holds good of the cereals, such as wheat, barley, oats, rice, and maize.   In all cases it seems reasonable to infer that the scruples which

[1] J. Teit, *The Thompson Indians of British Columbia*, p. 349 (*The Jesup North Pacific Expedition, Memoir of* the American Museum of Natural History, April, 1900).

savages manifest at eating the first fruits of any crop, and
the ceremonies which they observe before they overcome
their scruples, are due at least in large measure to a notion
that the plant or tree is animated by a spirit or even a deity,
whose leave must be obtained, or whose favour must be
sought before it is possible to partake with safety of the new
crop.   This indeed is plainly affirmed of the Aino : they call
the millet " the divine cereal," " the cereal deity," and they
pray to and worship him before they will eat of the cakes
made from the new millet.[1]   And even where the indwelling
divinity of the first fruits is not expressly affirmed, it
appears to be implied both by the solemn preparations made
for eating them and by the danger supposed to be incurred
by persons who venture to partake of them without observing the prescribed ritual.   In all such cases, accordingly, we
may not improperly describe the eating of the new fruits as a
sacrament or communion with a deity, or at all events with
a powerful spirit.

Among the usages which point to this conclusion are
the custom of employing either new or specially reserved
vessels to hold the new fruits,[2] and the practice of
purifying the persons of the communicants and even the
houses and streets of the whole town, before it is lawful
to engage in the solemn act of communion with the
divinity.[3]   Of all the modes of purification adopted on these
occasions none perhaps brings out the sacramental virtue of
the rite so clearly as the Creek and Seminole practice of
taking a purgative before swallowing the new corn.   The
intention is thereby to prevent the sacred food from being
polluted by contact with common food in the stomach of
the eater.   For the same reason Catholics partake of the
Eucharist fasting ; and among the pastoral Masai of Eastern
Africa the young warriors, who live on meat and milk
exclusively, are obliged to eat nothing but milk for so many
days and then nothing but meat for so many more, and
before they pass from the one food to the other they must
make sure that none of the old food remains in their
stomachs ; this they do by swallowing a very powerful

*The sanc-
tity of the
new fruits
indicated
in various
ways.*

*Care taken
to prevent
the contact
of sacred
and profane
food in the
stomach of
the eater.*

---

[1] See above, p. 52.   [2] See above, pp. 50, 53, 65, 66, 72, 81.
[3] See above, pp. 59, 60, 63, 69 *sq.*, 71, 73, 75 *sq.*, 82.

Contact
between
certain
foods in the
stomach of
the eater
forbidden.

purgative and emetic.[1]   Similarly, among the Suk, a tribe of British East Africa, no one may partake of meat and milk on the same day, and if he has chewed raw millet he is forbidden to drink milk for seven days.[2]   Among the Wataturu, another people of Eastern Africa akin to the Masai, a warrior who had eaten antelope's flesh might not drink of milk on the same day.[3]   Similarly among the Central Esquimaux the rules prohibiting contact between venison and the flesh of marine animals are very strict.   The Esquimaux themselves say that the goddess Sedna dislikes the deer, and therefore they may not bring that animal into contact with her favourites, the sea beasts.   Hence the meat of the whale, the seal, or the walrus may not be eaten on the same day with venison.   Both sorts of meat may not even lie on the floor of the hut or behind the lamps at the same time.   If a man who has eaten venison in the morning happens to enter a hut in which the flesh of seal is being cooked, he is allowed to eat venison on the bed, but it must be wrapt up before being carried into the hut, and he must take care to keep clear of the floor.   Before changing from one food to the other the Esquimaux must wash themselves.[4]   Again, just as the Esquimaux think that their

---

[1] Joseph Thomson, *Through Masai Land* (London, 1885), p. 430 ; P. Reichard, *Deutsch-Ostafrika* (Leipsic, 1892), p. 288 ; O. Baumann, *Durch Massailand zur Nilquelle* (Berlin, 1894), p. 162 ; M. Merker, *Die Masai* (Berlin, 1904), p. 33 ; M. Weiss, *Die Völkerstämme im Norden Deutsch-Ostafrikas* (Berlin, 1910), p. 380. However, the motive which underlies the taboo appears to be a fear of injuring by sympathetic magic the cows from which the milk is drawn. See my essay " Folk-lore in the Old Testament," in *Anthropological Essays presented to E. B. Tylor* (Oxford, 1907), pp. 164 *sq.* According to Reichard the warriors may partake of honey both with meat and with milk. Thomson does not mention honey and speaks of a purgative only. The periods during which meat and milk are alternately consumed vary, according to Reichard, from twelve to fifteen days. We may conjecture, therefore, that two of them,

making up a complete cycle, correspond to a lunar month, with reference to which the diet is perhaps determined.

[2] M. W. H. Beech, *The Suk, their Language and Folklore* (Oxford, 1911), p. 9. In both cases the motive, as with the Masai, is probably a fear of injuring the cattle, and especially of causing the cows to loose their milk. This is confirmed by other taboos of the same sort observed by the Suk. Thus they think that to eat the flesh of a certain forest pig would cause the cattle of the eater to run dry, and that if a rich man ate fish his cows would give no milk. See M. W. H. Beech, *op. cit.* p. 10.

[3] O. Baumann, *Durch Massailand zur Nilquelle* (Berlin, 1894), p. 171.

[4] Fr. Boas, " The Central Eskimo," *Sixth Annual Report of the Bureau of Ethnology* (Washington, 1888), p. 595 ; *id.*, " The Eskimo of Baffin Land and Hudson Bay," *Bulletin of the American Museum of Natural*

goddess would be offended if venison met seal or whale or walrus meat in the eater's stomach, so the Melanesians of Florida, one of the Solomon Islands, believe that if a man who has eaten pork or fish or shell-fish or the flesh of a certain sort of cuscus were to enter a garden immediately afterwards, the ghosts who preside over the garden and cause the fruits to grow would be angry and the crop would consequently suffer ; but three or four days after partaking of such victuals, when the food has quite left his stomach, he may enter the garden without offence to the ghosts or injury to the crop.[1] In like manner the ancient Greeks, of whose intellectual kinship with savages like the Esquimaux and the Melanesians we have already met with many proofs, laid it down as a rule that a man who had partaken of the black ram offered to Pelops at Olympia might not enter into the temple of Zeus, and that persons who had sacrificed to Telephus at Pergamus might not go up to the temple of Aesculapius until they had washed themselves,[2] just as the Esquimaux who have eaten venison must wash before they may partake of seal or whale or walrus meat. Again, at Lindus in Rhodes there was a sanctuary of some god or hero unknown into which no one who had partaken of goat's flesh or peas-pudding might enter for three days, and no one who had eaten cheese might enter for one day.[3] The prescribed interval was probably calculated to allow the obnoxious food to pass out of the body of the eater before he entered into the presence of the deity, who for some reason or other cherished an antipathy to these particular viands. At Castabus in the Carian Chersonese there was a sanctuary of Hemithea, which no one might approach who had either eaten pork or touched a pig.[4]

In some of the festivals which we have examined, as

History, vol. xv. part i. (New York, 1901) pp. 122-124. For more details see *Taboo and the Perils of the Soul*, pp. 208 *sqq.*

[1] Rev. R. H. Codrington, *The Melanesians* (Oxford, 1891), p. 134.

[2] Pausanias, v. 13. 3. We may assume, though Pausanias does not expressly say so, that persons who sacrificed to Telephus partook of the sacrifice.

[3] Dittenberger, *Sylloge Inscriptionum Graecarum*,[2] No. 576 (vol. ii. p. 267); Ch. Michel, *Recueil d'Inscriptions Grecques*, No. 723, p. 622. Further, no one who had suffered a domestic bereavement might enter the sanctuary for forty days. Hence the pollution of death was clearly deemed more virulent, or at all events more lasting, than the pollution of food.

[4] Diodorus Siculus, v. 62. 5.

The sacrament of
first-fruits
sometimes
combined
with a
sacrifice of
them to
gods or
spirits.

in the Cheremiss, Buru, Cham, Ewe, and Creek ceremonies, the sacrament of first-fruits is combined with a sacrifice or presentation of them to gods or spirits,[1] and in course of time the sacrifice of first-fruits tends to throw the sacrament into the shade, if not to supersede it. The mere fact of offering the first-fruits to the gods or spirits comes now to be thought a sufficient preparation for eating the new corn ; the higher powers having received their share, man is free to enjoy the rest. This mode of viewing the new fruits implies that they are regarded no longer as themselves instinct with divine life, but merely as a gift bestowed by the gods upon man, who is bound to express his gratitude and homage to his divine benefactors by returning to them a portion of their bounty. More examples of the sacrifice, as distinct from sacrament, of first-fruits will be given presently.[2]

§ 2. *Eating the God among the Aztecs*

Aztec custom of eating sacramentally a dough image of the god Huitzilopochtli or Vitzilipuztli as a mode of communion with the deity.

The custom of eating bread sacramentally as the body of a god was practised by the Aztecs before the discovery and conquest of Mexico by the Spaniards. Twice a year, in May and December, an image of the great Mexican god Huitzilopochtli or Vitzilipuztli was made of dough, then broken in pieces, and solemnly eaten by his worshippers. The May ceremony is thus described by the historian Acosta : " The Mexicans in the month of May made their principal feast to their god Vitzilipuztli, and two days before this feast, the virgins whereof I have spoken (the which were shut up and secluded in the same temple and were as it were religious women) did mingle a quantity of the seed of beets with roasted maize, and then they did mould it with honey, making an idol of that paste in bigness like to that of wood, putting instead of eyes grains of green glass, of blue or white ; and for teeth grains of maize set forth with all the ornament and furniture that I have said. This being finished, all the noblemen came and brought it an exquisite and rich garment, like unto that of the idol, wherewith they did attire it. Being thus clad and deckt, they did set it in an azured chair and in a litter to carry it on their shoulders.

[1] See above, pp. 51 *sq*., 54, 58, 60 *sq*., 64, 74.   [2] See below, pp. 109 *sqq*.

The morning of this feast being come, an hour before day all the maidens came forth attired in white, with new ornaments, the which that day were called the Sisters of their god Vitzilipuztli, they came crowned with garlands of maize roasted and parched, being like unto azahar or the flower of orange ; and about their necks they had great chains of the same, which went bauldrickwise under their left arm. Their cheeks were dyed with vermilion, their arms from the elbow to the wrist were covered with red parrots' feathers." Young men, dressed in red robes and crowned like the virgins with maize, then carried the idol in its litter to the foot of the great pyramid-shaped temple, up the steep and narrow steps of which it was drawn to the music of flutes, trumpets, cornets, and drums. " While they mounted up the idol all the people stood in the court with much reverence and fear. Being mounted to the top, and that they had placed it in a little lodge of roses which they held ready, presently came the young men, which strewed many flowers of sundry kinds, wherewith they filled the temple both within and without. This done, all the virgins came out of their convent, bringing pieces of paste compounded of beets and roasted maize, which was of the same paste whereof their idol was made and compounded, and they were of the fashion of great bones. They delivered them to the young men, who carried them up and laid them at the idol's feet, wherewith they filled the whole place that it could receive no more. They called these morsels of paste the flesh and bones of Vitzilipuztli. Having laid abroad these bones, presently came all the ancients of the temple, priests, Levites, and all the rest of the ministers, according to their dignities and antiquities (for herein there was a strict order amongst them) one after another, with their veils of diverse colours and works, every one according to his dignity and office, having garlands upon their heads and chains of flowers about their necks ; after them came their gods and goddesses whom they worshipped, of diverse figures, attired in the same livery ; then putting themselves in order about those morsels and pieces of paste, they used certain ceremonies with singing and dancing. By means whereof they were blessed and consecrated for the flesh and bones of this idol. This ceremony and blessing (whereby they were taken for the flesh and bones of the idol) being ended, they honoured those pieces in the same sort as their god.

Eating the flesh and bones of the god Vitzilipuztli sacramentally.

" Then come forth the sacrificers, who began the sacrifice of men in the manner as hath been spoken, and that day they did sacrifice a greater number than at any other time, for that it was the most solemn feast they observed. The sacrifices being ended, all the young men and maids came out of the temple attired as before, and being placed in order and rank, one directly against another, they danced by drums, the which sounded in praise of the feast, and of the idol which they did celebrate. To which song all the most ancient and greatest noblemen did answer dancing about them, making a great circle, as their use is, the young men and maids remaining always in the midst. All the city came to this goodly spectacle, and there was a commandment very strictly observed throughout all the land, that the day of the feast of the idol of Vitzilipuztli they should eat no other meat but this paste, with honey, whereof the idol was made. And this should be eaten at the point of day, and they should drink no water nor any other thing till after noon : they held it for an ill sign, yea, for sacrilege to do the contrary : but after the ceremonies ended, it was lawful for them to eat anything. During the time of this ceremony they hid the water from their little children, admonishing all such as had the use of reason not to drink any water ; which, if they did, the anger of God would come upon them, and they should die, which they did observe very carefully and strictly. The ceremonies, dancing, and sacrifice ended, they went to unclothe themselves, and the priests and superiors of the temple took the idol of paste, which they spoiled of all the ornaments it had, and made many pieces, as well of the idol itself as of the truncheons which they consecrated, and then they gave them to the people in manner of a communion, beginning with the greater, and continuing unto the rest, both men, women, and little children, who received it with such tears, fear, and reverence as it was an admirable thing, saying that they did eat the flesh and bones of God, wherewith they were grieved. Such as had any sick folks demanded thereof for them, and carried it with great reverence and veneration." [1]

From this interesting passage we learn that the ancient Mexicans, even before the arrival of Christian missionaries, were fully acquainted with the theological doctrine of transubstantiation and acted upon it in the solemn rites of their religion. They believed that by consecrating bread their priests could turn it into the very body of their god, so that all who thereupon partook of the consecrated bread entered into a mystic communion with the deity by receiving a portion of his divine substance into themselves. The doctrine of transubstantiation, or the magical conversion of bread into flesh, was also familiar to the Aryans of ancient India long before the spread and even the rise of Christianity. The Brahmans taught that the rice-cakes offered in sacrifice were substitutes for human beings, and that they were actually converted into the real bodies of men by the manipulation of the priest. We read that " when it (the rice-cake) still consists of rice-meal, it is the hair. When he pours water on it, it becomes skin. When he mixes it, it becomes flesh : for then it becomes consistent ; and consistent also is the flesh. When it is baked, it becomes bone : for then it becomes somewhat hard ; and hard is the bone. And when he is about to take it off (the fire) and sprinkles it with butter, he changes it into marrow. This is the completeness which they call the fivefold animal sacrifice." [2] These remarkable transformations, daily wrought by the priest, on the rice-wafer, were, however, nothing at all to those which the gods themselves accomplished when

The doctrine of transubstantiation or the magical conversion of bread into flesh recognised by the ancient Aztecs and Brahmans.

[1] J. de Acosta, *Natural and Moral History of the Indies*, bk. v. ch. 24, vol. ii. pp. 356-360 (Hakluyt Society, London, 1880). I have modernised the old translator's spelling. Acosta's authority, which he followed without acknowledgment, was an anonymous writer of about the middle of the sixteenth century, whose manuscript, written in Spanish, was found in the library of the Franciscan monastery at Mexico in 1856. A French translation of it has been published. See *Manuscrit Ramirez, Histoire de l'Origine des Indiens qui habitent la Nouvelle-Espagne selon leurs traditions*, publié par D. Charnay (Paris, 1903), pp. 149-154. Acosta's description is followed by A. de Herrera (*General History of the vast Continent and Islands of America*, translated by Capt. John Stevens (London, 1725-1726), iii. 213-215).

[2] *The Satapatha-Brâhmana*, translated by J. Eggeling, Part i. (Oxford, 1882) p. 51 (*Sacred Books of the East,* vol. xii.).

they first instituted the rite. For the horse and the ox
which they sacrificed became a *bos gaurus* and a gayal
respectively ; the sheep was turned into a camel ; and the goat
was converted into a remarkable species of deer, enriched
with eight legs, which slew lions and elephants.[1] On the
whole it would seem that neither the ancient Hindoos nor
the ancient Mexicans had much to learn from the most
refined mysteries of Catholic theology.

The sacred
food not to
be defiled
by contact
with com-
mon food.

Now, too, we can perfectly understand why on the day
of their solemn communion with the deity the Mexicans
refused to eat any other food than the consecrated bread
which they revered as the very flesh and bones of their
God, and why up till noon they might drink nothing at all,
not even water. They feared no doubt to defile the portion
of God in their stomachs by contact with common things.
A similar pious fear led the Creek and Seminole Indians, as
we saw, to adopt the more thoroughgoing expedient of
rinsing out their insides by a strong purgative before they
dared to partake of the sacrament of first-fruits.[2] We can
now also conjecture the reason why Zulu boys, after eating
the flesh of the black bull at the feast of first-fruits, are
forbidden to drink anything till the next day.[3]

Aztec
custom of
killing the
god Huit-
zilopochtli
in effigy
and eating
him after-
wards.

At the festival of the winter solstice in December the
Aztecs killed their god Huitzilopochtli in effigy first and
ate him afterwards. As a preparation for this solemn
ceremony an image of the deity in the likeness of a man was
fashioned out of seeds of various sorts, which were kneaded
into a dough with the blood of children. The bones of the
god were represented by pieces of acacia wood. This image
was placed on the chief altar of the temple, and on the day
of the festival the king offered incense to it. Early next day
it was taken down and set on its feet in a great hall. Then
a priest, who bore the name and acted the part of the god
Quetzalcoatl, took a flint-tipped dart and hurled it into the
breast of the dough-image, piercing it through and through.
This was called " killing the god Huitzilopochtli so that his
body might be eaten." One of the priests cut out the heart
of the image and gave it to the king to eat. The rest of

---

[1] *Op. cit.* pp. 51 *sq.*, with the
translator's note.

[2] See above, pp. 73 *sqq.*

[3] Above, p. 68, note [3].

the image was divided into minute pieces, of which every man great and small, down to the male children in the cradle, received one to eat. But no woman might taste a morsel. The ceremony was called *teoqualo*, that is, " god is eaten." [1]

At another festival the Mexicans made little images like men, which stood for the cloud-capped mountains. These images were moulded of a paste of various seeds and were dressed in paper ornaments. Some people fashioned five, others ten, others as many as fifteen of them. Having been made, they were placed in the oratory of each house and worshipped. Four times in the course of the night offerings of food were brought to them in tiny vessels ; and people sang and played the flute before them through all the hours of darkness. At break of day the priests stabbed the images with a weaver's instrument, cut off their heads, and tore out their hearts, which they presented to the master of the house on a green saucer. The bodies of the images were then eaten by all the family, especially by the servants, " in order that by eating them they might be preserved from certain distempers, to which those persons who were negligent of worship to those deities conceived themselves to be subject." [2] In some cities of Mexico, as in Tlacopan and Coyohuacan, an idol was fashioned out of grains of various kinds, and the warriors ate it in the belief that the sacred food would increase their forces fourfold when they marched to the fight.[3] At certain festivals held thrice a year in Nicaragua all the men, beginning with the priests and chiefs, drew blood from their tongues and genital organs with sharp knives of flint, allowed it to drip on some

(marginal note: Mexican custom of eating images of dough.)

---

[1] H. H. Bancroft, *Native Races of the Pacific States* (London, 1875-1876), iii. 297-300 (after Torquemada) ; F. S. Clavigero, *History of Mexico*, translated by Ch. Cullen (London, 1807), i. 309 *sqq.* ; B. de Sahagun, *Histoire générale des choses de la Nouvelle-Espagne*, traduite et annotée par D. Jourdanet et R. Siméon (Paris, 1880), pp. 203 *sq.* ; J. G. Müller, *Geschichte der amerikanischen Urreligionen* (Bâle, 1867), p. 605 ; Brasseur de Bourbourg, *Histoire des Nations civilisées du Mexique et de l'Amérique Centrale* (Paris, 1857-1859),

iii. 531-534.

[2] F. S. Clavigero, *op. cit.* i. 311 ; B. de Sahagun, *op. cit.* pp. 74, 156 *sq.* ; J. G. Müller, *op. cit.* p. 606 ; H. H. Bancroft, *op. cit.* iii. 316 ; Brasseur de Bourbourg, *op. cit.* iii. 535. This festival took place on the last day of 16th month (which extended from 23rd December to 11th January). At another festival the Mexicans made the semblance of a bone out of paste and ate it sacramentally as the bone of the god. See Sahagun, *op. cit.* p. 33.

[3] Brasseur de Bourbourg, *op. cit.* iii. 539.

sheaves of maize, and then ate the bloody grain as a blessed food.[1]

Mexican
custom of
eating a
man as a
human em-
bodiment
of the god
Tetzcat-
lipoca.   But the Mexicans did not always content themselves with eating their gods in the outward and visible shape of bread or grain ; it was not even enough that this material vehicle of the divine life should be kneaded and fortified with human blood.   They craved, as it seems, after a closer union with the living god, and attained it by devouring the flesh of a real man, who, after he had paraded for a time in the trappings and received the honours of a god, was slaughtered and eaten by his cannibal worshippers.   The deity thus consumed in effigy was Tetzcatlipoca, and the man chosen to represent him and die in his stead was a young captive of handsome person and illustrious birth. During his captivity the youth thus doomed to play the fatal part of divinity was allowed to range the streets of Mexico freely, escorted by a distinguished train, who paid him as much respect as if he had been indeed the god himself instead of only his living image.   Twenty days before the festival at which the tragic mockery was to end, that he might taste all the joys of this transient world to which he must soon bid farewell, he received in marriage four women, from whom he parted only when he took his place in the last solemn procession.   Arrived at the foot of the sacred pyramid on the top of which he was to die, the sacrificers saluted him and led him up the long staircase.   On the summit five of them seized him and held him down on his back upon the sacrificial stone, while the high priest, after bowing to the god he was about to kill, cut open his breast and tore out the throbbing heart with the accustomed rites.   But instead of being kicked down the staircase and sent rolling from step to step like the corpses of common victims, the body of the dead god was carried respectfully down, and his flesh, chopped up small, was distributed among the priests and nobles as a blessed food.   The head, being severed from the trunk, was preserved in a sacred place along with the

---

[1] G. F. de Oviedo, *Histoire du Nicaragua* (Paris, 1840), p. 219. Oviedo's account is borrowed by A. de Herrera (*General History of the vast Continent and Islands of America,* translated by Capt. John Stevens, iii. 301).

white and grinning skulls of all the other victims who had lived and died in the character of the god Tetzcatlipoca.[1]

The custom of entering into communion with a god by eating of his effigy survived till lately among the Huichol Indians of Mexico. In a narrow valley, at the foot of a beetling crag of red rock, they have a small thatched temple of the God of fire, and here down to recent years stood a small image of the deity in human form roughly carved out of solidified volcanic ash. The idol was very dirty and smeared with blood, and in his right side was a hole, which owed its existence to the piety and devotion of his worshippers. For they believed that the power of healing and a knowledge of mysteries could be acquired by eating a little of the god's holy body, and accordingly shamans, or medicine-men, who desired to lay in a stock of these accomplishments, so useful in the exercise of their profession, were wont to repair to the temple, where, having deposited an offering of food or a votive bowl, they scraped off with their finger-nails some particles of the god's body and swallowed them. After engaging in this form of communion with the deity they had to abstain from salt and from all carnal converse with their wives for five months.[2] Again, the Malas, a caste of pariahs in Southern India, communicate with the goddess Sunkalamma by eating her effigy. The communion takes place at marriage. An image of the goddess in the form of a truncated cone is made out of rice and green gram cooked together, and it is decorated with a nose jewel, garlands, and other religious symbols. Offerings of rice, frankincense, camphor, and a coco-nut are then made to the image, and a ram or he-goat is sacrificed. After the sacrifice has been presented, all the persons assembled prostrate themselves in silence before the image, then they break it in pieces, and distributing the pieces among themselves they swallow them. In this way they are, no doubt, believed to absorb the divine

[marginal note] Communion with a god by eating of his effigy among the Huichol Indians of Mexico and the Malas of Southern India.

[1] J. de Torquemada, *Monarquia Indiana*, lib. x. cap. 14, vol. ii. pp. 259 *sqq.* (Madrid, 1723); Brasseur de Bourbourg, *op. cit.* iii. 510-512.

[2] C. Lumholtz, *Unknown Mexico* (London, 1903), ii. 166-171. When Mr. Lumholtz revisited the temple in 1898, the idol had disappeared. It has probably been since replaced by another. The custom of abstaining both from salt and from women as a mode of ceremonial purification is common among savage and barbarous peoples. See above, p. 75 (as to the Yuchi Indians), and *Totemism and Exogamy*, iv. 224 *sqq.*

Catholic custom of eating effigies of the Madonna.

essence of the goddess whose broken body has just passed into their stomachs.[1] In Europe the Catholic Church has resorted to similar means for enabling the pious to enjoy the ineffable privilege of eating the persons of the Infant God and his Mother. For this purpose images of the Madonna are printed on some soluble and harmless substance and sold in sheets like postage stamps. The worshipper buys as many of these sacred emblems as he has occasion for, and affixing one or more of them to his food swallows the bolus. The practice is not confined to the poor and ignorant. In his youth Count von Hoensbroech and his devout mother used thus to consume portions of God and his Mother with their meals.[2]

§ 3. *Many Manii at Aricia*

Loaves called *Maniae* baked at Aricia.

Woollen effigies dedicated at Rome to Mania, the Mother or Grandmother of Ghosts, at the Compitalia.

We are now able to suggest an explanation of the proverb " There are many Manii at Aricia."[3] Certain loaves made in the shape of men were called by the Romans *maniae*, and it appears that this kind of loaf was especially made at Aricia.[4] Now, Mania, the name of one of these loaves, was also the name of the Mother or Grandmother of Ghosts,[5] to whom woollen effigies of men and women were dedicated at the festival of the Compitalia. These effigies were hung at the doors of all the houses in Rome ; one effigy was hung up for every free person in the house, and one effigy, of a different kind, for every slave. The reason was that on this day the ghosts of the dead were believed to be going about, and it was hoped that, either out of good nature or through simple inadvertence, they would carry off the effigies at the door instead of the living people

---

[1] E. Thurston, *Castes and Tribes of Southern India* (Madras, 1909), iv. 357 *sq.*

[2] Graf Paul von Hoensbroech, *14 Jahre Jesuit* (Leipsic, 1909-1910), i. 25 *sq.* The practice was officially sanctioned by a decree of the Inquisition, 29th July 1903.

[3] See *The Magic Art and the Evolution of Kings*, i. 22.

[4] Festus, ed. C. O. Müller, pp. 128, 129, 145. The reading of the last passage is, however, uncertain ("*et Ariciae genus panni fieri ; quod manici † appelletur* ").

[5] Varro, *De lingua latina*, ix. 61 ; Arnobius, *Adversus nationes*, iii. 41 ; Macrobius, *Saturn.* i. 7. 35 ; Festus, p. 128, ed. C. O. Müller. Festus speaks of the mother or grandmother of the *larvae* ; the other writers speak of the mother of the *lares*.

in the house.   According to tradition, these woollen figures were substitutes for a former custom of sacrificing human beings.[1]   Upon data so fragmentary and uncertain, it is impossible to build with confidence ; but it seems worth suggesting that the loaves in human form, which appear to have been baked at Aricia, were sacramental bread, and that in the old days, when the divine King of the Wood was annually slain, loaves were made in his image, like the paste figures of the gods in Mexico, India, and Europe, and were eaten sacramentally by his worshippers.[2] The Mexican sacraments in honour of Huitzilopochtli were also accompanied by the sacrifice of human victims.   The tradition that the founder of the sacred grove at Aricia was a man named Manius, from whom many Manii were descended, would thus be an etymological myth invented to

The loaves at Aricia perhaps sacramental bread made in the likeness of the King of the Wood.

[1] Macrobius, *l.c.* ; Festus, pp. 121, 239, ed. C. O. Müller. The effigies hung up for the slaves were called *pilae*, not *maniae*. *Pilae* was also the name given to the straw-men which were thrown to the bulls to gore in the arena. See Martial, *Epigr.* ii. 43. 5 *sq.* ; Asconius, *In Cornel.* p. 55, ed. Kiessling and Schoell.

[2] The ancients were at least familiar with the practice of sacrificing images made of dough or other materials as substitutes for the animals themselves. It was a recognised principle that when an animal could not be easily obtained for sacrifice, it was lawful to offer an image of it made of bread or wax. See Servius on Virgil, *Aen.* ii. 116 ; compare Pausanias, x. 18. 5. Poor people who could not afford to sacrifice real animals offered dough images of them (Suidas, *s.v.* βοῦς ἕβδομος ; compare Hesychius, *s.vv.* βοῦς, ἕβδομος βοῦς). Hence bakers made a regular business of baking cakes in the likeness of all the animals which were sacrificed to the gods (Proculus, quoted and emended by Chr. A. Lobeck, *Aglaophamus*, p. 1079). When Cyzicus was besieged by Mithridates and the people could not procure a black cow to sacrifice at the rites of Persephone, they made a cow of dough and placed it at the altar (Plutarch,

Lucullus, 10). In a Boeotian sacrifice to Hercules, in place of the ram which was the proper victim, an apple was regularly substituted, four chips being stuck in it to represent legs and two to represent horns (Julius Pollux, i. 30 *sq.*). The Athenians are said to have once offered to Hercules a similar substitute for an ox (Zenobius, *Cent.* v. 22). And the Locrians, being at a loss for an ox to sacrifice, made one out of figs and sticks, and offered it instead of the animal (Zenobius, *Cent.* v. 5). At the Athenian festival of the Diasia cakes shaped like animals were sacrificed (Schol. on Thucydides, i. 126, p. 36, ed. Didot). We have seen above (p. 25) that the poorer Egyptians offered cakes of dough instead of pigs. The Cheremiss of Russia sometimes offer cakes in the shape of horses instead of the real animals. See P. v. Stenin, "Ein neuer Beitrag zur Ethnographie der Tscheremissen," *Globus*, lviii. (1890) pp. 203 *sq.* Similarly a North-American Indian dreamed that a sacrifice of twenty elans was necessary for the recovery of a sick girl ; but the elans could not be procured, and the girl's parents were allowed to sacrifice twenty loaves instead. See *Relations des Jésuites*, 1636, p. 11 (Canadian reprint, Quebec, 1858).

explain the name *maniae* as applied to these sacramental
loaves. A dim recollection of the original connexion of the
loaves with human sacrifices may perhaps be traced in the
story that the effigies dedicated to Mania at the Compitalia
were substitutes for human victims. The story itself, however, is probably devoid of foundation, since the practice of
putting up dummies to divert the attention of ghosts or
demons from living people is not uncommon. As the
practice is both widely spread and very characteristic of the
manner of thought of primitive man, who tries in a thousand
ways to outwit the malice of spiritual beings, I may be
pardoned for devoting a few pages to its illustration, even
though in doing so I diverge somewhat from the strict line
of argument. I would ask the reader to observe that the
vicarious use of images, with which we are here concerned,
differs wholly in principle from the sympathetic use of them
which we examined before ; [1] and that while the sympathetic
use belongs purely to magic, the vicarious use falls within
the domain of religion.

Practice of putting up dummies to divert the attention of ghosts or demons from living people.

The Tibetans stand in fear of innumerable earth-demons,
all of whom are under the authority of Old Mother Khön-ma.
This goddess, who may be compared to the Roman Mania,
the Mother or Grandmother of Ghosts, is dressed in golden-
yellow robes, holds a golden noose in her hand, and rides on
a ram. In order to bar the dwelling-house against the foul
fiends, of whom Old Mother Khön-ma is mistress, an
elaborate structure somewhat resembling a chandelier is
fixed above the door on the outside of the house. It contains
a ram's skull, a variety of precious objects such as gold-leaf,
silver, and turquoise, also some dry food, such as rice, wheat,
and pulse, and finally images or pictures of a man, a woman,
and a house. " The object of these figures of a man, wife,
and house is to deceive the demons should they still come
in spite of this offering, and to mislead them into the belief
that the foregoing pictures are the inmates of the house, so
that they may wreak their wrath on these bits of wood and
so save the real human occupants." When all is ready, a
priest prays to Old Mother Khön-ma that she would be
pleased to accept these dainty offerings and to close the open

Tibetan custom of putting effigies at the doors of houses to deceive demons.

[1] See *The Magic Art and the Evolution of Kings*, i. 55 *sqq.*

doors of the earth, in order that the demons may not come
forth to infest and injure the household.[1]

Further, it is often supposed that the spirits of persons
who have recently departed this life are apt to carry
off with them to the world of the dead the souls of their
surviving relations. Hence the savage resorts to the
device of making up of dummies or effigies which he
puts in the way of the ghost, hoping that the dull-
witted spirit will mistake them for real people and so
leave the survivors in peace. Hence in Tahiti the priest
who performed the funeral rites used to lay some slips
of plantain leaf-stalk on the breast and under the arms of
the corpse, saying, " There are your family, there is your
child, there is your wife, there is your father, and there is
your mother. Be satisfied yonder (that is, in the world of
spirits). Look not towards those who are left in the world."
This ceremony, we are told, was designed " to impart contentment to the departed, and to prevent the spirit from
repairing to the places of his former resort, and so distressing
the survivors." [2] When the Galelareese bury a corpse, they
bury with it the stem of a banana-tree for company, in order
that the dead person may not seek a companion among the
living. Just as the coffin is being lowered into the earth,
one of the bystanders steps up and throws a young banana-
tree into the grave, saying, " Friend, you must miss your
companions of this earth ; here, take this as a comrade." [3]
In the Banks Islands, Melanesia, the ghost of a woman who
has died in childbed cannot go away to Panoi or ghost-land
if her child lives, for she cannot leave the baby behind.
Hence to bilk her ghost they tie up a piece of banana-
trunk loosely in leaves and lay it on her bosom in the grave.
So away she goes, thinking she has her baby with her, and
as she goes the banana-stalk keeps slipping about in the
leaves, and she fancies it is the child stirring at her breast.
Thus she is happy, till she comes to ghost-land and finds she
has been deceived ; for a baby of banana-stalk cannot pass

Effigies
buried with
the dead in
order to de-
ceive their
ghosts.

[1] L. A. Waddell, *The Buddhism of
Tibet* (London, 1895), pp. 484-486.
[2] W. Ellis, *Polynesian Researches*,
Second Edition (London, 1832-1836),
i. 402.

[3] M. J. van Baarda, " Fabelen,
Verhalen en Overleveringen der Galela-
reezen," *Bijdragen tot de Taal- Land-
en Volkenkunde van Nederlandsch-
Indië*, xlv. (1895) p. 539.

muster among the ghosts. So back she comes tearing in
grief and rage to look for the child ; but meantime the infant
has been artfully removed to another house, where the dead
mother cannot find it, though she looks for it everywhere.[1]
In the Pelew Islands, when a woman has died in childbed, her spirit comes and cries, "Give me the child!"
So to beguile her they bury the stem of a young banana-tree
with her body, cutting it short and laying it between her
right arm and her breast.[2] The same device is adopted for
the same purpose in the island of Timor.[3] In like circumstances negroes of the Niger Delta force a piece of the stem
of a plantain into the womb of the dead mother, in order to
make her think that she has her babe with her and so to
prevent her spirit from coming back to claim the living child.[4]
Among the Yorubas of West Africa, when one of twins dies,
the mother carries about, along with the surviving child, a
small wooden figure roughly fashioned in human shape and of
the sex of the dead twin. This figure is intended not merely
to keep the live child from pining for its lost comrade, but
also to give the spirit of the dead child something into which
it can enter without disturbing its little brother or sister.[5]
Among the Tschwi of West Africa a lady observed a sickly
child with an image beside it which she took for a doll.
But it was no doll, it was an effigy of the child's dead twin
which was being kept near the survivor as a habitation for
the little ghost, lest it should wander homeless and, feeling lonely, call its companion away after it along the dark
road of death.[6]

Fictitious
burials to
divert the
attention
of demons
from the
real burials.
At Onitsha, a town on the left bank of the Niger,
a missionary once met a funeral procession which he
describes as very singular. The real body had already been
buried in the house, but a piece of wood in the form of a

[1] Rev. R. H. Codrington, *The Melanesians* (Oxford, 1891), p. 275.

[2] J. Kubary, "Die Religion der
Pelauer," in A. Bastian's *Allerlei aus
Volks- und Menschenkunde* (Berlin,
1888), i. 9.

[3] W. M. Donselaar, "Aanteekenin-
gen over het eiland Saleijer," *Mededeelingen van wege het Nederlandsche Zendelinggenootschap*, i. (1857) p. 290.

[4] Le Comte C. N. de Cardi, "Ju-
ju laws and customs in the Niger
Delta," *Journal of the Anthropological
Institute*, xxix. (1899) p. 58.

[5] A. B. Ellis, *The Yoruba-speaking
Peoples of the Slave Coast* (London,
1894), p. 80.

[6] Miss Mary H. Kingsley, *Travels
in West Africa* (London, 1897), p.
473.

sofa and covered up was being borne by two persons on
their heads, attended by a procession of six men and six
women.   The men carried cutlasses and the women clapped
their hands as they passed along each street, crying, " This
is the dead body of him that is dead, and is gone into the
world of spirits."   Meantime the rest of the villagers had to
keep indoors.[1]   The sham corpse was probably intended as
a lure to draw away prowling demons from the real body.
So among the Angoni, who inhabit the western bank of
Lake Nyassa, there is a common belief that demons hover
about the dying and dead before burial in order to snatch
away their souls to join their own evil order.   Guns are
fired and drums are beaten to repel these spiritual foes,
but a surer way of baulking their machinations is to have a
mock funeral and so mislead and confound them.   A sham
corpse is made up out of anything that comes to hand, and
it is treated exactly as if it were what it pretends to be.
This lay figure is then carried some distance to a grave,
followed by a great crowd weeping and wailing as if their
hearts would break, while the rub-a-dub of drums and the
discharge of guns add to the uproar.   Meantime the real
corpse is being interred as quietly and stealthily as possible
near the house.   Thus the demons are baffled ; for when
the dummy corpse has been laid in the earth with every mark
of respect, and the noisy crowd has dispersed, the fiends swoop
down on the mock grave only to find a bundle of rushes or
some such trash in it ; but the true grave they do not know
and cannot find.[2]   Similarly among the Bakundu of the
Cameroons two graves are always made, one in the hut of
the deceased and another somewhere else, and no one knows
where the corpse is really buried.   The custom is apparently
intended to guard the knowledge of the real grave from
demons, who might make an ill use of the body, if not of
the soul, of the departed.[3]   In like manner the Kamilaroi
tribe of Australia are reported to make two graves, a real

[1] S. Crowther and J. C. Taylor, *The Gospel on the Banks of the Niger* (London, 1859), pp. 250 *sq.*
[2] J. Macdonald, " East Central African Customs," *Journal of the Anthropological Institute*, xxii. (1893) pp. 114 *sq.* ; *id., Myth and Religion* (London, 1893), pp. 155 *sq.* (from MS. notes of Dr. Elmslie).
[3] B. Schwarz, *Kamerun* (Leipsic, 1886), pp. 256 *sq.*; E. Reclus, *Nouvelle Géographie Universelle*, xiii. 68 *sq.*

one and an empty one, for the purpose of cheating a malevolent spirit called Krooben.[1]   So, too, some of the Nagas of Assam dig two graves, a sham grave made conspicuous on purpose to attract the notice of the evil spirits, and the real grave made inconspicuous to escape their attention : a figure is set up over the false grave.[2]   Isis is said to have made many false graves of the dead Osiris in Egypt in order that his foe Typhon might not be able to find the true one.[3]   In Bombay, if a person dies on an unlucky day, a dough figure of a man is carried on the bier with him and burnt with his corpse.   This is supposed to hinder a second death from occurring in the family,[4] probably because the demons are thought to take the dough figure instead of a real person.

Effigies used to cure or prevent sickness by deluding the demons of disease or inducing them to accept the effigies instead of the persons.   Again, effigies are often employed as a means of preventing or curing sickness ; the demons of disease either mistake the effigies for living people or are persuaded or compelled to enter them, leaving the real men and women well and whole.[5]   Thus the Alfoors of Minahassa, in Celebes, will sometimes transport a sick man to another house, while they leave on his bed a dummy made up of a pillow and clothes. This dummy the demon is supposed to mistake for the sick man, who consequently recovers.[6]   Cure or prevention of this sort seems to find especial favour with the Dyaks of Borneo.   Thus, when an epidemic is raging among them, the Dyaks of the Katoengouw river set up wooden images at their doors in the hope that the demons of the plague may be deluded into carrying off the effigies instead of the people.[7]   Among the Oloh Ngadju of Borneo, when a sick man is supposed to be suffering from the assaults of a ghost, puppets of dough or rice-meal are made and thrown under

---

[1] J. Fraser, "The Aborigines of New South Wales," *Journal and Proceedings of the Royal Society of New South Wales*, xvi. (1882) p. 229 ; A. W. Howitt, *Native Tribes of South-East Australia* (London, 1904), p. 467.

[2] This I learned from Dr. Burton Brown (formerly of 3 Via Venti Setembri, Rome), who lived for some time among the Nagas.

[3] Strabo, xvii. 1. 23, p. 803 ; Plutarch, *Isis et Osiris*, 18.

[4] *Panjab Notes and Queries*, ii. p. 39, § 240 (December 1884).

[5] Some examples of this vicarious use of images as substitutes for the sick have been given in an earlier part of this work. See *Taboo and the Perils of the Soul*, pp. 62 *sq.*

[6] N. Graafland, *De Minahassa*, (Rotterdam, 1869), i. 326.

[7] P. J. Veth, *Borneo's Wester-Afdeeling* (Zaltbommel, 1854-56), ii. 309.

the house as substitutes for the patient, who thus rids himself
of the ghost.   So if a man has been attacked by a crocodile
and has contrived to escape, he makes a puppet of dough or
meal and casts it into the water as a vicarious offering ;
otherwise the water-god, who is conceived in the shape of a
crocodile, might be angry.[1]   In certain of the western districts of Borneo if a man is taken suddenly and violently
sick, the physician, who in this part of the world is generally
an old woman, fashions a wooden image and brings it seven
times into contact with the sufferer's head, while she says :
" This image serves to take the place of the sick man ; sickness, pass over into the image."   Then, with some rice, salt,
and tobacco in a little basket, the substitute is carried to the
spot where the evil spirit is supposed to have entered into
the man.   There it is set upright on the ground, after the
physician has invoked the spirit as follows : " O devil, here
is an image which stands instead of the sick man.   Release
the soul of the sick man and plague the image, for it is
indeed prettier and better than he."   Similar substitutes are
used almost daily by these Dyaks for the purpose of drawing off evil influences from anybody's person.   Thus, when
an Ot Danom baby will not stop squalling, its maternal
grandmother takes a large leaf, fashions it into a puppet to
represent the child, and presses it against the infant's body.
Having thus decanted the spirit, so to speak, from the baby
into the puppet, she pierces the effigy with little arrows from
a blow-gun, thereby killing the spirit that had vexed her
child.[2]   Similarly in the island of Dama, between New
Guinea and Celebes, where sickness is ascribed to the agency
of demons, the doctor makes a doll of palm-leaf and lays it,
together with some betel, rice, and half of an empty egg-
shell, on the patient's head.   Lured by this bait the demon
quits the sufferer's body and enters the palm-leaf doll, which
the wily doctor thereupon promptly decapitates.   This may

[1] F. Grabowsky, " Ueber verschiedene weniger bekannte Opfer bei den
Oloh   Ngadju   in Borneo,"   *Internationales Archiv für Ethnographie*, i.
(1888) pp. 132 *sq.*

[2] E. L. M. Kühr, " Schetsen uit

Borneo's Westerafdeeling," *Bijdragen
tot de Taal- Land- en Volkenkunde
van Nederlandsch-Indië*, xlvii. (1897)
pp. 60 *sq.*   For another mode in which
these same Dyaks seek to heal sickness
by means of an image, see *Taboo and
the Perils of the Soul*, pp. 55 *sq.*

reasonably be supposed to make an end of the demon and of the sickness together.[1]   A Dyak sorcerer, being called in to pre-scribe for a little boy who suffered from a disorder of the stomach, constructed two effigies of the boy and his mother out of bundles of clothes and offered them, together with some of the parents' finery, to the devil who was plaguing the child ; it was hoped that the demon would take the effigies and leave the boy.[2]   Batta magicians can conjure the demon of disease out of the patient's body into an image made out of a banana-tree with a human face and wrapt up in magic herbs ; the image is then hurriedly removed and thrown away or buried beyond the boundaries of the village.[3] Sometimes the image, dressed as a man or a woman accord-ing to the sex of the patient, is deposited at a cross-road or other thoroughfare, in the hope that some passer-by, see-ing it, may start and cry out, " Ah ! So-and-So is dead " ; for such an exclamation is supposed to delude the demon of disease into a belief that he has accomplished his fell purpose, so he takes himself off and leaves the sufferer to get well.[4] The Mai Darat, a Sakai tribe of the Malay Peninsula, attribute all kinds of diseases to the agency of spirits which they call *nyani* ; fortunately, however, the magician can induce these maleficent beings to come out of the sick person and take up their abode in rude figures of grass, which are hung up outside the houses in little bell-shaped shrines decorated with peeled sticks.[5]

Effigies used to divert the attention of demons in Nias and various parts of Asia.

In the island of Nias people fear that the spirits of murdered infants may come and cause women with child to miscarry.   To divert the unwelcome attention of these sprites from a pregnant woman an elaborate mechanism has been contrived.   A potent idol called Fangola is set up beside her bed to guard her slumbers during the hours of darkness from

[1] J. G. F. Riedel, *De sluik- en kroesharige rassen tusschen Selebes en Papua* (The Hague, 1886), p. 465.

[2] H. Ling Roth, " Low's Natives of Borneo," *Journal of the Anthropological Institute,* xxi. (1892) p. 117.

[3] B. Hagen, " Beiträge zur Kenntniss der Battareligion," *Tijdschrift voor Indische Taal- Land- en Volkenkunde,* xxviii. (1883) p. 531.

[4] M. Joustra, " Het leven, de zeden en gewoonten der Bataks," *Mededeel-ingen van wege het Nederlandsche Zendelinggenootschap,* xlvi. (1902) pp. 413 *sq.*

[5] N. Annandale and H. C. Robinson, " Some Preliminary Results of an Ex-pedition to the Malay Peninsula," *Journal of the Anthropological Institute,* xxxii. (1902) p. 416.

the evil things that might harm her; another idol, connected
with the first by a chain of palm-leaves, is erected in the large
room of the house ; and lastly a small banana-tree is planted
in front of the second idol.   The notion is that the sprites,
scared away by the watchful Fangola from the sleeping
woman, will scramble along the chain of palm-leaves to the
other idol, and then, beholding the banana-tree, will mistake
it for the woman they were looking for, and so pounce upon
it instead of her.[1]   In Bhutan, when the Lamas make noisy
music to drive away the demon who is causing disease, little
models of animals are fashioned of flour and butter and the
evil spirit is implored to enter these models, which are then
burnt.[2]   So in Tibet, when a man is very ill and all other
remedies have failed, his friends will sometimes, as a last
resort, offer an image of him with some of his clothes to
the Lord of Death, beseeching that august personage to
accept the image and spare the man.[3]   A Burmese mode
of curing a sick man is to bury a small effigy of him in a
tiny coffin, after which he ought certainly to recover.[4]   In
Siam, when a person is dangerously ill, the magician
models a small image of him in clay and carrying it
away to a solitary place recites charms over it which
compel the malady to pass from the sick man into the
image.   The sorcerer then buries the image, and the sufferer
is made whole.[5]   So, too, in Cambodia the doctor fashions
a rude effigy of his patient in clay and deposits it in some
lonely spot, where the ghost or demon takes it instead of the
man.[6]   The same ideas and the same practices prevail much
further to the north among the tribes on the lower course of
the River Amoor.   When a Goldi or a Gilyak shaman has
cast out the devil that caused disease, an abode has to be
provided for the homeless devil, and this is done by making

[1] Fr. Kramer, "Der Götzendienst
der Niasser," *Tijdschrift voor Indische
Taal- Land- en Volkenkunde*, xxxiii.
(1890) p. 489.
[2] A. Bastian, *Die Völkerstämme am
Brahmaputra* (Berlin, 1883), p. 73.
[3] Sarat Chandra Das, *Journey to
Lhasa and Central Tibet* (London,
1902), p. 134.
[4] ShwayYoe, *The Burman* (London,

1882), ii. 138.
[5] Pallegoix, *Description du Royaume
Thai ou Siam* (Paris, 1854), ii. 48 *sq.*
Compare A. Bastian, *Die Völker des
östlichen Asien* (Leipsic and Jena,
1866-1871), iii. 293, 486 ; E. Young,
The Kingdom of the Yellow Robe
(Westminster, 1898), p. 121.
[6] J. Moura, *Le Royaume du Cambodge* (Paris, 1883), i. 176.

a wooden idol in human form of which the ejected demon takes possession.[1]

Effigies used to divert ghostly and other evil influence from people in China.

The Chinese of Amoy make great use of cheap effigies as means of diverting ghostly and other evil influence from people. These effigies are kept in stock and sold in the shops which purvey counterfeit paper money and other spurious wares for the use of simple-minded ghosts and gods, who accept them in all good faith instead of the genuine articles. Nothing could well be cruder than the puppets that are employed to relieve sufferers from the many ills which flesh is heir to. They are composed of two bamboo splinters fastened together crosswise with a piece of paper pasted on one side to represent a human body. Two other shreds of paper, supposed to stand for boots, distinguish the effigy of a man from the effigy of a woman. Armed with one of these "substitutes for a person," as they are called, you may set fortune at defiance. If a member of your family, for example, is ailing, or has suffered any evil whatever, or even is merely threatened by misfortune, all that you have to do is to send for one of these puppets, pass it all over his body while you recite an appropriate spell, and then burn the puppet. The maleficent influence is thus elicited from the person of the sufferer and destroyed once for all. If your child has tumbled into one of those open sewers which yawn for the unwary in the streets, you need only fish him out, pass the puppet over his filthy little body, and say: "This contact (of the substitute) with the front of the body brings purity and prosperity, and the contact with the back gives power to eat till an old, old, old age ; the contact with the left side establishes well-being for years and years, and the contact with the right side bestows longevity ; happy fate, come ! ill fate, be transferred to the substitute !" So saying you burn the substitute, by choice near the unsavoury spot where the accident happened ; and if you are a careful man you will fetch a pail of water and wash the ashes away. Moreover, the child's head should be shaven quite clean ; but if the sufferer was an adult, it is enough to lay bare with the razor

---

[1] A. Woldt, " Die Kultus-Gegenstände der Golden und Giljaken," *Internationales Archiv für Ethnographie*, i. (1888) pp. 102 *sq.*

a small patch on his scalp to let out the evil influence.[1]   In
Corea effigies are employed on much the same principle for
the purpose of prolonging life.   On the fourteenth and the
fifteenth day of the first month all men and women born under
the Jen or "Man" star make certain straw images dressed
in clothes and containing a number of the copper cash which
form the currency of the country.   Strictly speaking, there
should be as many cash in the image as the person whom
it represents has lived years ; but the rule is not strictly
observed.   These images are placed on the path outside
the house, and the poor people seize them and tear them
up in order to get the cash which they contain.   The
destruction of the image is supposed to save the person
represented from death for ten years.   Accordingly the
ceremony need only be performed once in ten years,
though some people from excess of caution appear to
observe it annually.[2]

The Abchases of the Caucasus believe that sickness
is sometimes caused by Mother Earth.   So in order to
appease her and redeem the life of the sick man, an
innocent maiden will make a puppet in human form,
richly clad, and bury it in the earth, saying, " Instead of the
sick man, play and delight yourself with this." [3]   The Ewe
negroes of Togoland, in West Africa, think that the spirits of
all living people come from heaven, where they live in the
intervals between their incarnations.   Life in Amedzowe, as
they call that heavenly region, which lies a little to the east
of the town of Ho, is very like life on earth.   There are
fields there and wildernesses and forests.   Also there are
all kinds of food, such as yams and maize and likewise stock-
yams, not to speak of cotton ; in fact, all these things came
from heaven just as men themselves did.   Moreover, everybody has his spiritual mother in heaven and his spiritual
aunt, also his spiritual uncle, his spiritual grandfather, and

Effigies used as substitutes to save the lives of people among the Abchases of the Caucasus and the Ewe negroes of West Africa.

---

[1] J. J. M. de Groot, *The Religious
System of China*, vi. (Leyden, 1910)
pp. 1103 *sq.* ; for a description of the
effigies or "substitutes for a person"
see *id.*, vol. v. (Leyden, 1907) p.
920.   Can the monkish and clerical
tonsure have been originally designed

in like manner to let out the evil
influence through the top of the head?
[2] T. Watters, "Some Corean
Customs and Notions," *Folk-lore*, vi.
(1895) pp. 82 *sq.*
[3] N. v. Seidlitz, "Die Abchasen,"
Globus, lxvi. (1894) p. 54.

so on, just as on earth. Now the spirits in heaven are apt to resent it when one of their number quits them to go and be born as a child on earth ; and sometimes they will pursue the truant and carry him back to the celestial country, and that is what we call death. Little children are most commonly fetched away by their mother in heaven ; for she wearies for them and comes and lays an invisible hand on the child, and it sickens and dies. If you hear a child whimpering of nights, you may be sure that its mother from heaven has laid her hand on it and is drawing it away to herself. If the child grows very sick and its earthly mother fears that it will die, she will mould two figures of clay, a man and a woman, and offer them in exchange to the heavenly mother, saying, " O thou bearer and mother of children ! instead of the child that has gone away from thee we bring thee here in exchange these clay men. Take them and withdraw thy hand from the child in this visible world." Grown-up people also, when they fall sick, will sometimes make images of clay and offer them as substitutes to the messengers who have come from heaven to fetch them away. These images are deposited with other offerings, such as cowry-shells and a musket, by the roadside ; and if the messengers accept them instead of the sick man, he re-covers.[1] During an epidemic of small-pox the Ewe negroes will sometimes clear a space outside of the town, where they erect a number of low mounds and cover them with as many little clay figures as there are people in the place. Pots of food and water are also set out for the refreshment of the spirit of small-pox who, it is hoped, will take the clay figures and spare the living folk ; and to make assurance doubly sure the road into the town is barricaded against him.[2]

Among the Nishga Indians of British Columbia when

[1] J. Spieth, *Die Ewe - Stämme* (Berlin, 1906), pp. 502-506, 512, 513, 838, 848, 910. It is a disputed point in Ewe theology whether there are many spiritual mothers in heaven or only one. Some say that there are as many spiritual mothers as there are individual men and women ; others doubt this and say that there is only one spiritual mother, and that she is the wife of God (*Mawu*) and gave birth to all spirits that live in heaven, both men and women.

[2] G. Binetsch, " Beantwortung mehrerer Fragen über unser Ewe-Volk und seine Anschauungen," *Zeitschrift für Ethnologie*, xxxviii. (1906) p. 37.

a medicine-man dreams a dream which portends death to
somebody, he informs the person whose life is threatened, and
together they concert measures to avert the evil omen. The
man whose life is at stake has a small wooden figure called
a *shigigiadsqu* made as like himself as the skill of the wood-
carver will allow, and this he hangs round his neck by a string
so that the figure lies exactly over his heart. In this position
he wears it long enough to allow the heat of his body to be
imparted to it, generally for about four days. On the fourth
day the medicine-man comes to the house, arrayed in his
bearskin and other insignia of office and bringing with him
a wisp of teased bark and a toy canoe made of cedar-bark.
Thus equipped, he sings a doleful ditty, the death-song of
the tribe. Then he washes the man over the region of the
heart with the wisp of bark dipped in water, places the wisp,
together with the wooden image, in the canoe, and after again
singing the death-chant, commits image, wisp, and canoe to
the flames, where they are all consumed. The death-chant
is now changed to a song of joy, and the man who was
lately in fear of his life joins in. He may well be gay, for
has he not given death the slip by devoting to destruction,
not merely a wisp saturated with the dangerous defilement
of his body, but also a substitute made in his own likeness
and impregnated with his very heart's warmth?[1]

With these examples before us we may fairly conclude
that the woollen effigies, which at the festival of the
Compitalia might be seen hanging at the doors of all the
houses in ancient Rome, were not substitutes for human
victims who had formerly been sacrificed at this season, but
rather vicarious offerings presented to the Mother or Grandmother of Ghosts, in the hope that on her rounds through
the city she would accept or mistake the effigies for the
inmates of the house and so spare the living for another
year. It is possible that the puppets made of rushes, which
in the month of May the pontiffs and Vestal Virgins annually
threw into the Tiber from the old Sublician bridge at Rome,[2]

---

[1] *The Illustrated Missionary News,* April 1st, 1891, pp. 59 *sq.*

[2] As to the custom see Varro, *De lingua latina,* v. 45 ; Ovid, *Fasti,* v. 621 *sqq.* ; Dionysius Halicarnasensis,

Antiquit. Roman. i. 38 ; Plutarch, *Quaestiones Romanae,* 32 and 86. For various explanations which have been proposed, see L. Preller, *Römische Mythologie* [3] ii. 134 *sqq.* ; W. Mann-

had originally the same significance ; that is, they may have been designed to purge the city from demoniac influence by diverting the attention of the demons from human beings to the puppets and then toppling the whole uncanny crew, neck and crop, into the river, which would soon sweep them far out to sea. In precisely the same way the natives of Old Calabar used periodically to rid their town of the devils which infested it by luring the unwary demons into a number of lamentable scarecrows, which they afterwards flung into the river.[1] This interpretation of the Roman custom is supported to some extent by the evidence of Plutarch, who speaks of the ceremony as " the greatest of purifications."[2] However, other explanations of the rite have been proposed : indeed these puppets of rushes have been a standing puzzle to Roman antiquaries in ancient and modern times.

hardt, *Antike Wald- und Feldkulte*, pp. 265 *sqq.* ; *Journal of Philology*, xiv. (1885) p. 156 note ; R. von Ihering, *Vorgeschichte der Indoeuropäer*, pp. 430-434 ; W. Warde Fowler, *The Roman Festivals of the Period of the Republic* (London, 1899), pp. 111 *sqq.* ; *id.*, *The Religious Experience of the Roman People* (London, 1911), pp. 54 *sq.*, 321 *sqq.* ; G. Wissowa, *Gesammelte Abhandlungen zur römischen Religions- und Stadtgeschichte* (Munich, 1904), pp. 211-229. The ceremony was observed on the fifteenth of May.

[1] See *The Golden Bough*, Second Edition, iii. 107.

[2] Plutarch, *Quaest. Roman.* 86.

CHAPTER XI

THE SACRIFICE OF FIRST-FRUITS

IN the preceding chapter we saw that primitive peoples often partake of the new corn and the new fruits sacramentally, because they suppose them to be instinct with a divine spirit or life. At a later age, when the fruits of the earth are conceived as created rather than as animated by a divinity, the new fruits are no longer partaken of sacramentally as the body and blood of a god ; but a portion of them is offered to the divine beings who are believed to have produced them. Originally, perhaps, offerings of first-fruits were supposed to be necessary for the subsistence of the divinities, who without them must have died of hunger ;[1] but in after times they seem to be looked on rather in the light of a tribute or mark of homage rendered by man to the gods for the good gifts they have bestowed on him. Sometimes the first-fruits are presented to the king, perhaps in his character of a god ; very often they are made over to the spirits of the human dead, who are sometimes thought to have it in their power to give or withhold the crops. Till the first-fruits have been offered to the deity, the dead, or the king, people are not at liberty to eat of the new crops. But, as it is not always possible to draw a sharp line between the sacrament and the sacrifice of first-fruits, it may be well to round off this part of the subject by giving some examples of the latter. The sacrifice of first-fruits to gods is probably later than the custom of partaking of them sacramentally.

The Ovambo or Ovakuanjama of South-West Africa stand in great fear of the spirits of the dead, who are believed to exercise a powerful influence over the living ; in particular the spirits of dead chiefs can give or withhold rain, a matter of vital importance in the parched region of Sacrifice of first-fruits among the Ovambo of South-West Africa.

[1] See above, vol. i. pp. 231 sqq.

Ovamboland.   Accordingly the people pay great respect to
the spirits of the departed, and they hold a thanksgiving
festival in their honour at the close of the harvest.   When
the new corn has been reaped and ground, a portion of it
is made into porridge and carried to the quarters of the
principal wife.   Here all the inhabitants of the kraal
assemble ; the head of the family takes some of the porridge,
dips it in melted fat, and throws it to the east, saying, " Take
it, ye spirits of the East ! "   Then he does the same towards
the west, saying, " Take it, ye spirits of the West ! "   This
is regarded as a thank-offering presented to the spirits of the
dead for not visiting the people with sickness while they were
cultivating the fields, and especially for sending the rain.[1]

Among the Basutos, when the corn has been threshed
and winnowed, it is left in a heap on the threshing-floor.
Before it can be touched a religious ceremony must be performed.   The persons to whom the corn belongs bring a
new vessel to the spot, in which they boil some of the grain.
When it is boiled they throw a few handfuls of it on the heap
of corn, saying, " Thank you, gods ; give us bread to-morrow
also ! "   When this is done the rest is eaten, and the pro-
vision for the year is considered pure and fit to eat.[2]   Here
the sacrifice of the first-fruits to the gods is the prominent
idea, which comes out again in the custom of leaving in the
threshing-floor a little hollow filled with grain, as a thank-
offering to these powerful beings.[3]   Still the Basutos retain
a lively sense of the sanctity of the corn in itself ; for, so long
as it is exposed to view, all defiled persons are carefully kept
from it.   If it is necessary to employ a defiled person in
carrying home the harvest, he remains at some distance
while the sacks are being filled, and only approaches to
place them upon the draught oxen.   As soon as the load is
deposited at the dwelling he retires, and under no pretext
may he help to pour the corn into the baskets in which it
is kept.[4]   The Makalaka worship a god called Shumpaoli,

[1] H. Tönjes, *Ovambaland, Land,
Leute, Mission* (Berlin, 1911), p. 195.

[2] Rev E. Casalis, *The Basutos* (London, 1861), pp. 251 *sq.*

[3] *Ibid.* p. 252.

[4] *Ibid.* pp. 252 *sq.*   In the southern
province of Ceylon "the threshers behave as if they were in a temple of the
gods when they put the corn into the
bags."   See C. J. R. Le Mesurier,
" Customs and Superstitions connected
with the Cultivation of Rice in the

whose image is to be found in the enclosure outside of their huts. The image consists of the head of an axe, a stone from the river, and a twig or long stalk of grass planted between them in the ground. About this god they scatter the first-fruits of their harvest, and when they brew beer they pour some of it on him.[1] Of the Bantu tribes of South Africa in general we are told that they might not eat of the new crops till the chief gave them leave to do so. When the millet was ripe he appointed a general assembly of the people at his residence, which was known as the Great Place ; he then performed certain rites, and in particular he offered a small quantity of the fresh grain to the spirits of his ancestors, either by laying it on their graves or by casting it into a stream. After that he granted the people permission to gather and eat the new corn.[2]

Among the Maraves or Zimbas, a tribe of the Upper Zambesi, bordering on the Portuguese territory, it is the custom that first-fruits of all produce must be offered to the spirits of the dead (*muzimos*), to whom they attribute all the good and ill that befall them. Every year at harvest-time the offerings are brought to these mighty beings. Small portions of all kinds of fruits, together with cooked fowls and *pombe* (the native intoxicant), are carried in procession, with songs, dances, and the beating of drums, to the burial-ground, which is always situated in a grove or a wilderness and is esteemed a sacred place ; no tree may be felled and no animal killed on the holy ground, for the natives believe that a spirit of the dead is present in everything within the precincts.[3] Among the Yaos of British Central Africa " offerings are made to the spirit world or to *mulungu* as the great agency in the affairs of human life. Outside the village, or beside the head-man's hut, may often be seen a rough shed. In this are placed the first-fruits of the new crop, green maize, beans, pumpkins, peas, etc., as a thankoffering from the villagers for their harvest. This is described as *kulomba*

Sacrifices of first-fruits in Central Africa.

Southern Province of Ceylon," *Journal of the Royal Asiatic Society*, N.S. xvii. (1885), p. 371.

[1] L. Decle, *Three Years in Savage Africa* (London, 1898), p. 173.

[2] G. McCall Theal, *Records of South-*

Eastern Africa, vii. (1901) p. 397.

[3] " Der Muata Cazembe und die Völkerstämme der Maravis, Chevas, Muembas, Lundas und andere von Süd-Afrika," *Zeitschrift für allgemeine Erdkunde* (Berlin), vi. (1856) pp. 272, 273.

mulungu, to worship *mulungu.*" [1] By *mulungu* the Yaos
mean primarily and strictly the soul of a dead person, which
is believed to influence the lives and fortunes of the
survivors, and therefore needs to be honoured and propitiated ; but they employ the word in an extended sense to
signify the aggregate of the spirits of all the dead, and
missionaries have adopted it as the nearest equivalent for the
word God.[2] Among the Winamwanga, a tribe of north-eastern
Rhodesia, between Lake Nyassa and Lake Tanganyika, it
is customary to offer the first beer and the first flour made
from the new harvest of millet to the spirits of the dead.   The
head of the family pours out some beer and a small quantity
of the new flour in a heap on the floor of his own house, after
which he prays to the spirits of his forefathers, thanks them
for the harvest, and invites them to come and partake of it
with the family.   The priest performs the same ceremony
at the shrine for the whole village.   The householder or the
priest speaks to the spirits as if they were sitting around
him.   Thus he may say, " O ye great spirits, fathers in the
spirit world, mothers in the spirit world, and all ye others,
bless us now.   Here is the food, and here is the offering, call
ye all of you each other."   Then after summoning the
dead by their names he may go on : " Come all of you and
partake of this offering.   Ye great spirits, all things of this
earth were known to you while yet ye were here.   Take
care of this your family, and of all these your children.
May we ever go in our ways in prosperity.   Oh! ye great
spirits, give to us food and all the produce of the land.
Drive ye away all illnesses from your family, ye great
spirits ; every evil spirit put far away from us, and whatever might seek to hurt us may it fly away on the wind.
Cause ye us to abide in peace." [3]   Among the Yombe of
Northern Rhodesia, to the west of Lake Tanganyika, no one
is allowed to partake of the new fruits until certain cere-

[1] Rev. A. Hetherwick, "Some
Animistic Beliefs among the Yaos of
British Central Africa," *Journal of the
Anthropological Institute,* xxxii. (1902)
pp. 94 *sq.*

[2] Rev. A. Hetherwick, *op. cit.* pp.
91-94.

[3] Dr. J. A. Chisholm, "Notes on
the Manners and Customs of the Winamwanga and Wiwa," *Journal of the
African Society,* vol. ix. No. 36 (July
1910), pp. 366 *sq.* Among the Winamwanga, as among the Maraves, the
human soul or spirit is called *muzimu*
(*op. cit.* p. 363).

monies have been performed. Escorted by a band of drummers, his medicine-men, and the village elders, the chief ascends the Kalanga Mountain until he reaches the hollow fastness which in former days his forefathers held against the marauding Angoni. Here the grandfather of the present chief lies buried. Before his tomb a bull is slain, and pots of freshly-brewed beer and porridge made from the first-fruits are deposited before the shrine. The ground is then carefully cleaned of weeds, and the blood of the bull is sprinkled on the freshly-turned-up soil and on the rafters of the little hut. After offering the customary prayers in thanksgiving for the harvest, and beseeching the spirits to partake with them of the first-fruits, the procession retires. On their return to the village, the carcase of the bull is divided, all partake of the fresh porridge and beer awaiting them, and the day closes with beer-drinking and dancing.[1]

The A-Kamba of British East Africa offer first-fruits to the spirits of their dead before anybody may eat of the new crop. Sometimes these offerings are piled on the graves of chiefs and left there along with the meat of a goat which has been sacrificed. Sometimes the offerings are made in a cleared place under the sacred wild fig tree (*mumbo*) of the village ; for the A-Kamba think that the spirits of the dead (*aïmu*) dwell in wild fig trees, and they build miniature huts at the foot of the trees for the accommodation of the ghosts. The clearing under the wild fig tree of the village is called the Place of Prayer (*ithembo*). When any crop is ripe, all the inhabitants of the district assemble, and a very old man and woman, chosen for the purpose, leave the crowd and go to the Place of Prayer, where they call aloud to the spirits of the dead and ask leave to eat the crop. The people then dance, and during the dance one of the women is sure to be seized with a fit of shaking and to cry aloud, which is deemed the answer of the spirits to the people's prayer.[2] Amongst the Baganda a man used to offer the first-fruits of a new garden to his god, imploring the blessing of the deity on the future

Sacrifices of first-fruits in East Africa.

---

[1] C. Gouldsbury and H. Sheane, *The Great Plateau of Northern Rhodesia* (London, 1911), pp. 294 *sq.*

[2] C. W. Hobley, *Ethnology of A-Kamba and other East African Tribes* (Cambridge, 1910), pp. 66, 85 *sq.*

crops.[1]   Among the Dinka of the White Nile no member
of a family may eat the new fruits until the father
or mother has scattered some of them over the court-
yard of the house in order to ensure the blessing of
God.[2]   When the millet is ripe, the Nubas of Jebel-Nuba,
a range of mountains in the eastern Sudan, observe the
following ceremony.   Every group of villages is presided
over by a sacred pontiff called a *cogiour* or *codjour*, who is
believed to act under the inspiration of a spirit named Laro.
So when it is known that the grain is ready to be cut, a
drum is beaten, the pontiff mounts his horse and, attended
by all the elderly men and women, repairs to his fields,
while the rest of the people betake themselves to their own
farms.   There the people whose eldest child is a boy break
five ears of corn, and those whose eldest child is a girl break
four.   But young unmarried people break five or four ears
according as they desire to have a boy or a girl for their
first-born.   All then return to the village and place the
ears they have gathered on the hedge which serves as an
enclosure.   When the beat of the drum and multitudinous
cries of joy announce the return of the pontiff, the people
take the gathered ears and advance to meet him.   He rides
at the head of a cavalcade composed of all the men who
have horses.   After that, attended by the elders, he retires
to his house, while the rest of the people deposit the ears of
corn in the cave of Laro, the being who inspires the holy
pontiff.   Feasting, drinking, and horse-races conclude the
ceremony.   At the races the young folk amuse themselves
by flinging stalks of millet before the horses to make them
shy and throw their riders.[3]

[1] Rev. J. Roscoe, *The Baganda*
(London, 1911), p. 428.

[2] *Annales de la Propagation de la
Foi*, lx. (1888) p. 57.   The account is
extracted from the letter of a Catholic
priest, himself a Dinka.   The name of
God, according to him, is *Den-dit*,
meaning " Great Rain."   The form of
the name agrees closely, and the
interpretation of it agrees exactly, with
the results of Dr. C. G. Seligmann's
independent enquiries, according to
which the name of the Dinka God
is *Dengdit*, "Great Rain," the word

for rain being *deng*.   See Dr. C. G.
Seligmann, in Dr. J. Hastings' *Encyclopaedia of Religion and Ethics*,
s.v. " Dinka," vol. iv. (Edinburgh,
1911) p. 707.

[3] " Coutumes étranges des indigènes
du Djebel-Nouba (Afrique centrale),
notes communiquées par les mission-
naires de Vérone," *Les Missions Catholiques*, xiv. (1882) p. 459.   As to the
Nubas and their pontiff see further
Stanislas Carceri, " Djebel-Nouba,"
Les Missions Catholiques, xv. (1883)
pp. 448-452.

The Igbiras, a pagan tribe at the confluence of the Niger and the Benue, bury their dead in their houses and have great faith in the power of the ghosts, whose guidance and protection they seek to ensure by periodical offerings of goats and cocks.   Also they offer the first-fruits of their crops to the dead, hanging bunches of the new grain over the burial-places in their huts.   The Igbiras also celebrate the festival of the new yams with great pomp.   It is their New Year's Day.   Sacrifices of fowls and goats are offered, and wine and oil are freely poured out.   The king takes a prominent part in the feast.[1] Among the Cross River natives, in the lower valley of the Niger, the eating of the new yams is an occasion of great rejoicing, but no one may partake of them until a portion has been ceremonially offered to the deities.   The festival is not held simultaneously but separately for each village according to the state of the crops.   High and low, old and young, men, women, and children dance to music on these joyful occasions.[2]   The Matse tribe of Ewe negroes in Togoland worship the Earth at the times when they dig the ripe yams in September, when they reap the ripe maize in November, and when they burn the grass in February.   The place where they offer sacrifices to the Earth goddess is called " the Wood of our Mother."   In the month of November the hunters, led by the Chief Huntsman and the High Priest, repair to the maize-fields, where they gather cobs of the ripe grain.   Some of these they deposit, with prayers, in the sacrificial place in the wood, but they keep the finest cobs for themselves.   After this sacrifice of the new corn to the Earth goddess everybody is free to get in his maize.[3]   Amongst the Hos, another Ewe tribe of Togoland, when a man is about to dig up his yam crop, he first of all digs up two yams which he had planted for the goddess Mawu Sodza.   These he holds up to her and prays, saying, " O Mawu Sodza, thou ship full of yams, give to me, and I will give to you ; pass me over, and I will pass you over.   Here are thy yams, which I have dug for thee.   When I dig mine, grant that I may have plenty."

---

[1] A. F. Mockler-Ferryman, *Up the Niger* (London, 1892), pp. 141 *sq.*
[2] Ch. Partridge, *Cross River Natives* (London, 1905), pp. 266 *sq.*
[3] J. Spieth, *Die Ewe-Stämme* (Berlin, 1906), pp. 795 *sq.*

Thereupon he begins to dig the crop.[1] Among the Bassari, another tribe of Togoland, no man may eat of the new yams until the people have paid a tribute of the first-fruits to the king. At such times long files of men, women, and children may be seen wending their way to the capital to render to the king his dues. But the king himself may not partake of the new yams until he has offered a portion of them, along with ten white fowls, to the fetish.[2] Before the Adeli of the Slave Coast may eat of the new yams, the owner of each farm must bring the first yams of his field to the fetish priest, who offers them to the fetish, after which he declares that the harvest may take place. The festival, accompanied by shooting and dancing, lasts several days ; it generally falls in August.[3]

First-fruits offered to kings in Madagascar and Burma.

Among the Betsileo of Madagascar the king used to receive first-fruits of all the crops, such as rice, maize, manioc, beans, and sweet potatoes : indeed this tribute of first-fruits formed a large part of his revenue.[4] The Hovas of Madagascar present the first sheaves of the new grain to the sovereign. The sheaves are carried in procession to the palace from time to time as the grain ripens.[5] So in Burma, when the *pangati* fruits ripen, some of them used to be taken to the king's palace that he might eat of them ; no one might partake of them before the king.[6] It has been suggested that the modern system of taxation may be directly derived from the ancient obligation of paying first-fruits to a sacred pontiff or king.[7]

Sacrifices of first-fruits in Assam and other parts of India.

Every year, when they gather their first crops, the Kochs of Assam offer some of the first-fruits to their ancestors, calling to them by name and clapping their hands.[8] Before they harvest any of their crops, the Garos, another people of Assam, deem it necessary to sacrifice the first-fruits of the

[1] J. Spieth, *op. cit.* p. 344. As to the goddess Mawu Sodza, see *ibid.* pp. 424 *sq.*

[2] H. Klose, *Togo unter deutscher Flagge* (Berlin, 1899), p. 504.

[3] L. Conradt, " Das Hinterland der deutschen Kolonie Togo," *Petermanns Mittheilungen,* xlii. (1896) p. 18.

[4] G. A. Shaw, " The Betsileo," *Antananarivo Annual and Madagascar Magazine, Reprint of the First Four Numbers* (Antananarivo, 1885), p. 346.

[5] J. Cameron, " On the Early Inhabitants of Madagascar," *Antananarivo Annual and Madagascar Magazine, Reprint of the First Four Numbers* (Antananarivo, 1885), p. 263.

[6] A. Bastian, *Die Völker des östlichen Asien,* ii. (Leipsic, 1866), p. 105.

[7] A. van Gennep, *Tabou et Totémisme à Madagascar* (Paris, 1904), p. 97.

[8] E. T. Dalton, *Descriptive Ethnology of Bengal* (Calcutta, 1872), p. 91.

crops to the gods. Thus, for example, they gather some ears of rice or millet, pound them between two stones, and offer them up on a piece of plantain stem.[1] In August, when the rice ripens, the Hos of Bengal offer the first-fruits of the harvest to Sing Bonga, who dwells in the sun. Along with the new rice a white cock is sacrificed ; and till the sacrifice has been offered no one may eat the new rice.[2] Among the Oraons of Bengal no one will partake of the new rice until some of it has been offered to the ancestors. A handful of it is cooked and spread on the ground, and a pot of rice-beer is brewed and some of the beer also spilt on the ground. Before drinking every one dips his finger in his cup and lets fall some drops in honour of the ancestors. Further, a whity grey fowl is killed, and the eldest of the family, addressing the ancestral spirits, says, " O old mothers and fathers, you have always been so good to us on these days. Here we are rejoicing : we cannot forget you : come and rejoice with us." [3] In Ladakh the peasants offer the first two or three handfuls of the wheat-crop to the spirit who presides over agriculture. These offerings they attach to the tops of the pillars which support the roofs of their houses ; and thus the bands of straw and ears of wheat form a primitive sort of capital. Rams' horns are sometimes added to this decoration.[4] In the Himalayan districts of the North-Western provinces of India the fields and boundaries are under the protection of a beneficent local deity named Kshetrpal or Bhumiya. Every village possesses a small temple sacred to him. When a crop is sown, a handful of grain is sprinkled over a stone in the corner of the field nearest to the temple, in order that the god may protect the growing crop from hail, blight, and the ravages of wild beasts ; and at harvest he receives the first-fruits in order that he may save the garnered grain from the inroads of rats and insects.[5] Among the hill tribes near

[1] Major A. Playfair, *The Garos* (London, 1909), p. 94.

[2] E. T. Dalton, *op. cit.* p. 198 ; (Sir) H. H. Risley, *Tribes and Castes of Bengal, Ethnographic Glossary* (Calcutta, 1891-1892), ii. 104.

[3] Rev. P. Dehon, S.J., *Religion and Customs of the Uraons* (Calcutta, 1906), p. 137 (*Memoirs of the Asiatic Society*

of Bengal, vol. i. No. 9).

[4] *North Indian Notes and Queries,* i. 57, No. 428, quoting Moorcroft and Trebeck, *Travels in the Himalayan Provinces,* i. 317 *sq.*

[5] E. T. Atkinson, *The Himalayan Districts of the North-Western Provinces of India,* ii. (Allahabad, 1884) p. 825. As to Bhumiya see further

Sacrifices
of first-
fruits
among hill
tribes of
India.
Rajamahall, in India, when the *kosarane* grain is being reaped in November or early in December, a festival is held as a thanksgiving before the new grain is eaten. On a day appointed by the chief a goat is sacrificed by two men to a god called Chitariah Gossaih, after which the chief himself sacrifices a fowl. Then the vassals repair to their fields, offer thanksgiving, make an oblation to Kull Gossaih (who is described as the Ceres of these mountaineers), and then return to their houses to eat of the new *kosarane*. As soon as the inhabitants have assembled at the chief's house—the men sitting on one side and the women on the other—a hog, a measure of *kosarane*, and a pot of spirits are presented to the chief, who in return blesses his vassals, and exhorts them to industry and good behaviour ; " after which, making a libation in the names of all their gods, and of their dead, he drinks, and also throws a little of the *kosarane* away, repeating the same pious exclamations." Drinking and festivity then begin, and are kept up for several days. The same tribes have another festival at reaping the Indian corn in August or September. Every man repairs to his fields with a hog, a goat, or a fowl, which he sacrifices to Kull Gossaih. Then, having feasted, he returns home, where another repast is prepared. On this day it is customary for every family in the village to distribute to every house a little of what they have prepared for their feast. Should any person eat of the new *kosarane* or the new Indian corn before the festival and public thanksgiving at the reaping of these crops, the chief fines him a white cock, which is sacrificed to Chitariah.[1] In

Sacrifices
of first-
fruits in the
Central
Provinces
of India.
the Central Provinces of India the first grain of the season is commonly offered to the god Bhímsen or Bhím Deo.[2] When the new rice crop is ripe, the Gadbas, a primitive tribe of the Central Provinces, cook the first-fruits and serve them to the cattle in new bamboo baskets ; after that the men themselves

W. Crooke, *Popular Religion and Folk-lore of Northern India* (Westminster, 1896), i. 105-107, who observes (pp. 106 *sq.*): " To illustrate the close connection between this worship of Bhúmiya as the soil godling with that of the sainted dead, it may be noted that in some places the shrine of Bhúmiya is identified with the Jathera, which is the ancestral mound, sacred to the common ancestor of the village or tribe."

[1] Thomas Shaw, " The Inhabitants of the Hills near Rajamahall," *Asiatic Researches*, iv. (London, 1807) pp. 56 *sq.*

[2] *Panjab Notes and Queries*, i. p. 60, § 502 (February 1884).

partake of the new rice.[1]   The Nahals, a forest tribe of the
same region, worship the forest god Jharkhandi in the month
of Chait, and until this rite has been performed they may
not use the leaves or fruits of the *Butea frondosa, Phyllanthus
emblica,* and mango trees.   When the god is worshipped,
they collect branches and leaves of these trees and offer
cooked food to them : after that they begin to use the new
leaves, fruit, and timber.[2]   Again, when the Mannewars,
another forest tribe of the Central Provinces, pick the flowers
of the *mahua* tree (*Bassia latifolia*), they worship the tree and
offer it some of the liquor distilled from the new flowers,
along with a fowl and a goat.[3]   The principal festivals of the
Parjas, a small tribe of the Central Provinces, are the feast
of new vegetation in July, the feast of the new rice in
August or September, and the feast of the new mango crop
in April or May.   At these feasts the new season's crop is
eaten, and offerings of them are presented to the ancestors
of the family, who are worshipped on these occasions.[4]   In
the Punjaub, when sugar-cane is planted, a woman puts on
a necklace and walks round the field, winding thread on a
spindle;[5] and when the sugar-cane is cut the first-fruits are
offered on an altar, which is built close to the press and is
sacred to the sugar-cane god.   Afterwards the first-fruits are
given to Brahmans.   Also, when the women begin to pick
the cotton, they go round the field eating rice-milk, the first
mouthful of which they spit upon the field toward the west ;
and the first cotton picked is exchanged at the village shop
for its weight in salt, which is prayed over and kept in the
house till the picking is finished.[6]

Sacrifices of first-fruits in the Punjaub.

Among the ancient Hindoos the first-fruits were sacrificed

---

[1] *Central Provinces, Ethnographic
Survey,* iii. *Draft Articles on Forest
Tribes* (Allahabad, 1907) p. 45.

[2] *Op. cit.* iii. 73.

[3] *Op. cit.* v. (Allahabad, 1911) p.
66.

[4] *Op. cit.* vii. (Allahabad, 1911) p.
102.

[5] The practice is curiously unlike the
custom of ancient Italy, in most parts
of which women were forbidden by law
to walk on the highroads twirling a
spindle, because this was supposed to

injure the crops (Pliny, *Nat. Hist.*
xxviii. 28).   The purpose of the Indian
custom may be to ward off evil influences from the field, as Mr. W.
Crooke suggests (*Popular Religion and
Folk-lore of Northern India,* ii. 305,
"This forms a sacred circle which
repels evil influence from the crop").
Compare *The Magic Art and Evolution
of Kings,* i. 113 *sq.*

[6] D. C. J. Ibbetson, *Outlines of
Panjab Ethnography* (Calcutta, 1883),
p. 119.

Sacrifices
of first-
fruits
among the
ancient
Hindoos.
to the gods at the beginning of harvest, generally at the
new or the full moon.   There were two harvests in the
year; the barley was reaped in spring and the rice in
autumn.   From the new grain, whether barley or rice, a
sacrificial cake was prepared and set forth on twelve
potsherds for the two great gods Indra and Agni; a pap
or gruel of boiled grain, sodden either in water or milk, was
offered to the Visve Devah, that is, to the common mob of
deities; and a cake on one potsherd was presented to
Heaven and Earth.   The origin of these sacrifices of first-
fruits was explained by the following myth.   They say that
the gods and their powerful rivals the Asuras once strove
with each other for the mastery.   In this strife the Asuras
defiled, both by magic and by poison, the plants on which
men and beasts subsist; for thus they hoped to get the better
of the gods.   Therefore neither man nor beast could eat
food, and for lack of it they well nigh perished.   When the
gods heard of it, they said one to the other, "Come let
us rid the plants of the defilement," and they did so by
means of the sacrifice.   But they could not agree as to
which of them should receive the sacrifices, so to decide this
delicate question they ran a race, and Indra and Agni came
in first; that is why the cake is offered to them on twelve
potsherds, while the common mob of the gods have to put up
with a simple pap or gruel.   To this day, therefore, he who
offers the first-fruits to the gods does it either because no
one will then be able to defile the plants, neither by magic
nor yet by poison; or perhaps he does it because the gods
did so before him.   Be that as it may, certain it is that
he thereby renders both kinds of plants wholesome and
innocuous, both the plants which men eat and the plants
on which cattle graze; that indeed is the reason why the
sacrificer sacrifices the first-fruits.   And the priest's fee for
the sacrifice is the first-born calf of the season, which is, as
it were, the first-fruit of the cattle.[1]

The Kachins of Upper Burma worship the spirit (*nat*)
of the earth every year before they sow their crops.   The
worship is performed by the chief on behalf of all the

[1] *The Satapatha Brâhmana*, trans-
lated by Julius Eggeling, Part i.
(Oxford, 1882), pp. 369-373 (*Sacred
Books of the East*, vol. xii.).

villagers, who contribute their offerings.   The priest afterwards determines by exorcism which particular household
shall start sowing first in order that the crop may be a good
one.   Then the household on which the lot has fallen goes
out and sows its fields.   When the crop is ripe, it may not
be reaped until the household which was the first to sow its
fields has gathered the first-fruits and offered them to its
own domestic spirits (*nats*).   This is usually done before the
crop is quite ripe, in order that the reaping of the other
crops may not be delayed.[1]   The Chins, another people of
Upper Burma, eat the first-fruits of their corn as a religious
rite, but before doing so they offer some of the new corn or
vegetables to their dead ancestors.   They also offer the first-
fruits to the goddess Pok Klai, a single glance of whose
eyes is enough to give them a plentiful harvest of rice.[2]
Among the Thay of Indo-China the first-fruits of the
rice are offered at harvest to the guardian spirit of the
family before the household may partake of the new crop.
The guardian spirit of the family is the last ancestor who
died ; he mounts guard until he is relieved by his successor ;
his shrine is a corner of the house screened off by a low
trellis of bamboo.   But besides the first-fruits offered him
at harvest this guardian spirit receives some of the parched
grain in spring, at the time when the first thunder of the
season is heard to mutter.   The grain which is presented
to him on this occasion was plucked from the crop before
the rice was quite ripe, and it has been carefully kept to
be offered to him when the first peal of thunder in spring
announces the reviving energies of nature.   When all is
ready, the rice is served up together with fish, which have
been caught for the purpose, on a table set in the corner
which is sacred to the guardian spirit.   A priest drones out
a long invitation to the spirit to come and feast with his
children ; then the family sits down to table and consumes
the offerings.   At the close of the banquet the daughter-in-
law of the deceased ancestor hangs up a basket containing

[1] (Sir) J. G. Scott and J. P. Hardiman, *Gazetteer of Upper Burma and
the Shan States*, Part i. vol. i. (Rangoon, 1900), pp. 425 *sq.*

[2] Rev. G. Whitehead, "Notes on
the Chins of Burma," *Indian Anti-
quary*, xxxvi. (1907) p. 207.

rice and fish for his use in the corner, after which she closes
the shrine for another year.[1]   In Corea the first-fruits of all
the crops used to be offered to the king with religious
pomp, and he received almost divine honours from his
subjects.[2]   This suggests that, as I have already conjectured, the common practice of presenting the first-fruits
to kings is founded on a belief in their divinity.

Sacrifices
of first-
fruits in
the East
Indies.   In the island of Tjumba, East Indies, a festival is held
after harvest.   Vessels filled with rice are presented as a
thankoffering to the gods.   Then the sacred stone at the
foot of a palm-tree is sprinkled with the blood of a sacrificed
animal ; and rice, with some of the flesh, is laid on the
stone for the gods.   The palm-tree is hung with lances and
shields.[3]   The Dyaks of Borneo hold a feast of first-fruits
when the paddy or unhusked rice is ripe.   The priestesses,
accompanied by a gong and drum, go in procession to the
farms and gather several bunches of the ripe paddy.   These
are brought back to the village, washed in coco-nut water, and
laid round a bamboo altar, which at the harvest festivals is
erected in the common room of the largest house.   The
altar is gaily decorated with white and red streamers, and is
hung with the sweet-smelling blossom of the areca palm.
The feast lasts two days, during which the village is tabooed ;
no one may leave it.   Only fowls are killed, and dancing
and gong-beating go on day and night.   When the festival
is over the people are free to get in their crops.[4]   The
pounding of the new paddy is the occasion of a harvest
festival which is celebrated all over Celebes.   The religious
ceremonies which accompany the feast were witnessed by
Dr. B. F. Matthes in July 1857.   Two mats were spread on
the ground, each with a pillow on it.   On one of the pillows
were placed a man's clothes and a sword, on the other a
woman's clothes.   These were seemingly intended to represent the deceased ancestors.   Rice and water were deposited
before the two dummy figures, which were also sprinkled
with the new paddy.   Moreover, dishes of rice were set

[1] A. Bourlet, "Les Thay," *An-*
thropos, ii. (1907) pp. 627-629.

[2] Ch. Dallet, *Histoire de l'Eglise*
de Corée (Paris, 1874), i. p. xxiv.

[3] Fr. Junghuhn, *Die Battaländer*
auf Sumatra (Berlin, 1847), ii. 312.

[4] Spenser St. John, *Life in the*
Forests of the Far East[2] (London,
1863), i. 191.

down for the rest of the family and the slaves of the
deceased. This was the end of the ceremony.[1] In Minahassa, a district of Celebes, the people have a festival of
"eating the new rice." Fowls or pigs are killed; some
of the flesh, with rice and palm-wine, is set apart for the
gods, and then the eating and drinking begin.[2] The
people of Kobi and Sariputi, two villages on the north-
east coast of Ceram, offer the first-fruits of the paddy,
in the form of cooked rice, with tobacco and other things,
to their ancestors as a token of gratitude. The ceremony is called "feeding the dead."[3] In the Tenimber
and Timor-laut Islands, East Indies, the first-fruits of the
paddy, along with live fowls and pigs, are offered to the
matmate. The *matmate* are the spirits of their ancestors,
which are worshipped as guardian-spirits or household gods.
They are supposed to enter the house through an opening in
the roof, and to take up their abode temporarily in their
skulls, or in images of wood or ivory, in order to partake of
the offerings and to help the family. They also assume the
form of birds, pigs, crocodiles, turtles, sharks, and so forth.[4]
In Amboyna, after the rice or other harvest has been
gathered in, some of the new fruits are offered to the gods,
and till this is done, the priests may by no means eat of
them. A portion of the new rice, or whatever it may be, is
boiled, and milk of the coco-nut is poured on it, mixed with
Indian saffron. It is then taken to the place of sacrifice and
offered to the god. Some people also pour out oil before
the deity; and if any of the oil is left over, they take
it home as a holy and priceless treasure, wherewith they
smear the forehead and breast of sick people and whole
people, in the firm conviction that the oil confers all kinds of
blessings.[5] In the Kei Islands, to the south-west of New
Guinea, the first-fruits are offered to Lir majoran, the god of
husbandry, when the harvest is ripe.[6] After the rice has

---

[1] B. F. Matthes, *Beknopt Verslag
mijner reizen in de Binnenlanden van
Celebes, in de jaren 1857 en 1861*, p. 5
(*Verzameling van Berigten betreffende
de Bijbelverspreiding*, Nos. 96-99).

[2] N. Graafland, *De Minahassa* (Rotterdam, 1869), i. 165.

[3] J. G. F. Riedel, *De sluik- en*
*kroesharige rassen tusschen Selebes en
Papua* (The Hague, 1886), p. 107.

[4] Riedel, *op. cit.* pp. 281, 296 *sq.*

[5] Fr. Valentyn, *Oud en nieuw Oost-
Indiën* (Dordrecht and Amsterdam,
1724-1726), iii. 10.

[6] C. M. Pleyte, "Ethnographische
Beschrijving der Kei-Eilanden," *Tijd-*

been reaped, the people of Nias deck the images of their ancestors with wreaths, and offer to them the first dishful of boiled rice, while they thank them for the blessings they have bestowed on the family.[1]   The Irayas and Catalangans of Luzon, tribes of the Malay stock, but of mixed blood, worship chiefly the souls of their ancestors under the name of *anitos*, to whom they offer the first-fruits of the harvest. The *anitos* are household deities ; some of them reside in pots in the corners of the houses ; and miniature houses, standing near the family dwelling, are especially sacred to them.[2]   When the Bagobos of the Philippines have got in their harvest of rice or maize, they will neither eat of it nor sell so much as a grain till they have made a pretence of feeding all their agricultural implements.[3]

Sacrifices of first-fruits in New Guinea.
The Bukaua of German New Guinea think that the spirits of their dead have power to make the fruits of the earth to grow.   Accordingly when they have cleared a patch in the forest for cultivation and are planting their crops, they take particular care to plant slips near the tree-stumps which have been left standing in the field, because the spirits of their long dead ancestors are supposed to perch on them.   While they plant, they call out the names of the dead, praying them to guard the field, so that their children, the living, may have food to eat and not suffer hunger.   And similarly, when they plant stones shaped like taro bulbs in the ground, which are supposed to produce a fine crop of taro, they pray to their forefathers to grant them an abundance of the fruits.   When the crops are ripe, the people fetch bundles of taro, clusters of bananas, sugar-canes, and vegetables from the fields and bring them back solemnly to the village ; a feast is prepared and a portion of the new fruits, along with tobacco, betel, and dog's flesh, is put in a coco-nut shell and set on a scaffold in the house of the owner of the field, while he prays to the spirits of

schrift van het Nederlandsch Aardrijks-kundig Genootschap, Tweede Serie, **x.** (1893) p. 801.

[1] Fr. Kramer, "Der Götzendienst der Niasser," *Tijdschrift voor Indische Taal- Land- en Volkenkunde*, xxxiii. (1890) p. 482.

[2] C. Semper, *Die Philippinen und ihre Bewohner* (Würzburg, 1869), p. 56.

[3] F. Blumentritt, "Das Stromgebiet des Rio Grande de Mindano," *Peter-manns Mittheilungen*, xxxvii. (1891) p. 111.

his forefathers, saying, " Ye who have guarded our field as we asked you to do, there is something for you ; now look on us favourably also for the time to come." Afterwards, while the people are feasting, the owner privily stirs the contents of the coco-nut shell with his finger, and then calls the attention of the others to it as a proof that the spirits have partaken of the offering provided for them. Finally the food remaining in the shell is consumed by the banqueters.[1]

In certain tribes of Fiji " the first-fruits of the yam harvest are presented to the ancestors in the Nanga [sacred enclosure] with great ceremony before the bulk of the crop is dug for the people's use, and no man may taste of the new yams until the presentation has been made. The yams thus offered are piled in the Great Nanga, and are allowed to rot there. If any one were impiously bold enough to appropriate them to his own use, he would be smitten with madness. The mission teacher before mentioned told me that, when he visited the Nanga he saw among the weeds with which it was overgrown, numerous yam vines which had sprung up out of the piles of decayed offerings. Great feasts are made at the presentations of the first-fruits, which are times of public rejoicing, and the Nanga itself is frequently spoken of as the *Mbaki*, or Harvest." [2] In other parts of Fiji the practice with regard to the first-fruits seems to have been different, for we are told by another observer that " the first-fruits of the yams, which are always presented at the principal temple of the district, become the property of the priests, and form their revenue, although the pretence of their being required for the use of the god is generally kept up." [3] In Tana, one of the New Hebrides, the general name for gods appeared to be *aremha*, which meant " a dead man." The spirits of departed ancestors were among the gods of the people. Chiefs who reached an advanced age were deified after their death, addressed by name, and prayed to on various occasions. They were supposed to preside especially over the growth of the yams and fruit-trees. The first-fruits

Sacrifices of first-fruits in Fiji and the New Hebrides.

[1] Stefan Lehner, " Bukaua," in R. Neuhauss's *Deutsch Neu-Guinea*, iii. (Berlin, 1911) pp. 434-436.

[2] Rev. Lorimer Fison, " The Nanga, or Sacred Stone Enclosure, of Waini-mala, Fiji," *Journal of the Anthropological Institute*, xiv. (1885) p. 27.

[3] J. E. Erskine, *Journal of a Cruise among the Islands of the Western Pacific* (London, 1853), p. 252.

were presented to them.   A little of the new fruit was laid on a stone, or on a shelving branch of the tree, or on a rude temporary altar, made of a few sticks lashed together with strips of bark, in the form of a table, with its four feet stuck in the ground.   All being quiet, the chief acted as high priest, and prayed aloud as follows : " Compassionate father ! here is some food for you ; eat it ; be kind to us on account of it."   Then all the people shouted.   This took place about noon, and afterwards the assembled people feasted and danced till midnight or morning.[1]

Sacrifices of first-fruits in the Solomon Islands.

In Florida, one of the Solomon Islands, the canarium nut is much used in the native cookery, but formerly none might be eaten till the sacrifice of the first-fruits had been offered to the ghosts of the dead.   This was done on behalf of a whole village by a man who inherited a knowledge of the way in which the sacrifice should be offered, and who accordingly had authority to open the season.   When he saw that the time had come, he raised a shout early in the morning, then climbed a tree, cracked the nuts, ate some himself, and put some on the stones in his sacred place for the particular ghost whom he worshipped.   Then all the people might gather the nuts for themselves.   The chief offered food, in which the new nuts were mixed, on the stones of the village sanctuary ; and every man who revered a ghost of his own did the same in his private sanctuary.[2] This sacrifice of first-fruits was witnessed by Mr. Woodford at the village of Aola, in the neighbouring island of Guadal-canar.   The canarium nuts, or Solomon Island almonds, had been ripe for a week, and Mr. Woodford had expressed a wish to taste them, but he was told that this was quite impossible till the offering to the ghost had been made.   As a native put it, " Devil he eat first ; all man he eat behind." All the inhabitants of the village adjourned to the sea-shore in groups of ten or twelve to perform the sacrifice.   The party to which Mr. Woodford attached himself swept a space clean beneath the spreading branches of a Barringtonia, and there constructed half-a-dozen tiny altars, each about six inches square, out of dry sticks.   On these altars they laid

[1] G. Turner, *Samoa* (London, 1884), pp. 318 *sq.*

[2] Rev. R. H. Codrington, *The Melanesians* (Oxford, 1891), pp. 132 *sq.*

offerings of yams, taros, bananas, and a little flesh ; and a few of the nuts were skinned and set up on sticks round about the altars.   Fire was then made by the friction of wood, for matches might not be used for this purpose, though probably every man had a box of them in his bag. With the sacred flame thus produced the altars were kindled and the offerings consumed.   When this was done, the women produced large flat cakes baked of a paste of pounded nuts, and these were eaten by all.[1]   In Saa, another of the Solomon Islands, when the yams are ripe, the people fetch some from each garden to offer to the ghosts.   Early in the morning all the male members of a family assemble at the sanctuary of the particular ancestral ghosts whom they revere.   One of them goes with a yam into the holy place and cries with a loud voice to the ghosts, " This is yours to eat," and with that he sets the yam beside the skull which is in the sanctuary.   The others call quietly upon all the ancestors and present their yams, which are many in number, because one from each garden is given to each of the ghosts.   Moreover, if any man has a relic of the dead at home, such as a head, or bones, or hair, he takes back a yam to his house and places it beside the head or whatever it may be.   In the same island, as in Florida, the new canarium nuts may not be eaten until the first-fruits have been offered to the ghosts.   Moreover, the first flying-fish of the season must be sacrificed to these spirits of the dead before the living are allowed to partake of the fish. The ghosts to whom the flying-fish are offered have the form of sharks.   Some of them have sanctuaries ashore, where images of sharks are set up ; and the flying-fish are laid before these images.   Other shark-ghosts have no place on shore ; so the fish offered to them are taken out to sea and shredded into the water, while the names of the ghosts are called out.[2]

In some of the Kingsmill Islands the god most commonly worshipped was called Tubuériki.   He was represented by a flat coral stone, of irregular shape, about three feet

Sacrifices of first-fruits in the Kingsmill Islands.

---

[1] C. M. Woodford, *A Naturalist among the Head-hunters, being an Account of Three Visits to the Solomon Islands* (London, 1890), pp. 26-28.

[2] Rev. R. H. Codrington, *The Melanesians*, p. 138.

long by eighteen inches wide, set up on end in the open air.
Leaves of the coco-nut palm were tied about it, considerably
increasing its size and height. The leaves were changed
every month, that they might be always fresh. The worship
paid to the god consisted in repeating prayers before the
stone, and laying beside it a portion of the food prepared by
the people for their own use. This they did at their daily
meals, at festivals, and whenever they specially wished
to propitiate the deity. The first-fruits of the season were
always offered to him. Every family of distinction had one
of these stones which was considered rather in the light of
a family altar than as an idol.[1]

Sacrifices
of first-
fruits in the
Tonga
Islands.

In the Tonga Islands the first-fruits of the year were
offered with solemn ceremony to the sacred chief Tooitonga,
who was regarded as divine. The ceremony generally took
place about October, and the people believed that if the rite
were neglected the vengeance of the gods would fall in a
signal manner upon them. The following is a description of
the festival as it was celebrated in the days when a European
flag rarely floated among the islands of the Pacific : "*Inachi*.
This word means, literally, a share or portion of anything
that is to be or has been distributed out : but in the sense
here mentioned it means that portion of the fruits of the
earth, and other eatables, which is offered to the gods in the
person of the divine chief Tooitonga, which allotment is
made once a year, just before the yams in general are
arrived at a state of maturity ; those which are used in this
ceremony being of a kind which admit of being planted
sooner than others, and, consequently, they are the first
fruits of the yam season. The object of this offering is to
insure the protection of the gods, that their favour may be
extended to the welfare of the nation generally, and in
particular to the productions of the earth, of which yams are
the most important.

"The time for planting most kinds of yams is about the
latter end of July, but the species called *caho-caho*, which is
always used in this ceremony, is put in the ground about a
month before, when, on each plantation, there is a small

---

[1] Horatio Hale, *United States Exploring Expedition, Ethnography and
Philology* (Philadelphia, 1846), p 97.

piece of land chosen and fenced in, for the purpose of growing a couple of yams of the above description. As soon as they have arrived at a state of maturity, the *How* [the King] sends a messenger to Tooitonga, stating that the yams for the *inachi* are fit to be taken up, and requesting that he would appoint a day for the ceremony : he generally fixes on the tenth day afterwards, reckoning the following day for the first. There are no particular preparations made till the day before the ceremony : at night, however, the sound of the conch is heard occasionally in different parts of the islands, and as the day of the ceremony approaches it becomes more frequent, so that the people of almost every plantation sound the conch three or four times, which, breaking in upon the silence of the night, has a pleasing effect, particularly at Vavaoo, where the number of woods and hills send back repeated echoes, adding greatly to the effect. The day before the ceremony, the yams are dug up, and ornamented with a kind of ribbons prepared from the inner membrane of the leaf of a species of pandanus, and dyed red ; when thus prepared, it is called *mellecoola* and is wrapped round the yam, beginning at one end, and running round spirally to the other, when it is brought back in the opposite direction, the turns crossing each other in a very neat manner. As the ceremony is always performed at the island where Tooitonga chooses to reside, the distant islands must make these preparations two or three days beforehand, that the yams, etc., may be sent in time to Vavaoo, where we will suppose the affair is to take place. The ninth day then is employed in preparing and collecting the yams and other provisions, such as fish, cava root, and *mahoa*, and getting ready mats, *gnatoo*, and bundles of *mellecoola :* but the yams only are to be carried in the procession about to be described. . . .

" The sun has scarcely set when the sound of the conch begins again to echo through the island, increasing as the night advances. At the Mooa [capital], and all the plantations, the voices of men and women are heard singing *Nófo óooa tegger gnaoóe, óooa gnaoóe,* ' Rest thou, doing no work ; thou shalt not work.' This increases till midnight, men generally singing the first part of the sentence, and the women the last, to produce a more pleasing effect : it then subsides for three or four hours, and again increases as the sun rises.   Nobody, however, is seen stirring out in the public roads till about eight o'clock, when the people from all quarters of the island are seen advancing towards the Mooa, and canoes from all the other islands are landing their men ; so that all the inhabitants of Tonga seem approaching by sea and land, singing and sounding the conch.   At the Mooa itself the universal bustle of preparation is seen and heard ; and the different processions entering from various quarters, of men and women, all dressed up in new *gnatoos*, ornamented with red ribbons and wreaths of flowers, and the men armed with spears and clubs, betoken the importance of the ceremony about to be performed.   Each party brings in its yams in a basket, which is carried in the arms with great care, by the principal vassal of the chief to whom the plantation may belong. The baskets are deposited in the *maldi*[1] (in the *Mooa*), and some of them begin to employ themselves in slinging the yams, each upon the centre of a pole about eight or nine feet long, and four inches diameter.   The proceedings are regulated by attending matabooles.[2]   The yams being all slung, each pole is carried by two men upon their shoulders, one walking before the other, and the yam hanging between them, ornamented with red ribbons.   The procession begins to move towards the grave of the last Tooitonga (which is generally in the neighbourhood, or the grave of one of his family will do), the men advancing in a single line, every two bearing a yam, with a slow and measured pace, sinking at every step, as if their burden were of immense weight.   In the meantime the chiefs and matabooles are seated in a semicircle before the grave, with their heads bowed down, and their hands clasped before them."   The procession then marched round the grave twice or thrice in a great circle, the conchs blowing and the men singing. Next the yams, still suspended from the poles, were de-

The first-fruits of the yams deposited on the grave of the last Tooitonga (divine chief).

---

[1] The *maldi* is "a piece of ground, generally before a large house, or chief's grave, where public ceremonies are principally held" (W. Mariner, *Tonga Islands, Vocabulary*).

[2] The *mataboole* is "a rank next below chiefs or nobles" (*ibid.*).

posited before the grave, and their bearers sat down beside them.   One of the *matabooles* of Tooitonga, seating himself before the grave, a little in advance of the men, now addressed the gods generally, and afterwards particularly, mentioning the late Tooitonga, and the names of several others.   He thanked them for their divine bounty in favouring the land with the prospect of so good a harvest, and prayed that their beneficence might be continued in future. When he had finished, the men rose and resumed their loads, and after parading two or three times before the grave, marched back to the *malái* the same way they came, singing and blowing the conchs as before.   The chiefs and *matabooles* soon followed to the same place, where the yams had been again deposited and loosened from the poles, though they still retained their ornaments.   Here the company sat down in a great circle, presided over by Tooitonga, while the king and other great chiefs retired into the background among the mass of the people.   Then the other articles that formed part of the *inachi* were brought forward, consisting of dried fish, mats, etc., which, with the yams, were divided into shares by one of the *matabooles* of Tooitonga.   About a fourth was allotted to the gods, and appropriated by the priests ; about a half fell to the king ; and the remainder belonged to Tooitonga. The materials of the *inachi* having been carried away, the company set themselves to drink *cava*.   Some *cava* root was brought and prepared ; a large quantity of provisions, perhaps a hundred and fifty baskets-full, was set forth, and a small part of it was distributed to be eaten with the *cava*. While the infusion was preparing, a *mataboole* made a speech to the people, saying that, as they had performed this important ceremony, the gods would protect them and grant them long lives, if only they continued to observe the religious rites and to pay due respect to the chiefs.   When the *cava* was all drunk, the circle separated, and the provisions were shared out to each chief according to his rank. The day concluded with wrestling, boxing, and so forth, and then the night dances began.   When these were ended, the people went home perfectly assured of the protection of the gods   At this ceremony, we are informed, the quantity

of provisions distributed was incredible, and the people
looked upon it as a very heavy tribute.[1]

Signifi-
cance of the
presenta-
tion of first-
fruits to the
divine chief
at the grave
of his pre-
decessor.

In this Tongan festival the solemn presentation of the
first-fruits to the divine chief at the grave of his predecessor
is highly significant: it confirms the conclusion which we
have already reached, that wherever the first-fruits are paid
to the chief, it is rather in his religious than in his civil
capacity that he receives them.   It is true that the king of
Tonga received a large share of the first-fruits, indeed a
larger share than was allotted to the divine chief; but it is
very noticeable that while the division of the first-fruits was
taking place under the presidency of the divine chief, the
king and the other great chiefs retired from the scene and
mingled with the mass of the people, as if to indicate that
as mere laymen they had no right to participate in a
religious rite of such deep solemnity.

Sacrifices
of first-
fruits in
Samoa and
other parts
of Poly-
nesia.

The Samoans used to present the first-fruits to the
spirits (*aitus*) and chiefs.[2]   For example, a family whose
god was in the form of an eel presented the first-fruits of
their taro plantations to the eel.[3]   In Tahiti "the first fish
taken periodically on their shores, together with a number
of kinds regarded as sacred, were conveyed to the altar.
The first-fruits of their orchards and gardens were also
taumaha, or offered, with a portion of their live stock, which
consisted of pigs, dogs, and fowls, as it was supposed death
would be inflicted on the owner or the occupant of the land,
from which the god should not receive such acknowledgment."[4]   In Huahine, one of the Society Islands, the
first-fruits were presented to the god Tani.   A poor person
was expected to bring two of the earliest fruits gathered, of
whatever kind; a *raatira* had to bring ten, and chiefs and
princes had to bring more, according to their rank and
riches.   They carried the fruits to the temple, where they
threw them down on the ground, with the words, "Here,

[1] W. Mariner, *Account of the
Natives of the Tonga Islands*, Second
Edition (London, 1818), ii. 78, 196-
203.   As to the divine chief Tooitonga
see *Taboo and the Perils of the Soul*,
p. 21.

[2] Ch. Wilkes, *Narrative of the*

United States Exploring Expedition,
New Edition (New York, 1851), ii.
133.

[3] G. Turner, *Samoa*, pp. 70 *sq.*

[4] W. Ellis, *Polynesian Researches*,
Second Edition (London, 1832-1836),
i. 350.

Tani, I have brought you something to eat."[1]   The chief
gods of the Easter Islanders were Make-Make and Haua.
To these they offered the first of all the produce of the
ground.[2]   Amongst the Maoris the offering of the first-fruits
of the sweet potatoes to Pani, son of Rongo, the god of
sweet potatoes, was a solemn religious ceremony.   The crop
of sweet potatoes (*kumara*) was sacred, and all persons
engaged in its cultivation were also sacred or tabooed ;
they might not quit the place nor undertake any other work.[3]

It has been affirmed that the old Prussians offered the
first-fruits of their crops and of their fishing to the god
Curcho, but doubt rests on the statement.[4]   We have seen
that the Athenians and other Greek peoples offered the
first-fruits of the wheat and barley harvests to Demeter and
Persephone at Eleusis.[5]   The Troezenians sacrificed the
first-fruits to Poseidon, whom they worshipped as the
guardian deity of their city.[6]   In Attica the first-fruits of
the vintage were presented to Icarius and Erigone.[7]   The
Romans sacrificed the first ears of corn to Ceres, and the
first of the new wine to Liber ; and until the priests had
offered these sacrifices, the people might not eat the new
corn nor drink the new wine.[8]   In various parts of ancient
Italy the vintage was solemnly inaugurated by the priests.
At Rome the duty devolved on the Flamen Dialis, who
sacrificed a lamb to Jupiter and then gathered the first
grapes over the entrails of the victim.   Till this ceremony
had been performed, the new wine might not be brought
into the city.[9]

Sacrifices of first-fruits among the old Prussians, Greeks, and Romans.

The Thompson River Indians of British Columbia used

[1] D. Tyerman and G. Bennet, *Journal of Voyages and Travels* (London, 1831), i. 284.

[2] Geiseler, *Die Oster-Insel* (Berlin, 1883), p. 31.

[3] E. Tregear, " The Maoris of New Zealand," *Journal of the Anthropological Institute*, xix. (1890) p. 110 ; R. Taylor, *Te Ika A Maui, or New Zealand and its Inhabitants*, Second Edition (London, 1870), pp. 165 *sq.* ; *Old New Zealand*, by a Pakeha Maori (London, 1884), pp. 103 *sq.*

[4] Chr. Hartknoch, *Alt und neues Preussen* (Frankfort and Leipsic, 1684),

p. 161 ; *id.*, *Dissertationes historicae de variis rebus Prussicis*, p. 163 (appended to his edition of P. de Dusburg's *Chronicon Prussiae*, Frankfort and Leipsic, 1679). Compare W. Mannhardt, *Die Korndämonen* (Berlin, 1868), p. 27.

[5] See above, vol. i. pp. 53 *sqq.*

[6] Plutarch, *Theseus*, 6.

[7] Hyginus, *Fabulae*, 130.

[8] Festus, *s.v.* " Sacrima," p. 319, ed. C. O. Müller ; Pliny, *Nat. Hist.* xviii. 8.

[9] Varro, *De lingua Latina*, vi. 16, ed. C. O. Müller.

K

Sacrifices
of first-
fruits
among the
Indians of
America.
to offer the first berries of the season to the earth, or more
generally to the mountains.   The offering was made by an
old grey-haired person, who danced and held out the fruit
towards the mountain-tops.   The rest of the people painted
their faces red and danced for some time.[1]   The Okanaken
Indians of British Columbia " observed first-fruits ceremonies.
When the first berries or roots were ripe, the chief would
send out his wife or eldest daughter to gather a portion.
The whole community would then come together, and
prayers would be offered to those spirits of the sky who
were supposed to preside over the operations of nature,
portions of the fruit or roots would be distributed to all
present, after which any one was free to gather all he or
she desired ; but no one would think of picking a berry
or digging a root until after the feast had been held." [2]
When the ears of maize were formed, the Quiches of Central
America gathered the first-fruits and carried them to the
priests ; moreover, they baked loaves or cakes, which they
offered to the idol who guarded their fields, but afterwards
these cakes were given to the poor or the infirm to eat.[3]   It
was the custom of the Arkansas Indians to offer the first-fruits
of the ripe maize and melons to the Master of Life ; even
children would die of hunger rather than touch the new
fruits before this offering had been made.   Some of the
new maize, melons, and other fruits were minced up with
the carcase of a dog in the presence of the old men, who
alone were privileged to assist at this solemn rite.   Then,
after performing certain ceremonies, the old men began to
dance, and some young girls, wound up to a pitch of
frenzy, threw themselves on the offering and bolted it
in an instant.   Thereupon the old men seized the damsels
and ducked them in the river Arkansas, which had a
sobering influence on the minds of the devotees.[4]   From
this account we may perhaps infer that in eating the new

[1] James Teit, *The Thompson In-
dians of British Columbia*, p. 345
(*The Jesup North Pacific Expedition,
Memoir of the American Museum of
Natural History*, April, 1900).

[2] C. Hill Tout, " Report on the
Ethnology of the Okanaken of British
Columbia," *Journal of the R. Anthropo-*

logical Institute, xli. (1911) p. 132.

[3] Brasseur de Bourbourg, *Histoire
des Nations civilisées du Mexique et
de l'Amérique-Centrale* (Paris, 1857-
1859), ii. 566.

[4] *Annales de l'Association de la
Propagation de la Foi*, i. (Paris and
Lyons, 1826) p. 386.

fruits the girls were believed to be inspired by the Master
of Life, who thus consumed the offering by deputy. The
chief solemnity of the Natchez, an Indian tribe on the Lower
Mississippi, was the Harvest Festival or the Festival of New
Fire.   An early account of this ceremony has been already
submitted to the reader,[1] but it may not be amiss to add
here for comparison the later description by Chateaubriand,
which differs from the other in some particulars, and lays
stress on the sacrifice rather than on the sacrament of first-
fruits.   According to Chateaubriand, then, when the time
for the festival drew near, a crier went through the villages
calling upon the people to prepare new vessels and new
garments, to wash their houses, and to burn the old grain,
the old garments, and the old utensils in a common fire.
He also proclaimed an amnesty to criminals.   Next day he
appeared again, commanding the people to fast for three
days, to abstain from all pleasures, and to make use of the
medicine of purification.   Thereupon all the people took
some drops extracted from a root which they called the
" root of blood."   It was a kind of plantain and distilled a
red liquor which acted as a violent emetic.   During their
three days' fast the people kept silence.   At the end of it
the crier proclaimed that the festival would begin on the
following day.   So next morning, as soon as it began to
grow light in the sky, the people streamed from all quarters
towards the temple of the Sun.   The temple was a large
building with two doors, one opening to the east, the other
to the west.   On this morning the eastern door of the
temple stood open.   Facing the eastern door was an altar,
placed so as to catch the first beams of the rising sun.   An
image of a *chouchouacha* (a small marsupial) stood upon the
altar ; on its right was an image of a rattlesnake, on its left
an image of a marmoset.   Before these images a fire of
oak-bark burned perpetually.   Once a year only, on the
eve of the Harvest Festival, was the sacred flame suffered
to die out.   To the right of the altar, on the morning of
this holy day, stood the great chief, who took his title and
traced his descent from the Sun.   To the left of the altar
stood his wife.   Round them were grouped, according to

Chateau-
briand's
description
of the har-
vest festival
among the
Natchez.

[1] Above, pp. 77 *sqq.*

their ranks, the war chiefs, the sachems, the heralds, and the young braves. In front of the altar were piled bundles of dry reeds, stacked in concentric rings.

The high priest, standing on the threshold of the temple, kept his eyes fixed on the eastern horizon. Before presiding at the festival he had to plunge thrice into the Mississippi. In his hands he held two pieces of dry wood which he kept rubbing slowly against each other, muttering magic words. At his side two acolytes held two cups filled with a kind of black sherbet. All the women, their backs turned to the east, each leaning with one hand on her rude mattock and supporting her infant with the other, stood in a great semicircle at the gate of the temple. Profound silence reigned throughout the multitude while the priest watched attentively the growing light in the east. As soon as the diffused light of dawn began to be shot with beams of fire, he quickened the motion of the two pieces of wood which he held in his hands ; and at the moment when the upper edge of the sun's disc appeared above the horizon, fire flashed from the wood and was caught in tinder. At the same instant the women outside the temple faced round and held up their infants and their mattocks to the rising sun.

The great chief and his wife now drank the black liquor. The priests kindled the circle of dried reeds ; fire was set to the heap of oak-bark on the altar, and from this sacred flame all the hearths of the village were rekindled. No sooner were the circles of reeds consumed than the chief's wife came from the temple and placing herself at the head of the women marched in procession to the harvest-fields, whither the men were not allowed to follow them. They went to gather the first sheaves of maize, and returned to the temple bearing them on their heads. Some of the sheaves they presented to the high priest, who laid them on the altar. Others they used to bake the unleavened bread which was to be eaten in the evening. The eastern door of the sanctuary was now closed, and the western door was opened.

When day began to decline, the multitude assembled once more at the temple, this time at its western gate, where they formed a great crescent, with the horns turned towards the west. The unleavened bread was held up and presented to the setting sun, and a priest struck up a hymn in praise of his descending light. When darkness had fallen the whole plain twinkled with fires, round which the people feasted ; and the sounds of music and revelry broke the silence of night.[1]

[1] Chateaubriand, *Voyage en Amérique*, pp. 130-136 (Michel Lévy, Paris, 1870).

CHAPTER XII

HOMOEOPATHIC MAGIC OF A FLESH DIET

Custom of killing and eating the corn-spirit sacramentally.

THE practice of killing a god has now been traced amongst peoples who have reached the agricultural stage of society. We have seen that the spirit of the corn, or of other cultivated plants, is commonly represented either in human or in animal form, and that in some places a custom has prevailed of killing annually either the human or the animal representative of the god. One reason for thus killing the corn-spirit in the person of his representative has been given implicitly in an earlier part of this work : we may suppose that the intention was to guard him or her (for the corn-spirit is often feminine) from the enfeeblement of old age by transferring the spirit, while still hale and hearty, to the person of a youthful and vigorous successor. Apart from the desirability of renewing his divine energies, the death of the corn-spirit may have been deemed inevitable under the sickles or the knives of the reapers, and his worshippers may accordingly have felt bound to acquiesce in the sad necessity.[1]

Belief of the savage that by eating an animal or man he acquires the qualities of that animal or man.

But, further, we have found a widespread custom of eating the god sacramentally, either in the shape of the man or animal who represents the god, or in the shape of bread made in human or animal form. The reasons for thus partaking of the body of the god are, from the primitive standpoint, simple enough. The savage commonly believes that by eating the flesh of an animal or man he acquires not only the physical, but even the moral and intellectual qualities which were characteristic of that animal or man ; so when the creature is deemed divine, our simple savage naturally expects to

[1] See *The Dying God*, pp. 9 *sqq.*

138

absorb a portion of its divinity along with its material substance. It may be well to illustrate by instances this common faith in the acquisition of virtues or vices of many kinds through the medium of animal food, even when there is no pretence that the viands consist of the body or blood of a god. The doctrine forms part of the widely ramified system of sympathetic or homoeopathic magic.

Thus, for example, the Creeks, Cherokee, and kindred tribes of North American Indians "believe that nature is possest of such a property, as to transfuse into men and animals the qualities, either of the food they use, or of those objects that are presented to their senses ; he who feeds on venison is, according to their physical system, swifter and more sagacious than the man who lives on the flesh of the clumsy bear, or helpless dunghill fowls, the slow-footed tame cattle, or the heavy wallowing swine. This is the reason that several of their old men recommend, and say, that formerly their greatest chieftains observed a constant rule in their diet, and seldom ate of any animal of a gross quality, or heavy motion of body, fancying it conveyed a dullness through the whole system, and disabled them from exerting themselves with proper vigour in their martial, civil, and religious duties."[1] The Zaparo Indians of Ecuador "will, unless from necessity, in most cases not eat any heavy meats, such as tapir and peccary, but confine themselves to birds, monkeys, deer, fish, etc., principally because they argue that the heavier meats make them unwieldy, like the animals who supply the flesh, impeding their agility, and unfitting them for the chase."[2] Similarly some of the Brazilian Indians would eat no beast, bird, or fish that ran, flew, or swam slowly, lest by partaking of its flesh they should lose their agility and be unable to escape from their enemies.[3] The Caribs abstained from the flesh of pigs lest it should cause them to have small eyes

Beliefs of the American Indians as to the homoeopathic magic of the flesh of animals.

---

[1] James Adair, *History of the American Indians* (London, 1775), p. 133.

[2] Alfred Simson, *Travels in the Wilds of Ecuador* (London, 1887), p. 168 ; *id.*, in *Journal of the Anthropological Institute*, vii. (1878) p. 503.

[3] A. Thevet, *Les Singularitez de la France Antarctique, autrement nommée Amerique* (Antwerp, 1558), p. 55 ; *id.*, *La Cosmographie Universelle* (Paris, 1575), ii. pp. 929, [963], 940 [974] ; J. Lerius, *Historia Navigationis in Brasiliam, quae et America dicitur* (1586), pp. 126 *sq.*

like pigs ; and they refused to partake of tortoises from a fear that if they did so they would become heavy and stupid like the animal.[1]   Among the Fans of West Africa men in the prime of life never eat tortoises for a similar reason ; they imagine that if they did so, their vigour and fleetness of foot would be gone.   But old men may eat tortoises freely, because having already lost the power of running they can take no harm from the flesh of the slow-footed creature.[2] Some of the Chiriguanos of eastern Bolivia would not touch the flesh of the vicuña, because they imagined that if they ate it they would become woolly like the vicuña.[3]   On the other hand the Abipones of Paraguay ate the flesh of jaguars in order to acquire the courage of the beast ;[4] indeed the number of jaguars which they consumed for this object is said to have been very great, and with a like intent they eagerly devoured the flesh of bulls, stags, boars, and ant-bears, being persuaded that by frequently partaking of such food they increased their strength, activity, and courage.   On the other hand they all abhorred the thought of eating hens, eggs, sheep, fish, and tortoises, because they believed that these tender viands begot sloth and listlessness in their bodies and cowardice in their minds.[5]   The Thompson Indians of British Columbia would not eat the heart of the fool-hen, nor would they allow their dogs to devour the bird, lest they should grow foolish like the bird.[6]

Bushman beliefs as to the homoeopathic magic of the flesh of animals.   While many savages thus fear to eat the flesh of slow-footed animals lest they should themselves become slow-footed, the Bushmen of South Africa purposely ate the flesh of such creatures, and the reason which they gave for doing so exhibits a curious refinement of savage philosophy.   They imagined that the game which they pursued would be influenced sympathetically by the food in the body of the

---

[1] Rochefort, *Histoire Naturelle et Morale des Îles Antilles*, Seconde Edition (Rotterdam, 1665), p. 465.

[2] C. Cuny, "De Libreville au Cameroun," *Bulletin de la Société de Géographie* (Paris), vii. Série, xvii. (1896) p. 342.

[3] R. Southey, *History of Brazil*, ii. (London, 1817) p. 373 ; *id.*, iii. (London, 1819) p. 164.

[4] P. Lozano, *Descripcion Chorographica del Gran Chaco* (Cordova, 1733), p. 90.

[5] M. Dobrizhoffer, *Historia de Abiponibus* (Vienna, 1784), i. 289 *sq.*

[6] J. Teit, *The Thompson Indians of British Columbia*, p. 348 (*The Jesup North Pacific Expedition, Memoir of the American Museum of Natural History*, April, 1900).

hunter, so that if he had eaten of swift-footed animals, the quarry would be swift-footed also and would escape him; whereas if he had eaten of slow-footed animals, the quarry would also be slow-footed, and he would be able to overtake and kill it. For that reason hunters of gemsbok particularly avoided eating the flesh of the swift and agile springbok; indeed they would not even touch it with their hands, because they believed the springbok to be a very lively creature which did not go to sleep at night, and they thought that if they ate springbok, the gemsbok which they hunted would likewise not be willing to go to sleep, even at night. How, then, could they catch it?[1]

Certain tribes on the Upper Zambesi believe in transmigration, and every man in his lifetime chooses the kind of animal whose body he wishes at death to enter. He then performs an initiatory rite, which consists in swallowing the maggots bred in the putrid carcase of the animal of his choice; thenceforth he partakes of that animal's nature. And on the occasion of a calamity, while the women are giving themselves up to lamentation, you will see one man writhing on the ground like a boa constrictor or a crocodile, another howling and leaping like a panther, a third baying like a jackal, roaring like a lion, or grunting like a hippopotamus, all of them imitating the characters of the various animals to perfection.[2] Clearly these people imagine that the soul or vital essence of the animal is manifested in the maggots bred in its decaying carcase; hence they imagine that by swallowing the maggots they imbue themselves with the very life and spirit of the creature which they desire to become. The Namaquas abstain from eating the flesh of hares, because they think it would make them faint-hearted as a hare. But they eat the flesh of the lion, or drink the blood of the leopard or lion, to get the courage and strength of these beasts.[3] The Bushmen will not give their children a jackal's heart to eat, lest it should make them timid like the jackal;

Other African beliefs as to the homoeopathic magic of the flesh of animals.

---

[1] W. H. I. Bleek and C. L. Lloyd, *Specimens of Bushman Folklore* (London, 1911), pp. 271-275.

[2] A. Bertrand, *The Kingdom of the Barotsi, Upper Zambezia* (London, 1899), p. 277, quoting the description given by the French missionary M. Coillard.

[3] Theophilus Hahn, *Tsuni-‖ Goam, the Supreme Being of the Khoi-Khoi* (London, 1881), p. 106.

but they give them a leopard's heart to eat to make them brave like the leopard.[1]   When a Wagogo man of German East Africa kills a lion, he eats the heart in order to become brave like a lion ; but he thinks that to eat the heart of a hen would make him timid.[2]   Among the Ja-luo, a tribe of Nilotic negroes, young men eat the flesh of leopards in order to make themselves fierce in war.[3]   The flesh of the lion and also that of the spotted leopard are sometimes cooked and eaten by native warriors in South-Eastern Africa, who hope thereby to become as brave as lions.[4]   When a Zulu army assembles to go forth to battle, the warriors eat slices of meat which is smeared with a powder made of the dried flesh of various animals, such as the leopard, lion, elephant, snakes, and so on ; for thus it is thought that the soldiers will acquire the bravery and other warlike qualities of these animals.   Sometimes if a Zulu has killed a wild beast, for instance a leopard, he will give his children the blood to drink, and will roast the heart for them to eat, expecting that they will thus grow up brave and daring men.   But others say that this is dangerous, because it is apt to produce courage without prudence, and to make a man rush heedlessly on his death.[5]   Among the Wabondei of Eastern Africa the heart of a lion or leopard is eaten with the intention of making the eater strong and brave.[6]   In British Central Africa aspirants after courage consume the flesh and especially the hearts of lions, while lecherous persons eat the testicles of goats.[7]   Among the Suk of British East Africa the fat and heart of a lion are sometimes given to children to eat in order that they may become strong ; but they are not allowed to know what they are eating.[8]   Arab women

[1] W. H. I. Bleek and L. C. Lloyd, *Specimens of Bushman Folklore* (London, 1911), p. 373.

[2] Rev. H. Cole, "Notes on the Wagogo of German East Africa," *Journal of the Anthropological Institute*, xxxii. (1902) p. 318.

[3] Sir Harry Johnston, *The Uganda Protectorate*, Second Edition (London, 1904), ii. 787.

[4] Rev. J. Macdonald, *Light in Africa*, Second Edition (London, 1890), p. 174 ; *id.*, in *Journal of the*

Anthropological Institute, xix. (1890) p. 282.

[5] Rev. H. Callaway, *Religious System of the Amazulu*, p. 438, note 16.

[6] O. Baumann, *Usambara und seine Nachbargebiete* (Berlin, 1891), p. 128.

[7] Sir H. H. Johnston, *British Central Africa* (London, 1897), p. 438 ; J. Buchanan, *The Shire Highlands*, p. 138.

[8] M. W. H. Beech, *The Suk, their Language and Folklore* (Oxford, 1911), p. 11.

in North Africa give their male children a piece of a lion's heart to eat to make them fearless.[1] The flesh of an elephant is thought by the Ewe-speaking peoples of West Africa to make the eater strong.[2] Before they go forth to fight, Wajagga warriors drink a magical potion, which often consists of shavings of the horn and hide of a rhinoceros mixed with beer ; this is supposed to impart to them the strength and force of the animal.[3] When a serious disease has attacked a Zulu kraal, the medicine-man takes the bone of a very old dog, or the bone of an old cow, bull, or other very old animal, and administers it to the healthy as well as to the sick people, in order that they may live to be as old as the animal of whose bone they have partaken.[4] So to restore the aged Aeson to youth, the witch Medea infused into his veins a decoction of the liver of the long-lived deer and the head of a crow that had outlived nine generations of men.[5] In antiquity the flesh of deer and crows was eaten for other purposes than that of prolonging life. As deer were supposed not to suffer from fever, some women used to taste venison every morning, and it is said that in consequence they lived to a great age without ever being attacked by a fever ; only the venison lost all its virtue if the animal had been killed by more blows than one.[6] Again, ancient diviners sought to imbue themselves with the spirit of prophecy by swallowing vital portions of birds and beasts of omen ; for example, they thought that by eating the hearts of crows or moles or hawks they took into their bodies, along with the flesh, the prophetic soul of the creature.[7]

Ancient beliefs as to the homoeopathic magic of the flesh of animals.

---

[1] J. Shooter, *The Kafirs of Natal and the Zulu Country* (London, 1857), p. 399.

[2] A. B. Ellis, *The Ewe-speaking Peoples of the Slave Coast of West Africa* (London, 1890), p. 99.

[3] M. Merker, *Rechtsverhältnisse und Sitten der Wadschagga* (Gotha, 1902), p. 38 (*Petermanns Mitteilungen, Ergänzungsheft*, No. 138).

[4] Rev. H. Callaway, *Nursery Tales, Traditions, and Histories of the Zulus* (Natal and London, 1868), p. 175 note.

[5] Ovid, *Metam.* vii. 271 *sqq.* As to the supposed longevity of deer and crows, see L. Stephani, in *Compte Rendu de la Commission Archéologique* (St. Petersburg), 1863, pp. 140 *sq.*, and my note on Pausanias, viii. 10. 10.

[6] Pliny, *Nat. Hist.* viii. 119.

[7] Porphyry, *De Abstinentia*, ii. 48 : οἱ γοῦν ζῴων μαντικῶν ψυχὰς δέξασθαι βουλόμενοι εἰς ἑαυτούς, τὰ κυριώτατα μόρια καταπιόντες, οἷον καρδίας κοράκων ἢ ἀσπαλάκων ἢ ἱεράκων, ἔχουσι παριοῦσαν τὴν ψυχὴν καὶ χρηματίζουσαν ὡς θεὸν καὶ εἰσιοῦσαν εἰς αὐτοὺς ἅμα τῇ ἐνθέσει τῇ τοῦ σώματος. Pliny also mentions the custom of eating the heart of a mole, raw and palpitating, as a means of acquiring skill in divination (*Nat. Hist.* xxx. 19).

Beliefs of
the Dyaks
and Aino
as to the
homoeo-
pathic
magic of
the flesh of
animals.

Among the Dyaks of North-West Borneo young men and warriors may not eat venison, because it would make them as timid as deer ; but the women and very old men are free to eat it.[1] However, among the Kayans of the same region, who share the same view as to the ill effect of eating venison, men will partake of the dangerous viand provided it is cooked in the open air, for then the timid spirit of the animal is supposed to escape at once into the jungle and not to enter into the eater.[2] The Aino of Japan think that the otter is a very forgetful animal, and they often call a person with a bad memory an " otter head." There-fore it is a rule with them that " the otter's head must not lightly be used as an article of food, for unless people are very careful they will, if they eat it, become as forgetful as that creature. And hence it happens that when an otter has been killed the people do not usually eat the head. But if they are seized with a very strong desire for a feast of otter's head, they may partake thereof, providing proper precautions are taken. When eating it the people must take their swords, knives, axes, bows and arrows, tobacco-boxes and pipes, trays, cups, garden tools, and everything they possess, tie them up in bundles with carrying slings, and sit with them attached to their heads while in the act of eating. This feast may be partaken of in this way, and no other. If this method be carefully adhered to, there will be no danger of forgetting where a thing has been placed, otherwise loss of memory will be the result." [3] On the other hand the Aino believe that the heart of the water-ousel is exceedingly wise, and that in speech the bird is most eloquent. Therefore whenever he is killed, he should be at once torn open and his heart wrenched out and swallowed before it has time to grow cold or suffer damage of any kind. If a man swallows it thus, he will become very fluent and wise, and will be able to argue down all his adversaries.[4] In Northern India people fancy that if you eat the eyeballs

[1] Spenser St. John, *Life in the Forests of the Far East*, Second Edition (London, 1863), i. 186, 206.

[2] W. H. Furness, *Home-life of Borneo Head-hunters* (Philadelphia, 1902), p. 71 ; compare *id.*, pp. 166 *sq.*

[3] Rev. J. Batchelor, *The Ainu and their Folk-lore* (London, 1901), pp. 511-513.

[4] Rev. J. Batchelor, *op. cit.* p. 337.

of an owl you will be able like an owl to see in the dark.[1]

When the Kansas Indians were going to war, a feast used to be held in the chief's hut, and the principal dish was dog's flesh, because, said the Indians, the animal who is so brave that he will let himself be cut in pieces in defence of his master, must needs inspire valour.[2] On extraordinary occasions the bravest warriors of the Dacotas used to perform a dance at which they devoured the livers of dogs raw and warm in order thereby to acquire the sagacity and bravery of the dog. The animals were thrown to them alive, killed, and cut open ; then the livers were extracted, cut into strips, and hung on a pole. Each dancer grabbed at a strip of liver with his teeth and chewed and swallowed it as he danced : he might not touch it with his hands, only the medicine-man enjoyed that privilege. Women did not join in the dance.[3] Men of the Buru and Aru Islands, East Indies, eat the flesh of dogs in order to be bold and nimble in war.[4] Amongst the Papuans of the Port Moresby and Motumotu districts, New Guinea, young lads eat strong pig, wallaby, and large fish, in order to acquire the strength of the animal or fish.[5] Some of the natives of Northern Australia fancy that by eating the flesh of the kangaroo or emu they are enabled to jump or run faster than before.[6] The Miris of Assam prize tiger's flesh as food for men ; it gives them strength and courage. But "it is not suited for women ; it would make them too strong-minded."[7] In Corea the bones of tigers fetch a higher price than those of leopards as a means of inspiring courage. A Chinaman in Seoul bought and ate a whole tiger to make himself brave and fierce.[8] The special seat of courage, according to the Chinese, is the gall-bladder ;

[1] W. Crooke, *Popular Religion and Folk-lore of Northern India* (Westminster, 1896), i. 279.

[2] Bossu, *Nouveaux Voyages aux Indes occidentales* (Paris, 1768), i. 112.

[3] H. R. Schoolcraft, *Indian Tribes of the United States*, ii. (Philadelphia, 1853) pp. 79 *sq.*

[4] J. G. F. Riedel, *De sluik- en kroesharige rassen tusschen Selebes en Papua* (The Hague, 1886), pp. 10, 262.

[5] James Chalmers, *Pioneering in New Guinea* (London, 1887), p. 166.

[6] *Journal of the Anthropological Institute*, xxiv. (1895) p. 179.

[7] E. T. Dalton, *Descriptive Ethnology of Bengal* (Calcutta, 1872), p. 33.

[8] *Proceedings of the Royal Geographical Society*, N.S., viii. (1886) p. 307.

so they sometimes procure the gall-bladders of tigers and bears, and eat the bile in the belief that it will give them courage.[1] Again, the Similkameen Indians of British Columbia imagine that to eat the heart of a bear inspires courage.[2]

Beliefs as to the homoeopathic magic of the flesh of wolves, bears, and serpents.

In Norse legend, Ingiald, son of King Aunund, was timid in his youth, but after eating the heart of a wolf he became very bold; Hialto gained strength and courage by eating the heart of a bear and drinking its blood;[3] and when Sigurd killed the dragon Fafnir and tasted his heart's blood, he acquired thereby a knowledge of the language of birds.[4] The belief that the language of birds or of animals in general can be learned by eating some part of a serpent appears to be ancient and wide-spread. Democritus is reported to have said that serpents were generated from the mixed blood of certain birds, and that therefore whoever ate a serpent would understand the bird language.[5] The Arabs in antiquity were supposed to be able to draw omens from birds because they had gained a knowledge of the bird language by eating either the heart or liver of a serpent; and the people of Paraka in India are said to have learned the language of animals in general by the same means.[6] Saxo Grammaticus relates how Rollo acquired all knowledge, including an understanding of the speech of animals, both wild and tame, by eating of a black serpent.[7] In Norway, Sweden, and Jutland down to the nineteenth century the flesh of a white snake was thought to confer supernatural wisdom on the eater;[8] it is a German and Bohemian superstition that whoever eats serpent's flesh understands the language of animals.[9] Notions of the same sort, based

---

[1] J. Henderson, "The Medicine and Medical Practice of the Chinese," *Journal of the North China Branch of the Royal Asiatic Society*, New Series, i. (Shanghai, 1865) pp. 35 *sq.* Compare Mrs. Bishop, *Korea and her Neighbours* (London, 1898), i. 79.

[2] Mrs. S. S. Allison, "Account of the Similkameen Indians of British Columbia," *Journal of the Anthropological Institute*, xxi. (1892) p. 313.

[3] P. E. Müller on Saxo Grammaticus, *Historia Danica* (Copenhagen, 1839-1858), vol. ii. p. 60.

[4] *Die Edda*, übersetzt von K. Simrock [8] (Stuttgart, 1882), pp. 180, 309.

[5] Pliny, *Hist. Natur.* x. 137, xxix. 72.

[6] Philostratus, *Vita Apollonii*, i. 20, iii. 9.

[7] Saxo Grammaticus, *Historia Danica*, ed. P. E. Müller (Copenhagen, 1839-1858), i. 193 *sq.*

[8] P. E. Müller, note in his edition of Saxo Grammaticus, vol. ii. p. 146.

[9] A. Wuttke, *Der deutsche Volksaberglaube* [2] (Berlin, 1869), p. 110, § 153; J. V. Grohmann, *Aberglauben*

no doubt on a belief in the extraordinary wisdom or subtlety of the serpent, often meet us in popular tales and traditions.[1]

In Morocco lethargic patients are given ants to swallow, and to eat lion's flesh will make a coward brave ;[2] but people abstain from eating the hearts of fowls, lest thereby they should be rendered timid.[3]   When a child is late in learning to speak, the Turks of Central Asia will give it the tongues of certain birds to eat.[4]   A North American Indian thought that brandy must be a decoction of hearts and tongues, "because," said he, " after drinking it I fear nothing, and I talk wonderfully."[5]   In Java there is a tiny earthworm which now and then utters a shrill sound like that of the alarum of a small clock.   Hence when a public dancing girl has screamed herself hoarse in the exercise of her calling, the leader of the troop makes her eat some of these worms, in the belief that thus she will regain her voice and will, after swallowing them, be able to scream as shrilly as ever.[6]   The people of Darfur, in Central Africa, think that the liver is the seat of the soul, and that a man may enlarge his soul by eating the liver of an animal.   "Whenever an animal is killed its

und Gebräuche aus Böhmen und Mähren (Prague and Leipsic, 1864), p. 230, § 1658.

[1] Grimm, Kinder- und Hausmärchen, No. 17 ; id., Deutsche Sagen [2] (Berlin, 1865-1866), No. 132 (vol. i. pp. 174-176) ; A. Kuhn und W. Schwartz, Norddeutsche Sagen, Märchen und Gebräuche (Leipsic, 1848), p. 154 ; A. Waldau, Böhmisches Märchenbuch (Prague, 1860), pp. 13 sqq. ; Von Alpenburg, Mythen und Sagen Tirols (Zurich, 1857), pp. 302 sqq. ; W. von Schulenburg, Wendische Volkssagen und Gebräuche aus dem Spreewald (Leipsic, 1880), p. 96 ; P. Sébillot, Traditions et Superstitions de la Haute-Bretagne (Paris, 1882), ii. 224 ; W. Grant Stewart, The Popular Superstitions and Festive Amusements of the High-landers of Scotland, New Edition (London, 1851), pp. 53, 56 ; J. F. Campbell, Popular Tales of the West Highlands, New Edition (Paisley and London, 1890), No. 47, vol. ii. pp. 377 sqq. ; E. Prym und A. Socin, Syrische Sagen und Maerchen (Göttin-

gen, 1881), pp. 150 sq.   On the serpent in relation to the acquisition by men of the language of animals, see further my article, "The Language of Animals," The Archaeological Review, i. (1888) pp. 166 sqq.   Sometimes serpents have been thought to impart a knowledge of the language of animals voluntarily by licking the ears of the seer.   See Apollodorus, Bibliotheca, i. 9. 11 sq. ; Porphyry, De abstinentia, iii. 4.

[2] A. Leared, Morocco and the Moors (London, 1876), p. 281.

[3] M. Quedenfelt, "Aberglaube und halb-religiöse Bruderschaft bei den Marokkanern," Verhandlungen der Berliner Gesellschaft für Anthropologie, Ethnologie und Urgeschichte, 1886, p. 682 (bound up with the Zeitschrift für Ethnologie, xviii. 1886).

[4] H. Vambery, Das Türkenvolk (Leipsic, 1885), p. 218.

[5] Charlevoix, Histoire de la Nouvelle France (Paris, 1744), vi. 8.

[6] P. J. Veth, "De leer der Sig-natuur," Internationales Archiv für Ethnographie, vii. (1894) pp. 140 sq.

liver is taken out and eaten, but the people are most careful not to touch it with their hands, as it is considered sacred ; it is cut up in small pieces and eaten raw, the bits being conveyed to the mouth on the point of a knife, or the sharp point of a stick.   Any one who may accidentally touch the liver is strictly forbidden to partake of it, which prohibition is regarded as a great misfortune for him."   Women are not allowed to eat liver, because they have no soul.[1]

The flesh and blood, but especially the hearts, of dead men eaten or drunk for the sake of acquiring the good qualities of the dead.

Again, the flesh and blood of dead men are commonly eaten and drunk to inspire bravery, wisdom, or other qualities for which the men themselves were remarkable, or which are supposed to have their special seat in the particular part eaten.   Thus among the mountain tribes of South-Eastern Africa there are ceremonies by which the youths are formed into guilds or lodges, and among the rites of initiation there is one which is intended to infuse courage, intelligence, and other qualities into the novices.   Whenever an enemy who has behaved with conspicuous bravery is killed, his liver, which is considered the seat of valour; his ears, which are supposed to be the seat of intelligence ; the skin of his forehead, which is regarded as the seat of perseverance ; his testicles, which are held to be the seat of strength ; and other members, which are viewed as the seat of other virtues, are cut from his body and baked to cinders.   The ashes are carefully kept in the horn of a bull, and, during the ceremonies observed at circumcision, are mixed with other ingredients into a kind of paste, which is administered by the tribal priest to the youths.   By this means the strength, valour, intelligence, and other virtues of the slain are believed to be imparted to the eaters.[2]   When Basutos of the mountains have killed a very brave foe, they immediately cut out his heart and eat it, because this is supposed to give them his courage and strength in battle.   At the close of the war the man who has slain such a foe is called before the chief and

---

[1] R. W. Felkin, " Notes on the For Tribe of Central Africa," *Proceedings of the Royal Society of Edinburgh*, xiii. (1884-1886) p. 218.

[2] Rev. J. Macdonald, "Manners, Customs, etc., of the South African Tribes,"*Journal of the Anthropological Institute*, xx. (1891) p. 116 ; *id.*, *Light in Africa* (London, 1890), p. 212.   Compare Rev. E. Casalis, *The Basutos* (London, 1861), pp. 257 *sq.* ; Dudley Kidd, *The Essential Kafir* (London, 1904), p. 309.

gets from the doctor a medicine which he chews with his food. The third day after this he must wash his body in running water, and at the expiry of ten days he may return to his wives and children.[1]   So an Ovambo warrior in battle will tear out the heart of his slain foe in the belief that by eating it he can acquire the bravery of the dead man.[2]   A similar belief and practice prevail among some of the tribes of British Central Africa, notably among the Angoni. These tribes also mutilate the dead and reduce the severed parts to ashes.   Afterwards the ashes are stirred into a broth or gruel, "which must be 'lapped' up with the hand and thrown into the mouth, but not eaten as ordinary food is taken, to give the soldiers courage, perseverance, fortitude, strategy, patience and wisdom."[3]   In former times whenever a Nandi warrior killed an enemy he used to eat a morsel of the dead man's heart to make himself brave.[4]   The Wagogo of German East Africa do the same thing for the same purpose.[5] When Sir Charles M'Carthy was killed by the Ashantees in 1824, it is said that his heart was devoured by the chiefs of the Ashantee army, who hoped by this means to imbibe his courage.   His flesh was dried and parcelled out among the lower officers for the same purpose, and his bones were long kept at Coomassie as national fetishes.[6]   The Amazons of Dahomey used to eat the hearts of foes remarkable for their bravery, in order that some of the intrepidity which animated them might be transfused into the eaters. In former days, if report may be trusted, the hearts of enemies who enjoyed a reputation for sagacity were also eaten, for the Ewe-speaking negro of these regions holds that the heart is the seat of the intellect as well as of courage.[7] Among the Yoruba-speaking negroes of the Slave Coast the

[1] Rev. J. Macdonald, in *Journal of the Anthropological Institute*, xx. (1891) p. 138; *id.*, *Light in Africa*, p. 220.
[2] H. Schinz, *Deutsch Südwest-Afrika* (Oldenburg and Leipsic, preface dated 1891), p. 320.
[3] J. Macdonald, "East Central African Customs," *Journal of the Anthropological Institute*, xxii. (1893) p. 111. Compare J. Buchanan, *The Shire Highlands*, p. 138; Sir H. H. Johnston, *British Central Africa*

(London, 1897), p. 438.
[4] A. C. Hollis, *The Nandi* (Oxford, 1909), p. 27.
[5] Rev. H. Cole, "Notes on the Wagogo of German East Africa," *Journal of the Anthropological Institute*, xxxii. (1902) p. 318.
[6] Rev. J. L. Wilson, *Western Africa* (London, 1856), pp. 167 *sq.*
[7] A. B. Ellis, *The Ewe-speaking Peoples of the Slave Coast* (London, 1890), pp. 99 *sq.*

priests of Ogun, the war-god, usually take out the hearts of human victims, which are then dried, crumbled to powder, mixed with rum, and sold to aspirants after courage, who swallow the mixture in the belief that they thereby absorb the manly virtue of which the heart is supposed to be the seat.[1]   Similarly, Indians of the Orinoco region used to toast the hearts of their enemies, grind them to powder, and then drink the powder in a liquid in order to be brave and valiant the next time they went forth to fight.[2]   The Nauras Indians of New Granada ate the hearts of Spaniards when they had the opportunity, hoping thereby to make themselves as dauntless as the dreaded Castilian chivalry.[3]   The Sioux Indians of North America used to reduce to powder the heart of a valiant enemy and swallow the powder, hoping thus to appropriate the dead man's valour.[4]   The Muskoghees also thought that to eat the heart of a foe would "communicate and give greater heart against the enemy.   They also think that the vigorous faculties of the mind are derived from the brain, on which account, I have seen some of their heroes drink out of a human skull ; they imagine, they only imbibe the good qualities it formerly contained."[5]   For a similar reason in Uganda a priest used to drink beer out of the skull of a dead king in order that he might be possessed by the king's spirit.[6]   Among the Esquimaux of Bering Strait, when young men had slain an enemy for the first time in war, they were wont to drink some of the blood and to eat a small piece of the heart of their victim in order to increase their bravery.[7]   In some tribes of North-Western Australia, when a man dies who had been a great warrior or hunter,

[1] A. B. Ellis, *The Yoruba-speaking Peoples of the Slave Coast* (London, 1894), p. 69.

[2] A. Caulin, *Historia Coro-graphica natural y evangelica dela Nueva Anda-lucia* (1779), p. 98.

[3] A. de Herrera, *General History of the vast Continent and Islands of America*, translated by Capt. J. Stevens (London, 1725-1726), vi. 187.

[4] F. de Castelnau, *Expédition dans les parties centrales de l'Amérique du Sud* (Paris, 1850-1851), iv. 382.

[5] James Adair, *History of the American Indians* (London, 1775), p. 135.

[6] Rev. J. Roscoe, "Notes on the Manners and Customs of the Baganda," *Journal of the Anthropological Institute*, xxxi. (1901) pp. 129 *sq.*; *id.*, "Further Notes on the Manners and Customs of the Baganda," *Journal of the Anthropological Institute*, xxxii. (1902) p. 45.

[7] E. W. Nelson, "The Eskimo about Bering Strait," *Eighteenth Annual Report of the Bureau of American Ethnology*, Part i. (Washington, 1899) p. 328.

his friends cut out the fat about his heart and eat it, because
they believe that it imparts to them the courage and cunning
of the deceased.[1]

But while the human heart is thus commonly eaten
for the sake of imbuing the eater with the qualities of
its original owner, it is not, as we have already seen,
the only part of the body which is consumed for this
purpose. Thus in New Caledonia the victors in a fight
used to eat the bodies of the slain, "not, as might be
supposed, from a taste for human flesh, but in order to
assimilate part of the bravery which the deceased was
supposed to possess."[2] Among the tribes about Mary-
borough in Queensland, when a man was killed in a ceremonial fight, it was customary for his friends to skin and
eat him, in order that his warlike virtues might pass into
the eaters.[3] Warriors of the Theddora and Ngarigo tribes
in South-Eastern Australia used to eat the hands and feet
of their slain enemies, believing that in this way they
acquired some of the qualities and courage of the dead.[4]
In the Dieri tribe of Central Australia, when a man had
been condemned and killed by a properly constituted party
of executioners, the weapons with which the deed was done
were washed in a small wooden vessel, and the bloody
mixture was administered to all the slayers in a prescribed
manner, while they lay down on their backs and the elders
poured it into their mouths. This was believed to give them
double strength, courage, and great nerve for any future
enterprise.[5] The Kamilaroi of New South Wales ate the
liver as well as the heart of a brave man to get his courage.[6]
In Tonquin also there is a popular superstition that the liver
of a brave man makes brave any who partake of it. Hence
when a Catholic missionary was beheaded in Tonquin in 1837,
the executioner cut out the liver of his victim and ate part of

Other parts than the heart are eaten for the purpose of acquiring the virtues of the deceased.

[1] E. Clement, "Ethnographical
Notes on the Western Australian
Aborigines,"*Internationales Archiv für
Ethnographie*, xvi. (1904) p. 8.

[2] O. Opigez, "Aperçu général sur la
Nouvelle-Calédonie," *Bulletin de la
Société de Géographie* (Paris), vii. Série,
vii. (1886) p. 433.

[3] A. W. Howitt, *Native Tribes of
South-East Australia* (London, 1904),
p. 753.

[4] A. W. Howitt, *op. cit.* p. 752.

[5] S. Gason, in *Journal of the Anthropological Institute*, xxiv. (1895) p.
172.

[6] Rev. W. Ridley, *Kamilaroi* (Sydney, 1875), p. 160.

it, while a soldier attempted to devour another part of it raw.[1] With a like intent the Chinese swallow the bile of notorious bandits who have been executed.[2] The Dyaks of Sarawak used to eat the palms of the hands and the flesh of the knees of the slain in order to steady their own hands and strengthen their own knees.[3] The Tolalaki, notorious head-hunters of Central Celebes, drink the blood and eat the brains of their victims that they may become brave.[4] The Italones of the Philippine Islands drink the blood of their slain enemies, and eat part of the back of their heads and of their entrails raw to acquire their courage. For the same reason the Efugaos, another tribe of the Philippines, suck the brains of their foes.[5] In like manner the Kai of German New Guinea eat the brains of the enemies they kill in order to acquire their strength.[6] Among the Kimbunda of Western Africa, when a new king succeeds to the throne, a brave prisoner of war is killed in order that the king and nobles may eat his flesh, and so acquire his strength and courage.[7] The notorious Zulu chief Matuana drank the gall of thirty chiefs, whose people he had destroyed, in the belief that it would make him strong.[8] It is a Zulu fancy that by eating the centre of the forehead and the eyebrow of an enemy they acquire the power of looking steadfastly at a foe.[9] In Tud or Warrior Island, Torres Straits, men would drink the sweat of renowned warriors, and eat the scrapings from

[1] *Annales de la Propagation de la Foi*, xi. (Lyons, 1838-1839) p. 258.

[2] J. Henderson, "The Medicine and Medical Practice of the Chinese," *Journal of the North China Branch of the Royal Asiatic Society*, New Series, i. (Shanghai, 1865) pp. 35 *sq.*

[3] A. C. Kruyt, "Het koppensnellen der Toradja's van Midden - Celebes, en zijne Beteekenis," *Verslagen en Mededeelingen der koninklijke Akademie van Wetenschappen*, Afdeeling Letter-kunde, Vierde Reeks, iii. (Amsterdam, 1899) p. 201.

[4] N. Adriani en A. C. Kruijt, "Van Posso naar Mori," *Mededeel-ingen van wege het Nederlandsche Zendelinggenootschap*, xliv. (1900) p. 162.

[5] F. Blumentritt, "Der Ahnencultus und die religiösen Anschauungen der Malaien des Philippinen - Archipels," *Mittheilungen der Wiener Geograph. Gesellschaft*, 1882, p. 154; *id.*, *Versuch einer Ethnographie der Philippinen* (Gotha, 1882), p. 32 (*Petermann's Mittheilungen, Ergänzungsheft*, No. 67).

[6] Ch. Keysser, "Aus dem Leben der Kaileute," in R. Neuhauss's *Deutsch Neu-Guinea*, iii. (Berlin, 1911) p. 131.

[7] L. Magyar, *Reisen in Süd-Afrika in den Jahren 1849-1857* (Buda-Pesth and Leipsic, 1859), pp. 273-276.

[8] Rev. J. Shooter, *The Kafirs of Natal* (London, 1857), p. 216.

[9] Rev. H. Callaway, *Nursery Tales, Traditions and Histories of the Zulus* (Natal and London, 1868), p. 163 note.

their finger-nails which had become coated and sodden with human blood. This was done " to make strong and like stone ; no afraid." [1] In Nagir, another island of Torres Straits, in order to infuse courage into boys a warrior used to take the eye and tongue of a man whom he had killed, and after mincing them and mixing them with his urine he administered the compound to the boy, who received it with shut eyes and open mouth seated between the warrior's legs.[2] Before every warlike expedition the people of Minahassa in Celebes used to take the locks of hair of a slain foe and dabble them in boiling water to extract the courage ; this infusion of bravery was then drunk by the warriors.[3] In New Zealand "the chief was an *atua* [god], but there were powerful and powerless gods ; each naturally sought to make himself one of the former ; the plan therefore adopted was to incorporate the spirits of others with their own ; thus, when a warrior slew a chief, he immediately gouged out his eyes and swallowed them, the *atua tonga*, or divinity, being supposed to reside in that organ ; thus he not only killed the body, but also possessed himself of the soul of his enemy, and consequently the more chiefs he slew the greater did his divinity become." [4]

Even without absorbing any part of a man's bodily substance it is sometimes thought possible to acquire his moral virtues through simple contact with his bones. Thus among the Toradjas of Central Celebes, when a youth is being circumcised he is made to sit on the skull of a slain foe in order to make him brave in war ; [5] and

Moral virtues of the dead acquired through simple contact with their bones.

---

[1] A. C. Haddon, "The Ethnography of the Western Tribe of Torres Straits," *Journal of the Anthropological Institute*, xix. (1890) p. 414, compare p. 312 ; *Reports of the Cambridge Anthropological Expedition to Torres Straits*, v. (Cambridge, 1904) p. 301.

[2] A. C. Haddon, *op. cit.* p. 420 ; *Reports of the Cambridge Anthropological Expedition to Torres Straits*, v. (Cambridge, 1904) pp. 301 *sq.*

[3] S. J. Hickson, *A Naturalist in North Celebes* (London, 1889), p. 216.

[4] R. Taylor, *Te Ika a Maui, or New Zealand and its Inhabitants*, Second Edition (London, 1870), p. 352. Compare *ibid.* p. 173 ; W. Ellis, *Polynesian Researches*, Second Edition (London, 1831-1836), i. 358 ; J. Dumont D'Urville, *Voyage autour du Monde et à la recherche de la Pérouse sur la corvette Astrolabe* (Paris, 1832-1833), ii. 547 ; E. Tregear, "The Maoris of New Zealand," *Journal of the Anthropological Institute*, xix. (1890) p. 108.

[5] A. C. Kruyt, " Het koppensnellen der Toradja's van Midden-Celebes,

when Scanderbeg, Prince of Epirus, was dead, the Turks, who had often felt the force of his arm in battle, are said to have imagined that by wearing a piece of his bones near their heart they should be animated with a strength and valour like his.[1]   A peculiar form of communion with the dead is practised by the Gallas of Eastern Africa.   They think that food from the house of a dead man, especially food that he liked, or that he cooked for himself, contains a portion of his life or soul.   If at the funeral feast a man eats some of that food, he fancies that he has thereby absorbed some of the life or soul of the departed, a portion of his spirit, intelligence, or courage.[2]

Savages sometimes seek to form a covenant of friendship with their dead foes by drinking their blood.

Strange as it may seem to us, one motive which induces a savage warrior to eat the flesh or drink the blood of the foe whom he has slain appears to be a wish to form an indissoluble covenant of friendship and brotherhood with his victim. For it is a widespread belief among savages that by transfusing a little of their blood into each other's bodies two men become kinsmen and allies; the same blood now circulating in the veins of both, neither can injure the other without at the same time injuring himself; the two have therefore given each other the strongest bond, the best possible hostages, for their good behaviour.[3]   Acting on this theory, the primitive warrior seeks to convert his slain foe into the firmest of friends by imbibing the dead man's blood or swallowing his flesh.   That at all events appears to be the idea at the root of the following customs.   When an Arawak Indian of British Guiana has murdered another, he repairs on the third night to the grave of his victim, and pressing a pointed stick through the corpse he licks off and swallows any blood that he finds adhering to the stick.   For he believes that if he did not taste his victim's blood, he would go mad and die; whereas by swallowing the blood he averts any ill consequences that might flow to him from the

en zijne Beteekenis," *Verslagen en Mededeelingen der koninklijke Akademie van Wetenschappen*, Afdeeling Letterkunde, Vierde Reeks, iii. (Amsterdam, 1899) p. 166.

[1] *The Spectator*, No. 316, March 3, 1712; Gibbon, *Decline and Fall*, ch. lxvii.

[2] Ph.   Paulitschke, *Ethnographie Nordost-Afrikas: die geistige Cultur der Danâkil, Galla und Somâl* (Berlin, 1896), p. 56.

[3] For examples of the blood-covenant see H. C. Trumbull, *The Blood Covenant* (London, 1887).   The custom is particularly common in Africa.

murder.[1]   The belief and practice of the Nandi are similar :
" To the present day, when a person of another tribe has been
slain by a Nandi, the blood must be carefully washed off the
spear or sword into a cup made of grass, and drunk by the
slayer.   If this is not done it is thought that the man will
become frenzied." [2]   So among the tribes of the Lower Niger
" it is customary and necessary for the executioner to lick the
blood that is on the blade " ; moreover, " the custom of licking
the blood off the blade of a sword by which a man has
been killed in war is common to all these tribes, and the
explanation given me by the Ibo, which is generally accepted,
is, that if this was not done, the act of killing would so
affect the strikers as to cause them to run amok among their
own people ; because the sight and smell of blood render
them absolutely senseless as well as regardless of all consequences.   And this licking the blood is the only sure remedy,
and the only way in which they can recover themselves." [3]
Among the Shans executioners believe that they would soon
fall ill and die if they did not taste the blood of their victims.[4]

The most probable explanation of these practices *Blood-*
seems to be that a manslayer is thought to be driven mad *covenant
formed by*
by the ghost of his victim, who takes possession of his *manslayers*
murderer's body and causes him to demean himself in a *with the
ghosts of*
frantic manner ; whereas, as soon as the slayer has tasted *their*
the blood of the slain, he becomes a blood-brother of his *victims.*
victim, whose ghost accordingly will do him no harm.[5]   This
hypothesis is strongly confirmed by the reason alleged for

[1] Rev. J. H. Bernau, *Missionary
Labours in British Guiana* (London,
1847), pp. 57 *sq.* ; R. Schomburgk,
Reisen in Britisch-Guiana (Leipsic,
1847-1848), ii. 497.

[2] A. C. Hollis, *The Nandi* (Oxford,
1909), p. 27.

[3] A. G. Leonard, *The Lower Niger
and its Tribes* (London, 1906), pp.
180, 181 *sq.*

[4] Mrs. Leslie Milne, *Shans at Home*
(London, 1910), p. 192.

[5] The Kukis of north-eastern India
believe that the ghost of an animal as
well as of a man will haunt its slayer
and drive him mad unless he performs

a ceremony called *ai.*   For example, a
man who has killed a tiger must dress
himself up as a woman, put flints into
the tiger's mouth, and eat eggs himself,
after which he makes a speech to the
tiger and gives it three cuts over the
head with a sword.   During this performance the principal performer must
keep perfectly grave.   Should he
accidentally laugh, he says, "The
porcupine laughed," referring to a
real porcupine which he carries in his
arms for the purpose.   See Lieut.-
Colonel J. Shakespeare, "The Kuki-
Lushai Clans," *Journal of the Royal
Anthropological Institute,* xxxix. (1909)
pp. 380 *sq.*

a similar custom formerly observed by the Maoris.   When a warrior had slain his foe in combat, he tasted his blood, believing that this preserved him from the avenging spirit of his victim ; for they imagined that " the moment a slayer had tasted the blood of the slain, the dead man became a part of his being and placed him under the protection of the *atua* or guardian-spirit of the deceased." [1]   In the light of these facts we can now explain the opinion, still widely held in Calabria, that if a murderer is to escape, he must suck his victim's blood from the reeking blade of the dagger with which he did the deed ; [2] and, further, we can see at least a glimmering of reason, however misapplied, in the confidence cherished by the Botocudos of Brazil, that if only they ate a morsel of the flesh of their enemies, the arrows of the fellow tribesmen of the slain would not be able to hit them.[3]   Indeed the evidence which I have just adduced suggests that the intention of forming a blood-covenant with the dead may have been a common motive for the cannibalism which has been so often practised by savage victors on the bodies of their victims.[4]   If that was so, it would to some extent mitigate the horror with which such a practice is naturally viewed by civilised observers ; since it would reveal the cannibal feast, no longer in the lurid light of a brutal outburst of blind rage and hatred against the vanquished, but in the milder aspect of a solemn rite designed to wipe out the memory of past hostilities and to establish a permanent relation of friendship and good fellowship with the dead.

Communion with the dead by swallowing their ashes.   Another mode of entering into communion with the dead by means of their bodily relics is to grind their bones to powder or to burn them to ashes, and then to swallow the powder or the ashes mixed with food or drink.   This method of absorbing the virtues or appropriating the souls

[1] J. Dumont D'Urville, *Voyage autour du Monde et à la recherche de la Pérouse* (Paris, 1832-1833), iii. 305.

[2] Vincenzo Dorsa, *La Tradizione greco-latina negli usi e nelle credenze popolari della Calabria Citeriore* (Cosenza, 1884), p. 138.

[3] F. de Castelnau, *Expédition dans les parties centrales de l'Amérique du Sud* (Paris, 1850-1851), iv. 382.

[4] Some of the evidence has already been cited by me in *Psyche's Task*, pp. 56-58.

of deceased kinsfolk has been practised by a number of Indian tribes of South America.   Thus the Tarianas, Tucanos, and other tribes in the valley of the Amazon, about a month after the funeral, disinter the corpse, which is then much decomposed, and put it in a great pan or oven over the fire till all the volatile parts are driven off with a most horrible stench, leaving only a black carbonaceous paste.   This paste is then pounded into a fine powder, and being mixed in several large vats of the native beer, the liquor is drunk by the assembled company until all is consumed.   They believe that thus the virtues of the deceased are transmitted to the drinkers.[1]   Similarly among the Xomanas and Passes of the Rio Negro and Japura River in Brazil, it was customary to burn the bones of the dead and mingle the ashes in their drink ; " for they fancied, that by this means they received into their own bodies the spirits of their deceased friends." [2]   We may suppose that a similar motive underlies the custom wherever it has been observed by the Indians of South America, even when this particular motive is not expressly alleged by our authorities. For example, the Retoroños, Pechuyos, and Guarayos of eastern Bolivia " manifested their feeling for the dead by a remarkable custom : when the body had mouldered they dug up the bones, reduced them to powder, and mingling it with maize, composed a sort of cake, which they considered it the strongest mark of friendship to offer and partake. Some of the first missionaries were regaled with this family bread, before they knew what they were eating." [3]   Again, in the province of Coro, in north-western Venezuela, when a chief died, they lamented him in the night, celebrating his actions ; then they parched his body at the fire, and reducing it to powder drank it up in their liquor, deeming this act the highest honour they could pay him.[4]   The Tauaré Indians of the Rio Enivra burn their dead, keep their ashes in hollow reeds, and eat a portion of the ashes with every

[1] A. R. Wallace, *Travels on the Amazon and Rio Negro*, Second Edition (London, 1889), ch. xvii. pp. 346 *sq.*
[2] R. Southey, *History of Brazil*, iii. (London, 1819) p. 722.

[3] R. Southey, *op. cit.* iii. 204.
[4] A. de Herrera, *The General History of the Vast Continent and Islands of America*, translated by Capt. John Stevens (London, 1725-1726), iv. 45.

meal.[1] So in antiquity Artemisia expressed her love and grief for her dead husband Mausolus by powdering his ashes and drinking them in water.[2] It is said that Mwamba, a recent king or chief of the Wemba in Northern Rhodesia, having detected one of his wives in an intrigue with another man, caused the guilty pair to be burned alive, while he watched their tortures from a raised seat. "Shortly after this, however, he would seem to have been stricken with remorse and the dread of Nemesis. The presiding witch-doctor was therefore ordered to collect the ashes of the twain, and decoct therefrom a potion), which was administered to the king to avert the avenging furies of evil spirits of the murdered pair, which might otherwise have hounded him into a fit of madness."[3] By drinking the ashes of his victims the king sought to identify himself with them and so to protect himself against their angry ghosts, just as we have seen that manslayers seek to protect themselves against the ghosts of their victims by drinking their blood.[4]

Savages attempt to inoculate themselves with moral and other virtues by

Just as the savage thinks that he can swallow the moral and other virtues in the shape of food, so he fondly imagines that he can inoculate himself with them. Here in Europe we as yet inoculate only against disease ; in Basutoland they have learned the art of inoculating not

[1] A. Reich und F. Stegelmann, "Bei den Indianern des Urubamba und des Envira," *Globus*, lxxxiii. (1903) p. 137. On similar custom practised by the American Indians see further De la Borde, *Relation de l'Origine, Mœurs, Coustumes, Religion, Guerres et Voyages des Caraibes Sauvages*, p. 37 (forming part of the *Recueil de divers Voyages faits en Afrique et en l'Amerique*, Paris, 1684) ; J. F. Lafitau, *Mœurs des Sauvages Ameriquains* (Paris, 1724), ii. 444-446; A. N. Cabeça de Vaca, *Relation et Naufrages* (Paris, 1837), p. 109 (in Ternaux Compans' *Voyages, Relations et Mémoires originaux pour servir à l'Histoire de la Découverte de l'Amérique*) ; R. Southey, *History of Brazil*, i. (Second Edition, London, 1822), Supplemental Notes, p. xxxvi. ; F. de Castelnau, *Expédition dans les parties centrales de l'Amérique du Sud* (Paris,

1850-1851), iv. 380; J. G. Müller, *Geschichte der amerikanischen Urreligionen* (Bâle, 1867), pp. 289 *sq.*; H. A. Coudreau, *La France Équinoxiale* (Paris, 1887), ii. 173 ; Theodor Koch, "Die Anthropophagie der südamerikanischen Indianer," *Internationales Archiv für Ethnographie*, xii. (1899) pp. 78-110; Th. Koch-Grünberg, *Zwei Jahre unter den Indianern* (Berlin, 1909-1910), ii. 152. Some Indians of Guiana rubbed their limbs with water in which the ashes of their dead were mingled. See A. Biet, *Voyage de la France Équinoxiale en l'Isle de Cayenne* (Paris, 1664), p. 392.

[2] Aulus Gellius, *Noctes Atticae*, x. 18 ; Valerius Maximus, iv. 6. 5.

[3] C. Gouldsbury and H. Sheane, *The Great Plateau of Northern Rhodesia* (London, 1911), p. 55.

[4] See above, p. 154 *sqq.*

merely against disease but against moral evil and public
calamity, against wild beasts and winter cold. For example,
if an epidemic is raging, if public affairs go ill, or war
threatens to break out, the chief, with paternal solicitude,
seeks to guard his people against the evils that menace
them by inoculating them with his own hand. Armed
with a lancet, he makes a slight incision in the temples of
each one, and rubs into the wound a pinch of magic
powder which has been carefully compounded of the ashes
of certain plants and animals. The plants and animals
whose ashes compose this sovereign medicine are always
symbolical ; in other words, they are supposed to be imbued
with the virtues which the chief desires to impart to his
people. They consist, for example, of plants whose foliage
withstands the rigours of winter ; mimosas, whose thorns
present an impenetrable barrier to all animals of the deer
kind ; the claws or a few hairs from the mane of a lion, the
bravest of beasts ; the tuft of hair round the root of the
horns of a bull, which is the emblem of strength and
fecundity ; the skin of a serpent ; the feathers of a kite or
a hawk.[1] So when the Barotsé wish to be swift of foot,
to cripple the fleeing game, and to ensure an abundant
catch, they scarify their arms and legs and rub into the
wounds a powder made of the burnt bones of various
beasts and birds.[2] Among some tribes of South-Eastern
Africa the same magic powder which is made from various
parts of slain foes, and is eaten by boys at circumcision,[3] is
used to inoculate the fighting-men in time of war. The
medicine-man makes an incision in the forehead of each
warrior, and puts the powder into the cut, thus infusing
strength and courage for the battle.[4] Among some Caffre
tribes the powdered charcoal with which the warriors are
thus inoculated in various parts of their bodies is procured
by burning the flesh of a live ox with a certain kind of

making cuts in their bodies and inserting in the cuts the ashes of animals and plants which they suppose to be endowed with the virtues in question.

---

[1] Rev. E. Casalis, *The Basutos*, (London, 1861), pp. 256 *sq.*

[2] E. Holub, *Sieben Jahre in Süd Afrika* (Vienna, 1881), ii. 361.

[3] See above, p. 148.

[4] J. Macdonald, "Manners, Customs, etc., of South African Tribes," *Journal of the Anthropological Institute*, xx. (1891) p. 133. The Barolong, a Bechuana tribe, observe a custom of this sort. See W. Joest, "Bei den Barolong," *Das Ausland*, 16th June 1884, p. 464.

wood or roots, to which magic virtue is attributed.[1] The
Basutos think that they can render themselves invulnerable by inoculation,[2] and the Zulus imagine that they can
protect themselves against snake-bite by similar means.
But the saving virtue of the inoculation is not permanent;
like vaccination, it has to be periodically renewed. Hence
every year, about October, Zulu men, women, and children
have a small piece of skin cut from the back of the left
hand, and the poison of a snake, mixed with spittle, is
rubbed into the wound. No snake will ever approach a
man who has thus been inoculated; and what is even more
curious, if the shadow of an inoculated man should touch
the shadow of a man who has not been inoculated, the
latter will fall down as if he had been shot, overcome by
the poison transmitted through the shadow: so exceedingly
virulent is the virus.[3] Among the Jukos, a tribe of the Benue
River in Northern Nigeria, before a hunter goes forth to
hunt elephants, he makes four cuts in his left arm and rubs
in "medicine"; this helps him to see the beast next day.[4]

The Zulus
think they
can inocu-
late them-
selves with
celestial
power.

Again, the Zulus know how to inoculate themselves not
merely with moral virtue, but even with celestial power.
For you must know that the Zulus have heaven-herds or
sky-herds, who drive away clouds big with hail and lightning,
just as herdsmen drive cattle before them. These heaven-
herds are in sympathy with the heaven. For when the
heaven is about to be darkened, and before the clouds
appear or the thunder mutters, the heart of the heaven-herd
feels it coming, for it is hot within him and he is excited
by anger. When the sky begins to be overcast, he too
grows dark like it; when it thunders, he frowns, that his
face may be black as the scowl of the angry heaven. Now
the way in which he thus becomes sympathetic with all
the changing moods of the inconstant heaven is this: he
eats the heaven and scarifies himself with it. And the way

[1] Col. Maclean, *A Compendium of
Kafir Laws and Customs* (Cape Town,
1866), p. 82.

[2] Father Porte, "Les reminiscences
d'un missionnaire du Basutoland," *Les
Missions Catholiques*, xxviii. (1896)
p. 149.

[3] Dudley Kidd, *Savage Childhood*

(London, 1906), p. 70, compare p.
43.

[4] Lieut. H. Pope-Hennessy, "Notes
on the Jukos and other Tribes of
the Middle Benue," *Anthropological
Reviews and Miscellanea*, p. (30); appended to *Journal of the Anthropological Institute*, xxx. (1900).

in which he eats the heaven and scarifies himself with it is as follows. When a bullock is struck by lightning, the wizard takes its flesh and puts it in a sherd and eats it while it is hot, mixed with medicine ; and thus he eats the heaven by eating the flesh, which came from the beast, which was struck by the lightning, which came down from the heaven. And in like manner he scarifies himself with the heaven, for he makes cuts in his body and rubs in medicine mixed with the flesh of a bullock that was struck by lightning.[1] In some Caffre tribes, when an animal or a man has been struck by lightning, the priest comes straightway and vaccinates every person in the kraal, apparently as a sort of insurance against lightning. He sets to work by tying a number of charms round the neck of every man and woman in the village, in order that they may have power to dig the dead man's grave ; for in these tribes beasts and men alike that have been struck by lightning are always buried, and the flesh is never eaten. Next a sacrificial beast is killed and a fire kindled, in which certain magic woods or roots are burned to charcoal, and then ground to powder. The priest thereupon makes incisions in various parts of the bodies of each inmate of the kraal, and rubs a portion of the powdered charcoal into the cuts ; the rest of the powder he mixes with sour milk, and gives to them all to drink. From the time the lightning strikes the kraal until this ceremony has been performed, the people are obliged to abstain entirely from the use of milk. Their heads are then shaved. Should a house have been struck by lightning it must be abandoned, with everything in it. Until all these rites have been performed, none of the people may leave the kraal or have any intercourse whatever with others ; but when the ceremonies have been duly performed, the people are pronounced clean, and may again associate with their neighbours. However, for some months afterwards none of the live stock of the kraal and few other things belonging to it are allowed to pass into other hands, whether by way of sale or of gift.[2] Hence it would appear that all persons in a

Some Caffres inoculate themselves against lightning.

---

[1] Rev. H. Callaway, *Religious System of the Amazulu*, pp. 380-382.
[2] Col. Maclean, *A Compendium of* *Kafir Laws and Customs* (Cape Town, 1866), pp. 83 *sq.*

village which has been struck by lightning are supposed to be infected with a dangerous virus, which they might communicate to their neighbours; and the vaccination is intended to disinfect them as well as to protect them against the recurrence of a like calamity. Young Carib warriors used to be inoculated for the purpose of making them brave and hardy. Some time before the ceremony the lad who was to be operated on caught a bird of prey of a particular sort and kept it in captivity till the day appointed. When the time was come and friends had assembled to witness the ceremony, the father of the boy seized the bird by its legs and crushed its head by beating it on the head of his son, who dared not wince under the rain of blows that nearly stunned him. Next the father bruised and pounded the bird's flesh, and steeped it in water together with a certain spice; after which he scored and slashed his son's body in all directions, washed his wounds with the decoction, and gave him the bird's heart to eat, in order, as it was said, that he might be the braver for it.[1]

Some savages attempt to acquire the physical and mental qualities of the dead by anointing themselves with their remains.
It is not always deemed necessary either that the mystical substance should be swallowed by the communicant, or that he should receive it by the more painful process of scarification and inoculation. Sometimes it is thought enough merely to smear or anoint him with it. Among some of the Australian blacks it used to be a common practice to kill a man, cut out his caul-fat, and rub themselves with it, in the belief that all the qualities, both physical and mental, which had distinguished the original owner of the fat, were thus communicated by its means to the person who greased himself with it.[2] The Kamilaroi tribe of New South Wales sometimes deposited their dead on the forks of trees, and lighting fires underneath caught the fat as it dropped; for they hoped with

---

[1] Du Tertre, *Histoire generale des Isles de S. Christophe, de la Guadeloupe, de la Martinique et autres dans l'Amerique* (Paris, 1654), pp. 417 sq.; *id., Histoire generale des Antilles* (Paris, 1667-1671), ii. 377; Rochefort, *Histoire Naturelle et Morale des Iles Antilles*[2] (Rotterdam, 1665), p. 556.

[2] R. Brough Smith, *Aborigines of Victoria* (Melbourne and London, 1878), i. p. xxix., ii. 313; A. W. Howitt, *Native Tribes of South-East Australia* (London, 1904), pp. 367 sqq.

the droppings to acquire the strength and courage of the deceased.[1] The Wollaroi, another tribe of New South Wales, used to place the dead on a stage, and the mourners sat under it and rubbed their bodies with the juices of putrefaction which exuded from the rotten body, believing that this made them strong. Others collected these juices in vessels, and the young men rubbed the stinking liquid into their persons in order to acquire the good qualities of the departed.[2] Wherever a like custom has been practised, as it has been, for example, by some of the natives of New Guinea, Timor Laut, and Madagascar,[3] we may conjecture that the motive has been similar. Again, the negroes of Southern Guinea regard the brain as the seat of wisdom, and think it a pity that, when a wise man dies, his brain and his wisdom should go to waste together. So they sever his head from his body and hang it up over a mass of chalk, which, as the head decays, receives the drippings of brain and wisdom. Any one who applies the precious dripping to his forehead is supposed to absorb thereby the intelligence of the dead.[4] Among the Beku, a tribe of dwarfs attached to the Fans in West Africa, the great charm for success in hunting is procured by killing a man and afterwards, when the corpse has begun to moulder in the grave, detaching the head from the body. The brain, heart, eyes and hairs of the body are then removed and mixed, according to a secret formula, with special incantations. When the compound is dry, the hunter rubs himself

---

[1] Rev. W. Ridley, *Kamilaroi* (Sydney, 1875), p. 160.

[2] A. W. Howitt, *Native Tribes of South-East Australia* (London, 1904), pp. 467, 468.

[3] J. Chalmers and W. W. Gill, *Work and Adventure in New Guinea* (London, 1885), pp. 130, 265, 308; J. G. F. Riedel, *De sluik- en kroesharige rassen tusschen Selebes en Papua* (The Hague, 1886), p. 308; Rev. J. Sibree, *The Great African Island* (London, 1880), p. 241. Other or the same peoples sometimes drink the juices of the decaying bodies of their kinsfolk, doubtless for a similar reason. See *Reports of the Cambridge Anthro-* pological Expedition to Torres Straits, vi. (Cambridge, 1906) p. 159; J. Chalmers and W. Gill, *op. cit.* pp. 27, 265; Ch. Wilkes, *Narrative of the United States Exploring Expedition*, New Edition (New York, 1851), ii. 139; J. G. F. Riedel, *op. cit.* p. 267; A. Bastian, *Indonesien*, ii. (Berlin, 1885) p. 95; *id.*, *Die Völker des Ostlichen Asien*, v. (Jena, 1869) p. 91; P. J. Veth, *Borneo's Westerafdeeling* (Zaltbommel, 1854-1856), ii. 270; J. Jacobs, *Eenigen Tijd onder de Baliers* (Batavia, 1883), p. 53.

[4] Rev. J. L. Wilson, *Western Africa* (London, 1856), p. 394.

with it " in order to acquire a dash of the higher power with which people are endowed in the other life, and in particular their invisibility." [1]   Among the Digger Indians of California, when a man died, it was customary to burn the body to ashes, mix the ashes with a thick resinous gum extracted from a pine-tree, and then smear the gum on the head of the mourner, where it was allowed to remain till it gradually wore away.[2]   The motive for the custom is not mentioned, but it was probably, like the motive for the parallel custom of swallowing the ashes of the dead, a desire to participate in the powers and virtues of the departed.   At a certain stage of the ceremonies by which, in the Andaman Islands, a boy is initiated into manhood, the chief takes the carcase of a boar and presses it heavily down on the shoulders, back, and limbs of the young man as he sits, silent and motionless, on the ground.   This is done to make him brave and strong.   Afterwards the animal is cut up, and its melted fat is poured over the novice, and rubbed into his body.[3]   The Arabs of Eastern Africa believe that an unguent of lion's fat inspires a man with boldness, and makes the wild beasts flee in terror before him.[4]   In the forests of North-western Brazil there lives a small falcon with a red beak which is so sharp-sighted that it can detect even a worm on the ground from a considerable height. When a Kobeua Indian has killed one of these birds, he pokes out its eyes and allows the fluid to drip into his own, believing that in this way they will be sharp-sighted like those of the falcon.[5]   Most of the Baperis, or Malekootoos, a Bechuana tribe of South Africa, revere or, as they say, sing the porcupine, which seems to be their totem, as the sun is the totem of some members of the tribe, and a species of ape the totem of others.   Those of them who have the porcupine for their totem swear by the animal, and lament if any one injures it.

The juices of animals are sometimes similarly applied for the same purpose.

[1] Mgr. Le Roy, " Les Pygmées," *Les Missions Catholiques*, xxix. (1897) p. 210.

[2] " Mourning for the Dead among the Digger Indians," *Journal of the Anthropological Institute*, iii. (1874) p. 530.

[3] E. H. Man, *Aboriginal Inhabit-* *ants of the Andaman Islands*, p. 66.

[4] Jerome Becker, *La Vie en Afrique* (Paris and Brussels, 1887), ii. 366.

[5] Th. Koch-Grünberg, *Zwei Jahre unter den Indianern* (Berlin, 1909-1910), ii. 153.

When a porcupine has been killed, they religiously gather up its bristles, spit on them, and rub their eyebrows with them, saying, " They have slain our brother, our master, one of ourselves, him whom we sing." They would fear to die if they ate of its flesh. Nevertheless they esteem it wholesome for an infant of the clan to rub into his joints certain portions of the paunch of the animal mixed with the sap of some plants to which they ascribe an occult virtue.[1] So at the solemn ceremony which is observed by the Central Australian tribes for the purpose of multiplying kangaroos, men of the kangaroo totem not only eat a little kangaroo flesh as a sacrament, but also have their bodies anointed with kangaroo fat. Doubtless the intention alike of the eating and of the anointing is to impart to the man the qualities of his totem animal, and thus to enable him to perform the ceremonies for the multiplication of the breed.[2]

In ancient Mexico the priests of the god Tezcatlipoca, before they engaged in religious rites which tried the nerve, used to smear their bodies with a magic ointment, which had the effect of banishing all fear, so that they would confront wild beasts in their dens or slaughter people in sacrifice with the utmost indifference. The ointment which had this marvellous property was compounded of the ashes of venomous reptiles and insects, such as spiders, scorpions, centipedes, and vipers, which were brayed up in a mortar along with living specimens of the same creatures, tobacco, soot, and the ashes of black caterpillars. This precious substance was then set before the god in little pots, because they said it was his victuals ; therefore they called it a divine food. And when the priests had besmeared them-

Magical ointment used by Mexican priests.

---

[1] T. Arbousset et F. Daumas, *Voyage d'Exploration au Nord-est de la Colonie du Cap de Bonne-Espérance* (Paris, 1842), pp. 349 *sq.*

[2] Spencer and Gillen, *Native Tribes of Central Australia* (London, 1899), pp. 204 *sq.* Men of other totem clans also partake of their totems sacramentally at these *Intichiuma* ceremonies (Spencer and Gillen, *op. cit.* pp. 202-206). As to the *Intichiuma* ceremonies, see *The Magic Art and the*

Evolution of Kings, i. 85 *sqq.* Another Central Australian mode of communicating qualities by external application is seen in the custom of beating boys on the calves of their legs with the leg-bone of an eagle-hawk ; strength is supposed to pass thereby from the bone into the boy's leg. See Spencer and Gillen, *op. cit.* p. 472 ; *Report on the Work of the Horn Scientific Expedition to Central Australia,* Part iv. (London and Melbourne, 1896), p. 180.

selves with it, they were ready to discharge the duties of their holy office by butchering their fellow men in the human shambles without one qualm of fear or one visiting of compassion. Moreover, an unction of this ointment was deemed a sovereign remedy for sickness and disease ; hence they named it " the divine physic" ; and sick people came from all quarters to the priests, as to their saviours, to have their ailing parts anointed with the divine physic and to be made whole.[1]

Qualities of a person, animal, or thing imparted by fumigation.
Sometimes the valuable qualities of an animal or of a person may be imparted to another by the more delicate and ethereal process of fumigation. This refined mode of cultivating the moral virtues is or used to be practised by the Caffres of South Africa. Thus in former times as soon as a baby was born, some dirt was scraped from the forearm and other parts of the father's body and mixed with special medicines. The mixture was then made to smoulder and the baby was fumigated or " washed" in the smoke. This ceremony was deemed of great importance, being the established way of communicating to the child a portion of the ancestral spirit (*itongo*) through the physical medium of the father's dirt, to which the spirit naturally adheres. But while the dirt was endowed with this spiritual potency, the moral character of the infant depended in a large measure on the nature of the medicines with which the dirt was compounded, and accordingly much thought and skill were devoted to their selection and preparation. Foremost among the ingredients was a meteorite, burnt to a cinder and ground to powder. The effect of this powder, well mixed with the dirt, and introduced into the orifices of the child's body by means of smoke, is to close the anterior fontanelle of the baby's skull, to strengthen the bones of that important part of his person, to communicate vigour to his mind and courage to his disposition, and in general to brace and harden his whole system with the strength and hardness of the

---

[1] *Manuscrit Ramirez, Histoire de l'Origine des Indiens qui habitent la Nouvelle Espagne selon leurs traditions,* publié par D. Charnay (Paris, 1903), pp. 171-173 ; J. de Acosta, *Natural and Moral History of the Indies* (Hak- luyt Society, London, 1880), ii. 364-367 ; E. Seler, *Altmexikanische Studien,* ii. (Berlin, 1899), pp. 43 *sq.* (*Veröffentlichungen aus dem königlichen Museum für Völkerkunde*).

meteorite.   Other ingredients which have a most beneficial
effect are the powdered whiskers of a leopard, the claws of a
lion, and the skin of a salamander.   The mode of administer-
ing the medicine is as follows.   You set fire to the compound, and while it smoulders, you hold the infant, wrapt
up in a blanket, over the burning mass so as to compel it to
inhale the smoke.   To make sure of producing the desired
effect, some of the powdered medicine is mixed with the baby's
food.[1]   In like manner by holding the smouldering feather
of a vulture under a baby's nose you render the child valiant
and brave like a vulture, and if you do the same with a
peacock's feather, your offspring will be, like a peacock,
impavid and never dismayed by thunder or other terrible
noises.[2]

It is now easy to understand why a savage should desire
to partake of the flesh of an animal or man whom he regards
as divine.   By eating the body of the god he shares in the
god's attributes and powers.   And when the god is a corn-
god, the corn is his proper body ; when he is a vine-god, the
juice of the grape is his blood ; and so by eating the bread
and drinking the wine the worshipper partakes of the real
body and blood of his god.   Thus the drinking of wine in
the rites of a vine-god like Dionysus is not an act of revelry,
it is a solemn sacrament.[3]   Yet a time comes when reasonable
men find it hard to understand how any one in his senses
can suppose that by eating bread or drinking wine he consumes the body or blood of a deity.   " When we call corn
Ceres and wine Bacchus," says Cicero, " we use a common
figure of speech ; but do you imagine that anybody is so
insane as to believe that the thing he feeds upon is a
god ? "[4] In writing thus the Roman philosopher little foresaw
that in Rome itself, and in the countries which have derived
their creed from her, the belief which he here stigmatises
as insane was destined to persist for thousands of years,

The savage custom of eating a god.

Cicero on transub-stantiation.

---

[1] Dudley Kidd, *Savage Childhood*
(London, 1906), pp. 12 *sq.*

[2] Dudley Kidd, *op. cit.* pp. 20 *sq.*

[3] On the custom of eating a god, see
also a paper by Felix Liebrecht, " Der
aufgegessene Gott," *Zur Volkskunde*
(Heilbronn, 1879), pp. 436-439 ; and

especially W. R. Smith, article " Sacrifice," *Encyclopaedia Britannica*, Ninth
Edition, vol. xxi. pp. 137 *sq.* On wine
as the blood of a god, see *Taboo and
the Perils of the Soul*, pp. 248 *sqq.*

[4] Cicero, *De natura deorum*, iii. 16.
41.

as a cardinal doctrine of religion, among peoples who pride themselves on their religious enlightenment by comparison with the blind superstitions of pagan antiquity.   So little can even the greatest minds of one generation foresee the devious track which the religious faith of mankind will pursue in after ages.

CHAPTER XIII

KILLING THE DIVINE ANIMAL

§ 1. *Killing the Sacred Buzzard*

In the preceding chapters we saw that many communities which have progressed so far as to subsist mainly by agriculture have been in the habit of killing and eating their farinaceous deities either in their proper form of corn, rice, and so forth, or in the borrowed shapes of animals and men. It remains to shew that hunting and pastoral tribes, as well as agricultural peoples, have been in the habit of killing the beings whom they worship. Among the worshipful beings or gods, if indeed they deserve to be dignified by that name, whom hunters and shepherds adore and kill are animals pure and simple, not animals regarded as embodiments of other supernatural beings. Our first example is drawn from the Indians of California, who living in a fertile country [1] under a serene and temperate sky, nevertheless rank near the bottom of the savage scale. Where a stretch of iron-bound coast breaks the long line of level sands that receive the rollers of the Pacific, there stood in former days, not far from the brink of the great cliffs, the white mission-house of San Juan Capistrano. Among the monks who here exercised over a handful of wretched Indians the austere discipline of Catholic Spain, there was a certain Father Geronimo Boscana who has bequeathed to us a precious record of the customs and superstitions of his savage flock. Thus he tells us that the

Hunting and pastoral tribes, as well as agricultural peoples, have been in the habit of killing and eating the beings whom they worship.

The Californian Indians used solemnly to kill the great buzzard which they adored; but they believed that though they slew it annually, it always came to life again.

---

[1] This does not refer to the Californian peninsula, which is an arid and treeless wilderness of rock and sand.

169

Acagchemem tribe adored the great buzzard, and that once a year they celebrated a great festival called *Panes* or bird-feast in its honour. The day selected for the festival was made known to the public on the evening before its celebration and preparations were at once made for the erection of a special temple (*vanquech*), which seems to have been a circular or oval enclosure of stakes with the stuffed skin of a coyote or prairie-wolf set up on a hurdle to represent the god Chinigchinich. When the temple was ready, the bird was carried into it in solemn procession and laid on an altar erected for the purpose. Then all the young women, whether married or single, began to run to and fro, as if distracted, some in one direction and some in another, while the elders of both sexes remained silent spectators of the scene, and the captains, tricked out in paint and feathers, danced round their adored bird. These ceremonies being concluded, they seized upon the bird and carried it to the principal temple, all the assembly uniting in the grand display, and the captains dancing and singing at the head of the procession. Arrived at the temple, they killed the bird without losing a drop of its blood. The skin was removed entire and preserved with the feathers as a relic or for the purpose of making the festal garment or *paelt*. The carcase was buried in a hole in the temple, and the old women gathered round the grave weeping and moaning bitterly, while they threw various kinds of seeds or pieces of food on it, crying out, "Why did you run away? Would you not have been better with us? you would have made *pinole* (a kind of gruel) as we do, and if you had not run away, you would not have become a *Panes*," and so on. When this ceremony was concluded, the dancing was resumed and kept up for three days and nights. They said that the *Panes* was a woman who had run off to the mountains and there been changed into a bird by the god Chinigchinich. They believed that though they sacrificed the bird annually, she came to life again and returned to her home in the mountains. Moreover they thought that "as often as the bird was killed, it became multiplied; because every year all the different Capitanes celebrated the same feast of *Panes*, and were firm in the opinion that the birds sacrificed were but one and the same female." [1]

The unity in multiplicity thus postulated by the Californians is very noticeable and helps to explain their motive for killing the divine bird. The notion of the life of a species as distinct from that of an individual, easy and obvious as it seems to us, appears to be one which the Californian savage cannot grasp. He is unable to conceive the life of the species otherwise than as an individual life, and therefore as exposed to the same dangers and calamities which menace and finally destroy the life of the individual. Apparently he imagines that a species left to itself will grow old and die like an individual, and that therefore some step must be taken to

Perhaps they hoped by the sacrifice of the individual bird to preserve the species

---

[1] Father Geronimo Boscana, " Chinigchinich ; a historical account of the origin, customs, and traditions of the Indians at the missionary establishment of St. Juan Capistrano, Alta California," appended to Alfred Robinson's *Life in California* (New York, 1846), pp. 291 *sq.* ; H. H. Bancroft, *Native Races of the Pacific States*, iii. 168. The mission station of San Juan Capistrano is described by R. H. Dana (*Two Years before the Mast*, chaps. xviii. and xxiv.). A favourable picture of the missions is drawn by G. H. von Langsdorf (*Reise um die Welt*, Frankfort, 1812, ii. pp. 134 *sqq.*), by Duflos de Mofras ("Fragment d'un Voyage en Californie," *Bulletin de la Société de Géographie* (Paris), ii. Série, xix. (1843) pp. 9-13), and by a writer (H. H.) in *The Century Magazine*, May, 1883, pp. 2-18. But the severe discipline of the Spanish monks is noticed by other travellers. We are told that the Indians laboured during the day in the fields to support their Spanish masters, were driven to church twice or thrice a day to hear service in a language which they did not understand, and at night were shut up in crowded and comfortless barracks, without windows and without beds. When the monks desired to make new proselytes, or rather to capture new slaves, they called in the aid of the soldiery, who attacked the Indian villages by night, lassoed the fugitives,

and dragged them back at their horses' tails to slavery in the missions. See O. von Kotzebue, *Reise um die Welt* (Weimar, 1830), ii. 42 *sqq.* ; F. W. Beechey, *Narrative of a Voyage to the Pacific and Beering's Strait* (London, 1831), ii. chap. i. ; A. Schabelski, "Voyage aux colonies russes de l'Amérique," *Bulletin de la Société de Géographie* (Paris), ii. Série, iv. (1835) pp. 216-218. A poet has described with prosaic accuracy the pastoral crook by which these good shepherds brought back their strayed lambs to the spiritual fold :—

" *Six horses sprang across the level ground*
    As six dragoons in open order dashed ;
Above their heads the lassos circled round,
    In every eye a pious fervour flashed ;
They charged the camp, and in one moment more
They lassoed six and reconverted four."
    (Bret Harte, *Friar Pedro's Ride*.)

In the verses inscribed *The Angelus, heard at the Mission Dolores*, 1868, and beginning

" *Bells of the Past, whose long-forgotten music*
    Still fills the wide expanse,"

the same poet shews that he is not insensible to the poetical side of those old Spanish missions, which have long passed away.

save from extinction the particular species which he regards as divine.   The only means he can think of to avert the catastrophe is to kill a member of the species in whose veins the tide of life is still running strong, and has not yet stagnated among the fens of old age.   The life thus diverted from one channel will flow, he fancies, more freshly and freely in a new one ; in other words, the slain animal will revive and enter on a new term of life with all the spring and energy of youth.   To us this reasoning is transparently absurd, but so too is the custom.   If a better explanation, that is, one more consonant with the facts and with the principles of savage thought, can be given of the custom, I will willingly withdraw the one here proposed.   A similar confusion, it may be noted, between the individual life and the life of the species was made by the Samoans.   Each family had for its god a particular species of animal ; yet the death of one of these animals, for example an owl, was not the death of the god, " he was supposed to be yet alive, and incarnate in all the owls in existence." [1]

§ 2. *Killing the Sacred Ram*

Ancient Egyptian sacrifice of a ram at the festival of Ammon.   The rude Californian rite which we have just considered has a close parallel in the religion of ancient Egypt.   The Thebans and all other Egyptians who worshipped the Theban god Ammon held rams to be sacred, and would not sacrifice them.   But once a year at the festival of Ammon they killed a ram, skinned it, and clothed the image of the god in the skin.   Then they mourned over the ram and buried it in a sacred tomb.   The custom was explained by a story that Zeus had once exhibited himself to Hercules clad in the fleece and wearing the head of a ram.[2]   Of course the ram in this case was simply the beast-god of Thebes, as the wolf was the beast-god of Lycopolis, and the goat was the beast-god of Mendes.   In other words, the ram was Ammon himself.   On the monuments, it is true, Ammon appears in semi-human form with the body of a man and the head of a

---

[1] G. Turner, *Samoa* (London, 1884), p. 21.   Compare *id.*, pp. 26, 61.

[2] Herodotus, ii. 42.   The custom has been already referred to above, p. 41.

ram.[1]   But this only shews that he was in the usual chrysalis
state through which beast-gods regularly pass before they
emerge as full-blown anthropomorphic gods.   The ram,
therefore, was killed, not as a sacrifice to Ammon, but as the
god himself, whose identity with the beast is plainly shewn
by the custom of clothing his image in the skin of the slain
ram.   The reason for thus killing the ram-god annually may
have been that which I have assigned for the general custom
of killing a god and for the special Californian custom of
killing the divine buzzard.   As applied to Egypt, this
explanation is supported by the analogy of the bull-god
Apis, who was not suffered to outlive a certain term of
years.[2]   The intention of thus putting a limit to the life of
the human god was, as I have argued, to secure him from
the weakness and frailty of age.   The same reasoning would
explain the custom—probably an older one—of putting the
beast-god to death annually, as was done with the ram of
Thebes.

One point in the Theban ritual—the application of the
skin to the image of the god—deserves particular attention.
If the god was at first the living ram, his representation by an
image must have originated later.   But how did it originate?
One answer to this question is perhaps furnished by the
practice of preserving the skin of the animal which is slain
as divine.   The Californians, as we have seen, preserved the
skin of the buzzard ; and the skin of the goat, which is killed
on the harvest-field as a representative of the corn-spirit, is
kept for various superstitious purposes.[3]   The skin in fact
was kept as a token or memorial of the god, or rather as
containing in it a part of the divine life, and it had only to
be stuffed or stretched upon a frame to become a regular
image of him.   At first an image of this kind would be
renewed annually,[4] the new image being provided by the

Use of the skin of the sacrificed animal.

---

[1] Ed. Meyer, *Geschichte des Alter-thums*,[2] i. 2 (Stuttgart and Berlin, 1909), p. 73 § 180.   Compare Sir J. G. Wilkinson, *Manners and Customs of the Ancient Egyptians* (London, 1878), iii. 1 *sqq.*

[2] Above, p. 36.

[3] Above, p. 170 ; vol. i. p. 285.

[4] The Italmens of Kamtchatka, at

the close of the fishing season, used to make the figure of a wolf out of grass. This figure they carefully kept the whole year, believing that it wedded with their maidens and prevented them from giving birth to twins ; for twins were esteemed a great misfortune. See G. W. Steller, *Beschreibung von dem Lande Kamtschatka* (Frankfort and

skin of the slain animal.   But from annual images to permanent images the transition is easy.   We have seen that
the older custom of cutting a new May-tree every year was
superseded by the practice of maintaining a permanent Maypole, which was, however, annually decked with fresh leaves
and flowers, and even surmounted each year by a fresh young
tree.[1]   Similarly when the stuffed skin, as a representative
of the god, was replaced by a permanent image of him in
wood, stone, or metal, the permanent image was annually
clad in the fresh skin of the slain animal.   When this stage
had been reached, the custom of killing the ram came
naturally to be interpreted as a sacrifice offered to the image,
and was explained by a story like that of Ammon and
Hercules.

§ 3. *Killing the Sacred Serpent*

The sacred
serpent of
Issapoo in
Fernando
Po.

West Africa appears to furnish another example of the
annual killing of a sacred animal and the preservation of its
skin.   The negroes of Issapoo, in the island of Fernando Po,
regard the cobra-capella as their guardian deity, who can do
them good or ill, bestow riches or inflict disease and death.
The skin of one of these reptiles is hung tail downwards from
a branch of the highest tree in the public square, and the
placing of it on the tree is an annual ceremony.   As soon
as the ceremony is over, all children born within the past
year are carried out and their hands made to touch the tail
of the serpent's skin.[2]   The latter custom is clearly a way of
placing the infants under the protection of the tribal god.
Similarly in Senegambia a python is expected to visit every
child of the Python clan within eight days after birth;[3] and
the Psylli, a Snake clan of ancient Africa, used to expose

Leipsic, 1774), pp. 327 *sq.*   According
to Chr. Hartknoch (*Dissertat. histor. de
variis rebus Prussicis,* p. 163; *Alt-
und neues Preussen,* Frankfort and
Leipsic, 1684, p. 161) the image of the
old Prussian god Curcho was annually
renewed.   But see W. Mannhardt, *Die
Korndämonen* (Berlin, 1868), p. 27.

[1] See *The Magic Art and the Evolution of Kings,* vol. ii. pp. 70 *sq.*

[2] T. J. Hutchinson, *Impressions of
Western Africa* (London, 1858), pp.
196 *sq.*   The writer does not expressly
state that a serpent is killed annually,
but his statement implies it.

[3] Dr. Tautain, "Notes sur les croyances et pratiques religieuses des Ban-
manas," *Revue d'Ethnographie,* iii.
(1885) p. 397.   Compare *Totemism
and Exogamy,* ii. 543 *sq.*

their infants to snakes in the belief that the snakes would
not harm true-born children of the clan.[1]

§ 4. *Killing the Sacred Turtles*

In the Californian, Egyptian, and Fernando Po customs
the animal slain may perhaps have been at some time or
other a totem, but this is very doubtful.[2]   At all events, in
all three cases the worship of the animal seems to have no
relation to agriculture, and may therefore be presumed to date
from the hunting or pastoral stage of society.   The same
may be said of the following custom, though the people who
practise it—the Zuni Indians of New Mexico—are now
settled in walled villages or towns of a peculiar type, and
practise agriculture and the arts of pottery and weaving.
But the Zuni custom is marked by certain features which
appear to place it in a somewhat different class from the
preceding cases.   It may be well therefore to describe it at
full length in the words of an eye-witness.

" With midsummer the heat became intense.   My brother
[*i.e.* adopted Indian brother] and I sat, day after day, in the
cool under-rooms of our house,—the latter [*sic*] busy with
his quaint forge and crude appliances, working Mexican
coins over into bangles, girdles, ear-rings, buttons, and what
not, for savage ornament.   Though his tools were wonderfully rude, the work he turned out by dint of combined
patience and ingenuity was remarkably beautiful.   One day
as I sat watching him, a procession of fifty men went hastily

---

[1] Varro in Priscian, x. 32, vol. i.
p. 524, ed. Keil ; Pliny, *Nat. Hist.*
vii. 14.   Pliny's statement is to be
corrected by Varro's.

[2] When I wrote *The Golden Bough*
originally I said that in these three cases
" the animal slain probably is, or once
was, a totem."   But this seems to me
less probable now than it did then.   In
regard to the Californian custom in
particular, there appears to be no good
evidence that within the area now
occupied by the United States totemism
was practised by any tribes to the west
of the Rocky Mountains.   See H.
Hale, *United States Exploring Expe-*

dition, *Ethnography and Philology*
(Philadelphia, 1846), p. 199 ; George
Gibbs, in *Contributions to North
American Ethnology* (Washington,
1877), i. 184 ; S. Powers, *Tribes of
California* (Washington, 1877), p. 5 ;
A. S. Gatschet, *The Klamath Indians
of South-western Oregon* (Washington,
1890), vol. i. p. cvi.   " California and
Oregon seem never to have had any
gentes or phratries " (A. S. Gatschet in
a letter to me, dated November 5th,
1888).   Beyond the very doubtful case
cited in the text, I know of no evidence that totemism exists in Fernando
Po.

down the hill, and off westward over the plain. They were solemnly led by a painted and shell-bedecked priest, and followed by the torch-bearing Shu-lu-wit-si, or God of Fire. After they had vanished, I asked old brother what it all meant.

" 'They are going,' said he, 'to the city of the Ka-ka and the home of our others.'

The return
of the pro-
cession
with the
turtles.
" Four days after, towards sunset, costumed and masked in the beautiful paraphernalia of the Ka-k'ok-shi, or ' Good Dance,' they returned in file up the same pathway, each bearing in his arms a basket filled with living, squirming turtles, which he regarded and carried as tenderly as a mother would her infant. Some of the wretched reptiles were carefully wrapped in soft blankets, their heads and fore-feet protruding,—and, mounted on the backs of the plume-bedecked pilgrims, made ludicrous but solemn caricatures of little children in the same position. While I was at supper upstairs that evening, the governor's brother-in-law came in. He was welcomed by the family as if a messenger from heaven. He bore in his tremulous fingers one of the much abused and rebellious turtles. Paint still adhered to his hands and bare feet, which led me to infer that he had formed one of the sacred embassy.

" 'So you went to Ka-thlu-el-lon, did you ?' I asked.

" ' E'e,' replied the weary man, in a voice husky with long chanting, as he sank, almost exhausted, on a roll of skins which had been placed for him, and tenderly laid the turtle on the floor. No sooner did the creature find itself at liberty than it made off as fast as its lame legs would take it. Of one accord, the family forsook dish, spoon, and drinking-cup, and grabbing from a sacred meal-bowl whole handfuls of the contents, hurriedly followed the turtle about the room, into dark corners, around water-jars, behind the grinding-troughs, and out into the middle of the floor again, praying and scattering meal on its back as they went. At last, strange to say, it approached the foot-sore man who had brought it.

" ' Ha !' he exclaimed with emotion ; 'see it comes to me again ; ah, what great favours the fathers of all grant me this day,' and, passing his hand gently over the sprawling animal, he inhaled from his palm deeply and long, at the same time invoking the favour of the gods.   Then he leaned his chin upon his hand, and with large, wistful eyes regarded h's ugly captive as it sprawled about, blinking its meal-bedimmed eyes, and clawing the smooth floor in memory of its native element.   At this juncture I ventured a question :

" ' Why do you not let him go, or give him some water ?

" Slowly the man turned his eyes toward me, an odd mixture of pain, indignation, and pity on his face, while the worshipful family stared at me with holy horror.

" ' Poor younger brother ! ' he said at last, ' know you not how precious it is ?   It die ?   It will *not* die ; I tell you, it cannot die.'

" ' But it will die if you don't feed it and give it water.'

" ' I tell you it *cannot* die ; it will only change houses to-morrow, and go back to the home of its brothers.   Ah, well !   How should *you* know ? ' he mused.   Turning to the blinded turtle again : ' Ah ! my poor dear lost child or parent, my sister or brother to have been !   Who knows which ?   Maybe my own great-grandfather or mother ! ' And with this he fell to weeping most pathetically, and, tremulous with sobs, which were echoed by the women and children, he buried his face in his hands.   Filled with sympathy for his grief, however mistaken, I raised the turtle to my lips and kissed its cold shell ; then depositing it on the floor, hastily left the grief-stricken family to their sorrows.   Next day, with prayers and tender beseechings, plumes, and offerings, the poor turtle was killed, and its flesh and bones were removed and deposited in the little river, that it might ' return once more to eternal life among its comrades in the dark waters of the lake of the dead.'   The shell, carefully scraped and dried, was made into a dance-rattle, and, covered by a piece of buckskin, it still hangs from the smoke-stained rafters of my brother's house.   Once a Navajo tried to buy it for a ladle ; loaded with indignant reproaches, he was turned out of the house.   Were any one to venture the suggestion that the turtle no longer lived, his remark would cause a flood of tears, and he would be

The turtle addressed as a dead relative.

The turtle killed.

reminded that it had only ' changed houses and gone to live
for ever in the home of " our lost others." ' "¹

*In this
custom is
expressed a
belief in the
transmigra-
tion of
human
souls into
turtles.*   In this custom we find expressed in the clearest way a
belief in the transmigration of human souls into the bodies
of turtles.² The theory of transmigration is held by the
Moqui Indians, who belong to the same race as the Zunis.
The Moquis are divided into totem clans—the Bear clan,
Deer clan, Wolf clan, Hare clan, and so on ; they believe that
the ancestors of the clans were bears, deer, wolves, hares, and
so forth ; and that at death the members of each clan become
bears, deer, and so on according to the particular clan to
which they belonged.³ The Zuni are also divided into clans,
the totems of which agree closely with those of the Moquis,
and one of their totems is the turtle.⁴ Thus their belief in
transmigration into the turtle is probably one of the regular
articles of their totem faith.⁵ What then is the meaning of
killing a turtle in which the soul of a kinsman is believed to
be present ? Apparently the object is to keep up a communication with the other world in which the souls of the
departed are believed to be assembled in the form of
turtles. It is a common belief that the spirits of the dead
return occasionally to their old homes ; and accordingly the
unseen visitors are welcomed and feasted by the living, and
then sent upon their way.⁶ In the Zuni ceremony the dead
are fetched home in the form of turtles, and the killing of the
turtles is the way of sending back the souls to the spirit-

¹ Frank H. Cushing, " My Adventures in Zuñi," *The Century Illustrated Monthly Magazine*, May 1883,
pp. 45 *sq.*
² Mr. Cushing, indeed, while he
admits that the ancestors of the Zuni
may have believed in transmigration,
says, " Their belief, to-day, however,
relative to the future life is spiritual-
istic." But the expressions in the text
seem to leave no room for doubting
that the transmigration into turtles is a
living article of Zuni faith.
³ H. R. Schoolcraft, *Indian Tribes
of the United States* (Philadelphia,
1853-1856), iv. 86. On the totem
clans of the Moquis, see J. G. Bourke,
Snake-Dance of the Moquis of Arizona
(London, 1884), pp. 116 *sq.*, 334 *sqq.*

⁴ For this information I am indebted
to the kindness of the late Captain J.
G. Bourke, 3rd Cavalry, U.S. Army,
author of the work mentioned in the
preceding note. In his letter Captain
Bourke gave a list of fourteen totem
clans of Zuni, which he received on the
20th of May 1881 from Pedro Dino (?),
Governor of Zuni.

⁵ It should be observed, however,
that Mr. Cushing omits to say whether
or not the persons who performed the
ceremony described by him had the
turtle for their totem. If they had not,
the ceremony need not have had anything to do with totemism.

⁶ See *Adonis, Attis, Osiris*, Second
Edition, pp. 301-318.

land. Thus the general explanation given above of the custom of killing a god seems inapplicable to the Zuni custom, the true meaning of which is somewhat obscure. Nor is the obscurity which hangs over the subject entirely dissipated by a later and fuller account which we possess of the ceremony. From it we learn that the ceremony forms part of the elaborate ritual which these Indians observe at the midsummer solstice for the purpose of ensuring an abundant supply of rain for the crops. Envoys are despatched to bring " their otherselves, the tortoises," from the sacred lake Kothluwalawa, to which the souls of the dead are believed to repair. When the creatures have thus been solemnly brought to Zuni, they are placed in a bowl of water and dances are performed beside them by men in costume, who personate gods and goddesses. " After the ceremonial the tortoises are taken home by those who caught them and are hung by their necks to the rafters till morning, when they are thrown into pots of boiling water. The eggs are considered a great delicacy. The meat is seldom touched except as a medicine, which is curative for cutaneous diseases. Part of the meat is deposited in the river with *kôhakwa* (white shell beads) and turquoise beads as offerings to Council of the Gods." [1] This account at all events confirms the inference that the tortoises are supposed to be reincarnations of the human dead, for they are called the " otherselves " of the Zuni ; indeed, what else should they be than the souls of the dead in the bodies of tortoises seeing that they come from the haunted lake ? As the principal object of the prayers uttered and of the dances performed at these midsummer ceremonies appears to be to procure rain for the crops, it may be that the intention of bringing the tortoises to Zuni and dancing before them is to intercede with the ancestral spirits, incarnate in the animals, that they may be pleased to exert their power over the waters of heaven for the benefit of their living descendants.

From a later account it appears that the custom is a mode of interceding with the ancestral spirits for rain.

[1] Mrs. Matilda Coxe Stevenson, " The Zuñi Indians," *Twenty-Third Annual Report of the Bureau of Ameri-* *can Ethnology* (Washington, 1904), pp. 148-162.

§ 5. *Killing the Sacred Bear*

Doubt also hangs at first sight over the meaning of the
bear-sacrifice offered by the Aino or Ainu, a primitive people
who are found in the Japanese island of Yezo or Yesso, as
well as in Saghalien and the southern of the Kurile Islands.
It is not quite easy to define the attitude of the Aino
towards the bear.   On the one hand they give it the name
of *kamui* or "god"; but as they apply the same word to
strangers,[1] it may mean no more than a being supposed
to be endowed with superhuman, or at all events extraordinary, powers.[2]   Again, it is said that "the bear is their
chief divinity";[3] "in the religion of the Aino the bear
plays a chief part";[4] "amongst the animals it is especially
the bear which receives an idolatrous veneration";[5] "they
worship it after their fashion"; "there is no doubt that this
wild beast inspires more of the feeling which prompts
worship than the inanimate forces of nature, and the Aino
may be distinguished as bear-worshippers."[6]   Yet, on the
other hand, they kill the bear whenever they can;[7] "in
bygone years the Ainu considered bear-hunting the most

---

[1] B. Scheube, "Der Baerencultus
und die Baerenfeste der Ainos," *Mittheilungen der deutschen Gesellschaft
b. S. und S. Ostasiens* (Yokohama),
Heft xxii. p. 45.

[2] We are told that the Aino have gods
for almost every conceivable object, and
that the word *kamui* "has various
shades of meaning, which vary if used
before or after another word, and
according to the object to which it is
applied."   "When the term *kamui* is
applied to good objects, it expresses the
quality of usefulness, beneficence, or of
being exalted or divine.   When applied
to supposed evil gods, it indicates that
which is most to be feared and dreaded.
When applied to devils, reptiles, and
evil diseases, it signifies what is most
hateful, abominable, and repulsive.
When applied as a prefix to animals,
fish or fowl, it represents the greatest
or fiercest, or the most useful for food
or clothing.   When applied to persons,

it is sometimes expressive of goodness,
but more often is a mere title of respect
and reverence."   See the Rev. J.
Batchelor, *The Ainu of Japan* (London, 1892), pp. 245-251; *id.*, *The
Ainu and their Folk-lore* (London,
1901), pp. 581 *sq.*   Thus the Aino
kamui appears to mean nearly the same
as the Dacotan *wakan*, as to which see
Taboo and the Perils of the Soul, p. 225,
note.

[3] W. Martin Wood, "The Hairy
Men of Yesso," *Transactions of the
Ethnological Society of London*, N.S.,
iv. (1866) p. 36.

[4] J. J. Rein, *Japan* (Leipsic, 1881-
1886), i. 446.

[5] H. von Siebold, *Ethnologische Studien über die Aino auf der Insel Yesso*
(Berlin, 1881), p. 26.

[6] Miss Isabella L. Bird, *Unbeaten
Tracks in Japan* (new edition, 1885),
p. 275.

[7] W. Martin Wood, *l.c.*

manly and useful way in which a person could possibly spend his time " ; [1] "the men spend the autumn, winter, and spring in hunting deer and bears. Part of their tribute or taxes is paid in skins, and they subsist on the dried meat "; [2] bear's flesh is indeed one of their staple foods ; they eat it both fresh and salted ; [3] and the skins of bears furnish them with clothing.[4] In fact, the worship of which writers on this subject speak appears to be paid chiefly to the dead animal. Thus, although they kill a bear whenever they can, " in the process of dissecting the carcass they endeavour to conciliate the deity, whose representative they have slain, by making elaborate obeisances and deprecatory salutations " ; [5] "when a bear has been killed the Ainu sit down and admire it, make their salaams to it, worship it, and offer presents of *inao* " ; [6] "when a bear is trapped or wounded by an arrow, the hunters go through an apologetic or propitiatory ceremony." [7] The skulls of slain bears receive a place of honour in their huts, or are set up on sacred posts outside the huts, and are treated with much respect : libations of millet beer, and of *sake*, an intoxicating liquor, are offered to them ; and they are addressed as " divine preservers " (*akoshiratki kamui*), or "precious divinities." [8] The skulls of foxes are also fastened to the sacred posts outside the huts ; they are regarded as charms against evil spirits, and are consulted as oracles.[9] Yet it is expressly said, " The live fox is revered just as little as the bear ; rather they avoid it as much as possible, considering it a wily animal." [10] The bear can hardly, therefore, be

[1] Rev. J. Batchelor, *The Ainu and their Folk-lore*, p. 471.
[2] Miss I. L. Bird, *op. cit.* p. 269.
[3] B. Scheube, *Die Ainos*, p. 4 (reprinted from *Mittheilungen d. deutsch. Gesell. b. S. und S. Ostasiens*, Yokohama).
[4] B. Scheube, "Baerencultus," etc., p. 45 ; W. Joest, in *Verhandlungen der Berliner Gesellschaft für Anthropologie, Ethnologie und Urgeschichte*, 1882, p. 188.
[5] W. Martin Wood, *l.c.*
[6] Rev. J. Batchelor, *The Ainu and their Folk-lore* (London, 1901), pp. 476 *sq.* As to the *inao* see below,

p. 186, note.
[7] Miss I. L. Bird, *op. cit.* p. 277.
[8] B. Scheube, *Die Ainos*, p. 15 ; H. von Siebold, *op. cit.* p. 26 ; W. Martin Wood, *l.c.* ; J. J. Rein, *Japan*, i. 447 ; Von Brandt, "The Ainos and Japanese," *Journal of the Anthropological Institute*, iii. (1874) p. 134 ; Miss Bird, *op. cit.* pp. 275, 276; Rev. J. Batchelor, *The Ainu and their Folk-lore*, pp. 495 *sq.*
[9] B. Scheube, *Die Ainos*, pp. 15, 16 ; Von Brandt, *l.c.* ; Rev. J. Batchelor, *The Ainu and their Folk-lore*, pp. 352-354, 504 *sq.*
[10] B. Scheube, *Die Ainos*, p. 16.

described as a sacred animal of the Aino, nor yet as a totem ; for they do not call themselves bears, and they kill and eat the animal freely.   However, they have a legend of a woman who had a son by a bear ; and many of them who dwell in the mountains pride themselves on being descended from a bear.   Such people are called " Descendants of the bear" (*Kimun Kamui sanikiri*), and in the pride of their heart they will say, " As for me, I am a child of the god of the mountains ; I am descended from the divine one who rules in the mountains," meaning by "the god of the mountains" no other than the bear.[1]   It is therefore possible that, as our principal authority, the Rev. J. Batchelor, believes, the bear may have been the totem of an Aino clan ; but even if that were so it would not explain the respect shewn for the animal by the whole Aino people.

Aino custom of catching a bear cub, rearing it for several years, and killing it at a solemn festival.But it is the bear-festival of the Aino which concerns us here.   Towards the end of winter a bear cub is caught and brought into the village.   If it is very small, it is suckled by an Aino woman, but should there be no woman able to suckle it, the little animal is fed from the hand or the mouth. If it cries loudly and long for its mother, as it is apt to do, its owner will take it to his bosom and let it sleep with him for a few nights, thus dispelling its fears and sense of loneliness. During the day it plays about in the hut with the children and is treated with great affection.   But when the cub grows big enough to pain people by hugging or scratching them, he is shut up in a strong wooden cage, where he stays generally for two or three years, fed on fish and millet porridge, till it is time for him to be killed and eaten.[2]   But "it is a peculiarly striking fact that the young bear is not kept merely to furnish a good meal ; rather he is regarded and

---

[1] Rev. J. Batchelor, *The Ainu and their Folk-lore*, pp. 8-10.   E. Reclus (*Nouvelle Géographie Universelle*, vii. 755) mentions a (Japanese ?) legend which attributes the hairiness of the Ainos to the suckling of their first ancestor by a bear.   But in the absence of other evidence this is no proof of totemism.

[2] B. Scheube, " Der Baerencultus und die Baerenfeste der Ainos," p. 45 ; Rev. J. Batchelor, *The Ainu and their Folk-lore*, pp. 483-485.   Mr. Batchelor formerly doubted or denied that the Aino women suckle the bear cubs (*The Ainu of Japan*, p. 173); but since then he has repeatedly seen them do it.   Once, while he was preaching, a cub was being passed round among all the young women present and suckled by each in turn.

honoured as a fetish, or even as a sort of higher being."[1]
In Yezo the festival is generally celebrated in September or
October.   Before it takes place the Aino apologise to their
gods, alleging that they have treated the bear kindly as long
as they could, now they can feed him no longer, and are
obliged to kill him.   A man who gives a bear-feast invites
his relations and friends ; in a small village nearly the whole
community takes part in the feast; indeed, guests from
distant villages are invited and generally come, allured
by the prospect of getting drunk for nothing.   The form of
invitation runs somewhat as follows : " I, so and so, am
about to sacrifice the dear little divine thing who resides
among the mountains.   My friends and masters, come ye to
the feast ; we will then unite in the great pleasure of sending
the god away.   Come." [2]   When all the people are assembled
in front of the cage, an orator chosen for the purpose
addresses the bear and tells it that they are about to send it
forth to its ancestors.   He craves pardon for what they are
about to do to it, hopes it will not be angry, and comforts it
by assuring the animal that many of the sacred whittled
sticks (*inao*) and plenty of cakes and wine will be sent
with it on the long journey.   One speech of this sort
which Mr. Batchelor heard ran as follows : " O thou
divine one, thou wast sent into the world for us to hunt.
O thou precious little divinity, we worship thee ; pray hear
our prayer.   We have nourished thee and brought thee up
with a deal of pains and trouble, all because we love thee so.
Now, as thou hast grown big, we are about to send thee to
thy father and mother.   When thou comest to them please
speak well of us, and tell them how kind we have been ;
please come to us again and we will sacrifice thee."   Having
been secured with ropes, the bear is then let out of the cage
and assailed with a shower of blunt arrows in order to rouse
it to fury.   When it has spent itself in vain struggles, it is
tied up to a stake, gagged and strangled, its neck being
placed between two poles, which are then violently com-
pressed, all the people eagerly helping to squeeze the

[1] J. J. Rein, *Japan* (Leipsic, 1881-
1886), i. 447.
[2] B. Scheube, "Der Baerencultus

und die Baerenfeste der Ainos," p. 45;
Rev. J. Batchelor, *The Ainu and their
Folk-lore*, pp. 485 *sq.*

animal to death. An arrow is also discharged into the
beast's heart by a good marksman, but so as not to shed
blood, for they think that it would be very unlucky if any of
the blood were to drip on the ground. However, the men
sometimes drink the warm blood of the bear "that the
courage and other virtues it possesses may pass into them";
and sometimes they besmear themselves and their clothes
with the blood in order to ensure success in hunting. When
the animal has been strangled to death, it is skinned and its
head is cut off and set in the east window of the house,
where a piece of its own flesh is placed under its snout,
together with a cup of its own meat boiled, some millet
dumplings, and dried fish. Prayers are then addressed to
the dead animal; amongst other things it is sometimes
invited, after going away to its father and mother, to return
into the world in order that it may again be reared for sacrifice. When the bear is supposed to have finished eating its
own flesh, the man who presides at the feast takes the cup
containing the boiled meat, salutes it, and divides the contents between all the company present : every person, young
and old alike, must taste a little. The cup is called "the
cup of offering" because it has just been offered to the dead
bear. When the rest of the flesh has been cooked, it is
shared out in like manner among all the people, everybody
partaking of at least a morsel ; not to partake of the feast
would be equivalent to excommunication, it would be to
place the recreant outside the pale of Aino fellowship.
Formerly every particle of the bear, except the bones, had to
be eaten up at the banquet, but this rule is now relaxed.
The head, on being detached from the skin, is set up on
a long pole beside the sacred wands (*inao*) outside of the
house, where it remains till nothing but the bare white skull
is left. Skulls so set up are worshipped not only at the
time of the festival, but very often as long as they last.
The Aino assured Mr. Batchelor that they really do believe
the spirits of the worshipful animals to reside in the skulls ;
that is why they address them as "divine preservers" and
"precious divinities."[1]

[1] Rev. J. Batchelor, *The Ainu and
their Folk-lore*, pp. 486-496. The   killing of the bear is described somewhat differently by Miss I. L. Bird

The ceremony of killing the bear was witnessed by Dr. B. Scheube on the tenth of August at Kunnui, which is a village on Volcano Bay in the island of Yezo or Yesso. As his description of the rite contains some interesting particulars not mentioned in the foregoing account, it may be worth while to summarise it.[1]

On entering the hut he found about thirty Aino present, men, women, and children, all dressed in their best. The master of the house first offered a libation on the fireplace to the god of the fire, and the guests followed his example. Then a libation was offered to the house-god in his sacred corner of the hut. Meanwhile the housewife, who had nursed the bear, sat by herself, silent and sad, bursting now and then into tears. Her grief was obviously unaffected, and it deepened as the festival went on. Next, the master of the house and some of the guests went out of the hut and offered libations before the bear's cage. A few drops were presented to the bear in a saucer, which he at once upset. Then the women and girls danced round the cage, their faces turned towards it, their knees slightly bent, rising and hopping on their toes. As they danced they clapped their hands and sang a monotonous song. The housewife and a few old women, who might have nursed many bears, danced tearfully, stretching out their arms to the bear, and addressing it in terms of endearment. The young folks were less affected ; they laughed as well as sang. Disturbed by the noise, the bear began to rush about his cage and howl lamentably. Next libations were offered at the *inao* (*inabos*) or sacred wands which stand outside of an Aino hut. These wands are about a couple of feet high, and are whittled at the top into spiral shavings.[2] Five new wands with bamboo

---

(*Unbeaten Tracks in Japan*, New Edition, 1885, pp. 276 *sq.*), but she did not witness the ceremony. She tells us that at Usu, on Volcano Bay, when the bear is being killed, the Aino shout, " We kill you, O bear ! Come back soon into an Aino." According to Dr. Siebold, a very respectable authority, the bear's own heart is frequently offered to the dead beast to assure him that he is still in life (*Ethnologische Studien über die Aino auf der Insel Yesso*, p. 26). This, however, is denied by Dr. Scheube, who says that the heart is eaten ("Baerencultus," p. 50 note). The custom may vary in different places.

[1] B. Scheube, "Der Baerencultus und die Baerenfeste der Ainos," *Mittheilungen der deutschen Gesellschaft b. S. und S. Ostasiens* (Yokohama), Heft xxii. pp. 46 *sqq.*

[2] B. Scheube, "Baerencultus," etc., p. 46 ; *id.*, *Die Ainos*, p. 15 ; Miss I.

leaves attached to them had been set up for the festival. This is regularly done when a bear is killed ; the leaves mean that the animal may come to life again. Then the bear was let out of his cage, a rope was thrown round his neck, and he was led about in the neighbourhood of the hut. While this was being done the men, headed by a chief, shot at the beast with arrows tipped with wooden buttons. Dr. Scheube had to do so also. Then the bear was taken before the sacred wands, a stick was put in his mouth, nine men knelt on him and pressed his neck against a beam. In five minutes the animal had expired without uttering a sound. Meantime the women and girls had taken post behind the men, where they danced, lamenting, and beating the men who were killing the bear. The bear's carcase was next placed on the mat before the sacred wands ; and a sword and quiver, taken from the wands, were hung round the beast's neck. Being a she-bear, it was also adorned with a necklace and ear-rings. Then food and drink were offered to it, in the shape of millet-broth, millet-cakes, and a pot of *sake*. The men now sat down on mats before the dead bear, offered libations to it, and drank deep. Meanwhile the women and girls had laid aside all marks of sorrow, and

---

L. Bird, *op. cit.* pp. 273 *sq.* As to these whittled wands (*inao*), which are so conspicuous about the Aino huts, see the Rev. J. Batchelor, *The Ainu and their Folk-lore*, pp. 89-95. He remarks (p. 92) : " I have often in-sisted both in my lectures and also in my writings that the Ainu do not wor-ship their *inao*, but that they make them as offerings to the deities, and set them up as signs showing reverence towards them. This, I must now remark, is true but in part, for while some of the ordinary or less important kinds are not worshipped, there are several others which are. Those *not* worshipped may almost always be regarded as offerings and charms pure and simple, while those which *are* worshipped must generally be regarded as messengers sent to the higher deities." On the whole Mr. Batchelor would describe the *inao* as fetishes of various degrees of power. See further P. Labbé, *Un*

bagne Russe, l'Isle de Sakhaline (Paris, 1903), pp. 194 *sq.*, who compares the use of these whittled sticks to the use of holy candles among Roman Catholics. In Borneo the search for camphor is attended by many superstitions ; among other things, when the searchers have found a tree which promises to yield much camphor "they plant near their hut a stake, whereof the outer surface has been cut into curled shavings and tufts down the sides and at the top" (W. H. Furness, *Home-life of Borneo Head-hunters*, Philadelphia, 1902, p. 168). According to some ancient authorities, the old Italians worshipped peeled sticks as gods or as the images of gods ; however, the statement seems no better than an etymological guess to explain the word *delubrum*. See Festus, *s.v.* "Delubrum," p. 73, ed. C. O. Müller ; Servius on Virgil, *Aen.* ii. 225.

danced merrily, none more merrily than the old women. When the mirth was at its height two young Aino, who had let the bear out of his cage, mounted the roof of the hut and threw cakes of millet among the company, who all scrambled for them without distinction of age or sex. The bear was next skinned and disembowelled, and the trunk severed from the head, to which the skin was left hanging. The blood, caught in cups, was eagerly swallowed by the men. None of the women or children appeared to drink the blood, though custom did not forbid them to do so. The liver was cut in small pieces and eaten raw, with salt, the women and children getting their share. The flesh and the rest of the vitals were taken into the house to be kept till the next day but one, and then to be divided among the persons who had been present at the feast. Blood and liver were offered to Dr. Scheube. While the bear was being disembowelled, the women and girls danced the same dance which they had danced at the beginning—not, however, round the cage, but in front of the sacred wands. At this dance the old women, who had been merry a moment before, again shed tears freely. After the brain had been extracted from the bear's head and swallowed with salt, the skull, detached from the skin, was hung on a pole beside the sacred wands. The stick with which the bear had been gagged was also fastened to the pole, and so were the sword and quiver which had been hung on the carcase. The latter were removed in about an hour, but the rest remained standing. The whole company, men and women, danced noisily before the pole ; and another drinking-bout, in which the women joined, closed the festival.

Perhaps the first published account of the bear-feast of the Aino is one which was given to the world by a Japanese writer in 1652. It has been translated into French and runs thus : " When they find a young bear, they bring it home, and the wife suckles it. When it is grown they feed it with fish and fowl and kill it in winter for the sake of the liver, which they esteem an antidote to poison, the worms, colic, and disorders of the stomach. It is of a very bitter taste, and is good for nothing if the bear has been killed in summer. This butchery begins in the first Japanese month. *Early Japanese account of the Aino festival of the bear.*

For this purpose they put the animal's head between two long poles, which are squeezed together by fifty or sixty people, both men and women. When the bear is dead they eat his flesh, keep the liver as a medicine, and sell the skin, which is black and commonly six feet long, but the longest measure twelve feet. As soon as he is skinned, the persons who nourished the beast begin to bewail him ; afterwards they make little cakes to regale those who helped them." [1]

The custom of rearing and killing bears among the Aino of Saghalien.

The Aino of Saghalien rear bear cubs and kill them with similar ceremonies. We are told that they do not look upon the bear as a god but only as a messenger whom they despatch with various commissions to the god of the forest. The animal is kept for about two years in a cage, and then killed at a festival, which always takes place in winter and at night. The day before the sacrifice is devoted to lamentation, old women relieving each other in the duty of weeping and groaning in front of the bear's cage. Then about the middle of the night or very early in the morning an orator makes a long speech to the beast, reminding him how they have taken care of him, and fed him well, and bathed him in the river, and made him warm and comfortable. " Now," he proceeds, "we are holding a great festival in your honour. Be not afraid. We will not hurt you. We will only kill you and send you to the god of the forest who loves you. We are about to offer you a good dinner, the best you have ever eaten among us, and we will all weep for you together. The Aino who will kill you is the best shot among us. There he is, he weeps and asks your forgiveness ; you will feel almost nothing, it will be done so quickly. We cannot feed you always, as you will understand. We have done enough for you ; it is now your turn to sacrifice yourself for us. You will ask God to send us, for the winter, plenty of otters and sables, and for the summer, seals and fish in abundance. Do not forget our messages, we love you much, and our children will never forget you." When the bear has partaken of his last meal amid the

---

[1] " Ieso-Ki, ou description de l'île d'Iesso, avec une notice sur la révolte de Samsay-in, composée par l'inter- prète Kannemon," printed in Malte-Brun's *Annales des Voyages*, xxiv. (Paris, 1814) p. 154.

general emotion of the spectators, the old women weeping
afresh and the men uttering stifled cries, he is strapped, not
without difficulty and danger, and being let out of the cage
is led on leash or dragged, according to the state of his
temper, thrice round his cage, then round his master's house,
and lastly round the house of the orator.   Thereupon he is
tied up to a tree, which is decked with sacred whittled sticks
(*inao*) of the usual sort ; and the orator again addresses him
in a long harangue, which sometimes lasts till the day is
beginning to break.   " Remember," he cries, " remember !
I remind you of your whole life and of the services we have
rendered you.   It is now for you to do your duty.   Do not
forget what I have asked of you.   You will tell the gods to
give us riches, that our hunters may return from the forest
laden with rare furs and animals good to eat ; that our
fishers may find troops of seals on the shore and in the sea,
and that their nets may crack under the weight of the fish.
We have no hope but in you.   The evil spirits laugh at us,
and too often they are unfavourable and malignant to us,
but they will bow before you.   We have given you food and
joy and health ; now we kill you in order that you may
in return send riches to us and to our children."   To this
discourse the bear, more and more surly and agitated, listens
without conviction ; round and round the tree he paces and
howls lamentably, till, just as the first beams of the rising
sun light up the scene, an archer speeds an arrow to his
heart.   No sooner has he done so, than the marksman
throws away his bow and flings himself on the ground, and
the old men and women do the same, weeping and sobbing.
Then they offer the dead beast a repast of rice and wild
potatoes, and having spoken to him in terms of pity and
thanked him for what he has done and suffered, they cut off
his head and paws and keep them as sacred things.   A
banquet on the flesh and blood of the bear follows.   Women
were formerly excluded from it, but now they share with the
men.   The blood is drunk warm by all present ; the flesh
is boiled, custom forbids it to be roasted.   And as the relics
of the bear may not enter the house by the door, and Aino
houses in Saghalien have no windows, a man gets up on the
roof and lets the flesh, the head, and the skin down through

the smoke-hole.   Rice and wild potatoes are then offered to the head, and a pipe, tobacco, and matches are considerately placed beside it.   Custom requires that the guests should eat up the whole animal before they depart : the use of salt and pepper at the meal is forbidden ; and no morsel of the flesh may be given to the dogs.   When the banquet is over, the head is carried away into the depth of the forest and deposited on a heap of bears' skulls, the bleached and moulder- ing relics of similar festivals in the past.[1]

Bear- festivals of the Gilyaks.

The Gilyaks, a Tunguzian people of Eastern Siberia,[2] hold a bear-festival of the same sort once a year in January. " The bear is the object of the most refined solicitude of an entire village and plays the chief part in their religious ceremonies." [3]   An old she-bear is shot and her cub is reared, but not suckled, in the village.   When the bear is big enough he is taken from his cage and dragged through the village. But first they lead him to the bank of the river, for this is believed to ensure abundance of fish to each family.   He is then taken into every house in the village, where fish, brandy, and so forth are offered to him.   Some people prostrate themselves before the beast.   His entrance into a house is supposed to bring a blessing ; and if he snuffs at the food offered to him, this also is a blessing.   Nevertheless they tease and worry, poke and tickle the animal continually, so that he is surly and snappish.[4]   After being thus taken to

---

[1] P. Labbé, *Un Bagne Russe, l'Isle de Sakhaline* (Paris, 1903), pp. 227, 232-258.   The Gilyaks of Saghalien similarly keep and sacrifice bears ; but the ceremonies are simpler, and they treat the animals with less respect than the Aino.   See P. Labbé, *op. cit.* pp. 261-267.

[2] They inhabit the banks of the lower Amoor and the north of Sa- ghalien.   See E. G. Ravenstein, *The Russians on the Amur* (London, 1861), p. 389.

[3] " Notes on the River Amur and the Adjacent Districts," translated from the Russian, *Journal of the Royal Geographical Society,* xxviii. (1858) p. 396.

[4] Compare the custom of pinching a frog before cutting off his head ; see

The Magic Art and the Evolution of Kings, ii. 86.   In Japan sorceresses bury a dog in the earth, tease him, then cut off his head and put it in a box to be used in magic.   See A. Bastian, *Die Culturländer des alten Amerika* (Berlin, 1878), i. 475 note, who adds " *wie im ostindischen Archi- pelago die Schutzseele gereizt wird.*" He probably refers to the Batta *Pang- hulu-balang.*   See H. von Rosenberg, *Der Malayische Archipel* (Leipsic, 1878), pp. 59 *sq.* ; W. Ködding, "Die Batakschen Götter," *Allgemeine Mis- sions-Zeitschrift,* xii. (1885) pp. 478 *sq.* ; J. B. Neumann, " Het Pane-en Bila-stroomgebied op het eiland Sum- atra," in *Tijdschrift van het Neder- landsch Aardrijkskundig Genootschap,* Tweede Serie, dl. iii. (1886) Afdeeling,

every house, he is tied to a peg and shot dead with arrows. His head is then cut off, decked with shavings, and placed on the table where the feast is set out. Here they beg pardon of the beast and worship him. Then his flesh is roasted and eaten in special vessels of wood finely carved. They do not eat the flesh raw nor drink the blood, as the Aino do. The brain and entrails are eaten last; and the skull, still decked with shavings, is placed on a tree near the house. Then the people sing and both sexes dance in ranks, as bears.[1]

One of these bear-festivals was witnessed by the Russian traveller L. von Schrenck and his companions at the Gilyak village of Tebach in January 1856. From his detailed report of the ceremony we may gather some particulars which are not noticed in the briefer accounts which I have just summarised. The bear, he tells us, plays a great part in the life of all the peoples inhabiting the region of the Amoor and Siberia as far as Kamtchatka, but among none of them is his importance greater than among the Gilyaks. The immense size which the animal attains in the valley of the Amoor, his ferocity whetted by hunger, and the frequency of his appearance, all combine to make him the most dreaded beast of prey in the country. No wonder, therefore, that the fancy of the Gilyaks is busied with him and surrounds him, both in life and in death, with a sort of halo of superstitious fear. Thus, for example, it is thought that if a Gilyak falls in combat with a bear, his soul transmigrates into the body of the beast. Nevertheless his flesh has an irresistible attraction for the Gilyak palate, especially when the animal has been kept in captivity for some time and fattened on fish, which gives the flesh, in the opinion of the Gilyaks, a peculiarly delicious flavour. But in order to

L. von Schrenck's description of a bear-festival among the Gilyaks of the Amoor

---

meer uitgebreide artikelen, No. 2, p. 306; Van Dijk, in *Tijdschrift voor Indische Taal- Land- en Volkenkunde*, xxxviii. (1895) pp. 307 *sq.*

[1] W. Joest, in B. Scheube, *Die Ainos*, p. 17; J. Deniker, "Les Ghiliaks d'après les derniers renseignements," *Revue d'Ethnographie*, ii. (1883) pp. 307 *sq.* (on the authority of Mr. Seeland); *Internationales Archiv für Ethnologie*, i. (1888) p. 102 (on the authority of Captain Jacobsen); *Archiv für Anthropologie*, xxvi. (1900) p. 796 (abstract of a Russian work on the Gilyaks by Dr. Seland or Seeland). What exactly is meant by "dancing as bears" ("*tanzen beide Geschlechter Reigentänze, wie Bären,*" Joest, *l.c.*) does not appear.

enjoy this dainty with impunity they deem it needful to
perform a long series of ceremonies, of which the intention
is to delude the living bear by a show of respect, and to
appease the anger of the dead animal by the homage paid
to his departed spirit. The marks of respect begin as soon
as the beast is captured. He is brought home in triumph
and kept in a cage, where all the villagers take it in turns
to feed him. For although he may have been captured or
purchased by one man, he belongs in a manner to the
whole village. His flesh will furnish a common feast, and
hence all must contribute to support him in his life. His
diet consists exclusively of raw or dried fish, water, and a
sort of porridge compounded of powdered fish-skins, train-
oil, and whortle-berries. The length of time he is kept in
captivity depends on his age. Old bears are kept only a
few months ; cubs are kept till they are full-grown. A
thick layer of fat on the captive bear gives the signal for
the festival, which is always held in winter, generally in
December but sometimes in January or February. At the
festival witnessed by the Russian travellers, which lasted a
good many days, three bears were killed and eaten. More
than once the animals were led about in procession and
compelled to enter every house in the village, where they
were fed as a mark of honour, and to shew that they were
welcome guests. But before the beasts set out on this
round of visits, the Gilyaks played at skipping-rope in
presence, and perhaps, as L. von Schrenck inclined to
believe, in honour of the animals. The night before they
were killed, the three bears were led by moonlight a long
way on the ice of the frozen river. That night no one in the
village might sleep. Next day, after the animals had been
again led down the steep bank to the river, and conducted
thrice round the hole in the ice from which the women of
the village drew their water, they were taken to an appointed place not far from the village, and shot to death
with arrows. The place of sacrifice or execution was
marked as holy by being surrounded with whittled sticks,
from the tops of which shavings hung in curls. Such sticks
are with the Gilyaks, as with the Aino, the regular symbols
that accompany all religious ceremonies. Before the bears

Bears led
in proces-
sion about
the village.

Slaughter
of the
bears.

received the fatal shafts from two young men chosen for the purpose, the boys were allowed to discharge their small but not always harmless arrows at the beasts. As soon as the carcases had been cut up, the skins with the heads attached to them were set up in a wooden cage in such a way as to make it appear that the animals had entered the cage and were looking out of it. The blood which flowed from the bears on the spot where they were killed was immediately covered up with snow, to prevent any one from accidentally treading on it, a thing which was strictly tabooed.

When the house has been arranged and decorated for their reception, the skins of the bears, with their heads attached to them, are brought into it, not however by the door, but through a window, and then hung on a sort of scaffold opposite the hearth on which the flesh is to be cooked. This ceremony of bringing the bears' skins into the house by the window was not witnessed by the Russian travellers, who only learned of it at second hand. They were told that when the thin disc of fish-skin, which is the substitute for a pane of glass in the window, has been replaced after the passage of the bear-skins, a figure of a toad made of birch bark is affixed to it on the outside, while inside the house a figure of a bear dressed in Gilyak costume is set on the bench of honour. The meaning of this part of the ceremony, as it is conjecturally interpreted by Von Schrenck, may be as follows. The toad is a creature that has a very evil reputation with the Gilyaks, and accordingly they attempt to lay upon it, as on a scapegoat, the guilt of the slaughter of the worshipful bear. Hence its effigy is excluded from the house and has to remain outside at the window, a witness of its own misdeeds ; whereas the bear is brought into the house and treated as an honoured guest, for fish and flesh are laid before it, and its effigy, dressed in Gilyak costume, is seated on the bench of honour.

The boiling of the bears' flesh among the Gilyaks is done only by the oldest men, whose high privilege it is ; women and children, young men and boys have no part in it. The task is performed slowly and deliberately, with a certain solemnity. On the occasion described by the Russian travellers the kettle was first of all surrounded with

Treatment of the bears skins.

Treatment of the bears flesh.

a thick wreath of shavings, and then filled with snow, for the use of water to cook bear's flesh is forbidden.   Meanwhile a large wooden trough, richly adorned with arabesques and carvings of all sorts, was hung immediately under the snouts of the bears ; on one side of the trough was carved in relief a bear, on the other side a toad.   When the carcases were being cut up, each leg was laid on the ground in front of the bears, as if to ask their leave, before being placed in the kettle ; and the boiled flesh was fished out of the kettle with an iron hook, and set in the trough before the bears, in order that they might be the first to taste of their own flesh.   As fast, too, as the fat was cut in strips it was hung up in front of the bears, and afterwards laid in a small wooden trough on the ground before them.   Last of all the inner organs of the beasts were cut up and placed in small vessels.   At the same time the women made bandages out of parti-coloured rags, and after sunset these bandages were tied round the bears' snouts just below the eyes " in order to dry the tears that flowed from them."   To each bandage, just below the eyes, was attached a figure of a toad cut out of birch bark.   The meaning of this appears to be, as Von Schrenck conjectured, as follows.   With the carving of his inner organs, the heart, liver, and so forth, the bear sees that his fate is sealed, and sheds some natural tears at his hard lot.   These tears trickle down his snout over the figure of the toad, which the poor deluded bear accordingly regards as the author of all the mischief.   For he cannot blame the Gilyaks, who have treated him so kindly.   Have they not received him as a guest in their house, set him on the seat of honour, given him of their best, and done nothing but with his knowledge and permission ?   Finally, have not their women shewn him the last delicate mark of attention by drying the tears that flow from his eyes and trickle down his nose ?   Surely then he cannot think that these kindly folk have done him any harm ; it was all the fault of the unprincipled toad.

Banquet on the bears' flesh.   Whatever may be thought of this explanation, as soon as the ceremony of wiping away poor bruin's tears had been performed, the assembled Gilyaks set to work in earnest to devour his flesh.   The broth obtained by boiling the meat had already been partaken of.   The wooden bowls, platters, and spoons out of which the Gilyaks eat the broth and flesh of the bears on these occasions are always made specially for the purpose at the festival and only then ; they are elaborately ornamented with carved figures of bears and other devices that refer to the animal or the festival, and the people have a strong superstitious scruple against parting with them.   While the festival lasts, no salt may be used in cooking the bear's flesh or indeed any other food ; and no flesh of any kind may be roasted, for the bear would hear the hissing and sputtering of the roasting flesh, and would be very angry.   After the bones had been picked clean they were put back in the kettle in which the flesh had been boiled.   And when the festal meal was over, an old man took his stand at the door of the house with a branch of fir in his hand, with which, as the people passed out, he gave a light blow to every one who had eaten of the bear's flesh or fat, perhaps as a punishment for their treatment of the worshipful animal.   In the afternoon of the same day the *Dance of the women.* women performed a strange dance.   Only one woman danced at a time, throwing the upper part of her body into the oddest postures, while she held in her hands a branch of fir or a kind of wooden castanets.   The other women meanwhile played an accompaniment in a peculiar rhythm by drumming on the beams of the house with clubs.   The dance reminded one of the Russian travellers of the bear-dance which he had seen danced by the women of Kamtchatka.   Von Schrenck believes, though he has not positive *Disposal of the skull and bones of the bear.* evidence, that after the fat and flesh of the bear have been consumed, his skull is cleft with an axe, and the brain taken out and eaten.   Then the bones and the skull are solemnly carried out by the oldest people to a place in the forest not far from the village.   There all the bones except the skull are buried.   After that a young tree is felled a few inches above the ground, its stump cleft, and the skull wedged into the cleft.   When the grass grows over the spot, the skull disappears from view, and that is the end of the bear.[1]

[1] L. von Schrenck, *Reisen und Forschungen im Amur-lande* (St. Petersburg, 1891), iii. 696-731.

Mr. L.
Sternberg's
description
of the bear-
festivals of
the Gilyaks.

Another description of the bear-festivals of the Gilyaks
has been given us by Mr. Leo Sternberg.[1]   It agrees substantially with the foregoing accounts, but a few particulars
in it may be noted.   According to Mr. Sternberg, the festival
is usually held in honour of a deceased relation : the next of
kin either buys or catches a bear cub and nurtures it for two
or three years till it is ready for the sacrifice.   Only certain
distinguished guests (*Narch-en*) are privileged to partake of
the bear's flesh, but the host and members of his clan eat a
broth made from the flesh ; great quantities of this broth are
prepared and consumed on the occasion.   The guests of
honour (*Narch-en*) must belong to the clan into which the
host's daughters and the other women of his clan are
married : one of these guests, usually the host's son-in-law,
is entrusted with the duty of shooting the bear dead with
an arrow.   The skin, head, and flesh of the slain bear are
brought into the house not through the door but through
the smoke-hole ; a quiver full of arrows is laid under the
head and beside it are deposited tobacco, sugar, and other
food.   The soul of the bear is supposed to carry off the souls
of these things with it on the far journey.   A special vessel
is used for cooking the bear's flesh, and the fire must be
kindled by a sacred apparatus of flint and steel, which
belongs to the clan and is handed down from generation to
generation, but which is never used to light fires except on
these solemn occasions.   Of all the many viands cooked for
the consumption of the assembled people a portion is placed
in a special vessel and set before the bear's head : this is
called " feeding the head."   After the bear has been killed,
dogs are sacrificed in couples of male and female.   Before
being throttled, they are fed and invited to go to their lord
on the highest mountain, to change their skins, and to return
next year in the form of bears.   The soul of the dead bear
departs to the same lord, who is also lord of the primaeval
forest ; it goes away laden with the offerings that have been
made to it, and attended by the souls of the dogs and also
by the souls of the sacred whittled sticks, which figure
prominently at the festival.

[1] L. Sternberg, " Die Religion der Giljaken," *Archiv für Religionswissenschaft*, viii. (1905) pp. 260-274.

The Goldi, neighbours of the Gilyaks, treat the bear in much the same way. They hunt and kill it; but sometimes they capture a live bear and keep him in a cage, feeding him well and calling him their son and brother. Then at a great festival he is taken from his cage, paraded about with marked consideration, and afterwards killed and eaten. " The skull, jaw-bones, and ears are then suspended on a tree, as an antidote against evil spirits; but the flesh is eaten and much relished, for they believe that all who partake of it acquire a zest for the chase, and become courageous." [1]

Bear-festivals of the Goldi.

The Orotchis, another Tunguzian people of the region of the Amoor, hold bear-festivals of the same general character. Any one who catches a bear cub considers it his bounden duty to rear it in a cage for about three years, in order at the end of that time to kill it publicly and eat the flesh with his friends. The feasts being public, though organised by individuals, the people try to have one in each Orotchi village every year in turn. When the bear is taken out of his cage, he is led about by means of ropes to all the huts, accompanied by people armed with lances, bows, and arrows. At each hut the bear and bear-leaders are treated to something good to eat and drink. This goes on for several days until all the huts, not only in that village but also in the next, have been visited. The days are given up to sport and noisy jollity. Then the bear is tied to a tree or wooden pillar and shot to death by the arrows of the crowd, after which its flesh is roasted and eaten. Among the Orotchis of the Tundja River women take part in the bear-feasts, while among the Orotchis of the River Vi the women will not even touch bear's flesh.[2]

Bear-festivals of the Orotchis.

In the treatment of the captive bear by these tribes there are features which can hardly be distinguished from worship. Such, for example, are the prayers offered to it both alive and dead; the offerings of food, including portions of its

Respect shewn by all these tribes for the bears which they kill and eat.

[1] E. G. Ravenstein, *The Russians on the Amur* (London, 1861), pp. 379 *sq.*; T. W. Atkinson, *Travels in the Regions of the Upper and Lower Amoor* (London, 1860), pp. 482 *sq.*

[2] E. H. Fraser, "The Fish-skin Tartars," *Journal of the China Branch of the Royal Asiatic Society for the year 1891-1892*, New Series, xxvi. 36-39. L. von Schrenck describes a bear-feast which he witnessed in 1855 among the Oltscha (*Reisen und Forschungen im Amur-lande*, iii. 723-728). The Oltscha are probably the same as the Orotchis.

own flesh, laid before the animal's skull ; and the Gilyak
custom of leading the living beast on to the ice of the river
in order to ensure a supply of fish, and of conducting him
from house to house in order that every family may receive
his blessing, just as in Europe a May-tree or a personal
representative of the tree-spirit used to be taken from door
to door in spring for the sake of diffusing among all and
sundry the fresh energies of reviving nature.[1]   Again, the
solemn participation in his flesh and blood, and particularly
the Aino custom of sharing the contents of the cup which
had been consecrated by being set before the dead beast, are
strongly suggestive of a sacrament, and the suggestion is
confirmed by the Gilyak practice of reserving special vessels
to hold the flesh and cooking it on a fire kindled by a sacred
apparatus which is never employed except on these religious
occasions.   Indeed our principal authority on Aino religion,
the Rev. John Batchelor, frankly describes as worship the
ceremonious respect which the Aino pay to the bear,[2] and
he affirms that the animal is undoubtedly one of their gods.[3]
Certainly the Aino appear to apply their name for god
(*kamui*) freely to the bear ; but, as Mr. Batchelor himself
points out,[4] that word is used with many different shades of
meaning and is applied to a great variety of objects, so that
from its application to the bear we cannot safely argue that
the animal is actually regarded as a deity.   Indeed we are
expressly told that the Aino of Saghalien do not consider
the bear to be a god but only a messenger to the gods, and
the message with which they charge the animal at its death
bears out the statement.[5]   Apparently the Gilyaks also look
on the bear in the light of an envoy despatched with
presents to the Lord of the Mountain, on whom the welfare
of the people depends.   At the same time they treat the
animal as a being of a higher order than man, in fact as a
minor deity, whose presence in the village, so long as he is
kept and fed, diffuses blessings, especially by keeping at bay
the swarms of evil spirits who are constantly lying in wait for

---

[1] *The Magic Art and the Evolution of Kings*, ii. 59 *sqq.*

[2] Rev. J. Batchelor, *The Ainu and their Folk-lore*, pp. 492, 493, 495, 496.

[3] *Op. cit.* p. 482.   Mr. Batchelor says " totem gods."

[4] *Op. cit.* pp. 580 *sqq.*

[5] See above, pp. 188 *sq.*

people, stealing their goods and destroying their bodies by sickness and disease. Moreover, by partaking of the flesh, blood, or broth of the bear, the Gilyaks, the Aino, and the Goldi are all of opinion that they acquire some portion of the animal's mighty powers, particularly his courage and strength. No wonder, therefore, that they should treat so great a benefactor with marks of the highest respect and affection.[1]

Some light may be thrown on the ambiguous attitude of the Aino to bears by comparing the similar treatment which they accord to other creatures. For example, they regard the eagle-owl as a good deity who by his hooting warns men of threatened evil and defends them against it ; hence he is loved, trusted, and devoutly worshipped as a divine mediator between men and the Creator. The various names applied to him are significant both of his divinity and of his mediatorship. Whenever an opportunity offers, one of these divine birds is captured and kept in a cage, where he is greeted with the endearing titles of " Beloved god" and " Dear little divinity." Nevertheless the time comes when the dear little divinity is throttled and sent away in his capacity of mediator to take a message to the superior gods or to the Creator himself. The following is the form of prayer addressed to the eagle-owl when it is about to be sacrificed : " Beloved deity, we have brought you up because we loved you, and now we are about to send you to your father. We herewith offer you food, *inao*, wine, and cakes ; take them to your parent, and he will be very pleased. When you come to him say, ' I have lived a long time among the Ainu, where an Ainu father and an Ainu mother reared me. I now come to thee. I have brought a variety of good things. I saw while living in Ainu-land a

Similar respect shewn by the Aino for the eagle-owls which they keep in cages and kill.

---

[1] This account of the attitude of the Gilyaks to the bear, and of their reasons for holding the festival, is the one given by Mr. Leo Sternberg. See his articles, "Die Religion der Giljaken," *Archiv für Religionswissenschaft*, viii. (1905) pp. 273 *sq.*, 456-458. He speaks of the bear as a minor deity (" *Er selbst ist ja eine Gottheit, wenn auch eine kleine* "). Mr. Sternberg and Mr. Batchelor, two of the best-informed writers on the subject, agree in denying that the slaughter of the bear at the festival is a sacrifice to the gods. See L. Sternberg, *op. cit.* p. 457 ; Rev. J. Batchelor, *The Ainu and their Folk-lore*, p. 482. As to the belief of the Gilyaks in evil spirits, which menace and destroy the life of man, see L. Sternberg, *op. cit.* pp. 460 *sqq.*

great deal of distress.   I observed that some of the people were possessed by demons, some were wounded by wild animals, some were hurt by landslides, others suffered shipwreck, and many were attacked by disease.   The people are in great straits.   My father, hear me, and hasten to look upon the Ainu and help them.'   If you do this, your father will help us." [1]

Similar respect shewn by the Aino for the eagles and hawks which they keep in cages and kill.

Again, the Aino keep eagles in cages, worship them as divinities, and ask them to defend the people from evil.   Yet they offer the bird in sacrifice, and when they are about to do so they pray to him, saying : " O precious divinity, O thou divine bird, pray listen to my words.   Thou dost not belong to this world, for thy home is with the Creator and his golden eagles.   This being so, I present thee with these *inao* and cakes and other precious things.   Do thou ride upon the *inao* and ascend to thy home in the glorious heavens. When thou arrivest, assemble the deities of thy own kind together and thank them for us for having governed the world.   Do thou come again, I beseech thee, and rule over us.   O my precious one, go thou quietly." [2]   Once more, the Aino revere hawks, keep them in cages, and offer them in sacrifice.   At the time of killing one of them the following prayer should be addressed to the bird : " O divine hawk, thou art an expert hunter, please cause thy cleverness to descend on me."   If a hawk is well treated in captivity and prayed to after this fashion when he is about to be killed, he will surely send help to the hunter.[3]

Advantages which the Aino hopes to reap from slaughtering the worshipful animals.

Thus the Aino hopes to profit in various ways by slaughtering the creatures, which, nevertheless, he treats as divine.   He expects them to carry messages for him to their kindred or to the gods in the upper world ; he hopes to partake of their virtues by imbibing parts of their bodies or in other ways ;   and apparently he looks forward to their bodily resurrection in this world, which will enable him again to catch and kill them, and again to reap all the benefits which he has already derived from their slaughter. For in the prayers addressed to the worshipful bear and the

[1] Rev. J. Batchelor, *The Ainu and their Folk-lore*, pp. 410-415.
[2] Rev. J. Batchelor, *op. cit.* pp.
432 *sq.*
[3] Rev. J. Batchelor, *op. cit.* p. 438.

worshipful eagle before they are knocked on the head the
creatures are invited to come again,[1] which seems clearly to
point to a faith in their future resurrection.   If any doubt
could exist on this head, it would be dispelled by the
evidence of Mr. Batchelor, who tells us that the Aino " are
firmly convinced that the spirits of birds and animals killed
in hunting or offered in sacrifice come and live again upon the
earth clothed with a body ; and they believe, further, that
they appear here for the special benefit of men, particularly
Ainu hunters." [2]   The Aino, Mr. Batchelor tells us, " con-
fessedly slays and eats the beast that another may come in
its place and be treated in like manner " ; and at the time
of sacrificing the creatures " prayers are said to them which
form a request that they will come again and furnish viands
for another feast, as if it were an honour to them to be thus
killed and eaten, and a pleasure as well.   Indeed such is the
people's idea." [3]   These last observations, as the context
shews, refer especially to the sacrifice of bears.

Thus among the benefits which the Aino anticipates
from the slaughter of the worshipful animals not the least
substantial is that of gorging himself on their flesh and
blood, both on the present and on many a similar occasion
hereafter ; and that pleasing prospect again is derived from
his firm faith in the spiritual immortality and bodily resurrection of the dead animals.   A like faith is shared by many
savage hunters in many parts of the world and has given rise
to a variety of quaint customs, some of which will be described presently.   Meantime it is not unimportant to observe
that the solemn festivals at which the Aino, the Gilyaks, and
other tribes slaughter the tame caged bears with demon-
strations of respect and sorrow, are probably nothing but an
extension or glorification of similar rites which the hunter performs over any wild bear which he chances to kill in the forest.
Indeed with regard to the Gilyaks we are expressly informed
that this is the case.   If we would understand the meaning
of the Gilyak ritual, says Mr. Sternberg, " we must above all
remember that the bear-festivals are not, as is usually but

The bear-festivals of these tribes are probably nothing but an extension of the similar rites which the hunter performs over any wild bear which he kills in the forest.

---

[1] See above, pp. 183, 184, 196.

[2] Rev. J. Batchelor, *The Ainu and*

their Folk-lore, p. 479.

[3] Rev. J. Batchelor, *op. cit.* pp.
481, 482.

falsely assumed, celebrated only at the killing of a house-bear but are held on every occasion when a Gilyak succeeds in slaughtering a bear in the chase. It is true that in such cases the festival assumes less imposing dimensions, but in its essence it remains the same. When the head and skin of a bear killed in the forest are brought into the village, they are accorded a triumphal reception with music and solemn cere-monial. The head is laid on a consecrated scaffold, fed, and treated with offerings, just as at the killing of a house-bear; and the guests of honour (*Narch-en*) are also assembled. So, too, dogs are sacrificed, and the bones of the bear are pre-served in the same place and with the same marks of respect as the bones of a house-bear. Hence the great winter festival is only an extension of the rite which is observed at the slaughter of every bear." [1]

The apparent contradic-tion in the behaviour of these tribes to bears is not so great as it seems to us at first sight. Savage logic.

Thus the apparent contradiction in the practice of these tribes, who venerate and almost deify the animals which they habitually hunt, kill, and eat, is not so flagrant as at first sight it appears to us: the people have reasons, and some very practical reasons, for acting as they do. For the savage is by no means so illogical and unpractical as to superficial observers he is apt to seem; he has thought deeply on the questions which immediately concern him, he reasons about them, and though his conclusions often diverge very widely from ours, we ought not to deny him the credit of patient and prolonged meditation on some fundamental problems of human existence. In the present case, if he treats bears in general as creatures wholly subservient to human needs and yet singles out certain individuals of the species for homage which almost amounts to deification, we must not hastily set him down as irrational and in-consistent, but must endeavour to place ourselves at his point of view, to see things as he sees them, and to divest ourselves of the prepossessions which tinge so deeply our own views of the world. If we do so, we shall probably discover that, however absurd his conduct may appear to us, the savage nevertheless generally acts on a train of reasoning which seems to him in harmony with the

---

[1] L. Sternberg, "Die Religion der Giljaken," *Archiv für Religionswissen-schaft*, viii. (1905) p. 272.

facts of his limited experience. This I propose to illustrate
in the following chapter, where I shall attempt to shew that
the solemn ceremonial of the bear-festival among the Ainos
and other tribes of north-eastern Asia is only a particularly
striking example of the respect which on the principles
of his rude philosophy the savage habitually pays to the
animals which he kills and eats.

CHAPTER XIV

THE PROPITIATION OF WILD ANIMALS BY HUNTERS

The savage believes that animals, like men, are endowed with souls which survive the death of their bodies.

THE explanation of life by the theory of an indwelling and practically immortal soul is one which the savage does not confine to human beings but extends to the animate creation in general. In so doing he is more liberal and perhaps more logical than the civilised man, who commonly denies to animals that privilege of immortality which he claims for himself. The savage is not so proud ; he commonly believes that animals are endowed with feelings and intelligence like those of men, and that, like men, they possess souls which survive the death of their bodies either to wander about as disembodied spirits or to be born again

The American Indians draw no sharp distinction between animals and men.

in animal form. Thus, for example, we are told that the Indian of Guiana does not see " any sharp line of distinction, such as we see, between man and other animals, between one kind of animal and another, or between animals—man included—and inanimate objects. On the contrary, to the Indian, all objects, animate and inanimate, seem exactly of the same nature except that they differ in the accident of bodily form. Every object in the whole world is a being, consisting of a body and spirit, and differs from every other object in no respect except that of bodily form, and in the greater or less degree of brute power and brute cunning consequent on the difference of bodily form and bodily habits." [1] Similarly we read that " in Cherokee mythology, as in that of Indian tribes generally, there is no essential difference between men and animals. In the primal genesis period they seem to be completely undifferentiated, and we

[1] E. F. im Thurn, *Among the Indians of Guiana* (London, 1883), p. 350.

find all creatures alike living and working together in harmony and mutual helpfulness until man, by his aggressiveness and disregard for the rights of the others, provokes their hostility, when insects, birds, fishes, reptiles, and fourfooted beasts join forces against him. Henceforth their lives are apart, but the difference is always one of degree only. The animals, like the people, are organized into tribes and have like them their chiefs and townhouses, their councils and ballplays, and the same hereafter in the Darkening land of Usunhiyi. Man is still the paramount power, and hunts and slaughters the others as his own necessities compel, but is obliged to satisfy the animal tribes in every instance, very much as a murder is compounded for, according to the Indian system, by 'covering the bones of the dead' with presents for the bereaved relatives."[1] To the same effect another observer of the North American Indians writes: "I have often reflected on the curious connexion which appears to subsist in the mind of an Indian between man and the brute creation, and found much matter in it for curious observation. Although they consider themselves superior to all other animals and are very proud of that superiority ; although they believe that the beasts of the forest, the birds of the air, and the fishes of the waters, were created by the Almighty Being for the use of man ; yet it seems as if they ascribe the difference between themselves and the brute kind, and the dominion which they have over them, more to their superior bodily strength and dexterity than to their immortal souls. All beings endowed by the Creator with the power of volition and self-motion, they view in a manner as a great society of which they are the head, whom they are appointed, indeed, to govern, but between whom and themselves intimate ties of connexion and relationship may exist, or at least did exist in the beginning of time. They are, in fact, according to their opinions, only the first among equals, the legitimate hereditary sovereigns of the whole animated race, of which they are themselves a constituent part. Hence, in their languages, those inflections of their nouns which we call *genders*, are not, as with us,

[1] J. Mooney, "Myths of the Cherokee," *Nineteenth Annual Report of* the *Bureau of American Ethnology,* Part i. (Washington, 1900) p. 261.

descriptive of the *masculine* and *feminine* species, but of the *animate* and *inanimate* kinds. Indeed, they go so far as to include trees and plants within the first of these descriptions. All animated nature, in whatever degree, is in their eyes a great whole, from which they have not yet ventured to separate themselves. They do not exclude other animals from their world of spirits, the place to which they expect to go after death."[1] Even Chinese authors "have roundly avowed themselves altogether unable to discover any real difference between men and animals," and they have drawn out the parallelism between the two in some detail.[2]

Some savages apparently fail to distinguish clearly even the bodies of animals from the bodies of men.

But it is not merely between the mental and spiritual nature of man and the animals that the savage traces a close resemblance ; even the distinction of their bodily form appears sometimes to elude his dull apprehension. An unusually intelligent Bushman questioned by a missionary "could not state any difference between a man and a brute —he did not know but a buffalo might shoot with bows and arrows as well as a man, if it had them."[3] In the opinion of the Gilyak, "the form and size of an animal are merely a sort of appearance. Every animal is in point of fact a real being like man, nay a Gilyak such as himself, but endowed with reason and strength which often surpass those of mere men."[4] Nor is it merely that in the mental fog the savage takes beasts for men ; he seems to be nearly as ready to take himself and his fellows for beasts. When the Russians first landed on one of the Alaskan islands the people took them for cuttle-fish, "on account of the buttons on their clothes."[5] We have seen how some savages identify themselves with animals of various sorts by eating the maggots bred in the rotting carcases of the beasts, and how thereafter, when occasion serves, they behave in their adopted

[1] Rev. John Heckewelder, "An Account of the History, Manners, and Customs of the Indian Nations who once inhabited Pennsylvania and the neighbouring States," *Transactions of the Historical and Literary Committee of the American Philosophical Society*, vol. i. (Philadelphia, 1819) pp. 247 *sq.*

[2] J. J. M. de Groot, *The Religious System of China*, iv. (Leyden, 1901) pp. 157 *sq.*

[3] John Campbell, *Travels in South Africa, being a Narrative of a Second Journey in the Interior of that Country* (London, 1822), ii. 34.

[4] L. Sternberg, "Die Religion der Giljaken," *Archiv für Religionswissenschaft*, viii. (1905) p. 248.

[5] I. Petroff, *Report on the Population, Industries, and Resources of Alaska*, p. 145.

characters by wriggling, roaring, barking, or grunting, according as they happen to be boa-constrictors, lions, jackals, or hippopotamuses.[1]   In the island of Mabuiag men of the Sam, that is, the Cassowary, totem think that cassowaries are men or nearly so.   "Sam he all same as relation, he belong same family," is the account they give of their kinship with the creature.   Conversely they hold that they themselves are cassowaries, or at all events that they possess some of the qualities of the long-legged bird.   When a Cassowary man went forth to reap laurels on the field of battle, he used to reflect with satisfaction on the length of his lower limbs : "My leg is long and thin, I can run and not feel tired ; my legs will go quickly and the grass will not entangle them."[2]   Omaha Indians believe that between a man and the creature which is his guardian spirit there subsists so close a bond that the man acquires the powers and qualities, the virtues and defects of the animal.   Thus if a man has seen a bear in that vision at puberty which determines an Indian's guardian spirit, he will be apt to be wounded in battle, because the bear is a slow and clumsy animal and easily trapped.   If he has dreamed of an eagle, he will be able to see into the future and foretell coming events, because the eagle's vision is keen and piercing.[3] Similarly, the Thompson Indians of British Columbia imagined that every man partook of the nature of the animal which was his guardian spirit ; for example, a man who had the grisly bear for his protector would prove a much fiercer warrior than one who had only a crow, a coyote, or a fox for his guardian spirit.   And before they set out on the war-path these Indians used to perform a mimic battle, in which each man, tricked out with paint and feathers, imitated the sounds of the animal that was his guardian spirit, grunting and whooping in character.[4]   The

---

[1] Above, p. 141.

[2] A. C. Haddon, "The Ethnography of the Western Tribe of Torres Straits," *Journal of the Anthropological Institute*, xix. (1890) p. 393 ; *id.*, *Head-hunters* (London, 1901), p. 133; *Reports of the Cambridge Anthropological Expedition to Torres Straits*, v.

(Cambridge, 1904) p. 166.

[3] Miss Alice C. Fletcher, *The Import of the Totem, a Study from the Omaha Tribe*, p. 6 (paper read before the American Association for the Advancement of Science, August 1897).

[4] James Teit, "The Thompson Indians of British Columbia," p. 356 (*The Jesup North Pacific Expedition.*

Bororos, a tribe of Indians in the heart of Brazil, will have it that they are parrots of a gorgeous red plumage which live in the Brazilian forest.   It is not merely that their souls will pass into these birds at death, but they themselves are actually identical with them in their life, and accordingly they treat the parrots as they might treat their fellow-tribesmen, keeping them in captivity, refusing to eat their flesh, and mourning for them when they die.   However, they kill the wild birds for their feathers, and, though they will not kill, they pluck the tame ones to deck their own naked brown bodies with the gaudy plumage of their feathered brethren.[1]

Hence the savage attempts to propitiate the animals which he kills and the other members of the species.

Thus to the savage, who regards all living creatures as practically on a footing of equality with man, the act of killing and eating an animal must wear a very different aspect from that which the same act presents to us, who regard the intelligence of animals as far inferior to our own and deny them the possession of immortal souls.   Hence on the principles of his rude philosophy the primitive hunter who slays an animal believes himself exposed to the vengeance either of its disembodied spirit or of all the other animals of the same species, whom he considers as knit together, like men, by the ties of kin and the obligations of the blood feud, and therefore as bound to resent the injury done to one of their number.   Accordingly the savage makes it a rule to spare the life of those animals which he has no pressing motive for killing, at least such fierce and dangerous animals as are likely to exact a bloody vengeance for the slaughter of one of their kind.   Crocodiles are animals of this sort.   They are only found in hot countries, where, as a rule, food is abundant and primitive man has therefore little reason to kill them for the sake of their tough and unpalatable flesh.[2]   Hence it is a custom with some savages

---

Memoir of the American Museum of Natural History, April 1900).

[1] K. von den Steinen, *Unter den Naturvölkern Zentral-Brasiliens* (Berlin, 1894), pp. 352 *sq.*, 512.   The Chambioa Indians of Central Brazil kept birds of the same species in captivity and used their brilliant feathers to cover enormous head-dresses or masks, some six feet high, which were worn by dancers in certain mystic

dances.   The masks were guarded in a special hut of each village, and no woman might see them under pain of death.   See F. de Castelnau, *Expédition dans les parties centrales de l'Amérique du Sud* (Paris, 1850-1851), i. 436 *sq.*, 440, 449-451.

[2] However, many savages hunt the crocodile for the sake of its flesh, which some of them even regard as a delicacy.   See H. von Wissmann, *My*

to spare crocodiles, or rather only to kill them in obedience to the law of blood feud, that is, as a retaliation for the slaughter of men by crocodiles.   For example, the Dyaks of Borneo will not kill a crocodile unless a crocodile has first killed a man.   "For why, say they, should they commit an act of aggression, when he and his kindred can so easily repay them?   But should the alligator take a human life, revenge becomes a sacred duty of the living relatives, who will trap the man-eater in the spirit of an officer of justice pursuing a criminal.   Others, even then, hang back, reluctant to embroil themselves in a quarrel which does not concern them.   The man-eating alligator is supposed to be pursued by a righteous Nemesis ; and whenever one is caught they have a profound conviction that it must be the guilty one, or his accomplice." [1]

When a Dyak has made up his mind to take vengeance on the crocodiles for the death of a kinsman, he calls in the help of a Pangareran, a man whose business it is to charm and catch crocodiles and to make them do his will.   While he is engaged in the discharge of his pro-

---

Second Journey through Equatorial Africa, from the Congo to the Zambesi (London, 1891), p. 298 ; Ch. Partridge, *Cross River Natives* (London, 1905), p. 149 ; A. F. Mocler-Ferryman, *Up the Niger* (London, 1892), p. 222 ; Captain G. Burrows, *The Land of the Pigmies* (London, 1898), p. 247 ; R. E. Dennett, "Bavili Notes," *Folklore*, xvi. (1905) p. 399 ; J. Halkin, *Quelques Peuplades du district de l'Uélé*, I. *Les Ababua* (Liége, 1907), p. 33 ; H. Reynolds, "Notes on the Azandé Tribe of the Congo," *Journal of the African Society*, No. xi. (April, 1904) p. 242 ; Brard, "Der Victoria-Nyansa," *Petermann's Mittheilungen*, xliii. (1897) p. 78 ; A. van Gennep, *Tabou et Totémisme à Madagascar* (Paris, 1904), p. 209 ; G. Kurze, "Sitten und Gebräuche der Lengua-Indianer," *Mitteilungen der Geographischen Gesellschaft zu Jena*, xxiii. (1905) p. 30 ; W. Barbrooke Grubb, *An unknown People in an unknown Land* (London, 1911), pp. 82 sq. ; *Census of India, 1901*, vol. xxvi., *Travancore* (Trivandrum, 1903), p. 353 ; Max Krieger, *Neu-Guinea* (Berlin, N.D.), p. 163 ; Spencer and Gillen, *Northern Tribes of Central Australia* (London, 1904), p. 770 ; W. E. Roth, *Ethnological Studies among the North-West-Central Queensland Aborigines* (Brisbane and London, 1897), p. 94 ; N. W. Thomas, *Natives of Australia* (London, 1906), p. 106.   In antiquity some of the Egyptians worshipped crocodiles, but others killed and ate them.   See Herodotus, ii. 69 ; Plutarch, *Isis et Osiris*, 50 ; Aelian, *De natura animalium*, x. 21.

[1] Rev. J. Perham, "Sea Dyak Religion," *Journal of the Straits Branch of the Royal Asiatic Society*, No. 10 (Singapore, 1883), p. 221.   Compare C. Hupe, "Korte verhandeling over de godsdienst zeden, enz. der Dajakkers," *Tijdschrift voor Neêrlands Indië*, 1846, dl. iii. 160 ; S. Müller, *Reizen en onderzoekingen in den Indischen Archipel* (Amsterdam, 1857), i. 238 ; M. T. H. Perelaer, *Ethnographische Beschrijving der Dajaks* (Zalt-Bommel, 1870), p. 7.

fessional duties the crocodile-catcher has to observe a
number of odd rules.   He may not go to anybody and may
not even pass in front of a window, because he is unclean.
He may not himself cook anything nor come near a fire.
If he would eat fruit, he may not peel or husk it himself,
but must get others to do it for him.   He may not even
chew his food, but is obliged to swallow it unchewed.   A
little hut is made for him on the bank of the river, where he
uses divination by means of the figure of a crocodile drawn
on a piece of bamboo for the purpose of determining whether
his undertaking will prosper.   The boat in which he em-
barks to catch the wicked man-eating crocodile must be
painted yellow and red, and in the middle of it lances are
erected with the points upward.   Then the man of skill
casts lots to discover whether the hook is to be baited with
pork, or venison, or the flesh of a dog or an ass.   In throwing the baited hook into the water he calls out : " Ye
crocodiles who are up stream, come down ; and ye crocodiles
who are down stream, come up ; for I will give you all good
food, as sweet as sugar and as fat as coco-nut.   I will give
you a pretty and beautiful necklace.   When you have got
it, keep it in your neck and body, for this food is very
pahuni," which means that it would be sinful not to eat it.
If a crocodile bites at the hook, the crocodile-catcher
bawls out, " Choose a place for yourself where you will lie ;
for many men are come to see you.   They are come joy-
fully and exultingly, and they give you a knife, a lance, and
a shroud."   If the crocodile is a female, he addresses her as
" Princess " ; if it is a male, he calls it " Prince."   The enchanter, who is generally a cunning Malay, must continue his
operations till he catches a crocodile in which traces are to be
found shewing that the animal has indeed devoured a human
being.   Then the death of the man is atoned for, and in order
not to offend the water-spirits a cat is sacrificed to the crocodiles.   The heads of the dead crocodiles are fastened on stakes
beside the river, where in time they bleach white and stand out
sharply against the green background of the forest.[1]   While
the captured crocodile is being hauled in to the bank, the

[1] F. Grabowsky, "Die Theogonie   *nationales Archiv für Ethnographie*,
der Dajaken auf Borneo," *Inter-*   v. (1892) pp. 119 *sq.*

subtle Dyaks speak softly to him and beguile him into offering no resistance ; but once they have him fast, with arms and legs securely pinioned, they howl at him and deride him for his credulity, while they rip up the belly of the infuriated and struggling brute to find the evidence of his guilt in the shape of human remains.   On one occasion Rajah Brooke of Sarawak was present at a discussion among a party of Dyaks as to how they ought to treat a captured crocodile. One side maintained that it was proper to bestow all praise and honour on the kingly beast, since he was himself a rajah among animals and was now brought there to meet the rajah ; in short, they held that praise and flattery were agreeable to him and would put him on his best behaviour.   The other side fully admitted that on this occasion rajah met rajah ; yet with prudent foresight they pointed to the dangerous consequences which might flow from establishing a precedent such as their adversaries contended for.   If once a captured crocodile, said they, were praised and honoured, the other crocodiles, on hearing of it, would be puffed up with pride and ambition, and being seized with a desire to emulate the glory of their fellow would enter on a career of man-eating as the road likely to lead them by the shortest cut to the temple of fame.[1]

The Minangkabauers of Sumatra have also a great respect for crocodiles.   Their celebrated law-giver Katoemanggoengan was indeed born again in the form of a crocodile ; and thus his descendants, including the rajah of Indrapoera and his family, are more or less distant cousins of the crocodiles, and enjoy the help and protection of the creatures in many ways, for example when they go on a journey.   The respect entertained for the animals is also attested by the ceremonies observed in some places when a crocodile has been caught.   A crowd of women then performs certain dances which closely resemble the dances performed when somebody has died.   Moreover, it is a rule with the

Ceremonies observed by the Minangkabauers of Sumatra at killing a crocodile.

---

[1] H. Ling Roth, *The Natives of Sarawak and British North Borneo* (London, 1896), i. 447 *sq*. Compare E. H. Gomes, *Seventeen years among the Sea Dyaks of Borneo* (London, 1911), pp. 56-60. Similarly the Kenyahs, Kayans, and Ibans, three tribes of Sarawak, will not kill crocodiles except in revenge for the death of one of their people. See C. Hose and W. MacDougall, "The Relations between Men and Animals in Sarawak," *Journal of the Anthropological Institute*, xxxi. (1901) pp. 186, 190, 199, compare *ib*. pp. 193 *sq*.

Minangkabauers that no cooking-pot may be washed in a river; to do so would be like offering the crocodiles the leavings of your food, and they would very naturally resent it. For the same reason in washing up the dinner or supper plates you must be careful not to make a splashing, or the crocodiles would hear it and take umbrage.[1]

Belief in the kinship of men with crocodiles among the Malays. Among the Malays of Patani Bay, in Siam, there is a family whose members may not kill a crocodile nor even be present when one of these ferocious reptiles is captured. The reason alleged for this forbearance is that the family claim kindred with a woman named Betimor, who was drowned in the river and afterwards turned into a crocodile. After her transformation she appeared to her father in a dream and told him what had become of her; so he went down to the river and made offerings to her of rice and wax tapers. There is a shrine on the spot where the woman was transformed into a crocodile, and any one may dedicate offerings there and pray to Toh Sri Lam; for so she has been called ever since her metamorphosis. Members of the crocodile family call on her for help in sickness and other misfortunes, and they will do so on behalf of other people for a proper consideration. Rice and wax tapers are the usual offerings.[2] In many islands of the Indian Archipelago, including Java, Sumatra, Celebes, Timor, and Ceram, this belief in a kinship of men with crocodiles assumes a peculiar form. The people imagine that women are often delivered of a child and a crocodile at the same birth, and that when this happens, the midwife carries the crocodile twin carefully down to the river and places it in the water. The family in which such a birth is thought to have happened, constantly put victuals into the river for their amphibious relation; and in particular the human twin, so long as he lives, goes down to the river at stated seasons to do his duty by his crocodile brother or sister; and if he were to fail to do so, it is the universal opinion

---

[1] J. L. van der Toorn, "Het animisme bij den Minangkabauer der Padangsche Bovenlanden," *Bijdragen tot de Taal- Land- en Volkenkunde van Nederlandsch-Indië*, xxxix. (1890) pp. 75 *sq.*

[2] Nelson Annandale, "Primitive Beliefs and Customs of the Patani Fishermen," *Fasciculi Malayenses, Anthropology*, i. (April, 1903) pp. 76-78.

that he would be visited with sickness or death for his unnatural conduct. Large parties of these crocodile people periodically go out in a boat furnished with great plenty of provisions and all kinds of music, and they row backwards and forwards, with the music playing, in places where crocodiles do most abound. As they do so they sing and weep by turns, each of them invoking his animal kinsfolk, till the snout of one of the brutes bobbs up from the water, whereupon the music stops, and food, betel, and tobacco are thrown into the river. By these delicate attentions they hope to recommend themselves to the formidable creatures.[1]

The crocodiles about the island of Damba in the Victoria Nyanza were sacred and might not be molested in any way. Hence they multiplied and became dangerous ; people made offerings to them in the hope of being spared by the monsters when they crossed in the ferries. From time to time batches of men were brought down to the beach and sacrificed to the crocodiles. Their arms and legs were broken so that they could not stir from the spot ; then they were laid out in a row on the shore, and the crocodiles came and dragged them into the water. On the island there was a temple dedicated to the crocodiles, and here an inspired medium resided who gave oracular responses. Under the influence of the spirit he wagged his head from side to side, opening his jaws and snapping them together, just as a crocodile does.[2] No doubt the spirit which possessed him in these moments of fine frenzy was supposed to be that of a crocodile. Similarly in other parts of Uganda men were inspired by the ghosts or spirits of lions, leopards, and serpents, and in that state of exaltation they uttered oracles, roaring like a lion, growling like a leopard, or grovelling and wriggling like a serpent, according to the nature of the spirit by which they were possessed.[3] Crocodiles abound in the Albert Nyanza Lake and its tributaries. In many places they are extremely dangerous,

Crocodiles respected in Africa.

[1] *Voyages of Captain James Cook round the World* (London, 1809), ii. 316-319.

[2] Rev. J. Roscoe, *The Baganda* (London, 1911), p. 336.

[3] Rev. J. Roscoe, *op. cit.* pp. 318, 322, 335.

but the Alur tribe of that region only hunt them when they
have dragged away a man; and they think that any one
who has taken away a crocodile's eggs must be on his guard
when he walks near the bank of the river, for the crocodiles
will try to avenge the injury by seizing him.[1]   In general
the Foulahs of Senegambia dare not kill a crocodile from
fear of provoking the vengeance of the relations and friends
of the murdered reptile; but if the sorcerer gives his consent
and passes his word that he will guarantee them against the
vengeance of the family of the deceased, they will pluck up
courage to attack one of the brutes.[2]

Crocodiles
respected in
Madagas-
car.

Like the Dyaks, the natives of Madagascar never kill a
crocodile "except in retaliation for one of their friends who
has been destroyed by a crocodile.   They believe that the
wanton destruction of one of these reptiles will be followed
by the loss of human life, in accordance with the principle of
lex talionis."   The people who live near the lake Itasy in
Madagascar make a yearly proclamation to the crocodiles,
announcing that they will revenge the death of some of their
friends by killing as many crocodiles in return, and warning
all well-disposed crocodiles to keep out of the way, as they
have no quarrel with them, but only with their evil-minded
relations who have taken human life.[3]   Various tribes of
Madagascar believe themselves to be descended from crocodiles, and accordingly they view the scaly reptile as, to all
intents and purposes, a man and a brother.   If one of the
animals should so far forget himself as to devour one of his
human kinsfolk, the chief of the tribe, or in his absence an
old man familiar with the tribal customs, repairs at the head
of the people to the edge of the water, and summons the
family of the culprit to deliver him up to the arm of justice.
A hook is then baited and cast into the river or lake.   Next
day the guilty brother, or one of his family, is dragged ashore,
and after his crime has been clearly brought home to him by
a strict interrogation, he is sentenced to death and executed.
The claims of justice being thus satisfied and the majesty of

[1] Fr. Stuhlmann, *Mit Emin Pascha
ins Herz von Afrika* (Berlin, 1894), pp.
510 *sq.*

[2] A. Raffenel, *Voyage dans l'Afrique*

occidentale (Paris, 1846), pp. 84 *sq.*

[3] J. Sibree, *The Great African
Island* (London, 1880), p. 269.

the law fully vindicated, the deceased crocodile is lamented
and buried like a kinsman ; a mound is raised over his relics
and a stone marks the place of his head.[1]   The Malagasy,
indeed, regard the crocodile with superstitious veneration as
the king of the waters and supreme in his own element.
When they are about to cross a river they pronounce a
solemn oath, or enter into an engagement to acknowledge
his sovereignty over the waters.   An aged native has been
known to covenant with the crocodiles for nearly half an
hour before plunging into the stream.   After that he lifted
up his voice and addressed the animal, urging him to do
him no harm, since he had never hurt the crocodile ;
assuring him that he had never made war on any of his
fellows, but on the contrary had always entertained the
highest veneration for him ; and adding that if he wantonly
attacked him, vengeance would follow sooner or later ; while
if the crocodile devoured him, his relations and all his race
would declare war against the beast.   This harangue occupied
another quarter of an hour, after which the orator dashed
fearlessly into the stream.[2]

Again, the tiger is another of those dangerous beasts   *Tigers
whom the savage prefers to leave alone, lest by killing one of   respected in
Sumatra.*
the species he should excite the hostility of the rest.   No
consideration will induce a Sumatran to catch or wound
a tiger except in self-defence or immediately after a tiger
has destroyed a friend or relation.   When a European has
set traps for tigers, the people of the neighbourhood have
been known to go by night to the place and explain to the
animals that the traps are not set by them nor with their
consent.[3]   If it is necessary to kill a tiger which has wrought
much harm in the village, the Minangkabauers of Sumatra
try to catch him alive in order to beg for his forgiveness
before despatching him, and in ordinary life they will not
speak evil of him or do anything that might displease him.
For example, they will not use a path that has been un-
trodden for more than a year, because the tiger has chosen

---

[1] Father Abinal, "Croyances fabu-
leuses des Malgaches," *Les Missions
Catholiques*, xii. (1880) p. 527 ; A.
van Gennep, *Tabou et Totémisme à
Madagascar* (Paris, 1904), pp. 283 *sq.*

[2] W. Ellis, *History of Madagascar*
(London, N.D.), i. 57 *sq.*

[3] W. Marsden, *History of Sumatra*
(London, 1811), p. 292.

that path for himself, and would deem it a mark of disrespect were any one else to use it.   Again, persons journey-
ing by night will not walk one behind the other, nor keep
looking about them, for the tiger would think that this
betrayed fear of him, and his feelings would be hurt by the
suspicion.   Neither will they travel bareheaded, for that also
would be disrespectful to the tiger ; nor will they knock off
the glowing end of a firebrand, for the flying sparks are like
the tiger's glistering eyes, and he would treat this as an
attempt to mimic him.[1]   The population of Mandeling,
a district on the west coast of Sumatra, is divided into clans,
one of which claims to be descended from a tiger.   It is
believed that the animal will not attack or rend the members
of this clan, because they are his kinsmen.   When members
of the clan come upon the tracks of a tiger, they enclose
them with three little sticks as a mark of homage ; and when
a tiger has been shot, the women of the clan are bound

Ceremonies to offer betel to the dead beast.[2]   The Battas of Sumatra
at killing seldom kill a tiger except from motives of revenge, observing
tigers in
Sumatra the rule an eye for an eye and a tooth for a tooth, or, as
and they express it, " He who owes gold must pay in gold ;
Bengal he who owes breath (that is, life) must pay with breath."
Nor can the beast be attacked without some · ceremony ;
only weapons that have proved themselves able to kill may
be used for the purpose.   When the tiger has been killed,
they bring the carcase to the village, set offerings before
it, and burn incense over it, praying the spirit of the tiger to
quit its material envelope and enter the incense pot.   As
soon as the soul may be supposed to have complied with
this request, a speaker explains to the spirits in general
the reasons for killing the tiger, and begs them to set forth
these reasons to the departed soul of the beast, lest the latter
should be angry and the people should suffer in consequence.
Then they dance round the dead body of the tiger till they
can dance no longer, after which they skin the carcase and

---

[1] J. L. van der Toorn, "Het animisme bij den Minangkabauer der
Padangsche Bovenlanden," *Bijdragen
tot de Taal- Land- en Volkenkunde van
Nederlandsch Indië*, xxxix. (1890) pp.
74, 75 *sq.*

[2] H. Ris, " De onderafdeeling Man-
dailing Oeloe en Pahantan en hare
Bevolking," *Bijdragen tot de Taal-
Land- en Volkenkunde van Nederlandsch Indië*, xlvi. (1896) pp. 472
sq.

bury it.[1]   The inhabitants of the hills near Rajamahall, in
Bengal, believe that if any man kills a tiger without divine
orders, either he or one of his relations will be devoured by
a tiger.   Hence they are very averse to killing a tiger,
unless one of their kinsfolk has been carried off by one of
the beasts.   In that case they go out for the purpose of
hunting and slaying a tiger ; and when they have succeeded
they lay their bows and arrows on the carcase and invoke
God, declaring that they slew the animal in retaliation for
the loss of a kinsman.   Vengeance having been thus taken,
they swear not to attack another tiger except under similar
provocation.[2]   The natives of Cochin China have a great
respect for the tiger, whom they regard as a terrible divinity.
Yet they set traps for him and leave no stone unturned to
catch him.   Once he is ensnared, they offer him their excuses
and condolences for the painful position in which he finds
himself.[3]

The Indians of Carolina would not molest snakes when
they came upon them, but would pass by on the other side
of the path, believing that if they were to kill a serpent, the
reptile's kindred would destroy some of their brethren, friends,
or relations in return.[4]   So the Seminole Indians spared
the rattlesnake, because they feared that the soul of the
dead rattlesnake would incite its kinsfolk to take vengeance.
Once when a rattlesnake appeared in their camp they
entreated an English traveller to rid them of the creature.
When he had killed it, they were glad but tried to scratch
him as a means of appeasing the spirit of the dead snake.[5]
Soon after the Iowas began to build their village near the
mouth of Wolf River, a lad came into the village and
reported that he had seen a rattlesnake on a hill not far off.
A medicine-man immediately repaired to the spot, and finding the snake made it presents of tobacco and other things
which he had brought with him for the purpose.   He also

*Snakes,
especially
rattle-
snakes,
respected
by the
North
American
Indians.*

---

[1] G. G. Batten, *Glimpses of the
Eastern Archipelago* (Singapore, 1894),
p. 86.

[2] Th. Shaw, "On the Inhabitants
of the Hills near Rajamahall," *Asiatic
Researches*, Fourth Edition, iv. (London, 1807) p. 37.

[3] *Annales de l'Association de la Pro-*
pagation de la Foi, v. (1831) pp. 363 *sq.*

[4] J. Bricknell, *The Natural History
of North Carolina* (Dublin, 1737), p.
368.

[5] W. Bartram, *Travels through
North and South Carolina, Georgia,
East and West Florida*, etc. (London,
1792) pp. 258-261.

had a long talk with the animal, and on returning to his
people told them that now they might travel about in safety,
for peace had been made with the snakes.[1]   The Delaware
Indians also paid great respect to the rattlesnake, whom
they called their grandfather, and they would on no account
destroy one of the reptiles.   They said that the rattlesnake
guarded them and gave them notice of impending danger
by his rattle, and that if they were to kill a rattlesnake, the
rest of the species would soon hear of it and bite the Indians
in revenge.[2]   The Potawatomi Indians highly venerated the
rattlesnake for a similar reason, being grateful to it for the
timely warning which it often gave of the approach of an
enemy.   Yet a young man who desired to obtain a rattle
would have no hesitation in killing one of the snakes for the
purpose ; but he apologised profusely to the creature for the
liberty he took with it, explaining that he required the rattle
for the adornment of his person, and that no disrespect was
intended to the snake ; and in proof of his good will he
would leave a piece of tobacco beside the carcase.[3]   The
Cherokee regard the rattlesnake as the chief of the snake
tribe and fear and respect him accordingly.   Few Cherokee
will venture to kill a rattlesnake, unless they cannot help it,
and even then they must atone for the crime by craving
pardon of the snake's ghost either in their own person or
through the mediation of a priest, according to a set formula.
If these precautions are neglected, the kinsfolk of the dead
snake will send one of their number as an avenger of blood,
who will track down the murderer and sting him to death.
It is absolutely necessary to cut off the snake's head and
bury it deep in the earth and to hide the body in a hollow
log ; for if the remains were exposed to the weather, the
other snakes would be so angry that they would send
torrents of rain and all the streams would overflow their
banks.   If a Cherokee dreams of being bitten by a snake,

[1] H. R. Schoolcraft, *Indian Tribes
of the United States* (Philadelphia,
1853-1856), iii. 273.

[2] Rev. John Heckewelder, " An
Account of the History, Manners,
and Customs of the Indian Nations
who once inhabited Pennsylvania and
the neighbouring States," *Transactions
of the Historical and Literary Committee of the American Philosophical
Society*, i. (Philadelphia, 1819) p. 245.

[3] W. Keating, *Narrative of an
Expedition to the Source of St. Peter's
River* (London, 1825), i. 127.

he must be treated in exactly the same way as if he had
been really bitten ; for they think that he has actually been
bitten by the ghost of a snake, and that if the proper
remedies were not applied to the hurt, the place would swell
and ulcerate, though possibly not for years afterwards.[1]
Once when an Englishman attempted to kill a rattlesnake,
a party of Ojibway Indians, with whom he was travelling,
begged him to desist, and endeavoured to appease the snake,
addressing it in turns as grandfather, smoking over it, and
beseeching it to take care of their families in their absence,
and to open the heart of the British Agent so that he should
fill their canoe with rum.   A storm which overtook them
next day on Lake Huron was attributed by them to the
wrath of the insulted rattlesnake, and they sought to mollify
him by throwing dogs as sacrifices to him into the waves.[2]
The Kekchi Indians of Guatemala will not throw serpents
or scorpions into the fire, lest the other creatures of the same
species should punish them for the outrage.[3]

In Kiziba, a district of Central Africa, to the west of Lake
Victoria Nyanza, if a woman accidentally kills a snake with
her hoe while she is working in the field, she hastens in
great agitation to the snake-priest and hands him over the
hoe, together with two strings of cowries and an ox-hide,
begging him to appease the angry spirit of the slain serpent.
In this application she is accompanied and supported by all
the villagers, who share her fears and anxiety.   Accordingly
the priest beats his drum as a sign that no woman of the
village is to work in the fields till further notice.   Next he
wraps the dead serpent in a piece of the ox-hide and buries
it solemnly.   On the following day he performs a ceremony of
purification for the slaughter of the reptile.   He compounds
a medicine out of the guts of a leopard or hyaena and
earth or mud dissolved in water, and with this mixture
he disinfects all the houses in the village, beginning with

Ceremonies observed in Kiziba at the killing of a snake.

---

[1] J. Mooney, " Myths of the
Cherokee," *Nineteenth Annual Report
of the Bureau of American Ethnology,*
Part i. (Washington, 1900) pp. 294-
296.   Compare *id.,* pp. 456-458 ;
J. Adair, *History of the American
Indians* (London, 1775), pp. 237 *sq.*

[2] Henry, *Travels,* pp. 176-179,
quoted by J. Mooney, *op. cit.* pp.
457 *sq.*

[3] C. Sapper, "Die Gebräuche und
religiösen Anschauungen der Kekchí-
Indianer," *Internationales Archiv für
Ethnographie,* viii. (1895) p. 204.

the house of the woman who killed the serpent. Next he proceeds to the fields, where all the women of the village have collected their hoes. These he purifies by dipping them in the fluid and then twirling them about so as to make the drops of water fly off. From that moment the danger incurred by the slaughter of the reptile is averted. The spirit of the serpent is appeased, and the women may resume their usual labours in the fields.[1]

Ceremonies observed by the North American Indians and others at the killing of a wolf.

When the Kwakiutl Indians of British Columbia have slain a wolf they lay the carcase on a blanket and take out the heart, of which every person who helped to kill the beast must eat four morsels. Then they wail over the body, saying, "Woe! our great friend!" After that they cover the carcase with a blanket and bury it. A bow or gun that killed a wolf is regarded as unlucky, and the owner gives it away. These Indians believe that the slaying of a wolf produces a scarcity of game.[2] When the Tinneh Indians of Central Alaska have killed a wolf or a wolverine, the carcase is brought into the camp or village with great pomp. The people go forth to meet it, saying, "The chief is coming." Then the body is carried into a hut and propped up in a sitting posture; and the medicine-man spreads before it a copious banquet, to which every family in the village has contributed of its best. When the dead animal is supposed to have satisfied his hunger, the men consume the remains of the feast, but no woman is allowed to participate in what has been thus offered to the wolf or the wolverine.[3] No ordinary Cherokee dares to kill a wolf, if he can possibly help it; for he believes that the kindred of the slain beast would surely avenge its death, and that the weapon with which the deed had been done would be quite useless for the future, unless it were cleaned and exorcised by a medicine-man. However, certain persons who know the proper rites of atonement for such a crime can kill wolves with impunity, and they are sometimes hired to do so by people who have suffered from the raids of the

---

[1] H. Rehse, *Kiziba, Land und Leute* (Stuttgart, 1910), pp. 130 *sq.*

[2] Fr. Boas, in *Eleventh Report on the North-Western Tribes of Canada*, pp. 9 *sq.* (separate reprint from the *Report of the British Association for 1896*).

[3] Rev. J. Jetté, "On the Medicine-men of the Ten'a," *Journal of the Royal Anthropological Institute*, xxxvii. (1907) p. 158.

wolves on their cattle or fish-traps.   The professional wolf-killer prays to the animal whom he has bereaved of life, and seeks to avert the vengeance of the other wolves by laying the blame of the slaughter on the people of another settlement.   To purify the gun which has perpetrated the murder, he unscrews the barrel, inserts into it seven small sour-wood rods which have been heated in the fire, and then allows the barrel and its contents to lie in a running stream till morning.[1] When the Chuckchees of north-eastern Siberia have killed a wolf, they hold a festival, at which they cry, " Wolf, be not angry with us.   It was not we who killed you, it was the Russians who destroyed you." [2]   In ancient Athens any man who killed a wolf had to bury it by subscription.[3]

In Jebel-Nuba, a district of the eastern Sudan, it is forbidden to touch the nests or remove the young of a species of black birds, resembling our blackbirds, because the people believe that the parent birds would avenge the wrong by causing a stormy wind to blow, which would destroy the harvest.[4]   Some of the Sudanese negroes of Upper Egypt regard the great black raven (*Corvus umbrinus*) as their uncle and exact pecuniary compensation or blood-money from any one who has been so rash as to slay their sable relative.   Having satisfied their scruples on that head, they give the bird a solemn burial, carrying the corpse to the graveyard on a bier with flags and shouts of *la ill Allah*, just as if they were interring one of their kinsfolk.[5]   The Palenques of South America are very careful to spare harmless animals which are not good for food ; because they believe that any injury inflicted on such creatures would entail the sickness or death of their own children.[6]

But the savage clearly cannot afford to spare all animals. He must either eat some of them or starve, and when the question thus comes to be whether he or the animal must

Certain birds respected.

---

[1] J. Mooney, " Myths of the Cherokee," *Nineteenth Annual Report of the Bureau of American Ethnology*, Part i. (Washington, 1900) p. 265.

[2] T. de Pauly, *Description Ethno-graphique des Peuples de la Russie* (St. Petersburg, 1862), *Peuples de la Sibérie Orientale*, p. 7.

[3] Scholiast on Apollonius Rhodius, *Argonaut.* ii. 124.

[4] " Coutumes étranges des indigènes du Djebel-Nouba," *Les Missions Catholiques*, xiv. (1882) p. 458.

[5] C. B. Klunzinger, *Upper Egypt* (London, 1878), pp. 402 *sq.*

[6] Caulin, *Historia Coro - graphica natural y evangelica dela Nueva Andalucia*, p. 96 : " *Reusan mucho matar qualquier animal no comestibile que no sea nocibo*," etc.   Here *reusan* appears to be a misprint for *recusan*.

perish, he is forced to overcome his superstitious scruples and take the life of the beast. At the same time he does all he can to appease his victims and their kinsfolk. Even in the act of killing them he testifies his respect for them, endeavours to excuse or even conceal his share in procuring their death, and promises that their remains will be honourably treated. By thus robbing death of its terrors he hopes to reconcile his victims to their fate and to induce their fellows to come and be killed also. For example, it was a principle with the Kamtchatkans never to kill a land or sea animal without first making excuses to it and begging that the animal would not take it ill. Also they offered it cedar-nuts and so forth, to make it think that it was not a victim but a guest at a feast. They believed that this hindered

other animals of the same species from growing shy. For instance, after they had killed a bear and feasted on its flesh, the host would bring the bear's head before the company, wrap it in grass, and present it with a variety of trifles. Then he would lay the blame of the bear's death on the Russians, and bid the beast wreak his wrath upon them. Also he would ask the bear to inform the other bears how well he had been treated, that they too might come without fear. Seals, sea-lions, and other animals were treated by the Kamtchatkans with the same ceremonious respect. Moreover, they used to insert sprigs of a plant resembling bear's wort in the mouths of the animals they killed ; after which they would exhort the grinning skulls to have no fear but to go and tell it to their fellows, that they also might come and be caught and so partake of this splendid hospitality.[1] When the Ostiaks have hunted and killed a bear, they cut off its head and hang it on a tree. Then they gather round in a circle and pay it divine honours. Next they run towards the carcase uttering lamentations and saying, " Who killed you? It was the Russians. Who cut off your head? It was a Russian axe. Who skinned you? It was a knife made by a Russian." They explain, too, that the feathers which sped the arrow on its flight came from the wing of a strange bird, and that they did nothing but let the arrow go.

---

[1] G. W. Steller, *Beschreibung von dem Lande Kamtschatka* (Frankfort and Leipsic, 1774), pp. 85, 280, 331.

They do all this because they believe that the wandering ghost of the slain bear would attack them on the first opportunity, if they did not thus appease it.[1]   Or they stuff the skin of the slain bear with hay ; and after celebrating their victory with songs of mockery and insult, after spitting on and kicking it, they set it up on its hind legs, " and then, for a considerable time, they bestow on it all the veneration due to a guardian god." [2]   When a party of Koryak have killed a bear or a wolf, they skin the beast and dress one of themselves in the skin.   Then they dance round the skin-clad man, saying that it was not they who killed the animal, but some one else, generally a Russian.   When they kill a fox they skin it, wrap the body in grass, and bid him go tell his companions how hospitably he has been received, and how he has received a new cloak instead of his old one.[3]   A fuller account of the Koryak ceremonies is given by a more recent writer.   He tells us that when a dead bear is brought to the house, the women come out to meet it dancing with firebrands.   The bear-skin is taken off along with the head ; and one of the women puts on the skin, dances in it, and entreats the bear not to be angry, but to be kind to the people.   At the same time they offer meat on a wooden platter to the dead beast, saying, " Eat, friend."   Afterwards a ceremony is performed for the purpose of sending the dead bear, or rather his spirit, away back to his home.   He is provided with provisions for the journey in the shape of puddings or reindeer-flesh packed in a grass bag.   His skin is stuffed with grass and carried round the house, after which he is supposed to depart towards the rising sun.   The intention of the ceremonies is to protect the people from the wrath of the slain bear and his kinsfolk, and so to ensure success in future bear-hunts.[4]   The Finns used to try to

---

[1] *Voyages au Nord* (Amsterdam, 1727), viii. 41, 416 ; P. S. Pallas, *Reise durch verschiedene Provinzen des russischen Reichs* (St. Petersburg, 1771-1776), iii. 64 ; J. G. Georgi, *Beschreibung aller Nationen des russischen Reichs* (St. Petersburg, 1776), p. 83.

[2] A. Erman, *Travels in Siberia* (London, 1848), ii. 43.   For the veneration of the polar bear by the Samoyedes, who nevertheless kill and eat it, see *ibid.* pp. 54 *sq.*

[3] A. Bastian, *Der Mensch in der Geschichte* (Leipsic, 1860), iii. 26.

[4] W. Jochelson, *The Koryak* (Leyden and New York, 1908), pp. 88 *sq.* (*The Jesup North Pacific Expedition*, vol. vi., *Memoir of the American Museum of Natural History*).

persuade a slain bear that he had not been killed by them, but had fallen from a tree, or met his death in some other way ;[1] moreover, they held a funeral festival in his honour, at the close of which bards expatiated on the homage that had been paid to him, urging him to report to the other bears the high consideration with which he had been treated, in order that they also, following his example, might come and be slain.[2]   When the Lapps had succeeded in killing a bear with impunity, they thanked him for not hurting them and for not breaking the clubs and spears which had given him his death wounds ; and they prayed that he would not visit his death upon them by sending storms or in any other way.   His flesh then furnished a feast.[3]

Propitia-
tion of
slain bears
by the
North
American
Indians.   The reverence of hunters for the bear whom they regularly kill and eat may thus be traced all along the northern region of the Old World, from Bering's Straits to Lappland.   It reappears in similar forms in North America.   With the American Indians a bear hunt was an important event for which they prepared by long fasts and purgations.   Before setting out they offered expiatory sacrifices to the souls of bears slain in previous hunts, and besought them to be favourable to the hunters.   When a bear was killed the hunter lit his pipe, and putting the mouth of it between the bear's lips, blew into the bowl, filling the beast's mouth with smoke.   Then he begged the bear not to be angry at having been killed, and not to thwart him afterwards in the chase.   The carcase was roasted whole and eaten ; not a morsel of the flesh might be left over.   The head, painted red and blue, was hung on a post and addressed by orators, who heaped praise on the dead beast.[4]   When men of the Bear clan in the Otawa tribe killed a bear, they made him a feast of his own flesh, and addressed him thus : " Cherish us no grudge because we

[1] Max Buch, *Die Wotjäken* (Stutt-gart, 1882), p. 139.

[2] A. Featherman, *Social History of the Races of Mankind, Fourth Division, Dravido - Turanians*, etc. (London, 1891) p. 422.

[3] J. Scheffer, *Lapponia* (Frankfort, 1673), pp. 233 *sq.*   The Lapps "have still an elaborate ceremony in hunting the bear.   They pray and chant to his carcase, and for several days worship before eating it " (E. Rae, *The White Sea Peninsula* (London, 1881), p. 276).

[4] Charlevoix, *Histoire de la Nouvelle France* (Paris, 1744), v. 173 *sq.* ; Chateaubriand, *Voyage en Amérique*, pp. 172-181 (Paris, Michel Lévy, 1870).

have killed you.   You have sense ; you see that our children
are hungry.   They love you and wish to take you into their
bodies.   Is it not glorious to be eaten by the children
of a chief?"[1]   Amongst the Nootka Indians of British
Columbia, when a bear had been killed, it was brought in
and seated before the head chief in an upright posture, with
a chief's bonnet, wrought in figures, on its head, and its fur
powdered over with white down.   A tray of provisions was
then set before it, and it was invited by words and gestures
to eat.   After that the animal was skinned, boiled, and
eaten.[2]   The Assiniboins pray to the bear and offer sacrifices to it of tobacco, belts, and other valuable objects.   Moreover, they hold feasts in its honour, that they may win the
beast's favour and live safe and sound.   The bear's head is
often kept in camp for several days mounted in some suitable position and decked with scraps of scarlet cloth, neck-
laces, collars, and coloured feathers.   They offer the pipe to
it, and pray that they may be able to kill all the bears they
meet, without harm to themselves, for the purpose of anointing themselves with his fine grease and banqueting on his
tender flesh.[3]   The Ojibways will not suffer dogs to eat the
flesh or gnaw the bones of a bear, and they throw all the
waste portions into the fire.   They think that if the flesh
were desecrated, they would have no luck in hunting bears
thereafter.[4]   A trader of the eighteenth century has described
the endearments which a party of Ojibways lavished on a
she-bear which he had just killed.   They took her head in
their hands, stroked it and kissed it, and begged a thousand
pardons for her violent death ; they called her their relation
and grandmother, and begged her not to lay the fault at
their door, for indeed it was an Englishman who had killed

---

[1] *Lettres édifiantes et curieuses,*
Nouvelle Édition, vi. (Paris, 1781) p.
171.   L. H. Morgan states that the
names of the Otawa totem clans had
not been obtained (*Ancient Society,*
London, 1877, p. 167).   From the
Lettres édifiantes, vi. 168-171, he might
have learned the names of the Hare,
Carp, and Bear clans, to which may
be added the Gull clan, as I learn from
an extract from *The Canadian Journal*
(Toronto) for March 1858, quoted in

The Academy, 27th September 1884,
p. 203.
[2] *A Narrative of the Adventures
and Sufferings of John R. Jewitt,* p.
117 (Middletown, 1820), p. 133 (Edinburgh, 1824).
[3] De Smet, *Western Missions and
Missionaries* (New York, 1863), p. 139.
[4] A. P. Reid, "Religious Belief of
the Ojibois Indians," *Journal of the
Anthropological Institute,* iii. (1874)
p. 111.

her. Having severed the head from the body, they adorned
it with all the trinkets they could muster and set it up on a
scaffold in the lodge.   Next day pipes were lit and tobacco
smoke blown into the nostrils of the dead bear, and the
trader was invited to pay this mark of respect to the animal
as an atonement for having taken her life.   Before they
feasted on the bear's flesh, an orator made a speech in which
he deplored the sad necessity under which they laboured of
destroying their friends the bears ; for how otherwise could
they subsist ? [1]   Some of the Indians of the Queen Charlotte Islands, off the north-western coast of America, used
to mark the skins of bears, otters, and other animals with
four red crosses in a line, by way of propitiating the spirit
of the beast they had killed.[2] When the Thompson Indians
of British Columbia were about to hunt bears, they would
sometimes address the animal and ask it to come and be
shot.   They prayed the grisly bear not to be angry with the
hunter, nor to fight him, but rather to have pity on him and
to deliver himself up to his mercies.   The man who intended
to hunt the grisly bear had to be chaste for some time before
he set out on his dangerous adventure.   When he had killed
a bear, he and his companions painted their faces in alternate
perpendicular stripes of black and red, and sang the bear
song.   Sometimes the hunter also prayed, thanking the beast
for letting itself be killed so easily, and begging that its
mate might share the same fate.   After they had eaten the
flesh of the bear's head, they tied the skull to the top of a
small tree, as high as they could reach, and left it there.
Having done so, they painted their faces with alternate stripes
of red and black as before ; for if they failed to observe this
ceremony, the bears would be offended, and the hunters
would not be able to kill any more.   To place the heads of
bears or any large beasts on trees or stones was a mark of
respect to the animals.[3]   The Lillooet and Shuswap Indians

---

[1] Henry's *Travels*, pp. 143-145,
quoted by J. Mooney, "Myths of the
Cherokee," *Nineteenth Annual Report
of the Bureau of American Ethnology*,
Part i. (Washington, 1900), pp. 446
sp.

[2] A. Mackenzie, "Descriptive notes

on certain implements, weapons, etc.,
from Graham Island, Queen Charlotte
Islands, B.C.," *Transactions of the
Royal Society of Canada*, ix. (1891)
section ii. p. 58.

[3] James Teit, *The Thompson Indians
of British Columbia*, p. 347 (*The Jesup*

of the same region used to observe similar ceremonies at the killing of a bear.[1]

A like respect is testified for other dangerous creatures by the hunters who regularly trap and kill them. When Caffre hunters are in the act of showering spears on an elephant, they call out, " Don't kill us, great captain ; don't strike or tread upon us, mighty chief." [2] When he is dead they make their excuses to him, pretending that his death was a pure accident. As a mark of respect they bury his trunk with much solemn ceremony ; for they say that " the elephant is a great lord ; his trunk is his hand." [3] Before the Amaxosa Caffres attack an elephant they shout to the animal and beg him to pardon them for the slaughter they are about to perpetrate, professing great submission to his person and explaining clearly the need they have of his tusks to enable them to procure beads and supply their wants. When they have killed him they bury in the ground, along with the end of his trunk, a few of the articles they have obtained for the ivory, thus hoping to avert some mishap that would otherwise befall them.[4] Among the Wanyamwezi of Central Africa, when hunters have killed an elephant, they bury his legs on the spot where he fell and then cover the place with stones. The burial is supposed to appease the spirit of the dead elephant and to ensure the success of the hunters in future undertakings.[5] When the Baganda have killed an elephant, they extract the nerve from the tusk and bury it, taking care to mark the place of the burial. For they think that the ghost of the dead elephant attaches itself to the nerve, and that if a

Propitia-tion of slain elephants in Africa.

North Pacific Expedition, Memoir of the American Museum of Natural History, April 1900). The Thompson Indians used to be known as the Couteau or Knife Indians.

[1] J. Teit, *The Lillooet Indians* (Leyden and New York, 1906), p. 279 (*The Jesup North Pacific Expedition, Memoir of the American Museum of Natural History*) ; *id., The Shuswap* (Leyden and New York, 1909), pp. 602 *sq.* (*The Jesup North Pacific Expedition*).

[2] Stephen Kay, *Travels and Researches in Caffraria* (London, 1833),

p. 138.

[3] L. Alberti, *De Kaffers aan de Zuidkust van Afrika* (Amsterdam, 1810), p. 95. Alberti's information is repeated by H. Lichtenstein (*Reisen im südlichen Afrika,* Berlin, 1811-1812, i. 412) and by Cowper Rose (*Four Years in Southern Africa,* London, 1829, p. 155). The burial of the trunk is also mentioned by Kay, *l.c.*

[4] J. Shooter, *The Kafirs of Natal* (London, 1857), p. 215.

[5] Fr. Stuhlmann, *Mit Emin Pascha ins Herz von Afrika* (Berlin, 1894), p. 87.

hunter were to step over the nerve, the elephant's ghost would cause him to be killed by an elephant the next time he went forth to hunt the beasts.[1]

Propitiation of lions in Africa. In Latuka, a district of the Upper Nile, lions are much respected, and are only killed when they prove very troublesome and dangerous. There used to be in this region a Lion-chief, as he was called, who professed to have all lions under his control, and who actually kept several tame lions about his house. Whenever a lion was accidentally caught in a trap near the station of the Egyptian Government, this man would regularly present himself and demand the release of the noble animal. The favour was always granted, and planks were let down into the pit to enable the imprisoned lion to clamber up and escape.[2] Amongst some tribes of Eastern Africa, when a lion is killed, the carcase is brought before the king, who does homage to it by prostrating himself on the ground and rubbing his face on the muzzle of the beast.[3]

Propitiation of slain leopards in Africa. In some parts of Western Africa if a negro kills a leopard he is bound fast and brought before the chiefs for having killed one of their peers. The man defends himself on the plea that the leopard is chief of the forest and therefore a stranger. He is then set at liberty and rewarded. But the dead leopard, adorned with a chief's bonnet, is set up in the village, where nightly dances are held in its honour.[4] The leopard is held in great veneration by the Igaras of the Niger. They call it "father" (*atta*), though they do not object to kill the animal in the chase. When a dead leopard is brought into Idah, the capital, it is dressed up in white and borne on the heads of four men from house to house, amidst singing and beating of drums. Each householder gives a present of cowries or cloth to the owner of the leopard, and at last the carcase is buried with great ceremony and firing of guns. Should these rites be neglected, the people imagine that the spirit of the dead leopard will punish them.[5] Among the Ewe negroes of Togoland

[1] Rev. J. Roscoe, *The Baganda* (London, 1911), p. 447

[2] Fr. Stuhlmann, *Mit Emin Pascha ins Herz von Afrika* (Berlin, 1894), p. 785.

[3] J. Becker, *La Vie en Afrique* (Paris and Brussels, 1887), ii. 298 *sq.*, 305.

[4] A. Bastian, *Die deutsche Expedition an der Loango-Küste* (Jena, 1874-1875), ii. 243.

[5] A. F. Mockler-Ferryman, *Up the Niger* (London, 1892), p. 309.

"hunters who had killed buffaloes, leopards, or wild black swine observed in Agome for nine days the same, or very similar, ceremonies as are customary at the death of a woman, in order to prevent the soul of the slain beasts from avenging itself on them, a custom which is the less surprising because the mourning customs themselves are based on the fear of spirits, namely the spirits of the dead. The natives ascribe to the souls of these dangerous animals the power of killing the man who shot them, or of so blinding and enchanting him that in the chase he confuses animals and men and so incurs serious mishaps."[1]   The quaint ceremonies which these negroes observe for the purpose of avoiding the imaginary perils have been described by a German missionary. The leopard and the wild buffalo, he tells us, are believed to be animated by malignant souls which not only do the hunter a mischief while they still occupy the bodies of the living creatures, but even after death, in their disembodied state, continue to haunt and plague their slayer, sometimes egging on a serpent or a leopard to sting or bite him, sometimes blinding him so that he shoots a man for an animal, or cannot find his way home and goes groping about in the wilderness till he perishes miserably. If a man thus blinded and crazed should make his way back to the town, he is banished for life and sold into slavery ; his house and plantation are razed to the ground ; and his nearest relations are often given as bail into the hands of strangers. It is therefore a very serious matter indeed for a hunter to incur the wrath of a leopard's ghost, and it is quite natural that he should take all reasonable measures to guard himself against so threatening a calamity. Hence as soon as he has killed a leopard, he hurries back to the town and brings word of it to the other men who have slain leopards on former occasions, and who now assist him with their advice and experience. The first thing they do is to put a stalk of grass in his mouth as a sign that he may not speak.

---

[1] Lieut. Herold, "Bericht betreffend religiöse Anschauungen und Gebräuche der deutschen Ewe-Neger," *Mittheilungen von Forschungsreisenden und Gelehrten aus den deutschen Schutzgebieten,* v. Heft 4 (Berlin, 1892), p. 156.

Then they repair to the place where the leopard lies dead in the forest, and inform the animal of the reasons why he has been shot, namely, because he has stolen sheep, fowls, and pigs, and has killed men.   Next the drums are beaten and the people assemble in the open square of the town.   The dead leopard meanwhile has been fastened to a pole, and with his eyes bandaged and his face upturned to heaven, is solemnly carried about the town and set down before the houses of the principal folk, who reward the hero and his comrades with presents.   After the procession has gone the round, the leopard is tied to a tree, and the hunters paint the slayer with red and white so as to make him look like a leopard, except that the leopard's spots are only painted on the left side of his body; a basket painted in the same colours is clapped on his head, and magical strings of cowries are tied round his hands and feet.   Thus attired, he and the other heroes who have killed leopards crawl about on all fours and roar like leopards when anybody comes near them.   In his left hand every man grasps a bow for the slaughter of innocent cocks and hens, and with his right he grabbles about in the earth like an animal seeking what it may devour.   None of them may speak, they may only roar, but they do that in a masterly manner.   At the head of this imposing procession go two men armed with a thick cudgel and a spear respectively; and the rear is brought up by a third man, who is privileged to walk upright on his hind legs.   This favoured person is the cook, whose office it is to dress the fowls which the human leopards purloin in the course of their pilgrimage; indeed for nineteen days they are privileged, no doubt in their character of leopards, to rob the hen-roosts with impunity.   In the afternoon the carcase of the leopard is taken down, skinned, and cut up.   The titbits are sent to the chief and the other dignitaries, who eat them; and the remainder of the flesh is consumed by the common folk.   The skin, the teeth, the head, and the claws belong to the hunter who killed the beast.   But for nineteen days thereafter the slayer of the leopard must retain his peculiar costume: he may eat only warm-blooded animals and food seasoned with salt: he may not eat anything seasoned with pepper; and on no account may he taste fish, because they are cold-blooded creatures. A general feast, of which all the male inhabitants of the town partake, winds up the proceedings at the close of the nineteen days. A feature of the festivities is a dramatic representation of a leopard-hunt, which is carried out in every detail amid great excitement. If only all these ceremonies are strictly observed, the hunter need have no fear at all of being plagued by the leopard's ghost.[1]

The Baganda greatly fear the ghosts of buffaloes which they have killed, and they always appease these dangerous spirits. On no account will they bring the head of a slain buffalo into a village or into a garden of plantains : they always eat the flesh of the head in the open country. Afterwards they place the skull in a small hut built for the purpose, where they pour out beer as an offering and pray to the ghost to stay where he is and not to harm them.[2] Oddly enough the Baganda also dread the ghosts of sheep, which they believe would haunt and kill the butcher if they saw him give the fatal stroke. Hence when a man is about to slaughter a sheep, he gets another man to divert its attention, and coming up behind the unsuspecting animal he stuns it with the blow of an axe-handle ; then, before it can recover consciousness, he adroitly cuts its throat. In this way the ghost of the sheep is bamboozled and will not haunt the butcher. Moreover, when a sheep dies in a house, the housewife may not say bluntly to her husband, "The sheep is dead," or its ghost, touched to the quick, would certainly make her fall ill and might even kill her. She must put a finer point on the painful truth by saying, "I am unable to untie such and such a sheep." Her husband understands her, but the ghost of the animal does not, or at all events he does not resent so delicate an allusion to its melancholy decease.[3] Even the ghost of a fowl may haunt a Muganda

Propitiation of slain buffaloes and sheep in Uganda.

---

[1] H. Spieth, "Jagdgebräuche in Avatime," *Mitteilungen der geographischen Gesellschaft zu Jena*, ix. (1890) pp. 18-20. Compare H. Klose, *Togo unter deutscher Flagge* (Berlin, 1899), pp. 145-147. The ceremonies observed after the slaughter of a wild buffalo are of the same general character with variations in detail.

[2] Rev. J. Roscoe, "Further Notes on the Manners and Customs of the Baganda," *Journal of the Anthropological Institute*, xxxii. (1902) p. 54 ; *id.*, *The Baganda* (London, 1911), pp. 289, 448.

[3] Rev. J. Roscoe, *The Baganda* (London, 1911), pp. 288 *sq.* Another curious notion which the Baganda have

woman and make her ill, if she has accidentally killed it with her hoe and flung away the body in the long grass instead of carrying it to her husband and confessing her fault.[1]

Propitiation of dead whales among the Koryak. Another formidable beast whose life the savage hunter takes with joy, yet with fear and trembling, is the whale. After the slaughter of a whale the maritime Koryak of north-eastern Siberia hold a communal festival, the essential part of which " is based on the conception that the whale killed has come on a visit to the village ; that it is staying for some time, during which it is treated with great respect ; that it then returns to the sea to repeat its visit the following year ; that it will induce its relatives to come along, telling them of the hospitable reception that has been accorded to it. According to the Koryak ideas, the whales, like all other animals, constitute one tribe, or rather family, of related individuals, who live in villages like the Koryak. They avenge the murder of one of their number, and are grateful for kindnesses that they may have received." [2] As large whales are now rarely seen in the bays of the Okhotsk Sea, the Koryak at the present time generally celebrate the festival for a white whale. One such festival was witnessed by Mr. W. Jochelson, at the village of Kuel, in October 1900. A white whale had been caught in the nets, and as the sea was partially frozen, the carcase had to be brought ashore in a sledge. When it was seen nearing the beach, a number of women, arrayed in their long embroidered dancing-coats, went forth to meet and welcome it, carrying lighted fire-brands in their hands. To carry burning fire-brands from the hearth is the ancient Koryak fashion of greeting an honoured guest. Strictly speaking, the women who go forth to welcome a whale to the house should wear masks of sedge-grass on their faces as well as dancing-coats on their bodies, and should carry sacrificial alder branches as well as fire-

---

about sheep is that they give health to cattle and prevent them from being struck by lightning. Hence a sheep is often herded with cows to serve as a sort of lightning-conductor. See J. Roscoe, *op. cit.* p. 421.

[1] Rev. J. Roscoe, *op. cit.* pp. 423 *sq.* Further, "if a man's dog died in the house, his wife dared not touch it,

because she feared its ghost ; she would call her husband to take it away " (*op. cit.* p. 425).

[2] W. Jochelson, *The Koryak* (Leyden and New York, 1908), p. 66 (*The Jesup North Pacific Expedition*, vol. vi., *Memoir of the American Museum of Natural History*).

brands in their hands, but on the present occasion the women
dispensed with the use of masks.   They danced, shaking
their heads, moving their shoulders, and swinging their whole
bodies with arms outstretched, now squatting, now rising and
singing, "Ah! a guest has come." In spite of the cold and the
wind the sweat dripped from them, so violently did they dance,
and they sang and screamed till they were hoarse.   When the
sledge with its burden had reached the shore, one of the women
pronounced an incantation over the whale's head, and then
thrust alder branches and sacrificial grass into its mouth.
Next they muffled its head in a hood, apparently to prevent
the creature from witnessing the painful spectacle of its own
dissection.   After that the men cut up the carcase, and the
women collected the blood in pails.   Two seals, which
had also been killed, were included in the festivities which
followed.   The heads of all three animals were cut off and
placed on the roof of the house.   Next day the festival
began.   In the morning the women plaited travelling bags
of grass for the use of the whale, and made grass masks.
In the evening, the people having assembled in a large
underground house, some boiled pieces of the white whale
were placed in a grass bag and set before a wooden image
of a white whale, so that the animal, or its departed spirit,
was thus apparently supposed to be regaled with portions of
its own body ; for the white whale and the seals were treated
as honoured guests at the banquet.   To keep up the pretence,
the people were silent or spoke only in whispers for fear of
wakening the guests before the time.   At last the preparations were complete : fresh faggots piled on the hearth sent
up a blaze, illumining with an unsteady light the smoke-
blackened walls of the vast underground dwelling, which a
moment before had been shrouded in darkness ; and the
long silence was broken by the joyful cries of the women,
"Here dear guests have come !"   "Visit us often !"   "When
you go back to the sea, tell your friends to call on us also,
we will prepare just as nice food for them as for you."   With
these words they pointed to puddings set out temptingly on
the boards.   Next the host took a piece of the fat of the white
whale and threw it into the fire, saying, "We are burning it
in the fire for thee !"   Then he went to the domestic shrine,

placed lumps of fat before the rude effigies of the guardian spirits, and smeared fat on their mouths. The appetites of the higher powers having thus been satisfied, the people set to and partook of the good things provided for them, including the flesh of the white whale and the seals. Lastly, two old men practised divination by means of the shoulder-blade of a seal to discover whether the white whale would go back to the sea and call his fellows to come and be caught like himself. In order to extract this information from the bone burning coals were piled on it, and the resulting cracks were carefully scrutinised. To the delight of all present the omens proved favourable : a long transverse crack indicated the sea to which the spirit of the white whale would soon depart. Four days later the departure actually took place. It was a bright sunshiny wintry morning : the frost was keen ; and for more than a mile seaward the beach was covered with blocks of ice. In the great underground dwelling, where the feast had been held, the hearth had been turned into something like an altar. On it lay the heads of the white whale and the seals, and beside them travelling-bags of grass filled with puddings, which the souls of the animals were to take with them on their long journey. Beside the hearth knelt two women, their faces covered with grass masks and their heads bent over the bags, mumbling an incantation. The sunlight streamed down on them through the smoke-hole overhead, but spread only a dim twilight through the remoter recesses of the vast subterranean chamber. The masks worn by the women were intended to guard them against the spirit of the white whale, which was supposed to be hovering invisible in the air. The incantation over, the women rose from their knees and doffed their masks. A careful examination of a pudding, which had been offered in sacrifice to the white whale, now revealed the joyful intelligence that the spirit of the whale had accepted the sacrifice and was about to return to the sea. All that remained, therefore, to do was to speed him on his way. For that purpose two men ascended the roof, let down thongs through the smoke-hole, and hauled up the heads of the white whale and of the seals together with the travelling-bags of provisions. That concluded the despatch of the souls of the dead animals to their home in the great waters.[1]

When the inhabitants of the Isle of St. Mary, to the north of Madagascar, go a-whaling, they single out the young whales for attack and "humbly beg the mother's pardon, stating the necessity that drives them to kill her progeny, and requesting that she will be pleased to go below while the deed is doing, that her maternal feelings may not be outraged by witnessing what must cause her so much uneasiness."[2]   An Ajumba hunter having killed a female hippopotamus on Lake Azyingo in West Africa, the animal was decapitated and its quarters and bowels removed.   Then the hunter, naked, stepped into the hollow of the ribs, and kneeling down in the bloody pool washed his whole body with the blood and excretions of the animal, while he prayed to the soul of the hippopotamus not to bear him a grudge for having killed her and so blighted her hopes of future maternity ; and he further entreated the ghost not to stir up other hippopotamuses to avenge her death by butting at and capsizing his canoe.[3]   The ounce, a leopard-like creature, is dreaded for its depredations by the Indians of Brazil.   When they have caught one of these animals in a snare, they kill it and carry the body home to the village. There the women deck the carcase with feathers of many colours, put bracelets on its legs, and weep over it, saying, " I pray thee not to take vengeance on our little ones for having been caught and killed through thine own ignorance. For it was not we who deceived thee, it was thyself.   Our husbands only set the trap to catch animals that are good to eat : they never thought to take thee in it.   Therefore, let not thy soul counsel thy fellows to avenge thy death on our little ones ! "[4]   When the Yuracares Indians of Bolivia have killed great apes in their tropical forests, they bring the bodies home, set them out in a row on palm leaves with their heads

Propitia-
tion of
whales,
hippo-
potamuses
ounces,
and apes.

---

[1] W. Jochelson, *The Koryak* (Leyden and New York, 1908), pp. 66-76 (*The Jesup North Pacific Expedition*, vol. vi., *Memoir of the American Museum of Natural History*).

[2] Captain W. F. W. Owen, *Narrative of Voyages to explore the Shores of Africa, Arabia, and Madagascar* (London, 1833), i. 170.

[3] Rev. R. H. Nassau, *Fetichism in West Africa* (London, 1904), p. 204.

[4] A. Thevet, *La Cosmographie Universelle* (Paris, 1575), ii. 936 [970] sq.

all looking one way, sprinkle them with chicha, and say, " We love you, since we have brought you home." They imagine that the performance of this ceremony is very grati- fying to the other apes in the woods.[1]   Before they leave a temporary camp in the forest, where they have killed a tapir and dried the meat on a babracot, the Indians of Guiana invariably destroy this babracot, saying that should a tapir passing that way find traces of the slaughter of one of his kind, he would come by night on the next occasion when Indians slept at that place, and, taking a man, would babracot him in revenge.[2]

Propitia-
tion of dead
eagles. When a Blackfoot Indian has caught eagles in a trap and killed them, he takes them home to a special lodge, called the eagles' lodge, which has been prepared for their reception outside of the camp.   Here he sets the birds in a row on the ground, and propping up their heads on a stick, puts a piece of dried meat in each of their mouths in order that the spirits of the dead eagles may go and tell the other eagles how well they are being treated by the Indians.[3]   So when Indian hunters of the Orinoco region have killed an animal, they open its mouth and pour into it a few drops of the liquor they generally carry with them, in order that the soul of the dead beast may inform its fellows of the welcome it has met with, and that they too, cheered by the prospect of the same kind reception, may come with alacrity to be killed.[4]   A Cherokee hunter who has killed an eagle stands over the dead bird and prays it not to avenge itself on his tribe, because it is not he but a Spaniard who has done the cruel deed.[5]   When a Teton Deceiving
the ghosts
of spiders. Indian is on a journey and he meets a grey spider or a spider with yellow legs, he kills it, because some evil would befall him if he did not.   But he is very careful not to let the spider know that he kills it, for if the spider knew, his soul would go and tell the other spiders, and one of them

[1] A. d'Orbigny, *Voyage dans l'Amé- rique Méridionale*, iii. (Paris and Stras- burg, 1844) p. 202.

[2] E. F. im Thurn, *Among the Indians of Guiana* (London, 1883), p. 352.

[3] G. B. Grinnell, *Blackfoot Lodge Tales* (London, 1893), p. 240.

[4] A. Caulin, *Historia Coro-graphica natural y evangelica dela Nueva Anda- lucia Guayana y Vertientes del Rio Orinoco* (1779), p. 97.

[5] J. Mooney, " Myths of the Chero- kee," *Nineteenth Annual Report of the Bureau of American Ethnology*, Part i. (Washington, 1900) p. 282.

would be sure to avenge the death of his relation. So in crushing the insect, the Indian says, "O Grandfather Spider, the Thunder-beings kill you." And the spider is crushed at once and believes what is told him. His soul probably runs and tells the other spiders that the Thunder-beings have killed him ; but no harm comes of that. For what can grey or yellow-legged spiders do to the Thunder-beings ? [1]

But it is not merely dangerous creatures with whom the savage desires to keep on good terms. It is true that the respect which he pays to wild beasts is in some measure proportioned to their strength and ferocity. Thus the savage Stiens of Cambodia, believing that all animals have souls which roam about after their death, beg an animal's pardon when they kill it, lest its soul should come and torment them. Also they offer it sacrifices, but these sacrifices are proportioned to the size and strength of the animal. The ceremonies observed at the death of an elephant are conducted with much pomp and last seven days.[2] Similar distinctions are drawn by North American Indians. "The bear, the buffalo, and the beaver are manidos [divinities] which furnish food. The bear is formidable, and good to eat. They render ceremonies to him, begging him to allow himself to be eaten, although they know he has no fancy for it. We kill you, but you are not annihilated. His head and paws are objects of homage. . . . Other animals are treated similarly from similar reasons. . . . Many of the animal manidos, not being dangerous, are often treated with contempt—the terrapin, the weasel, polecat, etc." [3] The distinction is instructive. Animals which are feared, or are good to eat, or both, are treated with ceremonious respect ; those which are neither formidable nor good to eat are despised. We have had examples of reverence paid to animals which are both feared and eaten. It remains to prove that similar respect is shewn

The ceremonies of propitiation offered to slain animals vary with the more or less dangerous character of the creature.

Animals which, without being feared, are valued for their flesh or their skin, are also treated with respect.

[1] J. Owen Dorsey, "Teton Folk-lore Notes," *Journal of American Folk-lore*, ii. (1889) p. 134 ; *id.*, "A Study of Siouan Cults," *Eleventh Annual Report of the Bureau of Ethnology* (Washington, 1894), p. 479.

[2] H. Mouhot, *Travels in the Central*

Parts of Indo-China (London, 1864), i. 252 ; J. Moura, *Le Royaume du Cambodge* (Paris, 1883), i. 422.

[3] H. R. Schoolcraft, *Indian Tribes of the United States* (Philadelphia, 1853-1856), v. 420.

to animals which, without being feared, are either eaten or valued for their skins.

When Siberian sable-hunters have caught a sable, no one is allowed to see it, and they think that if good or evil be spoken of the captured sable no more sables will be caught. A hunter has been known to express his belief that the sables could hear what was said of them as far off as Moscow. He said that the chief reason why the sable hunt was now so unproductive was that some live sables had been sent to Moscow. There they had been viewed with astonishment as strange animals, and the sables cannot abide that. Another, though minor, cause of the diminished take of sables was, he alleged, that the world is now much worse than it used to be, so that nowadays a hunter will sometimes hide the sable which he has got instead of putting it into the common stock. This also, said he, the sables cannot abide.[1] A Russian traveller happening once to enter a Gilyak hut in the absence of the owner, observed a freshly killed sable hanging on the wall. Seeing him look at it, the housewife in consternation hastened to muffle the animal in a fur cap, after which it was taken down, wrapt in birch bark, and put away out of sight. Despite the high price he offered for it, the traveller's efforts to buy the animal were unavailing. It was bad enough, they told him, that he, a stranger, had seen the dead sable in its skin, but far worse consequences for the future catch of sables would follow if they were to sell him the animal entire.[2] Alaskan hunters

Bones of
sables and
beavers
kept out of
reach of
dogs, lest
the spirits
of the dead
animals
should be
offended.

preserve the bones of sables and beavers out of reach of the dogs for a year and then bury them carefully, " lest the spirits who look after the beavers and sables should consider that they are regarded with contempt, and hence no more should be killed or trapped." [3] The Shuswap Indians of British Columbia think that if they did not throw beaver-bones into the river, the beavers would not go into the traps any more, and that the same thing would happen were a dog to eat the flesh or gnaw the bone of a beaver.[4] Carrier Indians

---

[1] J. G. Gmelin, *Reise durch Sibirien* (Göttingen, 1751-1752), ii. 278.

[2] L. von Schrenck, *Reisen und Forschungen im Amur-lande*, iii. 564.

[3] W. Dall, *Alaska and its Resources*

(London, 1870), p. 89 ; *id.*, in *The Yukon Territory* (London, 1898), p. 89.

[4] Fr. Boas, in *Sixth Report on the North-Western Tribes of Canada*, p.

who have trapped martens or beavers take care to keep
them from the dogs ; for if a dog were to touch these
animals the Indians believe that the other martens or
beavers would not suffer themselves to be caught.[1] A
missionary who fell in with an old Carrier Indian asked
him what luck he had in the chase. "Oh, don't speak to me
about it," replied the Indian ; "there are beavers in plenty.
I caught one myself immediately after my arrival here, but
unluckily a dog got hold of it. You know that after that
it has been impossible for me to catch another." "Non-
sense," said the missionary ; "set your traps as if nothing
had happened, and you will see." "That would be useless,"
answered the Indian in a tone of despair, "quite useless.
You don't know the ways of the beaver. If a dog merely
touches a beaver, all the other beavers are angry at the
owner of the dog and always keep away from his traps."
It was in vain that the missionary tried to laugh or argue
him out of his persuasion ; the man persisted in abandoning
his snares and giving up the hunt, because, as he asserted,
the beavers were angry with him.[2] A French traveller,
observing that the Indians of Louisiana did not give the
bones of beavers and otters to their dogs, enquired the
reason. They told him there was a spirit in the woods who
would tell the other beavers and otters, and that after that
they would catch no more animals of these species.[3] The
Canadian Indians were equally particular not to let their
dogs gnaw the bones, or at least certain of the bones, of
beavers. They took the greatest pains to collect and
preserve these bones, and, when the beaver had been caught
in a net, they threw them into the river. To a Jesuit who
argued that the beavers could not possibly know what
became of their bones, the Indians replied, "You know
nothing about catching beavers and yet you will be prat-
ing about it. Before the beaver is stone dead, his soul

92 (separate reprint from the *Report of
the British Association for 1890*).

[1] A. G. Morice, "Notes, archæo-
logical, industrial, and sociological, on
the Western Dénés," *Transactions of
the Canadian Institute*, iv. (1892-93)
p. 108.

[2] A. G. Morice, *Au pays de l'Ours
Noir, chez les sauvages de la Colombie
Britannique* (Paris and Lyons, 1897),
p. 71.

[3] L. Hennepin, *Description de la
Louisiane* (Paris, 1683), pp. 97 *sq.*

takes a turn in the hut of the man who is killing him and makes a careful note of what is done with his bones. If the bones are given to the dogs, the other beavers would get word of it and would not let themselves be caught. Whereas, if their bones are thrown into the fire or a river, they are quite satisfied ; and it is particularly gratifying to the net which caught them."[1] Before hunting the beaver they offered a solemn prayer to the Great Beaver, and presented him with tobacco ; and when the chase was over, an orator pronounced a funeral oration over the dead beavers. He praised their spirit and wisdom. "You will hear no more," said he, "the voice of the chieftains who commanded you and whom you chose from among all the warrior beavers to give you laws. Your language, which the medicine-men understand perfectly, will be heard no more at the bottom of the lake. You will fight no more battles with the otters, your cruel foes. No, beavers ! But your skins shall serve to buy arms ; we will carry your smoked hams to our children ; we will keep the dogs from eating your bones, which are so hard."[2]

The elan, deer, and elk were treated by the American Indians with the same punctilious respect, and for the same

---

[1] *Relations des Jésuites*, 1634, p. 24 (Canadian reprint, Quebec, 1858). Nets are regarded by the Indians as living creatures who not only think and feel but also eat, speak, and marry wives. See F. Gabriel Sagard, *Le Grand Voyage du Pays des Hurons*, p. 256 (pp. 178 *sq.* of the reprint, Librairie Tross, Paris, 1865) ; S. Hearne, *Journey to the Northern Ocean* (London, 1795), pp. 329 *sq.* ; *Relations des Jésuites*, 1636, p. 109 ; *ibid.* 1639, p. 95 ; Charlevoix, *Histoire de la Nouvelle France* (Paris, 1744), v. 225 ; Chateaubriand, *Voyage en Amérique*, pp. 140 *sqq.* The Hebrews sacrificed and burned incense to their nets (Habakkuk i. 16). In some of the mountain villages of Annam the people, who are great hunters, sacrifice fowls, rice, incense, and gilt paper to their nets at the festival of the New Year. See Le R. P. Cadière, " Coutumes populaires de la

vallée du Nguôn-So'n," *Bulletin de l'École Française d'Extrême-Orient*, ii. (Hanoi, 1902) p. 381. When a net has caught little or nothing, the Ewe negroes think that it must be hungry ; so they call in the help of a priest, who commonly feeds the hungry net by sprinkling maize-flour and fish, moistened with palm oil, on its meshes. See G. Härtter, " Der Fischfang im Evheland," *Zeitschrift für Ethnologie*, xxxviii. (1906) p. 55.

[2] Chateaubriand, *Voyage en Amérique*, pp. 175, 178 (Paris, Michel Lévy Frères, 1870). They will not let the blood of beavers fall on the ground, or their luck in hunting them would be gone (*Relations des Jésuites*, 1633, p. 21). Compare the rule about not allowing the blood of kings to fall on the ground. See *Taboo and the Perils of the Soul*, pp. 241 *sqq.*

reason.   Their bones might not be given to the dogs nor
thrown into the fire, nor might their fat be dropped upon
the fire, because the souls of the dead animals were believed
to see what was done to their bodies and to tell it to the
other beasts, living and dead.   Hence, if their bodies were
ill-used, the animals of that species would not allow themselves to be taken, neither in this world nor in the world to
come.[1]   The houses of the Indians of Honduras were
encumbered with the bones of deer, the Indians believing
that if they threw the bones away, the other deer could not
be taken.[2]   Among the Chiquites of Paraguay a sick man
would be asked by the medicine-man whether he had not
thrown away some of the flesh of the deer or turtle, and if
he answered yes, the medicine-man would say, " That is
what is killing you.   The soul of the deer or turtle has
entered into your body to avenge the wrong you did it." [3]
Before the Tzentales of Southern Mexico and the Kekchis
of Guatemala venture to skin a deer which they have killed,
they lift up its head and burn copal before it as an offering ;
otherwise a certain being named Tzultacca would be angry
and send them no more game.[4]   Cherokee hunters ask
pardon of the deer they kill.   If they failed to do so, they
think that the Little Deer, the chief of the deer tribe, who
can never die or be wounded, would track the hunter to his
home by the blood-drops on the ground and would put the
spirit of rheumatism into him.   Sometimes the hunter, on
starting for home, lights a fire in the trail behind him to
prevent the Little Deer from pursuing him.[5]   Before they

[1] L. Hennepin, *Nouveau voyage d'un pais plus grand que l'Europe* (Utrecht, 1698), pp. 141 *sq.*; *Relations des Jésuites*, 1636, p. 109 ; F. Gabriel Sagard, *Le Grand Voyage du Pays des Hurons*, p. 255 (p. 178 of the reprint, Librairie Tross, Paris, 1865).   Not quite consistently the Canadian Indians used to kill every elan they could overtake in the chase, lest any should escape to warn their fellows (Sagard, *l.c.*).

[2] A. de Herrera, *General History of the vast Continent and Islands of America*, translated by Capt. John Stevens (London, 1725-1726), iv. 142.

[3] *Lettres édifiantes et curieuses*, Nou-

velle Édition, viii. (Paris, 1781) p. 339.

[4] C. Sapper, " Die Gebräuche und religiösen Anschauungen der Kekchí-Indianer," *Internationales Archiv für Ethnographie*, viii. (1895) pp. 195 *sq.*

[5] J. Mooney, " Cherokee Theory and Practice of Medicine," *American Journal of Folk-lore*, iii. (1890) pp. 45 *sq.*; *id.*, " Sacred Formulas of the Cherokees," *Seventh Annual Report of the Bureau of Ethnology* (Washington, 1891), pp. 320 *sq.*, 347 ; *id.*, " Myths of the Cherokee," *Nineteenth Annual Report of the Bureau of American Ethnology*, Part i. (Washington, 1900) pp. 263 *sq.*

went out to hunt for deer, antelope, or elk the Apaches used
to resort to sacred caves, where the medicine-men propitiated
with prayer and sacrifice the animal gods whose progeny
they intended to destroy.[1] The Indians of Louisiana bewailed bitterly the death of the buffaloes which they were
about to kill.   More than two hundred of them at a time
have been seen shedding crocodile tears over the approaching slaughter of the animals, while they marched in solemn
procession, headed by an old man who waved a pocket-
handkerchief at the end of a stick as an oriflamme, and by a
woman who strutted proudly along, bearing on her back
a large kettle which had been recently abstracted from
the baggage of some French explorers.[2]   The Thompson
Indians of British Columbia cherished many superstitious
beliefs and observed many superstitious practices in regard
to deer.   When a deer was killed, they said that the rest of
the deer would be well pleased if the hunters butchered the
animal nicely and cleanly.   To waste venison displeased the
animals, who after that would not allow themselves to be
shot by the hunter.   If a hunter was overburdened and had
to leave some of the venison behind, the other deer were
better pleased if he hung it up on a tree than if he let it
lie on the ground.   The guts were gathered and put where
the blood had been spilt in butchering the beast, and the
whole was covered up with a few fir-boughs.   In laying the
boughs on the blood and guts the man told the deer not to
grieve for the death of their friend and not to take it ill that
he had left some of the body behind, for he had done his
best to cover it.   If he did not cover it, they thought the
deer would be sorry or angry and would spoil his luck in the
chase.   When the head of a deer had to be left behind, they
commonly placed it on the branch of a tree, that it might
not be contaminated by dogs and women.   For the same
reason they burned the bones of the slain deer, lest they
should be touched by women or gnawed by dogs.   And
venison was never brought into a hut by the common door,
because that door was used by women ; it was taken in

---

[1] J. G. Bourke, "Religion of the
Apache Indians," *Folk-lore*, ii. (1891)
p. 438.

[2] L. Hennepin, *Description de
la Louisiane* (Paris, 1683), pp. 8a
sq.

through a hole made in the back of the hut. No hunter
would give a deer's head to a man who was the first or
second of a family, for that would make the rest of the deer
very shy and hard to shoot. And in telling his friends of
his bag he would generally call a buck a doe, and a doe he
would call a fawn, and a fawn he would call a hare. This
he did that he might not seem to the deer to brag.[1] The
Lillooet Indians of British Columbia threw the bones of
animals, particularly those of the deer and the beaver, into
the water, in order that the dogs should not defile or eat
them and thereby offend the animals. When the hunter
committed the bones to the water he generally prayed to
the dead animal, saying, " See ! I treat you respectfully.
Nothing shall defile you. Have pity on me, so I may kill
more of you ! May I be successful in hunting and
trapping ! "[2] The Canadian Indians would not eat the
embryos of the elk, unless at the close of the hunting
season ; otherwise the mother-elks would be shy and refuse
to be caught.[3]

Indians of the Lower Fraser River regard the porcupine
as their elder brother. Hence when a hunter kills one of these
creatures he asks his elder brother's pardon and does not eat
of the flesh till the next day.[4] The Sioux will not stick an
awl or needle into a turtle, for they are sure that, if they were
to do so, the turtle would punish them at some future time.[5]
Some of the North American Indians believed that each sort
of animal had its patron or genius who watched over and
preserved it. An Indian girl having once picked up a dead
mouse, her father snatched the little creature from her and
tenderly caressed and fondled it. Being asked why he did
so, he said that it was to appease the genius of mice, in
order that he might not torment his daughter for eating the

*Porcu-
pines,
turtles,
and mice
treated by
American
Indians
with cere-
monious
respect.*

---

[1] James Teit, *The Thompson Indians
of British Columbia*, pp. 346 *sq.*
(*The Jesup North Pacific Expedition,
Memoir of the American Museum of
Natural History*, April 1900).

[2] James Teit, *The Lillooet Indians*
(Leyden and New York, 1906), pp.
281 *sq.* (*The Jesup North Pacific
Expedition, Memoir of the American
Museum of Natural History*).

[3] *Relations des Jésuites*, 1634, p.
26 (Canadian reprint, Quebec, 1858).

[4] Fr. Boas, in " Ninth Report on
the North-Western Tribes of Canada,"
*Report of the British Association for
1894*, pp. 459 *sq.*

[5] H. R. Schoolcraft, *Indian Tribes
of the United States* (Philadelphia,
1853-1856), iii. 230.

mouse. With that he handed the mouse to the girl and she ate it.[1]

Dead foxes, turtles, deer, and pigs treated with ceremonious respect. When the Koryak have killed a fox, they take the body home and lay it down near the fire, saying, " Let the guest warm himself. When he feels warm, we will free him from his overcoat." So when the frozen carcase is thawed, they skin it and wrap long strips of grass round about it. Then the animal's mouth is filled with fish-roe, and the mistress of the house gashes the flesh and puts more roe or dried meat into the gashes, making believe that the gashes are the fox's pockets, which she thus fills with provisions. Then the carcase is carried out of the house, and the people say, " Go and tell your friends that it is good to visit yonder house. ' Instead of my old coat, they gave me a new one still warmer and with longer hair. I have eaten my fill, and had my pockets well stored. You, too, go and visit them.' " The natives think that if they neglected to observe this ceremonial they would have no luck in hunting foxes.[2] When a Ewe hunter of Togoland has killed an antelope of a particular kind (*Antilope leucoryx*), he erects an enclosure of branches, within which he places the lower jawbones of all the animals he has shot. Then he pours palm-wine and sprinkles meal on the bones, saying, " Ye lower jawbones of beasts, ye are now come home. Here is food, here is drink. Therefore lead your comrades (that is, the living beasts of the forest) hither also." [3] In the Timor-laut islands of the Indian Archipelago the skulls of all the turtles which a fisherman has caught are hung up under his house. Before he goes out to catch another, he addresses himself to the skull of the last turtle that he killed, and having inserted betel between its jaws, he prays the spirit of the dead animal to entice its kinsfolk in the sea to come and be caught.[4] In the Poso district of central Celebes hunters keep the jawbones of deer and wild pigs which they have killed and hang them up in their houses near the fire. Then they say

[1] Charlevoix, *Histoire de la Nouvelle France* (Paris, 1744), v. 443.

[2] W. Bogaras, *The Chuckchee* (Leyden and New York, 1904-1909), p. 409 (*The Jesup North Pacific Expedition*, vol. vii., *Memoir of the American Museum of Natural History*).

[3] J. Spieth, *Die Ewe - Stämme* (Berlin, 1906), pp. 389 *sq.*

[4] J. A. Jacobsen, *Reisen in die Inselwelt des Banda-Meeres* (Berlin, 1896), p. 234.

to the jawbones, " Ye cry after your comrades, that your grandfathers, or nephews, or children may not go away." Their notion is that the souls of the dead deer and pigs tarry near their jawbones and attract the souls of living deer and pigs, which are thus drawn into the toils of the hunter.[1]   Thus in all these cases the wily savage employs dead animals as decoys to lure living animals to their doom.

The Lengua Indians of the Gran Chaco love to hunt the ostrich, but when they have killed one of these birds and are bringing home the carcase to the village, they take steps to outwit the resentful ghost of their victim.   They think that when the first natural shock of death is passed, the ghost of the ostrich pulls himself together and makes after his body.   Acting on this sage calculation, the Indians pluck feathers from the breast of the bird and strew them at intervals along the track.   At every bunch of feathers the ghost stops to consider, " Is this the whole of my body or only a part of it ? "   The doubt gives him pause, and when at last he has made up his mind fully at all the bunches, and has further wasted valuable time by the zigzag course which he invariably pursues in going from one to another, the hunters are safe at home, and the bilked ghost may stalk in vain round about the village, which he is too timid to enter.[2]

Ghost of ostrich outwitted.

The Esquimaux of the Hudson Bay region believe that the reindeer are controlled by a great spirit who resides in a large cave near the end of Cape Chidley.   The outward form of the spirit is that of a huge white bear.   He obtains and controls the spirit of every reindeer that is slain or dies, and it depends on his good will whether the people shall have a supply of reindeer or not.   The sorcerer intercedes with this great spirit and prevails on him to send the deer to the hungry Esquimaux.   He informs the spirit that the people have in no way offended him, since he, the sorcerer, has taken great care that the whole of the meat was eaten up,

Esquimaux propitiation of the spirit who controls reindeer.

---

[1] A. C. Kruijt, " Een en ander aangaande het geestelijk en maatschappelijk leven van den Poso-Alfoer," *Mededeelingen van wege het Nederlandsche Zendelinggenootschap*, xli.   (1897) pp. 4 *sq.*

[2] W. Barbrooke Grubb, *An Unknown People in an Unknown Land* (London, 1911), pp. 125 *sq.*

and that last spring, when the does were returning to him to drop their young, none of the little or embryo fawns were devoured by the dogs. After long incantations the magician announces that the patron of the deer condescends to supply the Esquimaux with the spirits of the animals in a material form, and that soon there will be plenty in the land. He charges the people to fall on and slay and thereby win the approval of the spirit, who loves to see good folk enjoying themselves, knowing that so long as the Esquimaux refrain from feeding their dogs with the unborn young, the spirits of the dead reindeer will return again to his watchful care. The dogs are not allowed to taste the flesh, and until the supply is plentiful they may not gnaw the leg-bones, lest the guardian of the deer should take offence and send no more of the animals. If, unfortunately, a dog should get at the meat, a piece of his tail is cut off or his ear is cropped to let the blood flow.[1] Again, the Central Esquimaux hold that sea-mammals, particularly whales, ground-seals, and common seals, sprang from the severed fingers of the goddess Sedna, and that therefore an Esquimau must make atonement for every such animal that he kills. When a seal is brought into the hut, the woman must stop working till it has been cut up. After the capture of a ground seal, walrus, or whale they must rest for three days. Not all sorts of work, however, are forbidden, for they may mend articles made of sealskin, but they may not make anything new. For example, an old tent cover may be enlarged in order to build a larger hut, but it is not allowed to make a new one. Working on new deerskins is strictly forbidden. No skins of this kind obtained in summer may be prepared before the ice has formed and the first seal has been caught with the harpoon. Later on, as soon as the first walrus has been taken, the work must again stop until autumn comes round. Hence all families are eager to finish the work on deerskins as fast as possible, for until that is done the walrus season may not begin.[2] The Greenlanders are careful not to

Ceremonious treatment of sea-beasts by the Esquimaux.

[1] L. M. Turner, "Ethnology of the Ungava District, Hudson Bay Territory," *Eleventh Annual Report of the Bureau of Ethnology* (Washington, 1894), pp. 200 *sq.*

[2] Fr. Boas, "The Central Eskimo," *Sixth Annual Report of the Bureau of Ethnology* (Washington, 1888), p. 595; *id.*, "The Eskimo of Baffin Land and Hudson Bay," *Bulletin of*

fracture the heads of seals or throw them into the sea, but
pile them in a heap before the door, that the souls of the
seals may not be enraged and scare their brethren from the
coast.[1]

The Esquimaux about Bering Strait believe that the
souls of dead sea-beasts, such as seals, walrus, and whales,
remain attached to their bladders, and that by returning the
bladders to the sea they can cause the souls to be re-
incarnated in fresh bodies and so multiply the game which
the hunters pursue and kill.   Acting on this belief every
hunter carefully removes and preserves the bladders of all
the sea-beasts that he kills ; and at a solemn festival held
once a year in winter these bladders, containing the souls of
all the sea-beasts that have been killed throughout the
year, are honoured with dances and offerings of food in the
public assembly-room, after which they are taken out on the
ice and thrust through holes into the water ; for the simple
Esquimaux imagine that the souls of the animals, in high
good humour at the kind treatment they have experienced,
will thereafter be born again as seals, walrus, and whales,
and in that form will flock willingly to be again speared,
harpooned, or otherwise done to death by the hunters.
The ceremonies observed at these annual festivals of reincarnation are elaborate.   The assembly-room or dancing-
house (*kashim, kassigim,* or *kassigit*), in which the festival
is held, consists of a spacious semi-subterranean chamber
entered by a tunnel, which leads down to a large round
cellar under the floor of the house.   From the cellar you
ascend into the assembly-room through a hole in the floor.
Wooden benches run round the apartment, which is lit by
lamps.   An opening in the roof serves at once as a window
and a chimney.   Unmarried men sleep in the assembly-
room at all times ; they have no other home.   The festival
is commonly held in December, but it may fall as late as
January.   It lasts several days.   When the time is come

Annual
ceremony
of return-
ing the
bladders
of the sea-
beasts to
the sea in
order that
the animals
may come
to life
again.

---

the *American Museum of Natural
History,* xv. (1901) pp. 119 *sqq.* As
to the antagonism which these Esquimaux suppose to exist between marine
and terrestrial animals, see above, p.
84 ; and with regard to the taboos

observed by these Esquimaux after the
slaughter of sea-beasts, see *Taboo and
the Perils of the Soul,* pp. 205 *sqq.*

[1] D. Crantz, *History of Greenland*
(London, 1767), i. 216.

to celebrate it, each hunter brings into the assembly-room the inflated bladders of all the seals, walrus, and whales that he has killed during the year.   These are tied by the necks in bunches and hung up on seal spears, which are stuck in a row in the wall some six or eight feet above the floor.   Here food and water are offered to them, or rather to the spirits of the animals which are supposed to be present in the bladders ; and the spirits signify their acceptance of the offering by causing the bladders to swing to and fro, a movement which is really produced by a man sitting in a dark corner, who pulls a string attached to the bladders.   Further, the bladders are fumigated with torches of wild parsnip stalks, the aromatic smoke and red flames of which are believed to be well-pleasing to the souls of the animals dangling in the bladders.   Moreover to amuse the souls men execute curious dances before them to the music of drums.   First the dancers move slowly with a jerky action from side to side ; then they gallop obliquely with arms tossed up and down ; and lastly they hop and jump, always keeping perfect time to the beat of the drums. The dance is supposed to imitate the movements of seals and walrus ; and again the spirits signify their pleasure by making the bladders swing backwards and forwards.   During the continuance of the festival no loud noises may be made in the assembly-room for fear of alarming the souls of the animals in the bladders ; if any person makes a noise by accident, all the men present raise a chorus of cries in imitation of the notes of the eider duck to let the souls of the animals think that the unseemly disturbance proceeds from the birds and not from the people.   Further, so long as the festival lasts, no wood may be cut with an iron axe in the village, the men must keep rigidly apart from the women, and no female above the age of puberty may come near the bladders suspended in the assembly-room, the reason assigned being that such women are unclean and might offend the sensitive souls of the sea-beasts in the bladders.   But immature girls, being untainted by the pollution which attaches to adult women, may go about the bladders freely.   The last and crowning scene of the festival takes place at night or just at sunrise.   The spears

with the bladders attached to them are passed out by the
shaman into the open air through the smoke-hole in the
roof.   When all are outside, a huge torch of wild parsnip
stalks is lighted ; the chief shaman takes it on his shoulder,
and runs with it as fast as he can across the snow and out
on the ice.   Behind him troop all the men carrying each
his spear with the bladders of the sea-beasts dangling and
flapping from it ; and in the rear race the women, children,
and old men, howling, screaming and making a great uproar.
In the darkness the lurid flame of the torch shoots high into
the air, casting a red glare over the snowy landscape and
lighting up the swarm of fantastic, fur-clad figures that
stream along in wild excitement.   Arrived at a hole, which
had been cut on purpose in the sea-ice, the shaman plants
his burning torch beside it in the snow, and every man as
he comes up rips open his bladders and thrusts them, one
after the other, into the water under the ice.   This ends
the ceremony.   The souls of the dead seals, walrus, and
whales, are now ready to be born again in the depths of
the sea.   So all the people return contented to the village.
At St. Michael the men who have thrust the bladders
under the ice are obliged on their return to leap through
a fire of wild parsnip stalks, probably as a mode of ceremonial purification ; for after the dance and the offering of
food at the festival the chief shaman passes a lighted torch
of parsnip stalks round the assembly-room and the dancers,
for the express purpose of purifying them and averting any
evil influence that might bring sickness or ill luck on the
hunters.[1]

For like reasons, a tribe which depends for its subsistence, chiefly or in part, upon fishing is careful to treat the
fish with every mark of honour and respect.   The Indians
of Peru " worshipped the whale for its monstrous greatness.
Besides this ordinary system of worship, which prevailed

Fish treated with respect by fishing tribes.

---

[1] E. W. Nelson, "The Eskimo
about Bering Strait," *Eighteenth
Annual Report of the Bureau of
American Ethnology*, Part i. (Washington, 1899), pp. 379-393, 437.   Compare A. Woldt, *Captain Jacobsen's
Reise an der Nordwestküste Americas
1881-1883* (Leipsic, 1884), pp. 289-
291.   In the text the ceremony has
been described mainly as it was witnessed by Mr. E. W. Nelson at
Kushunuk, near Cape Vancouver, in
December, 1879.   As might have been
expected, the ritual varies in details
at different places.

The
Peruvian
Indians
worshipped
the various
sorts of fish
which they
caught.

throughout the coast, the people of different provinces adored the fish that they caught in greatest abundance ; for they said that the first fish that was made in the world above (for so they named Heaven) gave birth to all other fish of that species, and took care to send them plenty of its children to sustain their tribe.   For this reason they worshipped sardines in one region, where they killed more of them than of any other fish ; in others, the skate ; in others, the dogfish ; in others, the golden fish for its beauty ; in others, the crawfish ; in others, for want of larger gods, the crabs, where they had no other fish, or where they knew not how to catch and kill them.   In short, they had what-ever fish was most serviceable to them as their gods."[1]   The Kwakiutl Indians of British Columbia think that when a salmon is killed its soul returns to the salmon country. Hence they take care to throw the bones and offal into the sea, in order that the soul may reanimate them at the resurrection of the salmon.   Whereas if they burned the bones the soul would be lost, and so it would be quite impossible for that salmon to rise from the dead.[2]   In like manner the Otawa Indians of Canada, believing that the souls of dead fish passed into other bodies of fish, never burned fish bones, for fear of displeasing the souls of the fish, who would come no more to the nets.[3]   The Hurons also refrained from throwing fish bones into the fire, lest the souls of the fish should go and warn the other fish not to let themselves be caught, since the Hurons would burn their bones.   Moreover, they had men who preached to the fish and persuaded them to come and be caught.   A good preacher was much sought after, for they thought that the exhortations of a clever man had a great effect in drawing the fish to the nets.   In the Huron fishing village where the French missionary Sagard stayed, the preacher to the

Fish
treated
with re-
spect by
the North
American
Indians.

[1] Garcilasso de la Vega, *Royal Commentaries of the Yncas*, translated by C. R. Markham, First Part, bk. i. ch. 10, vol. i. pp. 49 *sq.* (Hakluyt Society, London, 1869-1871).   Compare *id.*, vol. ii. p. 148.

[2] Fr. Boas, in *Sixth Report on the North-Western Tribes of Canada*, pp. 61 *sq.* (separate reprint from the *Report*

of the British Association for 1890) ; *id.*, *Kwakiutl Texts*, ii. pp. 303 *sq.*, 305 *sq.*, 307, 317 (*Jesup North Pacific Expedition, Memoir of the American Museum of Natural History*, December, 1902).

[3] *Relations des Jésuites*, 1667, p. 12 (Canadian reprint, Quebec, 1858).

fish prided himself very much on his eloquence, which was
of a florid order.   Every evening after supper, having seen
that all the people were in their places and that a strict
silence was observed, he preached to the fish.   His text
was that the Hurons did not burn fish bones.   " Then
enlarging on this theme with extraordinary unction, he
exhorted and conjured and invited and implored the fish
to come and be caught and to be of good courage and to
fear nothing, for it was all to serve their friends who
honoured them and did not burn their bones." [1]   At
Bogadjim in German New Guinea an enchanter is employed
to lure the fish to their doom.   He stands in a canoe on
the beach with a decorated fish-basket beside him, and
commands the fish to come from all quarters to Bogadjim.[2]
When the Aino have killed a sword-fish, they thank the fish
for allowing himself to be caught and invite him to come
again.[3]   Among the Nootka Indians of British Columbia it
was formerly a rule that any person who had partaken of
bear's flesh must rigidly abstain from eating any kind of
fish for a term of two months.   The motive for the abstinence was not any consideration for the health of the eater,
but " a superstitious belief, that should any of their people
after tasting bear's flesh, eat of fresh salmon, cod, etc., the
fish, though at ever so great a distance off, would come to
the knowledge of it, and be so much offended thereat, as
not to allow themselves to be taken by any of the inhabitants." [4]   The disappearance of herring from the sea about   Herring re-
Heligoland in 1530 was attributed by the fishermen to the   spected by
misconduct of two lads who had whipped a freshly-caught   European
herring and then flung it back into the sea.[5]   A similar   fishermen.
disappearance of the herrings from the Moray Firth, in the
reign of Queen Anne, was set down by some people to a
breach of the Sabbath which had been committed by the
fishermen, while others opined that it was due to a quarrel

[1] F. Gabriel Sagard, *Le Grand
Voyage du Pays des Hurons*, pp. 255
sqq. (pp. 178 *sqq.* of the reprint,
Libraire Tross, Paris, 1865).

[2] B. Hagen, *Unter den Papuas*
(Wiesbaden, 1899), p. 270.

[3] Rev. J. Batchelor, *The Ainu and
their Folk-lore* (London, 1901), pp.

529 *sq.*

[4] *A Narrative of the Adventures
and Sufferings of John R. Jewitt*
(Middletown, 1820), p. 116.

[5] M. J. Schleiden, *Das Salz* (Leipsic,
1875), p. 47.   For this reference I am
indebted to my late friend W. Robertson Smith.

in which blood had been spilt in the sea.[1] For Scotch
fishermen are persuaded that if blood be drawn in a quarrel
on the coast where herring are being caught, the shoal will
at once take its departure and not return for that season at
least.   West Highland fishermen believe that every shoal of
herring has its leader which it follows wherever he goes.
This leader is twice as big as an ordinary herring, and the
fishermen call it the king of herring.   When they chance
to catch it in their nets they put it back carefully into the
sea ; for they would esteem it petty treason to destroy the

Compensa-
tion made
to fish for
catching
them.

royal fish.[2]   The natives of the Duke of York Island
annually decorate a canoe with flowers and ferns, lade it,
or are supposed to lade it, with shell-money, and set it
adrift to compensate the fish for their fellows who have
been caught and eaten.[3]   When the Tarahumares of Mexico
are preparing to poison the waters of a river for the purpose
of stupefying and catching the fish, they take the precaution
of first making offerings to the Master of the Fish by way
of payment for the fish of which they are about to bereave
him.   The offerings consist of axes, hats, blankets, girdles,
pouches, and especially knives and strings of beads, which
are hung to a cross or a horizontal bar set up in the middle
of the river.   However, the Master of the Fish, who is
thought to be the oldest fish, does not long enjoy these
good things ; for next morning the owners of the various
articles remove them from the river and appropriate them to
their usual secular purposes.[4]   It is especially necessary to
treat the first fish caught with consideration in order to
conciliate the rest of the fish, whose conduct may be supposed to be influenced by the reception given to those of
their kind which were the first to be taken.   Accordingly
the Maoris always put back into the sea the first fish caught,
" with a prayer that it may tempt other fish to come and be
caught." [5]   Among the Baganda " the first fish taken were

[1] Hugh Miller, *Scenes and Legends of the North of Scotland*, ch. xvii. pp. 256 *sq.* (Edinburgh, 1889).

[2] M. Martin, " Description of the Western Islands of Scotland," in Pinkerton's *Voyages and Travels*, iii. (London, 1809) p. 620.

[3] W. Powell, *Wanderings in a Wild Country* (London, 1883), pp. 66 *sq.*

[4] C. Lumholtz, *Unknown Mexico* (London, 1903), i. 403.

[5] R. Taylor, *Te Ika a Maui, or New Zealand and its Inhabitants*, Second Edition (London, 1870), p

treated ceremonially : some the fisherman took to the god
Mukasa ; the remainder his wife cooked, and he and she
both partook of them, and he afterwards jumped over her." [1]

Still more stringent are the precautions taken when the
fish are the first of the season.   On salmon rivers, when the
fish begin to run up the stream in spring, they are received
with much deference by tribes who, like the Indians of the
Pacific Coast of North America, subsist largely upon a fish
diet.   To some of these tribes the salmon is what corn is to
the European, rice to the Chinese, and seals to the Esquimaux.
Plenty of salmon means abundance in the camp and joy at
the domestic hearth ; failure of the salmon for a single season
means famine and desolation, silence in the village, and sad
hearts about the fire.[2]   Accordingly in British Columbia the
Indians used to go out to meet the first fish as they came
up the river : " They paid court to them, and would address
them thus : ' You fish, you fish ; you are all chiefs, you are ;
you are all chiefs.' " [3]   Amongst the Thlinkeet or Tlingit of
Alaska the first halibut of the season is carefully handled and
addressed as a chief, and a festival is given in his honour,
after which the fishing goes on.[4]   Among the tribes of the
Lower Fraser River when the first sockeye-salmon of the
season has been caught, the fisherman carries it to the chief
of his tribe, who delivers it to his wife.   She prays, saying
to the salmon, " Who has brought you here to make us
happy ?   We are thankful to your chief for sending you."
When she has cut and roasted the salmon according to
certain prescribed rules, the whole tribe is invited and partakes of the fish, after they have purified themselves by
drinking a decoction of certain plants which is regarded as
a medicine for cleansing the people.   But widowers, widows,
menstruous women, and youths may not eat of this particular
salmon.   Even later, when the fish have become plentiful
and these ceremonies are dispensed with, the same classes of

Cere-
monious
treatment
of the first
fish of the
season.

200 ; A. S. Thomson, *The Story of
New Zealand* (London, 1859), i. 202 ;
E. Tregear, "The Maoris of New
Zealand," *Journal of the Anthropologi-
cal Institute*, xix. (1890) p. 109.
   [1] Rev. J. Roscoe, *The Baganda*
(London, 1911), p. 395.

   [2] A. G. Morice, *Au pays de l'Ours
Noir* (Paris and Lyons, 1897), p. 28.
   [3] Sir John Lubbock, *Origin of
Civilisation* [4] (London, 1882), p. 277,
quoting *Metlahkatlah*, p. 96.
   [4] W. Dall, *Alaska and its Resources*
(London, 1870), p. 413.

persons are not allowed to eat fresh salmon, though they may partake of the dried fish. The sockeye-salmon must always be looked after carefully. Its bones have to be thrown into the river, after which the fish will revive and return to its chief in the west. Whereas if the fish are not treated with consideration, they will take their revenge, and the careless fisherman will be unlucky.[1] Among the Songish or Lkungen tribe of Vancouver Island it is a rule that on the day when the first salmon have been caught, the children must stand on the beach waiting for the boats to return. They stretch out their little arms and the salmon are heaped on them, the heads of the fish being always kept in the direction in which the salmon are swimming, else they would cease to run up the river. So the children carry them and lay them on a grassy place, carefully keeping the heads of the salmon turned in the same direction. Round the fish are placed four flat stones, on which the plant hog's wort (*Peucedanum leiocarpum*, Nutt.), red paint, and bulrushes are burnt as an offering to the salmon. When the salmon have been roasted each of the children receives one, which he or she is obliged to eat, leaving nothing over. But grown people are not allowed to eat the fish for several days. The bones of the salmon that the children have eaten may not touch the ground. They are kept in dishes, and on the fourth day an old woman, who pretends to be lame, gathers them in a huge basket and throws them into the sea.[2] The Tsimshian Indians of British Columbia observe certain ceremonies when the first olachen fish of the season are caught. The fish are roasted on an instrument of elder-berry wood, and the man who roasts them must wear his travelling dress, mittens, cape, and so forth. While this is being done the Indians pray that plenty of olachen may come to their fishing-ground. The fire may not be blown up, and in eating the fish they

---

[1] Fr. Boas, in "Ninth Report on the North-Western Tribes of Canada," *Report of the British Association for 1894*, p. 461. Compare J. Teit, *The Lillooet Indians* (Leyden and New York, 1906), pp. 280 *sq.* (*The Jesup North Pacific Expedition, Memoir of the American Museum of Natural History*); C. Hill Tout, in *Journal of the Anthropological Institute*, xxxv. (1905) p. 140; *id.*, *The Far West, the Home of the Salish and Déné* (London, 1907), pp. 170-172.

[2] Fr. Boas, in *Sixth Report on the North-Western Tribes of Canada*, pp. 16 *sq.* (separate reprint from the *Report of the British Association for 1890*).

may not cool it by blowing nor break a single bone. Everything must be neat and clean, and the rakes used for catching the fish must be kept hidden in the house.[1] In spring,
when the winds blow soft from the south and the salmon
begin to run up the Klamath river, the Karoks of California
dance for salmon, to ensure a good catch. One of the
Indians, called the Kareya or God-man, retires to the
mountains and fasts for ten days. On his return the people
flee, while he goes to the river, takes the first salmon of the
catch, eats some of it, and with the rest kindles the sacred
fire in the sweating-house. " No Indian may take a salmon
before this dance is held, nor for ten days after it, even if his
family are starving." The Karoks also believe that a fisherman will take no salmon if the poles of which his spearing-
booth is made were gathered on the river-side, where the
salmon might have seen them. The poles must be brought
from the top of the highest mountain. The fisherman will
also labour in vain if he uses the same poles a second year
in booths or weirs, " because the old salmon will have told
the young ones about them."[2] Among the Indians of the
Columbia River, " when the salmon make their first appearance in the river, they are never allowed to be cut crosswise,
nor boiled, but roasted ; nor are they allowed to be sold
without the heart being first taken out, nor to be kept over
night, but must be all consumed or eaten the day they are
taken out of the water. All these rules are observed for
about ten days."[3] They think that if the heart of a fish were
eaten by a stranger at the beginning of the season, they
would catch no more fish. Hence, they roast and eat the
hearts themselves.[4] There is a favourite fish of the Aino
which appears in their rivers about May and June. They
prepare for the fishing by observing rules of ceremonial
purity, and when they have gone out to fish, the women at

[1] *Id.*, in *Fifth Report on the North-
Western Tribes of Canada*, p. 51 (separate
reprint from the *Report of the British
Association for 1889*).

[2] Stephen Powers, *Tribes of California* (Washington, 1877), pp. 31 *sq.*

[3] Alex. Ross, *Adventures of the First
Settlers on the Oregon or Columbia

River (London, 1849), p. 97.

[4] Ch. Wilkes, *Narrative of the United
States Exploring Expedition*, New Edition (New York, 1851), iv. 324, v. 119,
where it is said, "a dog must never be
permitted to eat the heart of a salmon;
and in order to prevent this, they cut
the heart of the fish out before they
sell it."

home must keep strict silence or the fish would hear them and disappear. When the first fish is caught he is brought home and passed through a small opening at the end of the hut, but not through the door; for if he were passed through the door, "the other fish would certainly see him and disappear."[1] This may partly explain the custom observed by other savages of bringing game in certain cases into their huts, not by the door, but by the window, the smoke-hole, or by a special opening at the back of the hut.[2]

Some savages preserve the bones of the animals they kill in order that the animals may come to life again.

With some savages a special reason for respecting the bones of game, and generally of the animals which they eat, is a belief that, if the bones are preserved, they will in course of time be reclothed with flesh, and thus the animal will come to life again. It is, therefore, clearly for the interest of the hunter to leave the bones intact, since to destroy them would be to diminish the future supply of game. Many of the Minnetaree Indians "believe that the bones of those bisons which they have slain and divested of flesh rise again clothed with renewed flesh, and quickened with life, and become fat, and fit for slaughter the succeeding June."[3] Hence on the western prairies of America, the skulls of buffaloes may be seen arranged in circles and symmetrical piles, awaiting the resurrection.[4] After feasting on a dog, the Dacotas carefully collect the bones, scrape, wash, and bury them, "partly, as it is said, to testify to the dog-species, that in feasting upon one of their number no disrespect was meant to the species itself, and partly also from

[1] H. C. St. John, "The Ainos," *Journal of the Anthropological Institute,* ii. (1873) p. 253; *id., Notes and Sketches from the Wild Coasts of Nipon,* pp. 27 *sq.* Similarly it is a rule with the Aino to bring the flesh of bears and other game into the house, not by the door, but by the window or the smoke-hole. See Rev. J. Batchelor, *The Ainu and their Folk-lore* (London, 1901), p. 123; P. Labbé, *Un Bagne Russe* (Paris, 1903), pp. 255 *sq.*

[2] *Archiv für Anthropologie,* xxvi. (1900) p. 796 (as to the Gilyak of the Amoor); J. Scheffer, *Lapponia* (Frankfort, 1673), pp. 242 *sq.* ; C. Leemius, *De Lapponibus Finmarchiae eorumque lingua, vita, et religione pris-*

tina commentatio (Copenhagen, 1767), p. 503; *Revue d'Ethnographie,* ii. (1883) pp. 308 *sq.* ; *Journal of the Anthropological Institute,* vii. (1878) p. 207; Fr. Boas, "The Central Eskimo," in *Sixth Annual Report of the Bureau of Ethnology* (Washington, 1888), p. 595; *id.,* "The Eskimo of Baffin Land and Hudson Bay," *Bulletin of the American Museum of Natural History,* xv. (1901) p. 148; A. G. Morice, in *Transactions of the Canadian Institute,* iv. (1892-93) p. 108.

[3] E. James, *Expedition from Pittsburgh to the Rocky Mountains* (London, 1823), i. 257.

[4] D. G. Brinton, *Myths of the New World*[2] (New York, 1876), p. 278.

a belief that the bones of the animal will rise and reproduce another." [1]   Among the Esquimaux of Baffin Land and Hudson Bay, when a boy has killed his first seal, his mother gathers all the bones and throws them into a seal-hole. They think that these bones will become seals which the boy will catch in later life.[2]   The Yuracares Indians of Bolivia are at great pains to collect all the bones of the beasts, birds, and fishes which they eat, and to throw them into a stream, bury them in the depths of the forest, or burn them in the fire, " in order that the animals of the sort killed may not be angry and may allow themselves to be killed again." [3]   In sacrificing an animal the Lapps regularly put aside the bones, eyes, ears, heart, lungs, sexual parts (if the animal was a male), and a morsel of flesh from each limb. Then, after eating the remainder of the flesh, they laid the bones and the rest in anatomical order in a coffin and buried them with the usual rites, believing that the god to whom the animal was sacrificed would reclothe the bones with flesh and restore the animal to life in Jabme-Aimo, the sub-terranean world of the dead.   Sometimes, as after feasting on a bear, they seem to have contented themselves with thus burying the bones.[4]   Thus the Lapps expected the resurrec-tion of the slain animal to take place in another world, resembling in this respect the Kamtchatkans, who believed that every creature, down to the smallest fly, would rise from the dead and live underground.[5]   On the other hand, the North American Indians looked for the resurrection of the animals in the present world.   The habit, observed especially by Mongolian peoples, of stuffing the skin of a sacrificed

[1] W. H. Keating, *Expedition to the Source of St. Peter's River* (London, 1825), i. 452.

[2] Fr. Boas, "The Eskimo of Baffin Land and Hudson Bay," *Bulletin of the American Museum of Natural History*, xv. (1901) p. 161.

[3] A. d'Orbigny, *Voyage dans l'Amérique Méridionale*, iii. (Paris and Strasburg, 1844) p. 201. However, in this case a belief in the resurrection of the animals is not expressly affirmed, and the practice of burning the bones seems inconsistent with it.

[4] E. J. Jessen, *De Finnorum Lap-*
ponumque Norwegicorum religione pagana tractatus singularis, pp. 46 *sq.*, 52 *sq.*, 65 (bound with C. Leem's *De Lapponibus Finmarchiae eorumque lingua, vita et religione pristina com-mentatio*, Copenhagen, 1767). Com-pare Leem's work, pp. 418-420, 428 *sq.*; J. Acerbi, *Travels through Sweden, Finnland, and Lapland* (London, 1802), ii. 302.

[5] G. W. Steller, *Beschreibung von dem Lande Kamtschatka* (Frankfort and Leipsic, 1774), p. 269; S. Kraschen-innikow, *Beschreibung des Landes Kamtschatka* (Lemgo, 1766), p. 246.

animal, or stretching it on a framework,[1] points rather to a belief in a resurrection of the latter sort. The objection commonly entertained by primitive peoples to break the bones of the animals which they have eaten or sacrificed [2]

[1] See A. Erman, referred to above, p. 223; J. G. Gmelin, *Reise durch Sibirien* (Göttingen, 1751-1752), i. 274, ii. 182 *sq.*, 214; H. Vambery, *Das Türkenvolk* (Leipsic, 1885), pp. 118 *sq.* When a fox, the sacred animal of the Conchucos in Peru, had been killed, its skin was stuffed and set up (A. Bastian, *Die Culturländer des alten Amerika*, i. 443). Compare the *bouphonia*, above, pp. 4 *sqq.*

[2] At the annual sacrifice of the White Dog, the Iroquois were careful to strangle the animal without shedding its blood or breaking its bones; the dog was afterwards burned (L. H. Morgan, *League of the Iroquois*, Rochester, 1851, p. 210). It is a rule with some of the Australian blacks that in killing the native bear they may not break his bones. They say that the native bear once stole all the water of the river, and that if they were to break his bones or take off his skin before roasting him, he would do so again (R. Brough Smyth, *Aborigines of Victoria*, i. 447 *sqq.*). Some of the Queensland aborigines believe that if the bones or skulls of dugong were not put away in a heap or otherwise preserved, no more dugong would be caught (W. E. Roth, *North Queensland Ethnography*, Bulletin No. 5, Brisbane, 1903, p. 27). When the Tartars whom Carpini visited killed animals for eating, they might not break their bones but burned them with fire (Carpini, *Historia Mongalorum* (Paris, 1838), cap. iii. § i. 2, p. 620). North American Indians might not break the bones of the animals which they ate at feasts (Charlevoix, *Histoire de la Nouvelle France*, vi. 72). In the war feast held by Indian warriors after leaving home, a whole animal was cooked and had to be all eaten. No bone of it might be broken. After being stripped of the flesh the bones were hung on a tree (*Narrative of the Captivity and Adventures of John Tanner*, London, 1830,

p. 287). On St. Olaf's Day (29th July) the Karels of Finland kill a lamb, without using a knife, and roast it whole. None of its bones may be broken. The lamb has not been shorn since spring. Some of the flesh is placed in a corner of the room for the house-spirits, some is deposited on the field and beside the birch-trees which are destined to be used as May-trees next year (W. Mannhardt, *Antike Wald- und Feldkulte*, pp. 160 *sq.*, note). Some of the Esquimaux in skinning a deer are careful not to break a single bone, and they will not break the bones of deer while walrus are being hunted (Fr. Boas, "The Central Eskimo," *Sixth Annual Report of the Bureau of Ethnology* (Washington, 1888), pp. 595 *sq.*). The Innuit (Esquimaux) of Point Barrow, Alaska, carefully preserve unbroken the bones of the seals which they have caught and return them to the sea, either leaving them in an ice-crack far out from the land or dropping them through a hole in the ice. By doing so they think they secure good fortune in the pursuit of seals (*Report of the International Expedition to Point Barrow, Alaska* (Washington, 1885), p. 40). In this last custom the idea probably is that the bones will be reclothed with flesh and the seals come to life again. The Mosquito Indians of Central America carefully preserved the bones of deer and the shells of eggs, lest the deer or chickens should die or disappear (H. H. Bancroft, *Native Races of the Pacific States*, i. 741). In Syria at the present time people offer a sacrifice for a boy when he is seven days old, and they will not break a bone of the victim, "because they fear that if a bone of the sacrifice should be broken, the child's bones would be broken, too" (S. I. Curtiss, *Primitive Semitic Religion To-day*, Chicago, etc., 1902, p. 178). This last may be a later misinterpretation of the old custom. For West African cases of refusal to break the

may be based either on a belief in the resurrection of the animals, or on a fear of intimidating other creatures of the same species and offending the ghosts of the slain animals. The reluctance of North American Indians and Esquimaux to let dogs gnaw the bones of animals[1] is perhaps only a precaution to prevent the bones from being broken.

We have already seen that some rude races believe in a resurrection of men[2] as well as of beasts, and it is quite natural that people who entertain such a belief should take care of the bones of their dead in order that the original owners of the bones may have them to hand at the critical moment. Hence in the Mexican territories of Guazacualco and Yluta, where the Indians thought that the dead would rise again, the bones of the departed were deposited in baskets and hung up on trees, that their spirits might not be obliged to grub in the earth for them at the resurrection.[3]

Some savages preserve or destroy the bones of men in order to assist or prevent their resurrection.

---

bones of sacrificial victims, see J. Spieth, *Die Ewe-Stämme* (Berlin, 1906), pp. 458, 466, 480, 527, 712, 796, 824. Amongst the Narrinyeri of South Australia, when an animal was being cut up, the bystanders used to leap and yell as often as a bone was broken, thinking that if they did not do so their own bones would rot within them (A. W. Howitt, *Native Tribes of South-East Australia*, p. 763).

[1] *Relations des Jésuites*, 1634, p. 25 (Canadian reprint, Quebec, 1858); A. Mackenzie, *Voyages through the Continent of America* (London, 1801), p. civ. ; J. Dunn, *History of the Oregon Territory* (London, 1844), p. 99 ; F. Whymper, in *Journal of the Royal Geographical Society*, xxxviii. (1868) p. 228 ; *id.*, in *Transactions of the Ethnological Society*, N.S., vii. (1869) p. 174 ; A. P. Reid, "Religious Belief of the Ojibois Indians," *Journal of the Anthropological Institute*, iii. (1874) p. 111 ; Fr. Boas, "The Central Eskimo," *Sixth Annual Report of the Bureau of Ethnology* (Washington, 1888), p. 596 ; *id.*, "The Eskimo of Baffin Land and Hudson Bay," *Bulletin of the American Museum of Natural History*, xv. (1901) p. 123 ; E. W. Nelson, "The Eskimo about Bering Strait," *Eighteenth Annual

Report of the Bureau of American Ethnology, Part i. (Washington, 1899) pp. 438 *sq.* For more examples see above, pp. 225, 238 *sqq.*, 242 *sq.*, 246. After a meal the Indians of Costa Rica gather all the bones carefully and either burn them or put them out of reach of the dogs. See W. M. Gabb, *On the Indian Tribes and Languages of Costa Rica* (read before the American Philosophical Society, 20th Aug. 1875), p. 520 (Philadelphia, 1875). The custom of burning the bones to prevent the dogs getting them does not necessarily contradict the view suggested in the text. It may be a way of transmitting the bones to the spirit-land. The aborigines of Australia burn the bones of the animals which they eat, but for a different reason ; they think that if an enemy got hold of the bones and burned them with charms, it would cause the death of the person who had eaten the animal (*Native Tribes of South Australia*, Adelaide, 1879, pp. 24, 196).

[2] See *Taboo and the Perils of the Soul*, pp. 279 *sqq.*

[3] A. de Herrera, *General History of the vast Continent and Islands of America*, translated by Capt. John Stevens (London, 1725-1726), iv. 126.

On the other hand, the Luritcha tribe of Central Australia, who eat their enemies, take steps to prevent their coming to life again, which might prove very inconvenient, by destroying the bones and especially the skulls of the bodies on which they have banqueted.[1]

Unquestioning faith of savages in the immortality of animals.

The preceding review of customs observed by savages for the conciliation and multiplication of animals which they hunt and kill, is fitted to impress us with a lively sense of the unquestioning faith which primitive man reposes in the immortality of the lower creatures. He appears to assume as an axiom too obvious to be disputed that beasts, birds, and fishes have souls like his own, which survive the death of their bodies and can be reborn in other bodies to be again killed and eaten by the hunter. The whole series of customs described in the foregoing pages—customs which are apt to strike the civilised reader as quaint and absurd—

The savage faith in human immortality is commonly supposed to be deduced from a primitive theory of dreams.

rests on this fundamental assumption. A consideration of them suggests a doubt whether the current explanation of the savage belief in human immortality is adequate to account for all the facts. That belief is commonly deduced from a primitive theory of dreams. The savage, it is said, fails to distinguish the visions of sleep from the realities of waking life, and accordingly when he has dreamed of his dead friends he necessarily concludes that they have not wholly perished, but that their spirits continue to exist in some place and some form, though in the ordinary course of events they elude the perceptions of his senses. On this theory the conceptions, whether gross or refined, whether repulsive or beautiful, which savages and perhaps civilised men have formed of the state of the departed, would seem to be no more than elaborate hypotheses constructed to account for appearances in dreams ; these towering structures, for all their radiant or gloomy grandeur, for all the massy strength and solidity with which they present themselves to the imagination of many, may turn out on inspection to be mere visionary castles built of clouds and vapour, which a breath of reason suffices to melt into air.

[1] Baldwin Spencer and F. J. Gillen, *Native Tribes of Central Australia* (London, 1899), p. 475.

But even if we grant for the sake of argument that this theory offers a ready explanation of the widespread belief in human immortality, it is less easy to see how the theory accounts for the corresponding belief of so many races in the immortality of the lower animals.   In his dreams the savage recognises the images of his departed friends by those familiar traits of feature, voice, and gesture which characterised them in life.   But can we suppose that he recognises dead beasts, birds, and fishes in like manner ? that their images come before him in sleep with all the particular features, the minute individual differences, which distinguished them in life from their fellows, so that when he sees them he can say to himself, for example, " This is the very tiger that I speared yesterday ; his carcase is dead, but his spirit must be still alive "; or, " That is the very salmon I caught and ate this morning ; I certainly killed his body, but clearly I have not succeeded in destroying his soul " ? No doubt it is possible that the savage has arrived at his theory of animal immortality by some such process of reasoning, but the supposition seems at least more far-fetched and improbable than in the case of human immortality.   And if we admit the insufficiency of the explanation in the one case, we seem bound to admit it, though perhaps in a less degree, in the other case also.   In short, we conclude that the theory of dreams appears to be hardly enough by itself to account for the widespread belief in the immortality of men and animals ; dreams have probably done much to confirm that belief, but would they suffice to originate it ?   We may reasonably doubt it.

Accordingly we are driven to cast about for some more adequate explanation of this prevalent and deeply rooted persuasion.   In search of such an explanation perhaps we need go no further than the sense of life which every man feels in his own breast.[1] We have seen that to the savage death presents itself not as a natural necessity but as a lamentable accident or crime that cuts short an existence which, but for it, might have lasted for ever.[2] Thus arguing apparently from his own sensations he conceives of life as an indestructible

But can a theory of dreams account for the savage belief in the immortality of animals?

Apparently the savage conceives life as an indestructible form of energy.

---

[1] For this suggestion I am indebted to a hint thrown out in conversation by my friend Professor G. F. Stout.
[2] See *The Dying God*, p. 1.

kind of energy, which when it disappears in one form must necessarily reappear in another, though in the new form it need not be immediately perceptible by us; in other words, he infers that death does not destroy the vital principle nor even the conscious personality, but that it merely transforms both of them into other shapes, which are not the less real because they commonly elude the evidence of our senses. If I am right in thus interpreting the thought of primitive man, the savage view of the nature of life singularly resembles the modern scientific doctrine of the conservation of energy. According to that doctrine, no material energy ever perishes or is even diminished; when it seems to suffer diminution or extinction, all that happens is that a portion or the whole of it has been transmuted into other shapes which, though qualitatively different from, are quantitatively equivalent to, the energy in its original form. In short, if we listen to science, nothing in the physical world is ever lost, but all things are perpetually changing: the sum of energy in the universe is constant and invariable, though it undergoes ceaseless transformations.[1] A similar theory of the indestructibility of energy is implicitly applied by the savage to explain the phenomena of life and death, and logically enough he does not limit the application to human beings but extends it to the lower animals. Therein he shews himself a better reasoner than his civilised brother, who commonly embraces with avidity the doctrine of human immortality but rejects with scorn, as derogatory to human dignity, the idea that animals have immortal souls. And when he attempts to confirm his own cherished belief in a life after death by appealing to similar beliefs among savages and inferring from them a natural instinct of immortality, it is well to

Analogy of the conception to the modern scientific conception of the conservation of energy.

---

[1] The principle of the conservation of energy is clearly stated and illustrated by Balfour Stewart in his book *The Conservation of Energy*, Fourth Edition (London, 1877). The writer does not countenance the view that life is a form of energy distinct from and independent of physical and chemical forces; he regards a living being simply as a very delicately constructed machine in which the natural forces are in a state of unstable equilibrium. To avoid misapprehension it may be well to add that I do not pretend to argue either for or against the theory of life which appears to be implicitly adopted by the savage; my aim is simply to explain, not to justify or condemn, the mental attitude of primitive man towards these profound problems.

remind him that, if he stands by that appeal, he must, like
the savage, consistently extend the privilege of immortality
to the despised lower animals ; for surely it is improper for
him to pick and choose his evidence so as to suit his
prepossessions, accepting those parts of the savage creed
which tally with his own and rejecting those which do not.
On logical and scientific grounds he seems bound to believe
either more or less : he must hold that men and animals
are alike immortal or that neither of them is so.

We have seen that many savages look forward to a The resur-
joyful resurrection of men and beasts, if only a proper rection of
the body in
care is taken of their skeletons ; the same old bones, they tales and
imagine, will do duty over again in the next life, when legends.
they have been decently clad in a new garment of flesh.
This quaint fancy is reflected in many popular tales ; not
uncommonly the animal or man in the story comes to life
lame of a limb, because one of his bones has been eaten,
broken, or lost.[1]   In a Magyar tale, the hero is cut in pieces,
but the serpent-king lays the bones together in their proper
order, and washes them with water, whereupon the hero revives.
His shoulder-blade, however, has been lost, so the serpent-
king supplies its place with one of gold and ivory.[2]   Such
stories, as Mannhardt has seen, explain why Pythagoras,
who claimed to have lived many lives, one after the other,
was said to have exhibited his golden leg as a proof of his
supernatural pretensions.[3]   Doubtless he explained that at
one of his resurrections a leg had been broken or mislaid,
and that he had replaced it, like Miss Kilmansegg, with
one of gold.   Similarly, when the murdered Pelops was
restored to life, the shoulder which Demeter had eaten was
made good with one of ivory,[4] which was publicly exhibited

---

[1] W. Mannhardt, *Germanische Mythen* (Berlin, 1858), pp. 57-74 ; *id.*,
Baumkultus, p. 116 ; C. L. Rochholz,
Deutscher Glaube und Brauch (Berlin,
1867), i. 219 *sqq.* ; J. Curtin, *Myths
and Folk-lore of Ireland* (London, N.D.),
pp. 45 *sq.* ; E. Cosquin, *Contes populaires de Lorraine* (Paris, N.D.), ii. 25 ;
E. S. Hartland, "The Physicians of
Myddfai," *Archaeological Review*, i.

(1888) pp. 30 *sq.*   In folk-tales, as in
primitive custom, the blood is sometimes
not allowed to fall on the ground. See
E. Cosquin, *l.c.*

[2] W. Mannhardt, *Germanische Mythen*, p. 66.

[3] Jamblichus, *Vita Pythag.* 92, 135,
140 ; Porphyry, *Vita Pythag.* 28.

[4] Pindar, *Olymp.* i. 37 *sqq.*, with
the Scholiast.

at Elis down to historical times.[1]   The story that one of the members of the mangled Osiris was eaten by fish, and that, when Isis collected his scattered limbs, she replaced the missing member with one of wood,[2] may perhaps belong to the same circle of beliefs.

The sinew of the thigh regularly cut out and thrown away by some American Indians.

There is a certain rule observed by savage hunters and fishers which, enigmatical at first sight, may possibly be explained by this savage belief in resurrection.   A traveller in America in the early part of the nineteenth century was told by a half-breed Choctaw that the Indians "had an obscure story, somewhat resembling that of Jacob wrestling with an angel ; and that the full-blooded Indians always separate the sinew which shrank, and that it is never seen in the venison exposed for sale ; he did not know what they did with it.   His elder brother, whom I afterwards met, told me that they eat it as a rarity ; but I have also heard, though on less respectable authority, that they refrain from it, like the ancient Jews. A gentleman, who had lived on the Indian frontier, or in the nation, for ten or fifteen years, told me that he had often been surprised that the Indians always detached this sinew ; but it had never occurred to him to inquire the reason." [3] James Adair, who knew the Indians of the South-Eastern States intimately, and whose absurd theories appear not to have distorted his view of the facts, observes that " when in the woods, the Indians cut a small piece out of the lower part of the thighs of the deer they kill, lengthways and pretty deep.   Among the great number of venison-hams they bring to our trading-houses, I do not remember to have observed one without it. . . . And I have been assured by a gentleman of character, who is now an inhabitant of South Carolina, and well acquainted with the customs of the northern Indians, that they also cut a piece out of the thigh of every deer they kill, and throw it away ; and reckon it such a dangerous pollution to eat it as to occasion sickness and other misfortunes of sundry kinds, especially by spoiling their guns from shooting with proper force and direction." [4]

---

[1] Pliny, *Nat. Hist.* xxviii. 34.

[2] Plutarch, *Isis et Osiris,* 18.   This is one of the sacred stories which the pious Herodotus (ii. 48) concealed and the pious Plutarch divulged.

[3] Adam Hodgson, *Letters from North America* (London, 1824), i. 244.

[4] J. Adair, *History of the American Indians* (London, 1775), pp. 137 *sq.* This writer, animated by a curious

In more recent times the statement of Adair's informant has been confirmed by a French missionary, who has also published the " obscure story " to which the English traveller Hodgson refers.   The Loucheux and Hare-skin Indians who roam the bleak steppes and forests that stretch from Hudson's Bay to the Rocky Mountains, and northward to the frozen sea, are forbidden by custom to eat the sinew of the legs of animals.   To explain this custom they tell the following " sacred story."   Once upon a time a man found a burrow of porcupines, and going down into it after the porcupines he lost his way in the darkness, till a kind giant called " He who sees before and behind " released him by cleaving open the earth.   So the man, whose name was " Fireless and Homeless," lived with the kind giant, and the giant hunted elans and beavers for him, and carried him about in the sheath of his flint knife.   " But know, my son," said the giant, " that he who uses the sky as his head is angry with me, and has sworn my destruction.   If he slays me the clouds will be tinged with my blood ; they will be red with it, probably."   Then he gave the man an axe made of the tooth of a gigantic beaver, and went forth to meet his foe.   But from under the ice the man heard a dull muffled sound.   It was a whale which was making this noise because it was naked and cold.   Warned by the man, the giant went toward the whale, which took human shape, and rushed upon the giant.   It was the wicked giant, the kind giant's enemy. The two struggled together for a long time, till the kind giant cried, " Oh, my son ! cut, cut the sinew of the leg." The man cut the sinew, and the wicked giant fell down and was slain.   That is why the Indians do not eat the sinew of the leg.   Afterwards, one day the sky suddenly flushed a fiery red, so Fireless and Homeless knew that the kind giant was no more, and he wept.[1]

though not uncommon passion for discovering the ten lost tribes of Israel, imagined that he detected the missing Hebrews disguised under the red skins and beardless faces of the American Indians.

[1] É. Petitot, *Monographie des Dènè-Dindjie* (Paris, 1876), pp. 77, 81 *sq.* ; *id.*, *Traditions indiennes du Canada Nord-ouest* (Paris, 1886), pp. 132 *sqq.*, compare pp. 41, 76, 213, 264.   The story is told in a briefer form, though without any reference to the custom, by another French missionary.   See the letter of Mgr. Tache, in *Annales de la Propagation de la Foi*, xxiv. (1852) pp. 336 *sq.*

This myth, it is almost needless to observe, does not really explain the custom. People do not usually observe a custom because on a particular occasion a mythical being is said to have acted in a certain way. But, on the contrary, they very often invent myths to explain why they practise certain customs. Dismissing, therefore, the story of Fireless and Homeless as a myth invented to explain why the Indians abstain from eating a particular sinew, it may be suggested [1] that the original reason for observing the custom was a belief that the sinew in question was necessary to reproduction, and that deprived of it the slain animals could not come to life again and stock the steppes and prairies either of the present world or of the spirit land. We have seen that the resurrection of animals is a common article of savage faith, and that when the Lapps bury the skeleton of the male bear in the hope of its resurrection they are careful to bury the genital parts along with it. However, subsequent enquiries make it probable that the Indian practice of cutting out the hamstring of deer has no other object than that of preventing eaters of venison from going lame. Among the Cherokee, we are told, " on killing a deer the hunter always makes an incision in the hind quarter and removes the hamstring, because this tendon, when severed, draws up into the flesh ; ergo, any one who should unfortunately partake of the hamstring would find his limbs drawn up in the same manner." [2] Thus the superstition

[1] The first part of this suggestion is due to my friend W. Robertson Smith. See his *Lectures on the Religion of the Semites* [2] (London, 1894), p. 380, note 1. The Faleshas, a Jewish sect of Abyssinia, after killing an animal for food, " carefully remove the vein from the thighs with its surrounding flesh." See Halévy, " Travels in Abyssinia," in *Publications of the Society of Hebrew Literature*, Second Series, vol. ii. p. 220. Caffre men will not eat the sinew of the thigh ; " it is carefully cut out and sent to the principal boy at the kraal, who with his companions consider it as their right." See Col. Maclean, *Kafir Laws and Customs* (Cape Town, 1866), p. 151. Gallas who pride themselves on their descent will not eat the flesh of the biceps ; the reasons assigned for the custom are inconsistent and unsatisfactory. See Ph. Paulitschke, *Ethnographie Nordost-Afrikas : die materielle Cultur der Danâkil, Galla und Somâl* (Berlin, 1893), p. 154. When the Bushmen kill a hare, they cut out a sinew of the thigh and will not eat it, alleging as their reason that the hare was once a man, and that this particular sinew is still human flesh. See W. H. I. Bleek and L. C. Lloyd, *Specimens of Bushman Folklore* (London, 1911), pp. xxxix., 60 *sq.*, 63.

[2] J. Mooney, " Sacred Formulas of the Cherokees," *Seventh Annual Report of the Bureau of Ethnology* (Washington, 1891), p. 323. Compare *id.*,

seems to rest on the common principle of homoeopathic or imitative magic, that an eater infects himself with the qualities of the animal of whose flesh he partakes. Many instances of the application of that principle have met us already.[1]

But some hunters hamstring the game for a different purpose ; they hope thereby to prevent the dead beast or its ghost from getting up and running away. This is the motive alleged for the practice by Koui hunters in Laos ; they think that the spells which they utter in the chase may lose their magical virtue, and that the slaughtered animal may consequently come to life again and escape. To prevent that catastrophe they therefore hamstring the beast as soon as they have butchered it.[2] When an Esquimau of Alaska has killed a fox, he carefully cuts the tendons of all the animal's legs in order to prevent the ghost from reanimating the body and walking about.[3] But hamstringing the carcase is not the only measure which the prudent savage adopts for the sake of disabling the ghost of his victim. In old days, when the Aino went out hunting and killed a fox first, they took care to tie its mouth up tightly in order to prevent the ghost of the animal from sallying forth and warning its fellows against the approach of the hunter.[4] The Gilyaks of the Amoor River put out the eyes of the seals they have killed, lest the ghosts of the slain animals should know their slayers and avenge their death by spoiling the seal-hunt.[5] The custom of putting out the eyes of slaughtered animals appears to be not uncommon among primitive peoples, and we may suspect that even where a different reason is alleged for it, the true

Some hunters hamstring the dead game in order to lame the ghosts of the animals.

Some savages put out the eyes of dead game in order perhaps to blind the ghosts of the animals.

"Myths of the Cherokee," *Nineteenth Annual Report of the Bureau of American Ethnology*, Part i. (Washington, 1900) pp. 267, 447. In the last of these passages the writer quotes Buttrick, *Antiquities*, p. 12, as follows : "The Indians never used to eat a certain sinew in the thigh. . . . Some say that if they eat of the sinew they will have cramp in it on attempting to run. It is said that once a woman had cramp in that sinew, and therefore none must eat it."

[1] See above, pp. 138 *sqq.*

[2] É. Aymonier, *Notes sur le Laos* (Saigon, 1885), p. 23.

[3] E. W. Nelson, "The Eskimo about Bering Strait," *Eighteenth Annual Report of the Bureau of American Ethnology*, Part i. (Washington, 1899) p. 423.

[4] Rev. J. Batchelor, *The Ainu and their Folk-lore* (London, 1901), p. 504.

[5] L. von Schrenck, *Reisen und Forschungen im Amur - Lande*, iii. 546.

original motive was to blind the dangerous ghost of the injured creature, and so to incapacitate it for retaliating on the slayer. Thus, when a Samoyed has killed a wild reindeer, one of the first things he does is to cut out the eyes and throw them away "in order to ensure a good bag in future"; and he buries the eyes in some place where no woman or adult girl is likely to step over them, since that also would spoil his luck in the chase.[1] Among the tribes of South-east Africa hunters pluck out the right eye of any animal they have killed and pour a charmed medicine into the empty socket.[2] Among the Thompson Indians of British Columbia a man whose daughter has just arrived at puberty may not hunt or trap for a month, or he will have no luck. Moreover, he should cut off the head of the first grouse he snares, pluck out the eyes, and insert two small roots of the *Zygadenus elegans* Pursch. in the orbits and another in its mouth, and having done so he ought to hang up the bird's head above his pillow. If he neglects these precautions, he will not be able to snare any more grouse or other small game.[3] No doubt the ceremonial pollution contracted by his daughter at this critical period of her life is supposed to infect the hunter and render him unacceptable to the game;[4] hence it seems a mere elementary dictate of prudence to hoodwink the grouse effectually by putting out their eyes. Sometimes, perhaps, the cutting out of the eyes of fierce and powerful animals may be a rational, not a superstitious, precaution. Thus the Kamtchatkans, who stab with knives the eyes of slain bears before they cut the carcases up, allege as their reason for doing so that bears which seem to be dead

---

[1] P. S. Pallas, *Reise durch verschiedene Provinzen des Russischen Reichs* (St. Petersburg, 1771-1776), iii. 70.

[2] Rev. J. Macdonald, *Light in Africa*, Second Edition (London, 1890), p. 171.

[3] J. Teit, *The Thompson Indians of British Columbia*, p. 317 (*The Jesup North Pacific Expedition, Memoir of the American Museum of Natural History*, April, 1900).

[4] So among the Esquimaux of Bering Strait a girl at puberty is considered unclean. " A peculiar atmosphere is supposed to surround her at this time, and if a young man should come near enough for it to touch him it would render him visible to every animal he might hunt, so that his success as a hunter would be gone." See E. W. Nelson, "The Eskimo about Bering Strait," *Eighteenth Annual Report of the Bureau of American Ethnology*, Part i. (Washington, 1899) p. 291.

of their wounds will sometimes revive and kill their would-be killers.[1]

It appears to be a common custom with savage hunters to cut out the tongues of the animals which they kill. On the analogy of the foregoing customs we may conjecture that the removal of the tongues is sometimes a precaution to prevent the ghosts of the creatures from telling their sad fate to their sympathising comrades, the living animals of the same sort, who would naturally be frightened, and so keep out of the hunter's way. Thus, for example, Omaha hunters remove the tongue of a slain buffalo through an opening made in the animal's throat. The tongues thus removed are sacred and may not touch any tool or metal except when they are boiling in the kettles at the sacred tent. They are eaten as sacred food.[2] Indian bear-hunters cut out what they call the bear's little tongue (a fleshy mass under the real tongue) and keep it for good luck in hunting or burn it to determine, from its crackling and so on, whether the soul of the slain bear is angry with them or not.[3] In folk-tales the hero commonly cuts out the tongue of the wild beast which he has slain and preserves it as a token. The incident serves to shew that the custom was a common one, since folk-tales reflect with accuracy the customs and beliefs of a primitive age.[4] On the other hand, the

---

[1] P. Dobell, *Travels in Kamtchatka and Siberia* (London, 1830), i. 19.

[2] Rev. J. Owen Dorsey, "Omaha Sociology," *Third Report of the Bureau of Ethnology* (Washington, 1884), pp. 289 *sq.*

[3] J. G. Kohl, *Kitschi-Gami* (Bremen, 1859), ii. 251 *sq.*; Charlevoix, *Histoire de la Nouvelle France*, v. 173; Chateaubriand, *Voyage en Amérique*, pp. 179 *sq.*, 184.

[4] For examples of the incident, see J. F. Bladé, *Contes populaires recueillis en Agenais* (Paris, 1874), pp. 12, 14; G. W. Dasent, *Popular Tales from the Norse* (Edinburgh, 1859), pp. 133 *sq.* ("Shortshanks"); Aug. Schleicher, *Litauische Märchen* (Weimar, 1857), p. 58; Sepp, *Altbayerischer Sagenschatz* (Munich, 1876), p. 114; R. Köhler, on L. Gonzenbach's *Sicilianische Märchen* (Leipsic, 1870), ii. 230;

Apollodorus, *Bibliotheca*, iii. 13. 3; Schol. on Apollonius Rhodius, *Argonaut.* i. 517; W. Mannhardt, *Antike Wald- und Feldkulte*, p. 53; J. C. Poestion, *Lappländische Märchen* (Vienna, 1886), pp. 231 *sq.*; A. F. Chamberlain, in *Eighth Report on the North-Western Tribes of Canada*, p. 35 (separate reprint from the *Report of the British Association for 1892*); I. V. Zingerle, *Kinder und Hausmärchen aus Tirol*[2] (Gera, 1870), No. 25, p. 127; A. Kuhn und W. Schwartz, *Norddeutsche Sagen, Märchen und Gebräuche* (Leipsic, 1848), p. 342; S. Grundtvig, *Dänische Volksmärchen*, übersetzt von W. Leo (Leipsic, 1878), p. 289; A. Leskien und K. Brugmann, *Litauische Volkslieder und Märchen* (Strasburg, 1882), pp. 405 *sq.*, 409 *sq.*; A. und A. Schott, *Walachische Maerchen* (Stuttgart and Tübingen), No. 10,

Tongues of
animals cut
out in order
to confer
super-
human
knowledge
or power
on their
possessors.

tongues of certain animals, as the otter and the eagle, are torn out and sometimes worn round their necks by Thlinkeet and Haida shamans as a means of conferring superhuman knowledge and power on their possessors.[1] In particular, an otter's tongue is supposed to convey a knowledge of "the language of all inanimate objects, of birds, animals, and other living creatures" to the shaman, who wears it in a little bag hung round his neck.[2] When a Galla priest sacrifices an animal and decides that the omens are favourable, he cuts out the tongue, sticks his thumb through it, and so flays the animal.[3] In certain cases Gallas cut out the tongues of oxen and wear them on their heads as tokens.[4] In Bohemia a fox's tongue is worn as an amulet to make a timid person bold ;[5] in Oldenburg and Belgium it is a remedy for erysipelas.[6] In Bohemia the tongue of a male snake, if cut from the living animal on St. George's Eve and placed under a person's tongue, will confer the gift of eloquence.[7] The Homeric Greeks cut out the tongues of sacrificial victims and burned them.[8] According to some accounts, the tongues of the victims were assigned by the Greeks to Hermes, as the god of speech, or to his human representatives the heralds.[9]

p. 142 ; Chr. Schneller, *Märchen und Sagen aus Wälschtirol* (Innsbruck, 1867), No. 39, pp. 116 *sq.* ; G. Basile, *Pentamerone,* übertragen von F. Liebrecht (Breslau, 1846), i. 99; P. Sébillot, *Contes Populaires de la Haute-Bretagne* (Paris, 1885), No. 11, p. 80 ; E. Cosquin, *Contes Populaires de Lorraine* (Paris, N.D.), i. p. 61 ; J. Haltrich, *Deutsche Volksmärchen aus dem Sachsenlande in Siebenbürgen*[4] (Vienna and Hermannstadt, 1885), No. 24, pp. 104 *sqq.* ; Grimm, *Household Tales,* No. 60. The incident often occurs in the type of tale analysed by Mr. E. S. Hartland in his *Legend of Perseus* (vol. i. pp. 12, 17, 18, etc. ; vol. iii. pp. 6, 7, 8, etc.).

[1] Fr. Boas, in *Fifth Report on the North-Western Tribes of Canada,* p. 58 (separate reprint from the *Report of the British Association for 1889*) ; *id.,* in *Journal of American Folk-lore,* i. (1888) p. 218.

[2] See W. H. Dall, "Masks and Labrets," *Third Annual Report of the Bureau of Ethnology* (Washington,

1884), pp. 111 *sq.* Compare *id., Alaska and its Resources* (London, 1870), p. 425 ; Ivan Petroff, *Report on the Population, Industries, and Resources of Alaska,* p. 176.

[3] Ph. Paulitschke, *Ethnographie Nordost - Afrikas : die Geistige Cultur der Danâkil Galla und Somâl* (Berlin, 1896), p. 47.

[4] Ph. Paulitschke, *op. cit.* p. 156 ; *id., Ethnographie Nordost-Afrikas : die materielle Cultur,* etc. (Berlin, 1893), p. 226.

[5] J. V. Grohmann, *Aberglauben und Gebräuche aus Böhmen und Mähren* (Prague and Leipsic, 1864), p. 54, § 354.

[6] L. Strackerjan, *Aberglaube und Sagen aus dem Herzogthum Oldenburg* (Oldenburg, 1867), ii. 94, § 381 ; E. Monseur, in *Revue de l'Histoire des Religions,* xxxi. (1895) pp. 297 *sq.*

[7] J. V. Grohmann, *op. cit.* p. 81, § 576.

[8] Homer, *Od.* iii. 332, 341.

[9] Scholiast on Aristophanes, *Plutus,* 1110 ; Athenaeus, i. 28, p. 16 B ;

On the principles of sympathetic magic we might expect that heralds should taste the tongues of sacrificial victims to strengthen their voices, or to acquire the gift of tongues.[1]

The conjecture that the practice of cutting out the tongues of dead animals may sometimes be a precaution to prevent their ghosts from telling tales, is to some extent confirmed by a ceremony which the Bechuanas used to observe after a battle. It was customary with them on these occasions to sacrifice a fine black ox, called the expiatory victim (*pekou*), cut off the tip of its tongue, and extract one of its eyes together with a piece of the hamstring and a piece of the principal tendon of the shoulder ; and the severed parts were afterwards carefully fried, along with some medicinal herbs, in a horn by a medicine-man. The reasons for thus mutilating the animal were explained by a native to two French missionaries. " If we cut out and purify the victim's tongue," said he, " the motive is to induce the guardian deities to prevent the enemy from speaking ill of us. We ask also that the sinews of their feet and hands may fail them in the battle ; and that their eyes may not cast a covetous look on our herds." [2] In this custom the sacrificial ox appears to be treated as the ceremonial equivalent of the enemy ; accordingly by cutting out its tongue you obviously prevent your enemy from cursing you, for how can he curse you if he has no tongue ? Similarly, by hamstringing the beast you ensure that the legs and arms of your adversary will fail him in the battle, and by gouging out the ox's eye you make perfectly certain that the foe will never be able to cast a longing eye on your fat beeves. Thus for all practical purposes the mutilation of the ox is quite as effective as the mutilation of the enemy's dead, which is sometimes practised by savages from similar superstitious motives. For example, on the return from a field of battle the Baganda used to cut up one or two of the enemy's dead, scoop out the eyes, cut off the ears, and lay the limbs on the road taken by the returning army "to

Marginal notes: Bechuana custom of mutilating a sacrificial ox in order to inflict corresponding mutilations on the enemy. Mutilation of the corpses of enemies or other dangerous persons for the purpose of maiming their ghosts.

Paroemiographi Graeci, ed. Leutsch et Schneidewin, i. 415, No. 100.

[1] See further H. Gaidoz, "Les Langues coupées," *Mélusine*, iii. (1886-87) coll. 303-307 ; E. Monseur, *loc. cit.*

[2] T. Arbousset et F. Daumas, *Relation d'un Voyage d'Exploration au Nord-est de la Colonie du Cap de Bonne-Espérance* (Paris, 1842), pp. 562-564.

prevent evil following them." [1]   The nature of the evil which
the Baganda warriors feared to incur if they did not mutilate
the dead in this fashion, is not mentioned, but we may conjecture that by gouging out the eyes and ears of their
slain foes they hoped to make their angry ghosts blind
and deaf ; or perhaps, upon the principles of homoeopathic
magic, they counted on maiming their living foes in like
manner.   Some of the aborigines of Australia cut off the
thumbs of their dead enemies in order that their ghosts may
not be able to throw spears. [2]   Other Australian tribes burn
off the thumb nails of their own dead to prevent the poor
ghost from scratching a way for himself out of the grave. [3]
When the Tupi Indians of Brazil killed and ate a prisoner,
" the thumb was cut off because of its use in archery, an art
concerning which they were singularly superstitious ; what
was done with it does not appear, except that it was not
eaten like the rest." [4]   Perhaps these Indians, like the
Australians, thought by this mutilation to disarm the
dangerous ghost of their victim.   When any bad man died,
the Esquimaux of Bering Strait used to cut the sinews of
his arms and legs, " in order to prevent the shade from
returning to the body and causing it to walk at night as a
ghoul." [5]   In Travancore the ghosts of men who have been
hanged for murder are particularly dreaded ; so in order to
incapacitate them from roaming about and attacking people,
it used to be customary to slice off a criminal's heels with a
sword or hamstring him at the moment when he swung free
from the ladder. [6]   The Omaha Indians used to slit the soles
of a man who had been killed by lightning in order to
prevent his ghost from walking. [7]   Among the Awemba of

Disabling the ghost by mutilating his dead body.

[1] Rev. J. Roscoe, "Further Notes
on the Manners and Customs of the
Baganda," *Journal of the Anthropological Institute*, xxxii. (1902) p. 60.
This custom appears not to be mentioned by the writer in his book *The
Baganda* (London, 1911).

[2] A. Oldfield, "On the Aborigines
of Australia," *Transactions of the
Ethnological Society of London*, N.S.
iii. (1865) p. 287.

[3] E. M. Curr, *The Australian Race*
(Melbourne and London, 1886), i. 348,
381.

[4] R. Southey, *History of Brazil*,
vol. i. Second Edition (London, 1822),
p. 231.

[5] E. W. Nelson, "The Eskimo
about Bering Strait," *Eighteenth Annual Report of the Bureau of American
Ethnology*, part i. (Washington, 1899)
p. 423.

[6] Rev. S. Mateer, *The Land of
Charity* (London, 1871), pp. 203 *sq.*

[7] Rev. J. Owen Dorsey, "A Study
of Siouan Cults," *Eleventh Annual
Report of the Bureau of Ethnology*
(Washington, 1894), p. 420.

Northern Rhodesia murderers often inflicted shocking mutilations on the bodies of their victims. " This was done, it is said, to prevent the spirit of the murdered person from exacting vengeance, and even if only the joint of the first or the little finger were cut off, such mutilation would suffice for this purpose."[1] These examples suggest that many other mutilations which savages practise on their dead enemies may spring, not from the blind fury of hatred, but from a cool calculation of the best mode of protecting themselves against the very natural resentment of the ghosts ; by mutilating the corpse they apparently hope to maim the ghost and so to render him incapable of harming them. At all events it appears that in certain circumstances some savages treat the dead bodies of men and beasts much alike, by hamstringing them in order to prevent their ghosts from getting up and walking. So consistent and impartial is the primitive philosopher in his attitude to the spirit world.

[1] C. Gouldsbury and H. Sheane, *The Great Plateau of Northern Rhodesia* (London, 1911), p. 126.

CHAPTER XV

THE PROPITIATION OF VERMIN BY FARMERS

§ 1. *The Enemies of the Crops*

Propitiation of the vermin which infest crops and cattle in Europe. BESIDES the animals which primitive man dreads for their strength and ferocity, and those which he reveres on account of the benefits which he expects from them, there is another class of creatures which he sometimes deems it necessary to conciliate by worship and sacrifice. These are the vermin that infest his crops and his cattle. To rid himself of these deadly foes the farmer has recourse to many superstitious devices, of which, though some are meant to destroy or intimidate the vermin, others aim at propitiating them and persuading them by fair means to spare the fruits of the earth and the herds. Thus Esthonian peasants, in the island of Oesel, stand in great awe of the weevil, an insect which is exceedingly destructive to the grain. They give it a fine name, and if a child is about to kill a weevil they say, " Don't do it ; the more we hurt him, the more he hurts us." If they find a weevil they bury it in the earth instead of killing it. Some even put the weevil under a stone in the field and offer corn to it. They think that thus it is appeased and does less harm.[1] Amongst the Saxons of Transylvania, in order to keep sparrows from the corn, the sower begins by throwing the first handful of seed backwards over his head, saying, "That is for you, sparrows." To guard the corn against the attacks of leaf-flies (*Erdflöhe*) he shuts his eyes and scatters three handfuls of oats in different directions. Having made this offering to the leaf-flies he feels sure that

---

[1] J. B. Holzmayer, "Osiliana," *Verhandlungen der gelehrten Estni-* *schen Gesellschaft zu Dorpat*, vii. Heft 2 (Dorpat, 1872), p. 105 note.

they will spare the corn.   A Transylvanian way of securing
the crops against all birds, beasts, and insects, is this : after
he has finished sowing, the sower goes once more from end
to end of the field imitating the gesture of sowing, but with
an empty hand.   As he does so he says, " I sow this for the
animals ; I sow it for everything that flies and creeps, that
walks and stands, that sings and springs, in the name of
God   the   Father,   etc."[1]   The Huzuls of the Carpathians
believe that the bite of the weasel is poisonous and that the
animal commits ravages on the cattle.   Yet they take care
never to kill a weasel, lest the surviving kinsfolk of the
deceased   should   avenge   his   death   on   the   herds   of   his
murderer.   They even celebrate a festival of weasels either
on St. Matthew's day (9th August, old style, 21st August,
new style), or on St. Catherine's day (24th November, old
style, 6th December, new style).   On that day no work
may be done, lest the weasels should harm the herds.[2]   The
following is a German way of freeing a garden from caterpillars.   After sunset or at midnight the mistress of the
house, or another female member of the family, walks all
round the garden dragging a broom after her.   She must
not look behind her, and must keep murmuring, " Good
evening, Mother Caterpillar, you shall come with your
husband to church."   The garden gate is left open till
the following morning.[3]

The attempts thus made by European peasants to Similar
mollify the rage and avert the ravages of vermin have their attempts made to
counterpart in the similar observances of savages.   When propitiate
the Matabele find caterpillars in their fields they put an ear of vermin by savages.
corn in a calabash, fill the vessel up with caterpillars, and set it
down on a path leading to another village, hoping thus to
induce the insects to migrate thither.[4]   The Yabim of German
New Guinea imagine that the caterpillars and worms which
infest their fields of taro are animated by the souls of

[1] G. A. Heinrich, *Agrarische Sitten
und Gebräuche unter den Sachsen
Siebenbürgens* (Hermannstadt, 1880),
pp. 15 *sq.*

[2] R. F. Kaindl, *Die Huzulen*
(Vienna, 1894), pp. 79, 103 ; *id.*,
" Viehzucht und Viehzauber in den

Ostkarpaten," *Globus*, lxix. (1906) p.
387.
[3] E. Krause, "Abergläubische Kuren
und sonstiger Aberglaube in Berlin,"
Zeitschrift für Ethnologie, xv. (1883)
p. 93.
[4] L. Decle, *Three Years in Savage
Africa* (London, 1898), p. 160.

the human dead ; hence in order to rid the crops of these vermin they politely request the insects to leave the fields and repair to the village. " Ye locusts, worms, and cater-pillars," they say, " who have died or hanged yourselves, or have been killed by a falling log or devoured by a shark, go into the village."[1]   There is a certain ant whose de-structive ravages are dreaded by the people of Nias. Generally they wage war on it by means of traps and other devices ; but at the time of the rice-harvest they cease to call the insect by its common name, and refer to it under the title of Sibaia, a good spirit who is supposed to protect the crop from harm.[2]   In South Mirzapur, when locusts threaten to eat up the fruits of the earth, the people catch one, decorate his head with a spot of red lead, salaam to him, and let him go.   After these civilities he immediately departs along with his fellows.[3]   Among the Wajagga of German East Africa sorcerers attempt to rid the fields of locusts by catching one of the insects, tying its legs together, and letting it fly away, after charging the creature to lead the swarm to the lands of a neighbouring and hostile chief.[4]   The Wagogo, another tribe of German East Africa, catch one of the birds which infest their gardens, and, having drenched it with a charmed stuff, they release the bird in the hope that it may entice all its companions away into the forest.[5]

Sometimes in dealing with vermin the farmer aims at a judicious mean between undue severity and weak indulgence.

Sometimes in dealing with vermin the farmer aims at hitting a happy mean between excessive rigour on the one hand and weak indulgence on the other ; kind but firm, he tempers severity with mercy.   An ancient Greek treatise on farming advises the husbandman who would rid his lands of mice to act thus : " Take a sheet of paper and write on it as follows : ' I adjure you, ye mice here present, that ye neither injure me nor suffer another mouse to do so.   I give you

[1] Vetter, "Aberglaube unter dem Jabim-Stamme in Kaiser-Wilhelms-land," *Mitteilungen der Geographischen Gesellschaft zu Jena*, xii. (1893) pp. 95 *sq.*

[2] E. Modigliani, *Un Viaggio a Nias* (Milan, 1890), p. 626.

[3] W. Crooke, *Popular Religion and Folklore of Northern India* (West-minster, 1896), ii. 303.

[4] M. Merker, "Rechtsverhältnisse und Sitten der Wadschagga," *Peter-manns Mitteilungen, Ergänzungsheft* No. 138 (Gotha, 1902), pp. 35 *sq.*

[5] Rev. H. Cole, "Notes on the Wagogo of German East Africa," *Journal of the Anthropological Insti-tute*, xxxii. (1902) p. 320.

yonder field' (here you specify the field) ; 'but if ever I
catch you here again, by the Mother of the Gods I will rend
you in seven pieces.' Write this, and stick the paper on an
unhewn stone in the field before sunrise, taking care to keep
the written side up."[1] In the Ardennes they say that to
get rid of rats you should repeat the following words : " *Erat
verbum, apud Deum vestrum.* Male rats and female rats, I
conjure you, by the great God, to go out of my house, out of
all my habitations, and to betake yourselves to such and such
a place, there to end your days. *Decretis, reversis et desem-
barassis virgo potens, clemens, justitiae.*" Then write the
same words on pieces of paper, fold them up, and place one
of them under the door by which the rats are to go forth,
and the other on the road which they are to take. This
exorcism should be performed at sunrise.[2] Some years ago
an American farmer was reported to have written a civil
letter to the rats, telling them that his crops were short, that
he could not afford to keep them through the winter, that he
had been very kind to them, and that for their own good he
thought they had better leave him and go to some of his
neighbours who had more grain. This document he pinned
to a post in his barn for the rats to read.[3] The mouse
is one of the most dreaded enemies of the rice-crop in
Celebes. Many therefore are the prayers and incantations
which prudent farmers resort to for the purpose of keeping
the vermin from their fields. Thus, for example, a man
will run round his field, saying, " Pruner is your name.
Creep not through my rice. Be blind and deaf. Creep
not through my rice. If you must creep through rice,
go and creep through other rice." The following formula is
equally effective : " Pruner is your real name. Mouse is
your by-name. Down in the evening land is the stone
on which you ought to sit; in the west, in Java, is your
abode." Or again : " O Longtail, Longtail, eat not my

<hr/>

[1] *Geoponica*, xiii. 5. According to
the commentator, the field assigned to
the mice is a neighbour's, but it may
be a patch of waste ground on the
farmer's own land. The charm is said
to have been employed formerly in the
neighbourhood of Paris (A. de Nore,
Coutumes, Mythes et Traditions des

Provinces de France, Paris and Lyons,
1846, p. 383).

[2] A. Meyrac, *Traditions, Coutumes,
Légendes et Contes des Ardennes*
(Charleville, 1890), p. 176.

[3] *American Journal of Folk-lore*, xi.
(1898) p. 161.

rice. It is the rice of a prince. It is the field of one who is revered."[1] The Aino of Japan believe that God first created rats and mice at Erum kotan, which means " rat place." Indeed, there are a great many rats and mice there even now, and the people of the village worship mice and offer them libations and sacred sticks whittled at the top into shavings. Grateful for these attentions, the mice spare the gardens and will not nibble at the roots and the fruits. But if the people omit to worship the mice, or if they are rash enough to speak evil of them, the creatures are angry and eat up the garden produce. The havoc which rats and mice now work in the gardens of the Aino every year is attributed to the modern neglect of the people to worship the vermin.[2]

Sometimes a few of the vermin are treated with high distinction, while the rest are pursued with relentless rigour. Sometimes the desired object is supposed to be attained by treating with high distinction one or two chosen individuals of the obnoxious species, while the rest are pursued with relentless rigour. In the East Indian island of Bali, the mice which ravage the rice-fields are caught in great numbers, and burned in the same way that corpses are burned. But two of the captured mice are allowed to live, and receive a little packet of white linen. Then the people bow down before them, as before gods, and let them go.[3] In the Kangean archipelago, East Indies, when the mice prove very destructful to the rice-crop, the people rid themselves of the pest in the following manner. On a Friday, when the usual service in the mosque is over, four pairs of mice are solemnly united in marriage by the priest. Each pair is then shut up in a miniature canoe about a foot long. These canoes are filled with rice and other fruits of the earth, and the four pairs of mice are then escorted to the sea-shore just as if it were a real wedding. Wherever the procession passes the people beat with all their might on their rice-blocks. On reaching the shore, the canoes, with their little inmates, are launched and left to the mercy of the winds and

[1] G. Maan, " Eenige mededeelingen omtrent de zeden en gewoonten der Toerateya ten opzichte van den rijst-bouw," *Tijdschrift voor Indische Taal-Land- en Volkenkunde*, xlvi. (1903) pp. 329 *sq.*

[2] Rev. J. Batchelor, *The Ainu and their Folk-lore* (London, 1901), p. 509.

[3] R. van Eck, " Schetsen van het eiland Bali," *Tijdschrift voor Neder-landsch-Indië*, N.S., viii. (1879) p. 125.

waves.[1] When the farms of the Sea Dyaks or Ibans of Sarawak
are much pestered by birds and insects, they catch a specimen of each kind of vermin (one sparrow, one grasshopper,
and so on), put them in a tiny boat of bark well-stocked with
provisions, and then allow the little vessel with its obnoxious
passengers to float down the river.   If that does not drive
the pests away, the Dyaks resort to what they deem a
more effectual mode of accomplishing the same purpose.
They make a clay crocodile as large as life and set it up in
the fields, where they offer it food, rice-spirit, and cloth, and
sacrifice a fowl and a pig before it.   Mollified by these
attentions, the ferocious animal very soon gobbles up all the
creatures that devour the crops.[2]   In some parts of Bohemia
the peasant, though he kills field mice and grey mice without
scruple, always spares white mice.   If he finds a white mouse
he takes it up carefully, and makes a comfortable bed for it
in the window ; for if it died the luck of the house would be
gone, and the grey mice would multiply fearfully in the
dwelling.[3]   In Albania, if the fields or vineyards are ravaged
by locusts or beetles, some of the women will assemble with
dishevelled hair, catch a few of the insects, and march with
them in a funeral procession to a spring or stream, in which
they drown the creatures.   Then one of the women sings,
" O locusts and beetles who have left us bereaved," and the
dirge is taken up and repeated by all the women in chorus.
Thus by celebrating the obsequies of a few locusts and
beetles, they hope to bring about the death of them all.[4]
When caterpillars invaded a vineyard or field in Syria, the
virgins were gathered, and one of the caterpillars was taken
and a girl made its mother.   Then they bewailed and buried
it.   Thereafter they conducted the " mother " to the place
where the caterpillars were, consoling her, in order that all
the caterpillars might leave the garden.[5]   On the first of

Mock lamentations of women for insects which destroy the crops.

---

[1] J. L. van Gennep, " Bijdrage tot
de kennis van den Kangean-Archipel,"
*Bijdragen tot de Taal- Land- en Volken-
kunde van Nederlandsch-Indië,* xlvi.
(1896) p. 101.
    [2] C. Hose and W. McDougall,
" The Relations between Men and
Animals in Sarawak "*Journal of the
Anthropological Institute,* xxxi. (1901)

pp. 198 *sq.*
    [3] J. V. Grohmann, *Aberglauben und
Gebräuche aus Böhmen und Mähren*
(Prague and Leipsic, 1864), p. 60,
§ 405.
    [4] J. G. von Hahn, *Albanesische
Studien* (Jena, 1854), Heft i. p. 157.
    [5] Lagarde,*Reliquiae juris ecclesiastici
antiquissimae,* p. 135. For this passage

September, Russian girls "make small coffins of turnips and
other vegetables, enclose flies and other insects in them, and
then bury them with a great show of mourning."[1] In
South Africa a plague of caterpillars is removed by a
number of small Caffre girls, who go singing through the
fields. They wail as they pass through the languishing
crops, and thus invoke the aid and pity of some ancestral
spirits. The mournful rite ends with a dance on a plot of
ground overlooking the fields.[2]

Ceremony
performed
by Baronga
women
to drive
insects
from the
crops.

On the shore of Delagoa Bay there thrives a small brown
beetle which is very destructive to the beans and maize.
The Baronga call it *noonoo*. In December or January,
when the insects begin to swarm, women are sent to collect
them from the bean-stalks in shells. When they have done
so, a twin girl is charged with the duty of throwing the
insects into a neighbouring lake. Accompanied by a woman
of mature years and carrying the beetles in a calabash, the
girl goes on her mission without saying a word to any one.
At her back marches the whole troop of women, their arms,
waists, and heads covered with grass and holding in their
hands branches of manioc with large leaves which they wave
to and fro, while they chant the words, "*Noonoo*, go away!
Leave our fields! *Noonoo*, go away! leave our fields!"
The little girl throws her calabash with the beetles into the
water without looking behind her, and thereupon the women
bellow out obscene songs, which they never dare to utter
except on this occasion and at the ceremony for making
rain.[3]

Images
made of
vermin as
a charm to
get rid of
them.

Another mode of getting rid of vermin and other noxious
creatures without hurting their feelings or shewing them
disrespect is to make images of them. Apollonius of Tyana
is said to have cleared Antioch of scorpions by making a

I am indebted to my late friend W.
Robertson Smith, who kindly translated
it for me from the Syriac. It occurs in
the *Canons* of Jacob of Edessa, of which
a German translation has been published
by C. Kayser (*Die Canones Jacob's von
Edessa übersetzt und erläutert*, Leipsic,
1886 ; see pp. 25 *sq.*).

[1] W. R. S. Ralston, *Songs of the*

Russian People (London, 1872), p.
255.
[2] Dudley Kidd, *Savage Childhood, a
Study of Kafir Children* (London,
1906), p. 292.
[3] H. A. Junod, *Les Ba-ronga* (Neuchatel, 1898), pp. 419 *sq.* As to the
rain-making ceremony among the Ba-
ronga, see *The Magic Art and the
Evolution of Kings*, i. 267 *sq.*

bronze image of a scorpion and burying it under a small pillar in the middle of the city.[1] Further, it is reported that he freed Constantinople from flies by means of a bronze fly, and from gnats by means of a bronze gnat.[2] In the Middle Ages Virgil passed for an enchanter and is said to have rid Naples of flies and grasshoppers by bronze or copper images of these insects ; and when the waters of the city were infested by leeches, he made a golden leech, which put a stop to the plague.[3] It is reported that a mosque at Fez used to be protected against scorpions by an image of a bird holding a scorpion in its beak.[4] An Arab writer tells of a golden locust which guarded a certain town from a plague of locusts ; and he also mentions two brazen oxen which checked a murrain among cattle.[5] Gregory of Tours tells us that the city of Paris used to be free of dormice and serpents, but that in his lifetime, while they were cleaning a sewer, they found a bronze serpent and a bronze dormouse and removed them. " Since then," adds the good bishop, " dormice and serpents without number have been seen in Paris." [6] When their land was overrun with mice, the Philistines made golden images of the vermin and sent them out of the country in a new cart drawn by two cows, hoping that the real mice would simultaneously depart.[7] So when a swarm of serpents afflicted the Israelites in the desert, they made a serpent of brass and set it on a pole as a mode of staying the plague.[8]

[1] J. Malalas, *Chronographia*, ed. L. Dindorf (Bonn, 1831), p. 264.

[2] D. Comparetti, *Vergil in the Middle Ages* (London, 1895), p. 265. I have to thank Mr. J. D. May of Merton College, Oxford, for this and the following references to Comparetti's book.

[3] D. Comparetti, *op. cit.* pp. 259, 293, 341.

[4] E. Doutté, *Magie et Religion dans l'Afrique du Nord* (Algiers, 1908), p. 144.

[5] *Encyclopaedia Biblica*, iv. (London, 1903) col. 4395.

[6] Grégoire de Tours, *Histoire Ecclésiastique des Francs*, traduction de M. Guizot, Nouvelle Édition (Paris, 1874), viii. 33, vol. i. p. 514. For some stories of the same sort, see J. B. Thiers, *Traité des Superstitions* (Paris, 1679), pp. 306-308.

[7] 1 Samuel vi. 4-18. The passage in which the plague of mice is definitely described has been omitted in the existing Hebrew text, but is preserved in the Septuagint (1 Samuel v. 6, καὶ μέσον τῆς χώρας αὐτῆς ἀνεφύησαν μύες). See Dean Kirkpatrick's note on 1 Samuel v. 6 (*Cambridge Bible for Schools and Colleges*).

[8] Numbers xxi. 6-9.

§ 2. Mouse Apollo and Wolf Apollo

Greek gods who took titles from vermin.   Some of the Greek gods were worshipped under titles derived from the vermin or other pests which they were supposed to avert or exterminate. Thus we hear of Mouse Apollo,[1] Locust Apollo,[2] and Mildew Apollo ;[3] of Locust Hercules and Worm-killing Hercules ;[4] of Foxy Dionysus ;[5] and of Zeus the Fly-catcher or Averter of Flies.[6] If we could trace all these and similar worships to their origin, we should probably find that they were at first addressed, not to the high gods as the protectors of mankind, but to the baleful things themselves, the mice, locusts, mildew, and so forth, with the intention of flattering and soothing them, of disarming their malignity, and of persuading them to spare their worshippers. We know that the Romans worshipped the mildew, the farmer's plague, under its own proper name.[7] **Mouse (*Smintheus*) Apollo.** The ravages committed by mice among the crops both in ancient and modern times are notorious,[8] and according to

---

[1] Homer, *Iliad*, i. 39, with the Scholia and the comment of Eustathius ; Strabo, xiii. i. 48 and 63 ; Aelian, *Nat. Anim.* xii. 5 ; Clement of Alexandria, *Protrept.* ii 39, p. 34, ed. Potter ; Pausanias, x. 12. 5.

[2] Strabo, xiii. i. 64 ; Pausanias, i. 24. 8.

[3] Strabo, xiii. i. 64 ; Eustathius, on Homer, *Iliad*, i. 39, p. 34 ; Dittenberger, *Sylloge Inscriptionum Graecarum*,[2] No. 609 (vol. ii. p. 386).

[4] Strabo and Eustathius, *ll.cc.*

[5] Professor W. Ridgeway has pointed out that the epithet Bassareus applied to Dionysus (Cornutus, *Theologiae Graecae Compendium*, 30) appears to be derived from *bassara*, "a fox." See J. Tzetzes, *Schol. on Lycophron*, 771 ; W. Ridgeway, in *The Classical Review*, x. (1896) pp. 21 *sqq.* ; S. Reinach, *Cultes, Mythes, et Religions*, ii. (Paris, 1906) pp. 106 *sqq.*

[6] Pliny, *Nat. Hist.* x. 75 ; Pausanias, v. 14. 1, viii. 26. 7 ; Clement of Alexandria, *Protrept.* ii. 38, p. 33, ed. Potter.

[7] *Robigo* or personified as *Robigus*. See Varro, *Rerum rusticarum*, i. 1. 6 ;

id., *De lingua latina*, vi. 16 ; Ovid, *Fasti*, iv. 905 *sqq.* ; Tertullian, *De spectaculis*, 5 ; Augustine, *De civitate Dei*, iv. 21 ; Lactantius, *Divin. Instit.* i. 20 ; L. Preller, *Römische Mythologie*[3] (Berlin, 1881-1883), ii. 43 *sqq.*; W. Warde Fowler, *The Roman Festivals of the Period of the Republic* (London, 1899), pp. 88 *sqq.*

[8] Aristotle, *Hist. Anim.* vi. 37, p. 580 b 15 *sqq.* ; Aelian, *Nat. Anim.* xvii. 41 ; W. Warde Fowler, in *The Classical Review* vi. (1892) p. 413. In Laos, a province of Siam, the ravages committed by rats are terrible. From time to time whole armies of these destructive rodents appear and march across the country in dense columns and serried ranks, devouring everything as they go, and leaving famine, with all its horrors, in their train. See Lieut.-Col. Tournier, *Notice sur le Laos Français* (Hanoi, 1900), pp. 104, 135. So in Burma, the rats multiply in some years to such an extent that they cause a famine by destroying whole crops and granaries. See Max and Bertha Ferrars, *Burma* (London, 1900), pp. 149 *sq.*

a tradition which may be substantially correct the worship of the Mouse (Smintheus) Apollo was instituted to avert them.[1] The image of a mouse which stood beside Apollo's tripod in the god's temple in the Troad,[2] may be compared with the golden mice which the Philistines made for the purpose of ridding themselves of the vermin ; and the tame mice kept in his sanctuary, together with the white mice which lived under the altar,[3] would on this hypothesis be parallel to the white mice which the Bohemian peasant still cherishes as the best way of keeping down the numbers of their grey-coated brethren.[4] An Oriental counterpart of the Mouse Apollo is the ancient pillar or rude idol which the Chams of Indo-China call *yang-tikuh* or "god rat," and to which they offer sacrifices whenever rats infest their fields in excessive numbers.[5]

Another epithet applied to Apollo which probably admits of a similar explanation is Wolfish.[6] Various legends set forth how the god received the title of Wolfish because he exterminated wolves ;[7] indeed this function was definitely attributed to him by the epithet Wolf-slayer.[8] Arguing from the analogy of the preceding cases, we may suppose that at first the wolves themselves were propitiated by fair words and sacrifices to induce them to spare man and beast; and that at a later time, when the Greeks, or rather the enlightened portion of them, had outgrown this rude form of worship, they transferred the duty of keeping off the wolves to a beneficent deity who discharged the same useful office for other pests, such as mice, locusts, and mildew. A reminiscence of the direct propitiation of the fierce and dangerous beasts themselves is preserved in the legends told to explain the origin of the Lyceum or Place of Wolves at Athens and of the sanctuary of Wolfish Apollo at Sicyon. It is said that once, when Athens was infested by wolves, Apollo commanded sacrifices to be offered on the Place of Wolves and the smell

Wolfish Apollo.

[1] Polemo, cited by a scholiast on Homer, *Iliad*, i. 39 (ed. Im. Bekker). Compare Eustathius on Homer, *Iliad*, i. 39.

[2] Aelian, *Nat. Anim.* xii. 5.

[3] Aelian, *l.c.*

[4] See above, p. 279.

[5] E. Aymonier, "Les Tchames et leurs religions," *Revue de l'Histoire des Religions*, xxiv. (1891) p. 236.

[6] Λύκειος or Λύκιος, Pausanias, i. 19. 3 (with my note), ii. 9. 7, ii. 19. 3, viii. 40. 5 ; Lucian, *Anacharsis*, 7 ; Im. Bekker, *Anecdota Graeca* (Berlin, 1814-1821), i. 277, lines 10 *sq.*

[7] Pausanias, ii. 9. 7 ; Scholiast on Demosthenes, xxiv. 114, p. 736.

[8] Sophocles, *Electra*, 6.

proved fatal to the animals.[1] Similarly at Sicyon, when the flocks suffered heavily from the ravages of wolves, the same god directed the shepherds to set forth meat mixed with a certain bark, and the wolves devoured the tainted meat and perished.[2] These legends probably reflect in a distorted form an old custom of sacrificing to the wolves, in other words of feeding them to mollify their ferocity and win their favour. We know that such a custom prevailed among the Letts down to comparatively recent times. In the month of December, about Christmas time, they sacrificed a goat to the wolves, with strange idolatrous rites, at a cross-road, for the purpose of inducing the wolves to spare the flocks and herds. After offering the sacrifice they used to brag that no beast of theirs would fall a victim to the ravening maw of a wolf for all the rest of that year, no, not though the pack were to run right through the herd. Sacrifices of this sort are reported to have been secretly offered by the Letts as late as the seventeenth century;[3] and if we knew more of peasant life in ancient Greece we might find that on winter days, while Aristotle was expounding his philosophy in the Lyceum or Place of Wolves at Athens, the Attic peasant was still carrying forth, in the crisp frosty air, his offering to the wolves, which all night long had been howling round his sheepfold in a snowy glen of Parnes or Pentelicus.

[1] Scholiast on Demosthenes, xxiv. 114, p. 736.

[2] Pausanias, ii. 9. 7.

[3] P. Einhorn, *Reformatio gentis Letticae in Ducatu Curlandiae*, reprinted in *Scriptores rerum Livonicarum*, vol. ii. (Riga and Leipsic, 1848) p. 621. The preface of Einhorn's work is dated 17th July 1636.

CHAPTER XVI

THE TRANSMIGRATION OF HUMAN SOULS INTO ANIMALS

WITH many savages a reason for respecting and sparing certain species of animals is a belief that the souls of their dead kinsfolk are lodged in these creatures. Thus the Indians of Cayenne refuse to eat certain large fish, because they say that the soul of some one of their relations might be in the fish, and that hence in eating the fish they might swallow the soul.[1] The Piaroas Indians of the Orinoco believe that the tapir is their ancestor and that the souls of the dying transmigrate into animals of that species. Hence they will never hunt the tapir nor eat its flesh. It may even ravage their crops with impunity ; they will not attempt to ward it off or scare it away.[2] The Canelos Indians of Ecuador also believe in the transmigration of souls ; it is especially under the form of jaguars that they expect to be born again ; hence they refuse to attack a jaguar except by way of righteous retribution for some wrong he has done them.[3] The doctrine of transmigration finds favour also with the Quixos Indians ; an old man told the Italian traveller Osculati that the soul is a breath which passes from the human body into an animal, and on the death of the animal shifts its quarters to another body.[4] The Caingua Indians of Paraguay think that the souls of the dead which are unable to depart this earth are born again in the shape of animals ; for that reason many of

Many savages spare certain animals because they believe the souls of their dead to be lodged in them. Examples of this belief among the American Indians.

[1] A. Biet, *Voyage de la France Equinoxiale en l Isle de Cayenne* (Paris, 1664), p. 361.

[2] J. Chaffanjon, *L'Orénoque et le Caura* (Paris, 1889), p. 203.

[3] Levrault, "Rapport sur les provinces de Canélos et du Napo," *Bulletin de la Société de Géographie* (Paris), Deuxième Série, xi. (1839) p. 75.

[4] G. Osculati, *Esplorazione delle regioni equatorali lungo il Napo ed il fiume delle Amazzoni* (Milan, 1850), p. 114.

them refuse to eat the flesh of the domestic pig, because they say, "He was a man."[1] Once when a Spaniard was out hunting with two Piros Indians of Peru, they passed a deserted house in which they saw a fine jaguar. The Indians drew the Spaniard away, and when he asked why they did not attack the animal, they said : " It was our sister. She died at the last rains. We abandoned the hut and on the second night she came back. It was the beautiful jaguar."[2] Similarly a missionary remarked of the Chiriguanos Indians of Bolivia that they must have some idea of the transmigration of souls ; for one day, while he was talking with a woman of the tribe who had left her daughter in a neighbouring village, she started at sight of a fox passing near and exclaimed, " May it not be the soul of my daughter who has died ? "[3] The Colombian Indians in the district of Popayan will not kill the deer of their forests, and entertain such a respect for these animals that they view with horror and indignation any one who dares to eat venison in their presence. They say that the souls of persons who have led a good life are in the deer.[4] In like manner the Indians of California formerly refused to eat the flesh of large game, because they held that the bodies of all large animals contained the souls of past generations of men and women. However, the Indians who were maintained at the Spanish missions and received their rations in the form of beef, had to overcome their conscientious scruples in regard to cattle. Once a half-caste, wishing to amuse himself at the expense of the devout, cooked a dish of bear's flesh for them and told them it was beef. They ate heartily of it, but when they learned the trick that had been played on them, they were seized with retchings, which only ended with the reappearance of the obnoxious meat. A reproach hurled by the wild tribes at their brethren who had fallen under European influence was " They eat venison!"[5] Californian Indians have been known to plead for the life of an old grizzly she-bear, because they thought

[1] J. B. Ambrosetti, " Los Indios Caingua del alto Paraná (misiones)," *Boletin del Instituto Geografico Argentino*, xv. (Buenos Ayres, 1895) p. 740.

[2] Ch. Wiener, *Pérou et Bolivie* (Paris, 1880), p. 369.

[3] *Lettres édifiantes et curieuses*, Nouvelle Édition, viii. (Paris, 1781) pp. 335 *sqq.*

[4] Fr. Coreal, *Voyages aux Indes occidentales* (Amsterdam, 1722), ii. 132.

[5] H. R. Schoolcraft, *Indian Tribes of the United States* (Philadelphia, 1853-1856), v. 215 *sq.*

it housed the soul of a dead grandam, whose withered features had borne some likeness to the wrinkled face of the bear.[1]

The doctrine of the transmigration of human souls into animal bodies is viewed with great favour by the negroes of northern Guinea. In different parts of the coast different species of animals are accounted sacred, because they are supposed to be animated by the spirits of the dead. Hence monkeys near Fishtown, snakes at Whydah, and crocodiles near Dix Cove live in the odour of sanctity.[2] In the lagoon of Tendo, on the Ivory Coast of West Africa, there is a certain sacred islet covered with impenetrable scrub, on which no native dare set foot. It is peopled only by countless huge bats, which at evening quit the island by hundreds of thousands to fly towards the River Tanoe, which flows into the lagoon. The natives say that these bats are the souls of the dead, who retire during the day to the holy isle and are bound to present themselves every night at the abode of Tano, the great and good fetish who dwells by the river of his name. Paddling past the island the negroes will not look at it, but turn away their heads. A European in crossing the lagoon wished to shoot one of the bats, but his boatmen implored him to refrain, lest he should kill the soul of one of their kinsfolk.[3] In the Mopane country of South Africa there is, or used to be, no check on the increase of lions, because the natives, believing that the souls of their chiefs entered into the animals, never attempted to kill them ; on the contrary, whenever they met a lion they saluted him in the usual fashion by clapping their hands. Hence the country was so infested by lions that people, benighted in fields, often slept for safety in trees.[4] Similarly, the Makanga, who occupy the angle between the Zambesi and Shire rivers, refrain from killing lions because they believe that the spirits of dead chiefs enter into them.[5] The Amambwe universally suppose that their reigning chief turns at death into a lion.[6]

Belief of the transmigration of human souls into animals in Africa.

[1] H. R. Schoolcraft, *op. cit.* iii. 113.

[2] Rev. J. L. Wilson, *Western Africa* (London, 1856), p. 210.

[3] J. C. Reichenbach, " Étude sur le royaume d'Assinie," *Bulletin de la Société de Géographie* (Paris), vii. Série, xi. (1890) pp. 322 *sq.*

[4] D. Livingstone, *Missionary Tra-vels and Researches in South Africa* (London, 1857), p. 615.

[5] Miss A. Werner, *The Natives of British Central Africa* (London, 1906), p. 64.

[6] C. Gouldsbury and H. Sheane, *The Great Plateau of Northern Rhodesia* (London, 1911), p. 200.

The Bahima of Ankole, in Central Africa, also imagine that their dead kings are changed into lions. Their corpses are carried to a forest called Ensanzi, where they lie in state for several days. At the end of that time the body is supposed to burst and give forth a lion cub, which contains the spirit of the deceased king. The animal is nurtured by priests till it is grown up, when it is released and allowed to roam the forest with the other lions. It is the duty of the priests to feed and care for the lions and to hold communications with the dead kings when occasion arises. For that purpose the priests always live in a temple in the forest, where they receive frequent offerings of cattle for the lions. In this forest the lions are sacred and may not be killed, but in other parts of the country they may be slaughtered with impunity. Similarly, the Bahima think that at death the king's wives are changed into leopards ; the transformation takes place in like manner through the bursting of the dead bodies in a belt of the same sacred forest. There the leopards are daily fed with offerings of meat by priests, whose office is hereditary. Further, the Bahima are of opinion that the spirits of dead princes and princesses come to life again in the form of snakes, which burst from their dead bodies in another belt of the same forest : there is a temple in the forest where priests feed and guard the holy serpents. When the little snakes have issued from the corpses of the princes, they are fed with milk till they are big enough to go alone.[1] The El Kiboron clan of the Masai, in East Africa, imagine that when married men of the clan are buried, their bones turn into serpents. Hence the El Kiboron do not, like the other Masai, kill snakes : on the contrary they are glad to see the reptiles in the kraal and set out saucers of milk and honey for them on the ground. It is said that snakes never bite members of the clan.[2] The Ababu and other tribes of the Congo region believe that at death their souls trans-

[1] Rev. J. Roscoe, "The Bahima, *Journal of the Royal Anthropological Institute*, xxxvii. (1907) pp. 101 *sq.* Compare Major J. A. Meldon, "Notes on the Bahima of Ankole," *Journal of the African Society*, No. 22 (January, 1907), p. 151.

[2] M. Merker, *Die Masai* (Berlin, 1894), p. 202. The belief that the human dead are turned into serpents is common in Africa ; and the practice of offering milk to the reptiles appears to be not infrequent. See *Adonis, Attis, Osiris*,[2] pp. 71 *sq.*

migrate into the bodies of various animals, such as the hippopotamus, the leopard, the gorilla, and the gazelle ; and on no account would a man eat the flesh of an animal of the particular kind which he expects to inhabit in the next life.[1] Some of the Caffres of the Zambesi region, in Portuguese territory, who believe in the transmigration of human souls into the bodies of animals, judge of the species of animals into which a dead person has transmigrated by the resemblance which he bore to it in his life. Thus, the soul of a big burly man with prominent teeth will pass into an elephant ; a strong man with a long beard will become a lion ; an ugly man with a large mouth and thick lips will be a hyaena ; and so on. Animals supposed to be tenanted by the spirits of the dead are treated as sacred and invulnerable. When a Portuguese lady, named Dona Maria, to whom the blacks were much attached, had departed this life, it chanced that a hyaena came repeatedly by night to the village and carried off pigs and kids. The lady's old slaves would not do the creature the smallest hurt, saying, " It is Dona Maria, our good mistress. She is hungry and comes to her house seeking what she may devour." [2]

The belief that the souls of the dead transmigrate into the bodies of animals appears to be widely diffused among the tribes of Madagascar. Thus, for example, the souls of the Betsileo are thought after death to be reborn in boa-constrictors, crocodiles, and eels of a particular sort according to their rank in life. It is the nobles, or at all events the most illustrious of them, who have the privilege of turning into boa-constrictors at death. To facilitate the transformation the corpse of a dead noble is strapped to the central pillar of his house, and the products of decomposition are collected in a silver bowl. The largest of the worms which are bred in the putrid liquid is believed to contain the soul

[1] J. Halkin, *Quelques Peuplades du district de l'Uelé* (Liége, 1907), p. 102 ; *Notes Analytiques sur les Collections Ethnographiques du Musée du Congo, La Religion* (Brussels, 1906), p. 162.

[2] Father Courtois, " Scènes de la vie Cafre," *Les Missions Catholiques,* xv. (1883) p. 593. For more evidence of similar beliefs in Africa, see Father Courtois, " À travers le haut Zambèze," *Les Missions Catholiques,* xvi. (1884) p. 299 (souls of the dead in guineafowl) ; Father Lejeune, " Dans la forêt," *Les Missions Catholiques,* xxvii. (1895) p. 248 (souls of the dead in apes, owls, etc.).

of the dead nobleman and to develop in due time into a boa-constrictor. Accordingly these huge serpents are regarded as sacred by the Betsileo ; nobody would dare to kill one of them. The people go down on their knees to them and salute them, just as they would do to a real live nobleman. It is a happy day when a boa-constrictor deigns to visit the village which he formerly inhabited in human form. He receives an ovation from his family. They go forth to meet him, spread silk for him to crawl upon, and carry him off to the public square, where he is allowed to gorge himself with the blood of a sacrificed ox. The souls of commoners of good standing transmigrate into the bodies of crocodiles, and in their new form still serve their old masters, particularly by announcing to them the approach of the hour when they must shuffle out of the human frame into the frame of boa-constrictors. Lastly, the scum of the population turn at death into eels, and to render the change as easy for them as possible it is customary to remove the bowels from the corpse and throw them into a sacred lake. The eel that swallows the first mouthful becomes the domicile of the soul of the deceased. No Betsileo would eat such eels.[1] Again, the Antankarana, a tribe in the extreme north of Madagascar, believe that the spirits of their dead chiefs pass into crocodiles, while those of common folk are reborn in other animals.[2] Once more, the Tanala, a tribe of south-eastern Madagascar, suppose that the souls of their dead transmigrate into certain animals, such as scorpions and insects, which accordingly they will not kill or eat, believing that the creatures will in like manner abstain from injuring them.[3]

Some of the Nagas of Assam hold that the spirits of the departed, after undergoing a cycle of changes in a sub-terranean world, are reborn on earth in the form of butterflies or small house flies, only however in that shape to perish for

[1] Father Abinal, " Croyances fabu-leuses des Malgaches," *Les Missions Catholiques*, xii. (1880) pp. 549-551. A somewhat different account of the Betsileo belief in the transmigration of souls is given by another authority. See G. A. Shaw, " The Betsileo," *Antananarivo Annual and Madagascar Magazine, Reprint of the First Four*

Numbers (Antananarivo, 1885), p. 411. Compare A. van Gennep, *Tabou et Totémisme à Madagascar* (Paris, 1904), pp. 272 *sq.*, 283, 291.

[2] Rev. J. Sibree, *The Great African Island* (London, 1880), p. 270.

[3] " Das Volk der Tanala," *Globus*, lxxxix. (1906) p. 362.

ever. Hence, when these small flies light on the wine-cups of the living, the wassailers will not kill them for fear of destroying some one of their ancestors.[1] For a like reason the Angamis, one of the Naga tribes, carefully abstain from injuring certain species of butterfly.[2] At Ang Teng, a large village of Upper Burma, the river at a point above a dilapidated bridge swarms with fish, which the people hold sacred, because they imagine them to be their dead come to life again in a fishy form. In former days no one might kill one of these fish under pain of death. Once a Shan, caught fishing with some dead fish in his possession, was instantly haled away and killed.[8] The people of Kon-Meney in eastern Cochin China will not eat toads, because long ago the soul of one of their chiefs passed at death into a toad. In his new shape he appeared to his son in a dream, informed him of the transformation, and commanded him to sacrifice a pig, a fowl, and millet wine to his deceased parent, assuring him that if he complied with the injunction the rice would grow well. The dutiful son obeyed the author of his being ; the toad appeared in the rice-fields watching over the growth of the rice, and the crop was magnificent. For two generations the sacrifices were duly offered, the toad appeared at the time of sowing, and the granaries were full. Afterwards, however, the people neglected to sacrifice to the toad and were punished accordingly by failure of the crops and consequent famine.[4] Some of the Chams of Indo-China believe that the souls of the dead inhabit the bodies of certain animals, such as serpents, crocodiles, and so forth, the kind of animal varying with the family. The species of animals most commonly regarded as tenanted by the spirits of the departed are the rodents and active climbing creatures which abound in the country, such as squirrels. According to some people, these small animals are especially the abode of still-born infants or of children

[1] W. H. Furness, "The Ethnography of the Nagas of Eastern Assam," *Journal of the Anthropological Institute*, xxxii. (1902) p. 463.

[2] T. C. Hodson, *The Nāga Tribes of Manipur* (London, 1911), p. 159.

[3] (Sir) J. George Scott and J. P. Hardiman, *Gazetteer of Upper Burma and the Shan States* (Rangoon, 1900-1901), Part ii. vol. i. p. 26.

[4] Guerlach, "Chez les sauvages de la Cochinchine Orientale, Bahnar, Reungao, Sédang," *Les Missions Catholiques*, xxvi. (1894) pp. 143 *sq.*

who died young. The souls of these little ones appear in dreams to their mourning parents and say : " I inhabit the body of a squirrel. Honour me as such. Make me a present of a flower, a coco-nut, a cup of roasted rice," and so on. The parents discharge this pious duty, respect these familiar spirits, ascribe illnesses to their displeasure, pray to them for healing, and on their deathbed commend to their descendants the care of such and such a spirit, as a member of the family.[1]

Belief in the transmigration of human souls into animals in the Philippines, the Sandwich Islands, and the Pelew Islands.

The Igorrots of Cabugatan, in the Philippines, regard the eels in their stream as the souls of their forefathers. Hence instead of catching and eating them they feed them, till the eels become as tame as carp in a pond.[2] In the Sandwich Islands various people worshipped diverse kinds of animals, such as fowls, lizards, owls, rats, and so forth. If a man who adored sharks happened to have a child still-born, he would endeavour to lodge the soul of the dead infant in the body of a shark. For this purpose he laid the tiny body, together with a couple of roots of taro, some kava, and a piece of sugar-cane, on a mat, recited prayers over it, and then flung the whole into the sea, believing that by virtue of this offering the transmigration of the child's soul into the shark's body would be effected, and that henceforth the voracious monsters would spare all members of the family who might otherwise be exposed to their attacks. In the temples dedicated to sharks there were priests who, morning and evening, addressed prayers to the shark-idol, and rubbed their bodies with water and salt, which, drying on their skin, imparted to it an appearance of being covered with scales. They also wore red stuffs, uttered shrill cries, leaped over the sacred enclosure, and persuaded the credulous islanders that they knew the exact moment when the children thrown

---

[1] E. Aymonier, "Les Tchames et leurs religions," *Revue de l'histoire des Religions*, xxiv. (1891) p. 267. Compare D. Grangeon, "Les Cham et leurs superstitions," *Les Missions Catholiques*, xxviii. (1896) p. 46. According to the latter writer, white horses are specially set apart to serve as domiciles for these domestic deities. After its dedication such a horse is care-fully tended and never mounted again.

[2] F. Blumentritt, "Der Ahnencultus und die religiösen Anschauungen der Malaien des Philippinen - Archipels," *Mittheilungen der Wiener Geogr. Gesellschaft*, 1882, p. 164; *id., Versuch einer Ethnographie der Philippinen* (Gotha, 1882), p. 29 (*Petermanns Mittheilungen, Ergänzungsheft*, No 67).

into the sea were turned into sharks. For this revelation they were rewarded by the happy parents with a plentiful supply of little pigs, coco - nuts, kava, and so on.[1] The Pelew Islanders believed that the souls of their forefathers lived in certain species of animals, which accordingly they held sacred and would not injure. For this reason one man would not kill snakes, another would not harm pigeons, and so on ; but every one was quite ready to kill and eat the sacred animals of his neighbours.[2]

We have seen that the Battas of Sumatra seldom kill a tiger and never without performing an elaborate ceremony to appease the animal's ghost. The reason alleged for treating tigers with this respect is that the souls of the dead often transmigrate into these animals, and therefore in killing a tiger a man never knows whether he is not killing a relative of his own. If members of the totemic clan of the Tiger should happen to be in a village when the carcase of a slain tiger is brought into it, they are bound to pay special marks of honour to its remains by putting betel in its mouth. A priest offers food and drink to the dead tiger, addresses him as Grandfather, prays him not to be angry or frightened, and explains to the gods the reasons for putting the animal to death.[3] *Transmigration of human souls into tigers in Sumatra.*

The Kayans of Borneo think that when the human soul departs from the body at death it may take the form of an animal or bird. For example, if a deer were seen browsing near a man's grave, his relations would probably conclude that his soul had assumed the shape of a deer, and the whole family would abstain from eating venison lest they should annoy the deceased.[4] Most of the Kalamantans, *Belief in the transmigration of human souls into animals in Borneo.*

[1] L. de Freycinet, *Voyage autour du Monde*, ii. (Paris, 1829) pp. 595 *sq.*

[2] K. Semper, *Die Palau-Inseln im Stillen Ocean* (Leipsic, 1873), pp. 87 *sq.*, 193. These sacred animals were called *kalids*. A somewhat different account of the *kalids* of the Pelew Islanders is given by J. Kubary ("Die Religion der Pelauer," in A. Bastian's *Allerlei aus Volks- und Menschenkunde*, Berlin, 1888, i. 5 *sqq.*).

[3] W. D. Helderman, "De tijger en het bijgeloof der Bataks," *Tijdschrift*

voor Indische Taal- Land- en Volkenkunde, xxxiv. (1891) pp. 170-175. The account which this writer gives of the reception of a dead tiger by the Battas agrees with, and is probably the source of, Mr. Batten's account cited above (pp. 216 *sq.*).

[4] C. Hose, "The Natives of Borneo," *Journal of the Anthropological Institute*, xxiii. (1894) p. 165. Compare A. W. Nieuwenhuis, *In Centraal Borneo* (Leyden, 1900), i. 148 ; *id.*, *Quer durch Borneo* (Leyden, 1904-1907), i. 105.

another tribe of Borneo, will kill and eat deer freely, but there are exceptions to the rule. " Thus Damong, the chief of a Malanau household, together with all his people, will not kill or eat the deer *Cervulus muntjac,* alleging that an ancestor had become a deer of this kind, and that, since they cannot distinguish this incarnation of his ancestor from other deer, they must abstain from killing all deer of this species. We know of one instance in which one of these people refused to use again his cooking-pot which a Malay had borrowed and used for cooking the flesh of this deer. This superstition is still rigidly adhered to, although these people have been converted to Islam of recent years. . . The people of Miri, who also are Mohammedan Malanaus, claim to be related to the large deer (*Cervus equinus*) and some of them to the muntjac deer also. Now these people live in a country in which deer of all kinds abound, and they always make a clearing in the jungle around a tomb. On such a clearing grass grows up rapidly, and so the spot becomes attractive to deer as a grazing ground ; and it seems not improbable that it is through frequently seeing deer about the tombs that the people have come to entertain the belief that their dead relatives become deer or that they are in some other way closely related to the deer. The Bakongs, another group of Malanaus, hold a similar belief with regard to the bear-cat (*Arctictis*) and the various species of *Paradoxurus,* and in this case the origin of the belief is admitted by them to be the fact that on going to their graveyards they often see one of these beasts coming out of a tomb. These tombs are roughly constructed wooden coffins raised a few feet only from the ground, and it is probable that these carnivores make their way into them in the first place to devour the corpse, and that they then make use of them as lairs." [1] Among the Sea Dyaks, also, of Borneo the idea of metempsychosis is not unknown. One of them used to treat a snake with the greatest kindness, because he said it had been revealed to

---

According to the latter writer the Kayans or Bahaus in general abstain from the flesh both of deer and of grey apes, because they think that the souls of the dead may be in them.

[1] Ch. Hose and W. McDougall, "The Relations between Men and Animals in Sarawak," *Journal of the Anthropological Institute,* xxxi. (1901) p. 193.

him in a dream that the spirit of his grandfather dwelt in that snake.[1]

Some of the Papuans on the northern coast of New Guinea also believe in the transmigration of souls. They hold that at death the souls of human beings sometimes pass into animals, such as cassowaries, fish, or pigs, and they abstain from eating the animals of the sort in which the spirits of the dead are supposed to have taken up their abode.[2] For example, at Masur in Dutch New Guinea there are people who imagine that the spirits of their ancestors transmigrated into cassowaries, and accordingly they will not partake of the flesh of the long-legged bird.[3] In Simbang, a village at the mouth of the Bubui river in German New Guinea, there is a family who will not harm crocodiles, not merely because they fear the vengeance of the creatures, but also because they reckon crocodiles their kinsfolk and expect that they themselves will turn into crocodiles at death. As head of the family they recognise a certain aged crocodile, everywhere known as " old Butong," who is said to have been born of a woman at Simbang.[4] They think that while they are at work in the fields, and the houses stand empty, their ancestors come forth from the river and repair to the place in the roof where the mysterious bullroarers are kept, which make a humming sound at the initiatory rites of young men. But when the people return from the fields they find the houses as empty and silent as when they left them : the spirits of their forefathers have plunged into the river again. If a crocodile carries off anybody, the natives are sure that the brute must be a stranger, not one of their own crocodile kinsfolk, who never would do such a thing ; and if their neighbours at Yabim are so unfeeling as to kill a crocodile, the Bubui people protest against the outrage and demand satisfaction. Some Yabim

Belief in the transmigration of human souls into animals in New Guinea.

---

[1] E. H. Gomes, *Seventeen Years among the Sea Dyaks of Borneo* (London, 1911), p. 143.

[2] F. S. A. de Clercq, " De West en Noordkust van Nederlandsch Nieuw-Guinea," *Tijdschrift van het Koninklijk Nederlandsch Aardrijkskundig Genootschap*, Tweede Serie, x. (1893) p. 635.

[3] Max Krieger, *Neu-Guinea* (Berlin, N.D.), p. 404.

[4] K. Vetter, *Komm herüber und hilf uns !* iii. (Barmen, 1898) p. 22. Compare *id.*, in *Nachrichten über Kaiser Wilhelms-Land*, 1897, pp. 87 *sq.* ; B. Hagen, *Unter den Papuas* (Wiesbaden, 1899), p. 225.

people give out that after death their souls will be turned into certain fabulous cave-haunting swine, and accordingly their relatives refuse to spear or to eat the real wild swine. If these animals break into and ravage the fields, their human kinsfolk attempt to appease them with offerings of coco-nuts and other valuable articles.[1] Similarly in Tamara, an island off the coast of German New Guinea, the people will not eat pork, because it is their conviction that the souls of the dead transmigrate into the bodies of pigs.[2] The Kai people, who inhabit the rugged and densely wooded mountains inland from Finsch Harbour in German New Guinea, imagine that the gloomy depths of some wild ravines are haunted by the souls of the dead in the form of cuscuses and other animals. None but the owner has the right to kill game in these dark and awful gullies, and even he must propitiate the soul of every animal that he slays in such a spot. For this purpose he spreads out offerings on the carcase and presents them to the injured spirit, saying, "Take the gifts and leave us the animal, that we may eat it." After leaving the articles long enough to allow the soul of the beast to abstract and convey away the souls of the things, the hunter is free to cut up and consume the carcase. Some years ago, when heavy rains caused a land-slip in these wild mountains, and a house with its inmates was buried in the ruins, public opinion in the neighbourhood attributed the disaster to the misconduct of the deceased, who had failed to appease the soul of a boa-constrictor slain by them on haunted ground.[3]

Belief in the transmigration of human souls into animals in the Solomon Islands. In the Solomon Islands a man at the point of death would gather the members of his family about him and inform them of the particular sort of creature, say a bird or a butterfly, into which he proposed to trans-migrate. Henceforth the family would regard that species of animal as sacred and would neither kill nor injure it. If they fell in with a creature of the kind, it might be a

---

[1] H. Zahn, "Die Jabim," in R. Neuhauss, *Deutsch Neu-Guinea*, iii. (Berlin, 1911) p. 310.

[2] R. Parkinson, "Die Berlinhafen Section, ein Beitrag zur Ethnographie der Neu-Guinea Küste," *Internation-* *ales Archiv für Ethnographie*, xiii. (1900) p. 40.

[3] Ch. Keysser, "Aus dem Leben der Kaileute," in R. Neuhauss, *Deutsch Neu-Guinea*, iii. (Berlin, 1911) pp. 150 *sq.*

bird or a butterfly, they would say, "That is papa," and offer him a coco-nut.[1] In these islands sharks are very often supposed to be ghosts, for dying people frequently announce their intention of being sharks when they have put off their human shape. After that, if any shark remarkable for its size or colour is seen to haunt a certain shore or rock, it is taken to be somebody's ghost, and the name of the deceased is given to it. For example, at Ulawa a dreaded man-eating shark received the name of a dead man and was propitiated with offerings of porpoise teeth. At Saa, certain food, for example coco-nuts from particular trees, is reserved to feed such a ghost-shark, but men of whom it is positively known that after death they will be in sharks are allowed by anticipation to partake of the shark-food in the sacred place. Other men will sometimes join themselves to their company, and speaking with the voice of a shark-ghost will say, "Give me to eat of that food." If such a man happens to be really possessed of supernatural power, he will in due time become a shark-ghost himself; but it is perfectly possible that he may fail. In Savo not very long ago a certain man had a shark that he used to feed and to which he offered sacrifice. He swam out to it with food, called it by name, and it came to him. Of course it was not a common shark, but a ghost, the knowledge of which had been handed down to him from his ancestors. Alligators also may lodge the souls of dead Solomon Islanders. In the island of Florida a story was told of an alligator that used to come up out of the sea and make itself quite at home in the village in which the man whose ghost it was had lived. It went by the name of the deceased, and though there was one man in particular who had special connexion with it and was said to own it, the animal was on friendly terms with everybody in the place and would even let children ride on its back. But the village where this happened has not yet been identified.[2] In the same island the appearance of anything wonderful is taken as proof of a ghostly presence and stamps the place as sacred. For example, a man planted some coco-nut palms

---

[1] Mr. Sleigh of Lifu, quoted by Prof. E. B. Tylor, in *Journal of the Anthropological Institute*, xxviii. (1898) p. 147.

[2] R. H. Codrington, *The Melanesians* (Oxford, 1891), pp. 179 *sq.*

and almond trees in the bush and died not long afterwards. After his death there appeared among the trees a great rarity in the shape of a white cuscus. The animal was accordingly assumed to be the ghost of the departed planter and went by his name. The place became sacred, and no one would gather the fruits of the trees there, until two young men, who had been trained in the principles of Christianity, boldly invaded the sanctuary and appropriated the almonds and coco - nuts.[1] It must not be supposed, however, that the choice of transmigration open to a Solomon Islander is restricted to the animal kingdom ; he is free after death to become a vegetable, if he feels so disposed. When a mission-school was established in the island of Ulawa it was observed with surprise that the natives would not eat bananas and had ceased to plant the tree. Enquiry elicited the origin of the restriction, which was recent and well remembered. A man of great influence, dying not long before, had forbidden the eating of bananas after his death, saying that he would be in the banana. The older natives would still mention his name and say, " We cannot eat So-and-so."[2]

The doctrine of the transmigration of human souls into animals in ancient India.

The doctrine of the reincarnation of human souls in the bodies either of men or of animals, which meets us as an article of faith in so many savage tribes, has a special interest for the historian of thought, because it has been adopted more or less explicitly and employed, not merely as a philosophical theory, but as a means of enforcing moral lessons, by thinkers, teachers, and lawgivers among various civilised peoples, notably in ancient India and Greece. Thus in the most famous of old Indian law-books, *The Laws of Manu*, the penalties to be endured by evil-doers in future births are described with a precision which leaves

---

[1] R. H. Codrington, *op. cit.* p. 177.
[2] R. H. Codrington, *op. cit.* p. 33. East Indian evidence of the belief in transmigration into animals is collected by G. A. Wilken (" Het animisme bij de volken van den Indischen Archipel," *De Indische Gids,* June 1884, pp. 988 *sqq.*), who argues that this belief supplies the link between ancestor-worship and totemism. Compare the same writer's article "Iets over de Papoewas van de Geelvinksbaai," pp. 24 *sqq.* (separate reprint from *Bijdragen tot de Taal- Land- en Volkenkunde van Ned. Indië*, 5e Volgreeks ii.). Wilken's view on this subject is favoured by Professor E. B. Tylor (*Journal of the Anthropological Institute*, xxviii. (1898) pp. 146 *sq.*). See further, *Totemism and Exogamy*, iv. 45 *sqq.*

nothing to be desired : the degradation of the birth is exactly proportioned to the degree of moral guilt of the transgressor. For example, if a man has the temerity to censure his teacher, even though the censure is richly deserved, that rash man in his next birth will be an ass ; but if he defames his teacher falsely, he will be a dog ; and if he is so lost to all sense of propriety as to live at the expense of his teacher, he will be a worm.¹ A faithless wife in her next transmigration will be born a jackal.² A Brahman who misappropriates money which he has received for a sacrifice will hereafter be either a vulture or a crow for the period of one hundred years.³ Men who delight in doing hurt will be born as carnivorous animals, and those who eat forbidden food will be degraded into worms. As for thieves, their lot is a hard one, and it is harder in proportion to the value of the article stolen. A man who steals gems will be born a goldsmith ; a man who steals grain will be born a rat ; a man who steals honey will be born a stinging insect ; and a man who steals clarified butter will be born an ichneumon. The penalty for stealing silk is to become a partridge, for stealing linen a frog, for stealing vegetables a peacock, for stealing cooked food a porcupine, for stealing uncooked food a hedgehog, and for stealing molasses a flying-fox. And so on for the various degrees of moral turpitude throughout the entire range of the animal kingdom.⁴ Buddha himself, who gave an immense extension to the doctrine of transmigration by incorporating it in his religious or rather philosophical system, is traditionally said to have undergone many animal births of various sorts before he attained to his supreme dignity. Thus it is reported that he was once a hare, once a dog, twice a pig, twice a frog, four times a serpent, six times a snipe, ten times a lion, eleven times a deer, and eighteen times a monkey ; to say nothing of having been once a devil-dancer, twice a thief, eighty-three times an ascetic, and so on.⁵

The doctrine of transmigration in Buddhism.

---

¹ *The Laws of Manu*, ii. 201.
² *Id.*, v. 164.
³ *Id.*, xi. 25.
⁴ *Id.*, xii. 39-78.
⁵ Sir Monier Monier - Williams,

Buddhism, Second Edition (London, 1890), pp. 111 *sq.* Full, if not always authentic, particulars of the Buddha's manifold transmigrations are contained in the *Jatakas*, a large col-

The
doctrine of
the trans-
migration
of souls
taught in
ancient
Greece by
Pythagoras
and Em-
pedocles.

In ancient Greece also the theory of the transmigration of souls found favour with the early philosophers Pythagoras and Empedocles, both of whom, if we may trust tradition, appealed to their own personal experience in support of the doctrine. According to ancient writers, Pythagoras affirmed that he had been Euphorbus the Trojan in one of his former lives, and in proof of the assertion he identified the shield of Euphorbus among the Trojan spoils at Mycenae.[1] He would seem to have held that human souls can transmigrate into animals or even into plants ;[2] and we may suppose that the possibility of such transmigrations was at least one of the reasons he alleged for enjoining the strictest of his disciples neither to kill nor to eat animals and to abstain from certain vegetables, such as beans and mallows.[3] Certainly at a later time these principles were maintained and these precepts inculcated by Empedocles, who outdid the reminiscences of his predecessor by asserting that he himself in former lives had been a boy, a girl, a bush, a bird, and a fish.[4] Hence he denounced as a crime the practice of killing and eating animals, since according to him a man could never know but that in slaughtering and eating an animal he might be murdering and devouring one of his dead kinsfolk, it might be his father or mother, his son or daughter.[5] Thus from the doctrine of transmigration Empedocles logically drew the same practical conclusion as the savage, who abstains, for example, from killing and eating crocodiles or pigs because he believes the souls of his departed relations to be embodied in crocodiles or pigs : the only important difference between the savage and the

lection of stories which has been completely translated into English by the late Professor E. B. Cowell, Dr. W. H. D. Rouse, and other scholars (6 volumes, Cambridge, 1895-1907).

[1] Diodorus Siculus, x. 6. 1-3 ; Jamblichus, De Pythagorica vita, xiv. 63 ; Porphyry, Vita Pythag. 26 sq. ; Ovid, Metamorph. xv. 160 sqq. According to Heraclides Ponticus, the philosopher remembered his personal identity in four different human lives before he was born into the world as Pythagoras (Diogenes Laertius, Vit. Philosoph. viii. 1. 4 sq.). See further E. Rohde,

Psyche[3] (Leipsic and Tübingen, 1903), ii. 417 sqq.

[2] Diogenes Laertius, Vit. Philosoph. viii. 1. 4 and 36.

[3] Jamblichus, De Pythagorica vita, xxiv. 107-109 ; Sextus Empiricus, ix. 127-130 ; Aulus Gellius, iv. 11.

[4] Diogenes Laertius, Vit. Philosoph. viii. 2. 77 ; H. Diels, Die Fragmente der Vorsokratiker,[2] i. (Berlin, 1906) p. 208, frag. 117.

[5] Sextus Empiricus, ix. 129 ; H. Diels, op. cit. i. pp. 213 sq., frag. 137.

philosopher in this respect is that, whereas the savage venerates and spares only animals of one particular species on the ground of their possible affinity to himself, the philosopher on his own shewing was bound to abstain from all animals whatever, since according to him the spirits of his deceased relatives might be lurking in creatures of any species. Hence while a faith in transmigration imposes but few restrictions on the diet of a savage, since it leaves him free to partake of the flesh of every sort of animals but one, the creed of Empedocles logically cut him off from a flesh diet altogether and compelled him to live on vegetables alone ; indeed, if he had been rigidly logical, he must have denied himself the use of vegetables also and perished of hunger, since on his theory vegetables as well as animals may house the souls of the dead.[1] However, like a wise man he sacrificed logic to life, and contented himself with forbidding his disciples the use of a few vegetables, such as beans and laurels,[2] while he suffered them to browse freely on all the rest.

So far as we can gather the real opinions of Pythagoras and Empedocles from the traditional history of the one and the miserably mutilated writings of the other, they seem both, like Buddha, with whom they had much in common, to have used the old savage doctrine of the transmigration of souls mainly as a handle by which to impress on the minds of their followers the necessity of leading an innocent, pure, and even ascetic life in this world as the only means of ensuring a blissful or at all events an untroubled eternity in a world to come.[3] At least this is fairly certain for Empedocles, whose views are comparatively well known to us through the fragments of his philosophical writings. From these utterances of his, the genuineness of which seems to be beyond suspicion, we gather that the psychology of Empedocles was a curious blend of savagery and mysticism. He regarded the incarnation of the human soul in a body of any sort as a punishment for sin, a degradation, a fall from heaven, an

The doctrine of transmigration used by Pythagoras and Empedocles mainly to inculcate certain ethical precepts.

The pessimism of Empedocles unlike the ordinary Greek view of life ; its similarity to Buddhism.

---

[1] Compare Sextus Empiricus, ix. 127-130.
[2] Plutarch, *Quaest. Conviv.* iii. 1. 2. 7 ; Aulus Gellius, iv. 11. 9 ; H. Diels,

op. cit. i. p. 214, fragments 140, 141.
[3] As to Pythagoras in this respect, see E. Rohde, *Psyche*[3] (Tübingen and Leipsic, 1903), ii. 161 *sqq.*

exile from God, a banishment from a world of bliss to a world of woe.[1] He describes the earth as a cavern,[2] a joyless land, where men wander in darkness, a prey to murder and revenge, to swarms of foul fiends, to wasting sickness and decay.[3] He speaks with pity and contempt of the life of mortals as a wretched and miserable existence, begotten of strife and sighs and prolonged as a punishment for their sins through a series of transmigrations, until, by the exercise of virtue, they have been born again as prophets, poets, physicians, and princes, and so return at last to communion with the gods to live thenceforth free from pain and sorrow, immortal, incorruptible, divine.[4] This view of human destiny, this passionate scorn poured on the present world, this ecstatic aspiration after a blissful eternity, the reward of virtue in a world to come, are very alien from the cheerful serenity, the calm rationalism of the ordinary Greek attitude towards existence on earth.[5] In his profound conviction of the manifold sufferings inseparable from mortality, in his longing to put off the burden of the body or what he calls "the garment of flesh," [6] in his tenderness for the lower animals and his strong sense of kinship with them, Empedocles resembled Buddha, whose whole cast of thought, however, was tinged with a still deeper shade of melancholy, a more hopeless outlook on the future. Yet so close in some respects is the similarity between the two that we might incline to suppose a direct influence of Buddhism on Empedocles, were it not that the dates of the two great thinkers, so far as they can be ascertained, appear to exclude the supposition.[7]

[1] Plutarch, *De exilio,* 17 ; *id., De esu carnium,* i. 7. 4 ; Clement of Alexandria, *Strom.* iv. 4. 12, p. 569 ed. Potter ; Hippolytus, *Refutatio omnium Haeresium,* vii. 29, p. 388 ed. L. Duncker and F. G. Schneidewin ; H. Diels, *op. cit.* i. pp. 207 *sq.,* fragments 115, 119.

[2] Porphyry, *De antro nympharum,* 8.

[3] H. Diels, *op. cit.* i. pp. 208 *sq.,* frag. 121.

[4] Clement of Alexandria, *Strom.* iii. 3. 14, iv. 23. 152, v. 14. 123, pp. 516 *sq.,* 632, 722 ed. Potter ; H. Diels, *Die Fragmente der Vorsokra-*

tiker,[2] i. (Berlin, 1906) pp. 207, 209, 215 *sq.,* fragments 115, 124, 144-147.

[5] Empedocles is cited by Aristotle as an example of the melancholy which he believed to be characteristic of men of genius. See Aristotle, *Problem.* 30, p. 953 a 27 ed. Im. Bekker.

[6] Stobaeus, *Eclogae,* i. 41. 60 (vol. i. p. 331 ed. A. Meineke) ; Plutarch, *De esu carnium* ii. 4. 4 ; H. Diels, *op. cit.* i. p. 210, frag. 126.

[7] It seems to be fairly certain that Buddha died and Empedocles was born somewhere about the year 480 B.C. Hence it is difficult to suppose that the

But if on its ethical side the teaching of Empedocles may almost be described as Buddhism relieved of its deepest shadows, on its scientific side it curiously antici- pated some speculations which have deeply stirred the European mind in our own and our fathers' days. For to his savage psychology and religious mysticism Empe- docles superadded a comprehensive and grandiose theory of the material universe, which presents a close analogy to that of Herbert Spencer. The scientific doctrine of the conservation of energy or, as he preferred to call it, the persistence of force, which Spencer made the corner-stone of his system, has its counterpart in the Empedoclean doctrine of the conservation or indestructibility of matter, the sum of which, according to him, remains always constant, never under- going either increase or diminution.[1]   Hence all the changes that take place in the physical world, according to Empe- docles, resolve themselves into the integration and disintegra- tion of matter, the composition and decomposition of bodies, brought about by the two antagonistic forces of attraction and repulsion, which in mythical language he called love and hate.   And just as all particular things are evolved by the force of attraction and dissolved by the force of repulsion, a state of concentration or aggregation in the individual per- petually alternating with a state of diffusion or segregation, so it is also with the material universe as a whole.   It, too, alternately contracts and expands according as the forces of attraction and repulsion alternately prevail.   For it was the opinion of Empedocles that a long, perhaps immeasurable, period of time, during which the force of attraction prevails over the force of repulsion, is succeeded by an equally long period in which the force of repulsion prevails over the force of attraction, each period lasting till, the predominant force being spent, its action is first arrested and then reversed by the opposite force ; so that the material universe performs a

Analogy of the physical specula- tions of Empe- docles to those of Herbert Spencer.

ideas of the former should have per- colated from India to Greece, or rather to Sicily, in the lifetime of the latter. As to their respective dates see H. Oldenberg, *Buddha* [5] (Stuttgart and Berlin, 1906), pp. 115, 227 ; E. Zeller, *Die Philosophie der Griechen*, i.[4]

(Leipsic, 1876) p. 678 note [1]

[1] Plutarch, *Adversus Coloten*, 10 ; Aristotle, *De Xenophane*, 2, p. 975 a 39-b 4 ed. Im. Bekker ; H. Diels, *op. cit.* i. pp. 175, 176, fragments 8 and 12.

periodic and rhythmic movement of alternate contraction and expansion, which never ceases except at the moments when, the two opposite forces exactly balancing each other, all things come to rest and equilibrium for a time, only however to return, with the backward sweep of the cosmic pendulum, to their former state either of consolidation or of dispersion. Thus under the influence of attraction and repulsion matter is constantly oscillating to and fro : at the end of a period of contraction it is gathered up in a solid globe : at the end of a period of expansion it is diffused throughout space in a state of tenuity which nowadays we might describe as gaseous. And this gigantic see-saw motion of the universe as a whole has gone on and will go on for ever and ever.[1]

Herbert Spencer's theory of alternate periods of concentration and dissipation of matter.

The imposing generalisation thus formulated by Empedocles in the fifth century before our era was enunciated independently in the nineteenth century of our era by Herbert Spencer. Like his Greek predecessor, the modern English philosopher held that the material universe passes through alternate periods of concentration and dissipation, of evolution and dissolution, according as the forces of attraction and repulsion alternately prevail. The terms in which he sums up his general conclusions might be used with hardly any change to describe the conclusions of Empedocles. For the sake of comparison it may be well to subjoin the passage. It runs as follows :—

" Thus we are led to the conclusion that the entire process of things, as displayed in the aggregate of the visible Universe, is analogous to the entire process of things as displayed in the smallest aggregates.

" Motion as well as matter being fixed in quantity, it would seem that the change in the distribution of Matter which Motion effects, coming to a limit in whichever direction it is carried, the indestructible Motion thereupon necessitates a reverse distribution. Apparently, the universally

[1] The evidence, consisting of the testimonies of ancient authorities and the fragments of Empedocles's own writings, is fully collected by H. Diels in his excellent work *Die Fragmente der Vorsokratiker*, Zweite Auflage, i. (Berlin, 1906) pp. 158 *sqq.*, 173 *sqq.* Compare *Fragmenta Philosophorum* *Graecorum*, ed. F. G. A. Mullach, i. (Paris, 1875) pp. 1 *sqq.*; H. Ritter et L. Preller, *Historia Philosophiae Graecae et Latinae ex fontium locis contexta*, Editio Quinta (Gothae, 1875), pp. 91 *sqq.* ; F. Zeller, *Die Philosophie der Griechen*, i.[4] (Leipsic, 1876) pp. 678 *sqq.*

coexistent forces of attraction and repulsion, which, as we have seen, necessitate rhythm in all minor changes throughout the Universe, also necessitate rhythm in the totality of its changes—produce now an immeasurable period during which the attractive forces predominating, cause universal concentration, and then an immeasurable period during which the repulsive forces predominating, cause universal diffusion —alternate eras of Evolution and Dissolution. And thus there is suggested the conception of a past during which there have been successive Evolutions analogous to that which is now going on ; and a future during which successive other such Evolutions may go on—ever the same in principle but never the same in concrete result." [1]

The most recent researches in physical science tend apparently rather to confirm than to invalidate these general views of the nature of the universe ; for if modern physicists are right in regarding the constitution of matter as essentially electrical, the antagonistic forces of attraction and repulsion postulated by Empedocles and Spencer would resolve themselves into positive and negative electricity. On the other hand the atomic disintegration which is now known to be proceeding in certain of the chemical elements, particularly in uranium and radium, and which is probably proceeding in all, suggests a doubt whether the universe is really, as Spencer supposed, in process of integration and evolution and not rather in process of disintegration and dissolution ; or whether perhaps the apparent evolution of the organic world is not attended by a simultaneous dissolution of the inorganic, so that the fabric of the universe would be a sort of Penelope's web, which the great artificer weaves and unweaves at the same time.[2] With such a grave doubt to

Evolution or dissolution.

---

[1] Herbert Spencer, *First Principles*, Third Edition (London, 1875), pp. 536 *sq.*

[2] On the discovery of the atomic disintegration of certain chemical elements, and the general question (Evolution or Dissolution ?) raised by that discovery, see W. C. D. Whetham, " The Evolution of Matter," in *Darwin and Modern Science* (Cambridge, 1909), pp. 565-582, particularly his concluding paragraph : " In the strict sense of the word, the process of atomic disintegration revealed to us by the new science of radio-activity can hardly be called evolution. In each case radio-active change involves the breaking up of a heavier, more complex atom into lighter and simpler fragments. Are we to regard this process as characteristic of the tendencies in accord with which the universe has reached its present state, and is passing to its unknown future ? Or have

trouble the outlook on the future, we may perhaps say that Empedocles was wiser than Herbert Spencer in leaving, as he apparently did, the question undecided, whether during the epoch open to human observation the force of attraction or that of repulsion has been and is predominant, and consequently whether matter as a whole is integrating or disintegrating, whether all things are gradually evolving into more complex and concentrated forms, or are gradually dissolving and wasting away, through simpler and simpler forms, into the diffused tenuity of their primordial constituents.

Empe-
docles as a
forerunner
of Darwin.   Just as in his view of the constitution and history of the physical universe Empedocles anticipated to some extent the theories of Spencer, so in his view of the development of living beings he anticipated to some extent the theories of Darwin ; for he held that the existing species of animals have been evolved out of inorganic matter through intermediate sorts of monstrous creatures, which, being ill fitted to survive, gradually succumbed and were exterminated in the struggle for existence.[1]   Whether Empedocles himself clearly enunciated the principle of the survival of the fittest as well as the doctrine of evolution, we cannot say with certainty ; but at all events it is significant that Aristotle, after stating for the first time the principle of the survival of the fittest, illustrates it by a reference to Empedocles's theory of the extinction of monstrous forms in the past, as if he understood the theory to imply the principle.[2]

we chanced upon an eddy in a backwater, opposed to the main stream of advance? In the chaos from which the present universe developed, was matter composed of large highly complex atoms, which have formed the simpler elements by radio-active or rayless disintegration? Or did the primaeval substance consist of isolated electrons, which have slowly come together to form the elements, and yet have left here and there an anomaly such as that illustrated by the unstable family of uranium and radium, or by some such course are returning to their state of primaeval simplicity?"

[1] H. Diels, *Die Fragmente der Vorsokratiker*,[2] i. (Berlin, 1906) pp. 190 *sqq.* ; *Fragmenta Philosophorum Grae-*

corum, ed. F. G. A. Mullach, i. (Paris, 1875) pp. 8 *sqq.* ; H. Ritter und L. Preller, *Historia Philosophiae Graecae et Latinae ex fontium locis contexta*[5] (Gothae, 1875), pp. 102 *sq.* ; E. Zeller, *Die Philosophie der Griechen*, i.[4] (Leipsic, 1876) pp. 718 *sqq.*

[2] Aristotle, *Physic. Auscult.* ii. 8, p. 198 b 29 *sqq.*, ed. Im. Bekker ; ὅπου μὲν οὖν ἅπαντα συνέβη ὥσπερ κἂν εἰ ἕνεκά του ἐγίνετο, ταῦτα μὲν ἐσώθη ἀπὸ τοῦ αὐτομάτου συστάντα ἐπιτηδείως · ὅσα δὲ μὴ οὕτως, ἀπώλετο καὶ ἀπόλλυται, καθάπερ Ἐμπεδοκλῆς λέγει τὰ βουγενῆ ἀνδρόπρωρα. This passage is quoted by Darwin in the "Historical Sketch" prefixed to *The Origin of Species* with the remark, "We here see the principle of natural selection shadowed

It is a remarkable instance of the strange complexities Empe-
and seeming inconsistencies of human nature, that a man docles as a
whose capacious mind revolved ideas so far-reaching and pretender to divinity
fruitful, should have posed among his contemporaries as a
prophet or even as a god, parading the streets of his native city
bedecked with garlands and ribbons and followed by obsequi-
ous crowds of men and women, who worshipped him and
prayed to him that he would reveal to them the better way,
that he would give them oracles and heal their infirmities.[1]
In the character of Empedocles, as in that of another fore-
runner of science, Paracelsus, the sterling qualities of the
genuine student would seem to have been alloyed with a
vein of ostentation and braggadocio; but the dash of the
mountebank which we may detect in his composition probably
helped rather than hindered him to win for a time the favour
and catch the ear of the multitude, ever ready as they are to
troop at the heels of any quack who advertises his wares by
a loud blast on a brazen trumpet. With so many claims on
the admiration of the wise and the adulation of the foolish,
we may almost wonder that Empedocles did not become the
founder, if not the god, of a new religion. Certainly other
human deities have set up in business and prospered with
an intellectual stock-in-trade much inferior to that of the
Sicilian philosopher. Perhaps Empedocles lacked that perfect sincerity of belief in his own pretensions without which
it seems difficult or impossible permanently to impose on
the credulity of mankind. To delude others successfully it
is desirable, if not absolutely necessary, to begin by being
one's self deluded, and the Sicilian sage was probably too
shrewd a man to feel perfectly at ease in the character of
a god.

The old savage doctrine of the transmigration of souls,
which Empedocles furbished up and passed off on his dis-

---

forth, but how little Aristotle fully
comprehended the principle, is shown
by his remarks on the formation of
the teeth." Darwin omits Aristotle's
reference to Empedocles, apparently
deeming it irrelevant or unimportant.
Had he been fully acquainted with the
philosophical speculations of Empedocles, we can scarcely doubt that

Darwin would have included him among
the pioneers of evolution.

[1] Diogenes Laertius, *Vit. Philosoph.*
viii. 2. 62 ; H. Diels, *Die Fragmente
der Vorsokratiker,*[2] i. (Berlin, 1906) p.
205, frag. 112. Compare *The Magic
Art and the Evolution of Kings,* i.
390.

The
doctrine of
the trans-
migration
of souls in
Plato.
ciples as a philosophical tenet, was afterwards countenanced,
if not expressly affirmed, by another Greek philosopher of a
very different stamp, who united, as no one else has ever
done in the same degree, the highest capacity for abstract
thought with the most exquisite literary genius.   But if he
borrowed the doctrine from savagery, Plato, like his two pre-
decessors, detached it from its rude original setting and fitted
it into an edifying moral scheme of retributive justice.   For he
held that the transmigration of human souls after death into
the bodies of animals is a punishment or degradation en-
tailed on the souls by the weaknesses to which they had
been subject or the vices to which they had been addicted in
life, and that the kind of animal into which a peccant soul
transmigrates is appropriate to the degree and nature of its
weakness or guilt.   Thus, for example, the souls of gluttons,
sots, and rakes pass into the bodies of asses ; the souls of
robbers and tyrants are born again in wolves and hawks ;
the souls of sober quiet people, untinctured by philosophy,
come to life as bees and ants ; a bad poet may turn at death
into a swan or a nightingale ; and a bad jester into an ape.
Nothing but a rigid practice of the highest virtue and a
single-minded devotion to abstract truth will avail to restore
such degraded souls to their human dignity and finally raise
them to communion with the gods.[1]   Though the passages
in which these views are set forth have a mythical colouring
and are, like all Plato's writings, couched in dramatic form
and put into the mouths of others, we need not seriously
doubt that they represent the real opinion of the philosopher
himself.[2]   It is interesting and instructive to meet with the
old savage theory of the transmigration of souls thus mas-
querading under a flowing drapery of morality and sparkling
with the gems of Attic eloquence in the philosophic system
of a great Greek thinker.   So curiously alike may be the
solutions which the highest and the lowest intellects offer of

---

[1] Plato, *Phaedo*, pp. 81 B-84 C; *Republic*, x. pp. 617 D-620 D ; *Timaeus*,
pp. 41 D-42 D ; *Phaedrus*, p. 249 B.

[2] This is the view of E. Zeller
(*Die Philosophie der Griechen*, ii.[3]
Leipsic, 1875, pp. 706 *sqq.*), Sir W.

E. Geddes (on Plato, *Phaedo*, p. 81 E),
and J. Adam (on Plato, *Republic*, x.
p. 618 A).   We have no right, with
some interpreters ancient and modern,
to dissolve the theory into an allegory
because it does not square with oui
ideas.

those profound problems which in all ages have engaged the curiosity and baffled the ingenuity of mankind.[1]

[1] In our own time the theory of transmigration is favoured by Dr. McTaggart, who argues that human beings may have lived before birth and may live many, perhaps an infinite number of, lives after death. Like Plato he further suggests that the nature of the body into which a person transmigrates at death may be appropriate to and determined by his or her character in the preceding life. See J. McT. Ellis McTaggart, *Some Dogmas of Religion* (London, 1906), pp. 112-139. However, Dr. McTaggart seems only to contemplate the transmigration of human souls into human bodies ; he does not discuss the possibility of their transmigration into animals.

CHAPTER XVII

TYPES OF ANIMAL SACRAMENT

§ 1. *The Egyptian and the Aino Types of Sacrament*

The ambiguous behaviour of the Aino and the Gilyaks towards bears explained.
WE are now perhaps in a position to understand the ambiguous behaviour of the Aino and Gilyaks towards the bear. It has been shewn that the sharp line of demarcation which we draw between mankind and the lower animals does not exist for the savage. To him many of the other animals appear as his equals or even his superiors, not merely in brute force but in intelligence ; and if choice or necessity leads him to take their lives, he feels bound, out of regard to his own safety, to do it in a way which will be as inoffensive as possible not merely to the living animal, but to its departed spirit and to all the other animals of the same species, which would resent an affront put upon one of their kind much as a tribe of savages would revenge an injury or insult offered to a tribesman. We have seen that among the many devices by which the savage seeks to atone for the wrong done by him to his animal victims one is to shew marked deference to a few chosen individuals of the species, for such behaviour is apparently regarded as entitling him to exterminate with impunity all the rest of the species upon which he can lay hands. This principle perhaps explains the attitude, at first sight puzzling and contradictory, of the Aino towards the bear. The flesh and skin of the bear regularly afford them food and clothing ; but since the bear is an intelligent and powerful animal, it is necessary to offer some satisfaction or atonement to the bear species for the loss which it sustains in the death of so many of its members. This satisfaction or atonement is

made by rearing young bears, treating them, so long as they live, with respect, and killing them with extraordinary marks of sorrow and devotion. So the other bears are appeased, and do not resent the slaughter of their kind by attacking the slayers or deserting the country, which would deprive the Aino of one of their means of subsistence.

Thus the primitive worship of animals assumes two forms, which are in some respects the converse of each other. On the one hand, animals are worshipped, and are therefore neither killed nor eaten. On the other hand, animals are worshipped because they are habitually killed and eaten. In both forms of worship the animal is revered on account of some benefit, positive or negative, which the savage hopes to receive from it. In the former worship the benefit comes either in the positive form of protection, advice, and help which the animal affords the man, or in the negative one of abstinence from injuries which it is in the power of the animal to inflict. In the latter worship the benefit takes the material form of the animal's flesh and skin. The two forms of worship are in some measure antithetical: in the one, the animal is not eaten because it is revered; in the other, it is revered because it is eaten. But both may be practised by the same people, as we see in the case of the North American Indians, who, while they apparently revere and spare their totem animals,[1] also revere the animals and fish upon which they subsist. The aborigines of Australia have totemism in the most primitive form known to us; but, so far as I am aware, there is no clear evidence that they attempt, like the North American Indians, to conciliate the animals which they kill and eat. The means which the Australians adopt to secure a plentiful supply of game appear to be primarily based, not on conciliation, but on sympathetic magic,[2] a principle to which the North American

Two forms of the worship of animals.

[1] This is known, for example, of the Yuchi Indians, for among them "members of each clan will not do violence to wild animals having the form and name of their totem. For instance, the Bear clan people never molest bears." See F. G. Speck, *Ethnology of the Yuchi Indians* (Philadelphia, 1909), p. 70. But in spite of the attention which has been paid to American totemism, we possess very little information as to the vital point of the system, the relation between a man and his totemic animal. Compare *Totemism and Exogamy*, iii. 88 *sq.*, 311.

[2] See *The Magic Art and the Evolution of Kings*, i. 85 *sqq.* However, Collins reports that among the

Indians also resort for the same purpose.[1] Hence, as the Australians undoubtedly represent a ruder and earlier stage of human progress than the American Indians, it would seem that before hunters think of worshipping the game as a means of ensuring an abundant supply of it, they seek to attain the same end by sympathetic magic.   This, again, would shew—what there is good reason for believing—that sympathetic magic is one of the earliest means by which man endeavours to adapt the agencies of nature to his needs.

Two types of animal sacrament, the Egyptian and the Aino type.   Corresponding to the two distinct types of animal worship, there are two distinct types of the custom of killing the animal god.   On the one hand, when the revered animal is habitually spared, it is nevertheless killed—and sometimes eaten—on rare and solemn occasions.   Examples of this custom have been already given and an explanation of them offered.   On the other hand, when the revered animal is habitually killed, the slaughter of any one of the species involves the killing of the god, and is atoned for on the spot by apologies and sacrifices, especially when the animal is a powerful and dangerous one ; and, in addition to this ordinary and everyday atonement, there is a special annual atonement, at which a select individual of the species is slain with extraordinary marks of respect and devotion.   Clearly the two types of sacramental killing—the Egyptian and the Aino types, as we may call them for distinction—are liable to be confounded by an observer ; and, before we can say to which type any particular example belongs, it is necessary to ascertain whether the animal sacramentally slain belongs

natives of New South Wales the women were "compelled to sit in their canoe, exposed to the fervour of the mid-day sun, hour after hour, chaunting their little song, and inviting the fish beneath them to take their bait " (D. Collins, *An Account of the English Colony in New South Wales*, London, 1804, p. 387). This may have been a form of conciliation like that employed by the American Indians towards the fish and game. But the account is not precise enough to allow us to speak with confidence. It is sometimes reported that the Australians

attempt to appease the kangaroos which they have killed, assuring the animals of their affection and begging them not to come back after death to torment them.   But the writer who mentions the report disbelieves it. See Dom Théophile Bérengier, in *Les Missions Catholiques*, x. (1878) p. 197.

[1] G. Catlin, *O-Kee-pa, a Religious Ceremony, and other Customs of the Mandans* (London, 1867), Folium reservatum ; Lewis and Clarke, *Travels to the Source of the Missouri River* (London, 1815), i. 205 *sq.*

to a species which is habitually spared, or to one which is habitually killed by the tribe. In the former case the example belongs to the Egyptian type of sacrament, in the latter to the Aino type.

The practice of pastoral tribes appears to furnish examples of both types of sacrament. "Pastoral tribes," says a learned ethnologist, "being sometimes obliged to sell their herds to strangers who may handle the bones disrespectfully, seek to avert the danger which such a sacrilege would entail by consecrating one of the herd as an object of worship, eating it sacramentally in the family circle with closed doors, and afterwards treating the bones with all the ceremonious respect which, strictly speaking, should be accorded to every head of cattle, but which, being punctually paid to the representative animal, is deemed to be paid to all. Such family meals are found among various peoples, especially those of the Caucasus. When amongst the Abchases the shepherds in spring eat their common meal with their loins girt and their staves in their hands, this may be looked upon both as a sacrament and as an oath of mutual help and support. For the strongest of all oaths is that which is accompanied with the eating of a sacred substance, since the perjured person cannot possibly escape the avenging god whom he has taken into his body and assimilated." [1] This kind of sacrament is of the Aino or expiatory type, since it is meant to atone to the species for the possible ill-usage of individuals. An expiation, similar in principle but different in details, is offered by the Kalmucks to the sheep, whose flesh is one of their staple foods. Rich Kalmucks are in the habit of consecrating a white ram under the title of "the ram of heaven" or "the ram of the spirit." The animal is never shorn and never sold; but when it

Examples of animal sacraments among pastoral tribes.

Aino or expiatory type of animal sacrament among the Abchases and Kalmuck.

[1] A. Bastian, in *Verhandlungen der Berliner Gesellschaft für Anthropologie, Ethnologie, und Urgeschichte,* 1870-71, p. 59. J. Reinegg (*Beschreibung des Kaukasus,* Gotha, St. Petersburg, and Hildesheim, 1796-97, ii. 12 *sq.*) describes what seems to be a sacrament of the Abghazses (Abchases). It takes place in the middle of autumn. A white ox called Ogginn appears from a holy cave, which is also called Ogginn. It is caught and led about amongst the assembled men (women are excluded) amid joyful cries. Then it is killed and eaten. Any man who did not get at least a scrap of the sacred flesh would deem himself most unfortunate. The bones are then carefully collected, burned in a great hole, and the ashes buried there.

grows old and its owner wishes to consecrate a new one, the old ram must be killed and eaten at a feast to which the neighbours are invited. On a lucky day, generally in autumn when the sheep are fat, a sorcerer kills the old ram, after sprinkling it with milk. Its flesh is eaten ; the skeleton, with a portion of the fat, is burned on a turf altar ; and the skin, with the head and feet, is hung up.[1]

Egyptian type of animal sacrament among the Todas and Madi.

An example of a sacrament of the Egyptian type is furnished by the Todas, a pastoral people of Southern India, who subsist largely upon the milk of their buffaloes. Amongst them "the buffalo is to a certain degree held sacred" and "is treated with great kindness, even with a degree of adoration, by the people."[2] They never eat the flesh of the cow buffalo, and as a rule abstain from the flesh of the male. But to the latter rule there is a single exception. Once a year all the adult males of the village join in the ceremony of killing and eating a very young male calf, —seemingly under a month old. They take the animal into the dark recesses of the village wood, where it is killed with a club made from the sacred tree of the Todas (the *tûde* or *Millingtonia*). A sacred fire having been made by the rubbing of sticks, the flesh of the calf is roasted on the embers of certain trees, and is eaten by the men alone, women being excluded from the assembly. This is the only occasion on which the Todas eat buffalo flesh.[3] The Madi or Moru tribe of Central Africa, whose chief wealth is their cattle, though they also practise agriculture, appear to kill a lamb sacramentally on certain solemn occasions. The custom is thus described by Dr. Felkin : " A remarkable custom is observed at stated times—once a year,

[1] A. Bastian, *Die Völker des östlichen Asien*, vi. (Jena, 1871) pp. 632, note. On the Kalmucks as a people of shepherds and on their diet of mutton, see J. G. Georgi, *Beschreibung aller Nationen des russischen Reichs* (St. Petersburg, 1776), pp. 406 *sq.*, compare p. 207 ; B. Bergmann, *Nomadische Streifereien unter den Kalmücken* (Riga, 1804-5), ii. 80 *sqq.*, 122 ; P. S. Pallas, *Reise durch verschiedene Provinzen des russischen Reichs* (St. Petersburg, 1771-1776), i.

319, 325. According to Pallas, it is only rich Kalmucks who commonly kill their sheep or cattle for eating ; ordinary Kalmucks do not usually kill them except in case of necessity or at great merry-makings. It is, therefore, especially the rich who need to make expiation.

[2] W. E. Marshall, *Travels amongst the Todas* (London, 1873), pp. 129 *sq.*

[3] W. E. Marshall, *op. cit.* pp. 80 *sq.*, 130.

I am led to believe. I have not been able to ascertain what exact meaning is attached to it. It appears, however, to relieve the people's minds, for beforehand they evince much sadness, and seem very joyful when the ceremony is duly accomplished. The following is what takes place : A large concourse of people of all ages assemble, and sit down round a circle of stones, which is erected by the side of a road (really a narrow path). A very choice lamb is then fetched by a boy, who leads it four times round the assembled people. As it passes they pluck off little bits of its fleece and place them in their hair, or on to some other part of their body. The lamb is then led up to the stones, and there killed by a man belonging to a kind of priestly order, who takes some of the blood and sprinkles it four times over the people. He then applies it individually. On the children he makes a small ring of blood over the lower end of the breast bone, on women and girls he makes a mark above the breasts, and the men he touches on each shoulder. He then proceeds to explain the ceremony, and to exhort the people to show kindness. . . . When this discourse, which is at times of great length, is over, the people rise, each places a leaf on or by the circle of stones, and then they depart with signs of great joy. The lamb's skull is hung on a tree near the stones, and its flesh is eaten by the poor. This ceremony is observed on a small scale at other times. If a family is in any great trouble, through illness or bereavement, their friends and neighbours come together and a lamb is killed ; this is thought to avert further evil. The same custom prevails at the grave of departed friends, and also on joyful occasions, such as the return of a son home after a very prolonged absence."[1] The sorrow thus manifested by the people at the annual slaughter of the lamb clearly indicates that the lamb slain is a sacred or divine animal, whose death is mourned by his worshippers,[2] just as the death of the sacred buzzard was mourned by the Californians and the death of the Theban ram by the

---

[1] R. W. Felkin, " Notes on the Madi or Moru Tribe of Central Africa," *Proceedings of the Royal Society of Edinburgh,* xii. (1882-84) pp. 336 *sq.*

[2] Mutton appears to be now eaten by the tribe as a regular article of food (R. W. Felkin, *op. cit.* p. 307), but this is not inconsistent with the original sanctity of the sheep.

Egyptians. The smearing each of the worshippers with the blood of the lamb is a form of communion with the divinity ;[1] the vehicle of the divine life is applied externally instead of being taken internally, as when the blood is drunk or the flesh eaten.

§ 2. *Processions with Sacred Animals*

Form of communion with a sacred animal by taking it from house to house.

Effigy of a snake carried from house to house by members of the Snake tribe.

The form of communion in which the sacred animal is taken from house to house, that all may enjoy a share of its divine influence, has been exemplified by the Gilyak custom of promenading the bear through the village before it is slain.[2] A similar form of communion with the sacred snake is observed by a Snake tribe in the Punjaub. Once a year in the month of September the snake is worshipped by all castes and religions for nine days only. At the end of August the Mirasans, especially those of the Snake tribe, make a snake of dough which they paint black and red, and place on a winnowing basket. This basket they carry round the village, and on entering any house they say :—

> " *God be with you all !*
> *May every ill be far !*
> *May our patron's (Gugga's) word thrive !* "

Then they present the basket with the snake, saying :—

> " *A small cake of flour :*
> *A little bit of butter :*
> *If you obey the snake,*
> *You and yours shall thrive !* "

Strictly speaking, a cake and butter should be given, but it is seldom done. Every one, however, gives something, generally a handful of dough or some corn. In houses where there is a new bride or whence a bride has gone, or where a son has been born, it is usual to give a rupee and a quarter, or some cloth. Sometimes the bearers of the snake also sing :—

> " *Give the snake a piece of cloth,*
> *And he will send a lively bride !* "

---

[1] See W. R. Smith, *Religion of the Semites*[2] (London, 1894), pp. 344 *sqq.* As to communion by means of an external application, see above, pp. 162 *sqq.*

[2] See above, pp. 190, 192.

When every house has been thus visited, the dough snake is buried and a small grave is erected over it. Thither during the nine days of September the women come to worship. They bring a basin of curds, a small portion of which they offer at the snake's grave, kneeling on the ground and touching the earth with their foreheads. Then they go home and divide the rest of the curds among the children. Here the dough snake is clearly a substitute for a real snake. Indeed, in districts where snakes abound the worship is offered, not at the grave of the dough snake, but in the jungles where snakes are known to be. Besides this yearly worship, performed by all the people, the members of the Snake tribe worship in the same way every morning after a new moon. The Snake tribe is not uncommon in the Punjaub. Members of it will not kill a snake, and they say that its bite does not hurt them. If they find a dead snake, they put clothes on it and give it a regular funeral.[1]

Ceremonies closely analogous to this Indian worship of the snake have survived in Europe into recent times, and doubtless date from a very primitive paganism. The best-known example is the "hunting of the wren." By many European peoples — the ancient Greeks and Romans, the modern Italians, Spaniards, French, Germans, Dutch, Danes, Swedes, English, and Welsh—the wren has been designated the king, the little king, the king of birds, the hedge king, and so forth,[2] and has been reckoned amongst those birds which it is extremely unlucky to kill. In England it is supposed that if any one kills a wren or harries its nest, he will infallibly break a bone or meet with some dreadful misfortune within the year;[3] sometimes it is thought that

"Hunting the Wren" in Europe.

Sacred character of the wren in popular superstition.

---

[1] *Panjab Notes and Queries,* ii. p. 91, § 555 (March 1885).
[2] See Ch. Vallancey, *Collectanea de rebus Hibernicis,* iv. (Dublin, 1786) p. 97; J. Brand, *Popular Antiquities* (London, 1882 - 1883), iii. 195 *sq.* (Bohn's ed.); Rev. C. Swainson, *Folklore of British Birds* (London, 1886), p. 36; E. Rolland, *Faune populaire de la France,* ii. 288 *sqq.* The names for the bird are βασιλίσκος, *regulus, rex avium* (Pliny, *Nat. Hist.* viii. 90, x. 203), *re di siepe, reyezuelo, roitelet, roi*

des oiseaux, Zaunkönig, etc. On the custom of hunting the wren see further N. W. Thomas, "The Scape-Goat in European Folklore," *Folk-lore,* xvii. (1906) pp. 270 *sqq.,* 280; Miss L. Eckstein, *Comparative Studies in Nursery Rhymes* (London, 1906), pp. 172 *sqq.* Miss Eckstein suggests that the killing of the bird called "the king" may have been a mitigation of an older custom of killing the real king.
[3] J. Brand, *Popular Antiquities,* iii. 194.

the cows will give bloody milk.[1]   In Scotland the wren is called "the Lady of Heaven's hen," and boys say :—

> " *Malisons, malisons, mair than ten,*
> *That harry the Ladye of Heaven's hen !* "[2]

At Saint Donan, in Brittany, people believe that if children touch the young wrens in the nest, they will suffer from the fire of St. Lawrence, that is, from pimples on the face, legs, and so on.[3]   In other parts of France it is thought that if a person kills a wren or harries its nest, his house will be struck by lightning, or that the fingers with which he did the deed will shrivel up and drop off, or at least be maimed, or that his cattle will suffer in their feet.[4]

Hunting the Wren in the Isle of Man.

Notwithstanding such beliefs, the custom of annually killing the wren has prevailed widely both in this country and in France.   In the Isle of Man down to the eighteenth century the custom was observed on Christmas Eve or rather Christmas morning.   On the twenty-fourth of December, towards evening, all the servants got a holiday ; they did not go to bed all night, but rambled about till the bells rang in all the churches at midnight.   When prayers were over, they went to hunt the wren, and having found one of these birds they killed it and fastened it to the top of a long pole with its wings extended.   Thus they carried it in procession to every house chanting the following rhyme :—

> " *We hunted the wren for Robin the Bobbin,*
> *We hunted the wren for Jack of the Can,*
> *We hunted the wren for Robin the Bobbin,*
> *We hunted the wren for every one.*"

When they had gone from house to house and collected all the money they could, they laid the wren on a bier and carried it in procession to the parish churchyard, where they made a grave and buried it "with the utmost solemnity, singing dirges over her in the Manks language, which they call her knell ; after which Christmas begins."   The burial

---

[1] R. Chambers, *Popular Rhymes of Scotland*, New Edition (London and Edinburgh, N.D.), p. 188.

[2] *Ibid.* p. 186.

[3] P. Sébillot, *Traditions et Superstitions de la Haute-Bretagne* (Paris,

1882), ii. 214.

[4] A. Bosquet, *La Normandie Romanesque et Merveilleuse* (Paris and Rouen, 1845), p. 221 ; E. Rolland, *op. cit.* ii. 294 *sq.* ; P. Sébillot, *l.c.* ; Rev. C. Swainson, *op. cit.* p. 42.

over, the company outside the churchyard formed a circle and danced to music. About the middle of the nineteenth century the burial of the wren took place in the Isle of Man on St. Stephen's Day (the twenty-sixth of December). Boys went from door to door with a wren suspended by the legs in the centre of two hoops, which crossed each other at right angles and were decorated with evergreens and ribbons. The bearers sang certain lines in which reference was made to boiling and eating the bird. If at the close of the song they received a small coin, they gave in return a feather of the wren; so that before the end of the day the bird often hung almost featherless. The wren was then buried, no longer in the churchyard, but on the seashore or in some waste place. The feathers distributed were preserved with religious care, it being believed that every feather was an effectual preservative from shipwreck for a year, and a fisherman would have been thought very foolhardy who had not one of them.[1] Even to the present time, in the twentieth century, the custom is generally observed, at least in name, on St. Stephen's Day, throughout the Isle of Man.[2]

A writer of the eighteenth century says that in Ireland the wren "is still hunted and killed by the peasants on Christmas Day, and on the following (St. Stephen's Day) he is carried about, hung by the leg, in the centre of two hoops, crossing each other at right angles, and a procession made in every village, of men, women, and children, singing an Irish catch, importing him to be the king of all birds."[3]   Down to

Hunting the Wren in Ireland and England.

---

[1] G. Waldron, *Description of the Isle of Man* (reprinted for the Manx Society, Douglas, 1865), pp. 49 *sqq.*; J. Train, *Account of the Isle of Man* (Douglas, 1845), ii. 124 *sqq.*, 141.

[2] In *The Morning Post* of Wednesday, 27th December 1911, we read that "the observance of the ancient and curious custom known as 'the hunt of the wren' was general throughout the Isle of Man yesterday. Parties of boys bearing poles decked with ivy and streamers went from house to house singing to an indescribable tune a quaint ballad detailing the pursuit and death of the wren, subsequently demanding recompense, which is rarely

refused. Formerly boys actually engaged in the chase, stoning the bird to death with the object of distributing the feathers 'for luck.'" From this account we may gather that in the Isle of Man the hunting of the wren is now merely nominal and that the pretence of it is kept up only as an excuse for collecting gratuities. It is thus that the solemnity of ritual dwindles into the pastime of children. I have to thank Mrs. J. H. Deane, of 41 Iverna Court, Kensington, for kindly sending me the extract from *The Morning Post*.

[3] Ch. Vallancey, *Collectanea de rebus Hibernicis*, iv. (Dublin, 1786) p. 97; J. Brand, *Popular Antiquities*, iii. 195.

the present time the "hunting of the wren" still takes place in parts of Leinster and Connaught. On Christmas Day or St. Stephen's Day the boys hunt and kill the wren, fasten it in the middle of a mass of holly and ivy on the top of a broom-stick, and on St. Stephen's Day go about with it from house to house, singing :—

> "*The wren, the wren, the king of all birds,*
> *St. Stephen's Day was caught in the furze;*
> *Although he is little, his family's great,*
> *I pray you, good landlady, give us a treat.*"

Money or food (bread, butter, eggs, etc.) were given them, upon which they feasted in the evening.[1] In Essex a similar custom used to be observed at Christmas, and the verses sung by the boys were almost identical with those sung in Ireland.[2] In Pembrokeshire a wren, called the King, used to be carried about on Twelfth Day in a box with glass windows surmounted by a wheel, from which hung various coloured ribbons. The men and boys who carried it from house to house sang songs, in one of which they wished joy, health, love, and peace to the inmates of the house.[3]

Hunting the Wren in France.   In the first half of the nineteenth century similar customs were still observed in various parts of the south of France. Thus at Carcassone, every year on the first Sunday of December the young people of the street Saint Jean used to go out of the town armed with sticks, with which they beat the bushes, looking for wrens. The first to strike down one of these birds was proclaimed King. Then they returned to the town in procession, headed by the King, who carried the

---

[1] G. H. Kinahan, "Notes on Irish Folk-lore," *Folk-lore Record*, iv. (1881) p. 108 ; Rev. C. Swainson, *Folk-lore of British Birds*, pp. 36 *sq.* ; E. Rolland, *Faune populaire de la France*, ii. 297 ; Professor W. Ridgeway, in *Academy*, 10th May 1884, p. 332 ; T. F. Thiselton Dyer, *British Popular Customs* (London, 1876), p. 497 ; L. L. Duncan, "Further Notes from County Leitrim," *Folk-lore*, v. (1894) p. 197. The custom is still, or was down to a few years ago, practised in County Meath, where the verses sung are practically the same as those in the

text. Wrens are scarce in that part of the country, "but as the boys go round more for the fun of dressing up and collecting money, the fact that there is no wren in their basket is quite immaterial." These particulars I learn from a letter of Miss A. H. Singleton, dated Appey-Leix, Ireland, 24th February 1904.

[2] W. Henderson, *Folk-lore of the Northern Counties* (London, 1879), p. 125.

[3] Rev. C. Swainson, *op. cit.* pp. 40 *sq.*

wren on a pole.   On the evening of the last day of the year
the King and all who had hunted the wren marched through
the streets of the town to the light of torches, with drums
beating and fifes playing in front of them.   At the door
of every house they stopped, and one of them wrote with
chalk on the door *vive le roi !* with the number of the year
which was about to begin.   On the morning of Twelfth Day
the King again marched in procession with great pomp,
wearing a crown and a blue mantle and carrying a sceptre.
In front of him was borne the wren fastened to the top of a
pole, which was adorned with a verdant wreath of olive, of oak,
and sometimes of mistletoe grown on an oak.   After hearing
high mass in the parish church of St. Vincent, surrounded by
his officers and guards, the King visited the bishop, the mayor,
the magistrates, and the chief inhabitants, collecting money to
defray the expenses of the royal banquet which took place
in the evening and wound up with a dance.[1]   At Entraigues
men and boys used to hunt the wren on Christmas Eve.
When they caught one alive they presented it to the priest,
who, after the midnight mass, set the bird free in the church.
At Mirabeau the priest blessed the bird.   If the men failed
to catch a wren and the women succeeded in doing so, the
women had the right to mock and insult the men, and to
blacken their faces with mud and soot, when they caught
them.[2]   At La Ciotat, near Marseilles, a large body of men
armed with swords and pistols used to hunt the wren every
year about the end of December.   When a wren was caught
it was hung on the middle of a pole, which two men carried,
as if it were a heavy burden.   Thus they paraded round the
town ; the bird was weighed in a great pair of scales ; and
then the company sat down to table and made merry.[3]

The parallelism between this custom of " hunting the

[1] Madame Clément, *Histoire des Fêtes civiles et religieuses*, etc., *de la Belgique Méridionale* (Avesnes, 1846), pp. 466-468 ; A. De Nore, *Coutumes, Mythes et Traditions des provinces de France* (Paris and Lyons, 1846), pp. 77 *sqq.* ; E. Rolland, *Faune populaire de la France*, ii. 295 *sq.* ; J. W. Wolf, *Beiträge zur deutschen Mythologie*, ii. (Göttingen, 1857) pp. 437 *sq.*   The ceremony was abolished at the revo-

lution of 1789, revived after the restoration, and suppressed again after 1830.
[2] E. Rolland, *op. cit.* ii. 296 *sq.*
[3] C. S. Sonnini, *Travels in Upper and Lower Egypt*, translated from the French (London, 1800), pp. 11 *sq.* ; J. Brand, *Popular Antiquities*, iii. 198. The " hunting of the wren " may be compared with a Swedish custom. On the 1st of May children rob the

Religious processions with sacred animals.

wren " and some of those which we have considered, especially the Gilyak procession with the bear, and the Indian one with the snake, seems too close to allow us to doubt that they all belong to the same circle of ideas. The worshipful animal is killed with special solemnity once a year ; and before or immediately after death he is promenaded from door to door, that each of his worshippers may receive a portion of the divine virtues that are supposed to emanate from the dead or dying god. Religious processions of this sort must have had a great place in the ritual of European peoples in prehistoric times, if we may judge from the numerous traces of them

Ceremony of beating a man clad in a cow's skin in the Highlands of Scotland.

which have survived in folk-custom. A well-preserved specimen is the following, which lasted in the Highlands of Scotland and in St. Kilda down at least to the latter half of the eighteenth century. It was described to Dr. Samuel Johnson in the island of Coll.[1] Another description of it runs as follows : " On the evening before New Year's Day it is usual for the cowherd and the young people to meet together, and one of them is covered with a cow's hide. The rest of the company are provided with

magpies' nests of both eggs and young. These they carry in a basket from house to house in the village and shew to the housewives, while one of the children sings some doggerel lines containing a threat that, if a present is not given, the hens, chickens, and eggs will fall a prey to the magpie. They receive bacon, eggs, milk, etc., upon which they afterwards feast. See L. Lloyd, *Peasant Life in Sweden* (London, 1870), pp. 237 *sq.* The resemblance of such customs to the " swallow song " and " crow song " of the ancient Greeks (on which see Athenaeus, viii. 59 *sq.*, pp. 359, 360) is obvious and has been remarked before now. Probably the Greek swallow-singers and crow-singers carried about dead swallows and crows or effigies of them. The " crow song " is referred to in a Greek inscription found in the south of Russia (ἐξ δεκάδας λυκάβας κεκορώνικα). See *Compte Rendu* of the Imperial Archaeological Commission, St. Petersburg, 1877, pp. 276 *sqq.* In modern Greece and Macedonia it is still customary for children on 1st March to go about the streets singing spring songs and carrying a wooden swallow, which is kept turning on a cylinder. See J. Grimm, *Deutsche Mythologie*,[4] ii. 636 ; A. Witzschel, *Sagen, Sitten und Gebräuche aus Thüringen* (Vienna, 1878), p. 301 ; G. F. Abbott, *Macedonian Folk-lore* (Cambridge, 1903), p. 18 ; J. C. Lawson, *Modern Greek Folklore and ancient Greek Religion* (Cambridge, 1910), p. 35. The custom of making the image of the swallow revolve on a pivot, which is practised in Macedonia as well as Greece, may be compared with the pirouetting of the girl in the Servian rain-making ceremony. The meaning of these revolutions is obscure. See *The Magic Art and the Evolution of Kings*, i. 273, 275.

[1] S. Johnson, *A Journey to the Western Islands of Scotland*, pp. 128 *sq.* (*The Works of Samuel Johnson, LL.D.*, edited by the Rev. R. Lynam, London, 1825, vol. vi.).

staves, to the end of which bits of raw hide are tied. The person covered with the hide runs thrice round the dwelling-house, *deiseil—i.e.* according to the course of the sun ; the rest pursue, beating the hide with their staves, and crying [here follows the Gaelic], ' Let us raise the noise louder and louder ; let us beat the hide.' They then come to the door of each dwelling-house, and one of them repeats some verses composed for the purpose. When admission is granted, one of them pronounces within the threshold the *beannachad-thurlair*, or verses by which he pretends to draw down a blessing upon the whole family [here follows the Gaelic], ' May God bless the house and all that belongs to it, cattle, stones, and timber ! In plenty of meat, of bed and body-clothes, and health of men, may it ever abound ! ' Then each burns in the fire a little of the bit of hide which is tied to the end of the staff. It is applied to the nose of every person and domestic animal that belongs to the house. This, they imagine, will tend much to secure them from diseases and other misfortunes during the ensuing year. The whole of the ceremony is called *colluinn*, from the great noise which the hide makes. It is the principal remnant of superstition among the inhabitants of St. Kilda." [1]

A more recent writer has described the old Highland custom as follows. Towards evening on the last day of the year, or Hogmanay, as the day is called in Scotland, " men began to gather and boys ran about shouting and laughing, playing shinty, and rolling ' pigs of snow ' (*mucan sneachda*), *i.e.* large snowballs. The hide of the mart or winter cow (*seiche a mhairt gheamhraidh*) was wrapped round the head of one of the men, and he made off, followed by the rest, belabouring the hide, which made a noise like a drum, with switches. The disorderly procession went three times *deiseal*, according to the course of the sun (*i.e.* keeping the house on the right hand) round each house in the village, striking the walls and shouting on coming to a door :

Another description of the Highland custom.

---

[1] John Ramsay, *Scotland and Scotsmen in the Eighteenth Century* (Edinburgh and London, 1888), ii. 438 *sq.* The custom is clearly referred to in the " Penitential of Theodore," quoted by Kemble, *Saxons in England*, i. 525 ; Ch. Elton, *Origins of English History* (London, 1882), p. 411 : " *Si quis in Kal. Januar. in cervulo vel vitula vadit, id est in ferarum habitus se communicant, et vestiuntur pellibus pecudum et assumunt capita bestiarum*," etc.

> ‘ *The* calluinn *of the yellow bag of hide,*
> *Strike the skin (upon the wall)*
> *An old wife in the graveyard,*
> *An old wife in the corner,*
> *Another old wife beside the fire,*
> *A pointed stick in her two eyes,*
> *A pointed stick in her stomach,*
> *Let me in, open this.’*

"Before this request was complied with, each of the revellers had to repeat a rhyme, called *Rann Calluinn* (*i.e.* a Christmas rhyme), though, as might be expected when the door opened for one, several pushed their way in, till it was ultimately left open for all. On entering each of the party was offered refreshments, oatmeal bread, cheese, flesh, and a dram of whisky. Their leader gave to the goodman of the house that indispensable adjunct of the evening's mummeries, the *Caisein-uchd*, the breast-stripe of a sheep wrapped round the point of a shinty stick. This was then singed in the fire (*teallach*), put three times with the right-hand turn (*deiseal*) round the family, and held to the noses of all. Not a drop of drink was given till this ceremony was performed. The *Caisein-uchd* was also made of the breast-stripe or tail of a deer, sheep, or goat, and as many as chose had one with them."[1] Another writer who gives a similar account of the ceremony and of the verses sung by the performers, tells us that the intention of putting the burnt sheep-skin to the noses of the people was to protect them against witchcraft and every infection.[2] The explanation, which is doubtless correct, reminds us of the extraordinarily persistent hold which the belief in sorcery and witchcraft has retained on the minds of the European peasantry. Formerly, perhaps, pieces of the cow-hide in which the man was clad were singed and put to the noses of the people, just as in the Isle of Man a feather of the wren used to be given to each household. Similarly, as we have seen, the human victim whom the Khonds slew as a divinity was taken from house to house, and every one

---

[1] J. G. Campbell, *Witchcraft and Second Sight in the Highlands and Islands of Scotland* (Glasgow, 1902), pp. 230-232. Shinty is the Scotch name for hockey: the game is played with a ball and curved sticks or clubs.

[2] R. Chambers, *Popular Rhymes of Scotland*, New Edition (London and Edinburgh, N.D.), pp. 166 *sq.*

strove to obtain a relic of his sacred person.[1] Such customs are only another form of that communion with the deity which is attained most completely by eating the body and drinking the blood of the god.

§ 3. The Rites of Plough Monday

In the "hunting of the wren," and the procession with the man clad in a cow-skin, there is nothing to shew that the customs in question have any relation to agriculture. So far as appears, they may date from a time before the invention of husbandry when animals were revered as divine in themselves, not merely as divine because they embodied the corn-spirit ; and the analogy of the Gilyak procession of the bear and the Indian procession of the snake is in favour of assigning the corresponding European customs to this very early date. On the other hand, there are certain European processions of animals, or of men disguised as animals, which may perhaps be purely agricultural in their origin ; in other words, the animals which figure in them may have been from the first nothing but representatives of the corn-spirit conceived in animal shape. Examples of such dramatic and at the same time religious rites have been collected by W. Mannhardt, who says of them in general : " Not only on the harvest field and on the threshing-floor but also quite apart from them people loved to represent the corn-spirit dramatically, especially in solemn processions in spring and about the winter solstice, whereby they meant to depict the return of the beneficent powers of summer to the desolate realm of nature." [2] Thus, for example, in country districts of Bohemia it is, or used to be, customary during the last days of the Carnival for young men to go about in procession from house to house collecting gratuities. Usually a man or boy is swathed from head to foot in pease-straw and wrapt round in straw-ropes : thus attired he goes by the name of the Shrovetide or Carnival Bear (*Fast-nachtsbär*) and is led from house to house to the accompaniment of music and singing. In every house he dances with

Proces-sions of men disguised as animals, in which the animal seems to represent the corn-spirit.

The Shrovetide Bear in Bohemia.

---

[1] See above, vol. i. pp. 246 *sq.*

[2] W. Mannhardt, *Antike Wald- und Feldkulte* (Berlin, 1877), p. 183.

the girls, the maids, and the housewife herself, and drinks to the health of the good man, the good wife, and the girls. For this performance the mummer is regaled with food by the good wife, while the good man puts money in his box. When the mummers have gone the round of the village, they betake themselves to the ale-house, whither also all the peasants repair with their wives ; " for at Shrovetide, but especially on Shrove Tuesday, every one must dance, if the flax, the vegetables, and the corn are to thrive ; and the more and the higher they dance, the greater the blessing which the people expect to crown their exertions." In the Leitmeritz district the Shrovetide Bear, besides being wrapt in straw, sometimes wears a bear's mask to emphasise his resemblance to the animal. In the Czech villages the housewives pluck the pease-straw and other straw from the Shrovetide Bear and put it in the nests of their geese, believing that the geese will lay more eggs and hatch their broods better for the addition of this straw to their nests. For a similar purpose in the Saaz district the women put the straw of the Shrovetide Bear in the nests of their hens.[1] In these customs the dancing for the express purpose of making the crops grow high,[2] and the use of the straw to make the geese and hens lay more eggs, sufficiently prove that the Shrovetide Bear is conceived to represent the spirit of fertility both animal and vegetable ; and we may reasonably conjecture that the dances of the mummer with the women and girls are especially intended to convey to them the fertilising powers of the spirit whom the mummer personates.[3]

---

[1] O. Freiherr von Reinsberg-Düringsfeld, *Fest- Kalender aus Böhmen* (Prague, N.D., preface dated 1861), pp. 49 - 52. Compare E. Cortet, *Essai sur les Fêtes Religieuses* (Paris, 1867), p. 83. Similar processions with a Shrovetide Bear take place among some of the German peasantry of Moravia, though there the mummer is said to be wrapt in skins and furs rather than in straw and to personate Winter. See W. Müller, *Beiträge zur Volkskunde der Deutschen in Mähren* (Vienna and Olmütz,

1893), p. 431. This latter interpretation may be due to a misunderstanding of the old custom.

[2] On this custom see *The Magic Art and the Evolution of Kings*, i. 137 *sqq.*

[3] Real bears and other animals were formerly promenaded about both town and country with rags of coloured cloth attached to them. Scraps of these cloths and hairs of the animals were given, rather perhaps sold, to all who asked for them as preservatives against sickness and the evil eye. The practice was condemned by the Council of Con·

In some parts of Bohemia the straw-clad man in these Shrovetide processions is called, not the Bear, but the Oats-goat, and he wears horns on his head to give point to the name.[1] These different names and disguises indicate that in some places the corn-spirit is conceived as a bear and in others as a goat. Many examples of the conception of the corn-spirit as a goat have already been cited ;[2] the conception of him as a bear seems to be less common. In the neighbourhood of Gniewkowo, in Prussian Lithuania, the two ideas are combined, for on Twelfth Day a man wrapt in pease-straw to represent a Bear and another wrapt in oats-straw to represent a Goat go together about the village ; they imitate the actions of the two animals and perform dances, for which they receive a present in every house.[3] At Marburg in Steiermark the corn-spirit figures now as a wolf and now as a bear. The man who gave the last stroke at threshing is called the Wolf. All the other men flee from the barn, and wait till the Wolf comes forth ; whereupon they pounce on him, wrap him in straw to resemble a wolf, and so lead him about the village. He keeps the name of Wolf till Christmas, when he is wrapt in a goat's skin and led from house to house as a Pease-bear at the end of a rope.[4] In this custom the dressing of the mummer in a goat's skin seems to mark him out as the representative of a goat ; so that here the mythical fancy of the people apparently hesitates between a goat, a bear, and a wolf as the proper embodiment of the corn-spirit. In Scandinavia the conception of the spirit as a goat who appears at Christmas (*Julbuck*) appears to be common. Thus, for example, in Bergslagshärad (Sweden) it used to be customary at Christmas to lead about a man completely wrapt in corn-straw and wearing a goat's horns on his head : he personated the Yule goat.[5] In some parts of Sweden a regular feature of the little Christmas drama is a pretence of slaughtering the Yule-goat, who, however, comes to life again. The actor,

---

stance. See J. B. Thiers, *Traité des Superstitions* (Paris, 1679), pp. 315 *sq.* We need not suppose that these animals represented the corn-spirit.

[1] W. Mannhardt, *Antike Wald- und Feldkulte*, pp 183 *sq.*

[2] See above, vol. i. pp. 281 *sqq.*

[3] W. Mannhardt, *op. cit.* p. 190.

[4] W. Mannhardt, *op. cit.* p. 188.

[5] W. Mannhardt, *op. cit.* pp. 191-193.

hidden by a coverlet made of skins and wearing a pair of
formidable horns, is led into the room by two men, who make
believe to slaughter him, while they sing verses referring to
the mantles of various colours, red, blue, white, and yellow,
which they laid on him, one after the other. At the conclusion of the song, the Yule-goat, after feigning death,
jumps up and skips about to the amusement of the
spectators.[1] In Willstad after supper on Christmas evening,
while the people are dancing " the angel dance " for the sake
of ensuring a good crop of flax, some long stalks of the
Yule straw, either of wheat or rye, are made up into the
likeness of a goat, which is thrown among the dancers with
the cry, "Catch the Yule-goat!" The custom in Dalarne
is similar, except that there the straw-animal goes by the
name of the Yule-ram.[2] In these customs the identification
of the Yule-goat or the Yule-ram with the corn-spirit seems
unmistakable. As if to clinch the argument it is customary
in Denmark and Sweden to bake cakes of fine meal at
Christmas in the form of goats, rams, or boars. These are
called Yule-goats, Yule-rams, or Yule-boars ; they are often
made out of the last sheaf of corn at harvest and kept till
sowing-time, when they are partly mixed with the seed-corn
and partly eaten by the people and the plough-oxen in the
hope thereby of securing a good harvest.[3] It would seem
scarcely possible to represent the identification of the corn-
spirit with an animal, whether goat, ram, or boar, more
graphically ; for the last corn cut at harvest is regularly
supposed to house the corn-spirit, who is accordingly caught,
kept through the winter in the shape of an animal, and then
mixed with the seed in spring to quicken the grain before it
is committed to the ground. Examples of the corn-spirit
conceived as a wether and a boar have met us in a preceding
part of this work.[4] The pretence of killing the Yule-goat
and bringing him to life again was probably in origin a
magical rite to ensure the rebirth of the corn-spirit in spring.

The Straw-bear at Whittlesey. In England a custom like some of the preceding still
prevails at Whittlesey in Cambridgeshire on the Tuesday

---

[1] L. Lloyd, *Peasant Life in Sweden*
(London, 1870), pp. 184 *sq.*; W.
Mannhardt, *op. cit.* pp. 196 *sq.*

[2] W. Mannhardt, *op. cit.* p. 196.
[3] W. Mannhardt, *op. cit.* pp. 197 *sq.*
[4] See above, vol. i. pp. 275, 298 *sqq.*

after Plough Monday, as I learn from an obliging communication of Professor G. C. Moore Smith of Sheffield University. He writes : " When I was at Whittlesey yesterday I had the pleasure of meeting a ' Straw-bear,' if not two, in the street. I had not been at Whittlesey on the day for nearly forty years, and feared the custom had died out. In my boyhood the Straw - bear was a man completely swathed in straw, led by a string by another and made to dance in front of people's houses, in return for which money was expected. This always took place on the Tuesday following Plough-Monday. Yesterday the Straw-bear was a boy, and I saw no dancing. Otherwise there was no change." [1]

A comparison of this English custom with the similar Continental customs which have been described above, raises a presumption that the Straw-bear, who is thus led about from house to house, represents the corn-spirit bestowing his blessing on every homestead in the village. This interpretation is strongly confirmed by the date at which the ceremony takes place. For the date is the day after Plough Monday, and it can hardly be doubted that the old popular celebration of Plough Monday has a direct reference to agriculture. Plough Monday is the first Monday of January after Twelfth Day. On that day it used to be the custom in various parts of England for a band of sturdy swains to drag a gaily decorated plough from house to house and village to village, collecting contributions which were afterwards spent in rustic revelry at a tavern. The men who drew the plough were called Plough Bullocks ; they wore their shirts over their coats, and bunches of ribbons flaunted from their hats and persons. Among them there was always one who personated a much bedizened old woman called Bessy ; under his gown he formerly had a bullock's tail fastened to him behind, but this appendage was afterwards discarded. He skipped, danced and cut capers, and carried a money-box soliciting contributions from the onlookers. Some of the band, in addition to their ribbons, " also wore small bunches of corn in their hats, from which

The ceremonies of Plough Monday in England.

---

[1] Letter of Professor G. C. Moore Smith, dated The University, Sheffield, 13th January, 1909.

the wheat was soon shaken out by the ungainly jumping which they called dancing. Occasionally, if the winter was severe, the procession was joined by threshers carrying their flails, reapers bearing their sickles, and carters with their long whips, which they were ever cracking to add to the noise, while even the smith and the miller were among the number, for the one sharpened the plough-shares and the other ground the corn ; and Bessy rattled his box and danced so high that he shewed his worsted stockings and corduroy breeches ; and very often, if there was a thaw, tucked up his gown skirts under his waistcoat, and shook the bonnet off his head, and disarranged the long ringlets that ought to have concealed his whiskers." Sometimes among the mummers there was a Fool, who wore the skin of a calf with the tail hanging down behind, and wielded a stick with an inflated bladder tied to it, which he applied with rude vigour to the heads and shoulders of the human team. Another mummer generally wore a fox's skin in the form of a hood with the tail dangling on his back. If any churl refused to contribute to the money-box, the plough-bullocks put their shoulders to the plough and ploughed up the ground in front of his door.[1]

The object of the dances on Plough Monday is probably to ensure the growth of the corn. The clue to the meaning of these curious rites is probably furnished by the dances or rather jumps of the men who wore bunches of corn in their hats. When we remember how often on the Continent about the same time of year the peasants dance and jump for the express purpose

---

[1] R. Chambers, *The Book of Days* (London and Edinburgh, 1886), i. 94 *sq.*; J. Brand, *Popular Antiquities*, New Edition (London, 1883), i. 506 *sqq.*; T. F. Thiselton Dyer, *British Popular Customs* (London, 1876), pp. 37 *sqq.* ; O. Freiherr von Reinsberg-Düringsfeld, *Das festliche Jahr* (Leipsic, 1863), pp. 27 *sq.* Compare W. Mannhardt, *Baumkultus* (Berlin, 1875), pp. 557 *sq.* ; T. Fairman Ordish, " English Folk-drama," *Folk-lore*, iv. (1893) pp. 163 *sqq.*; *Folk-lore*, viii. (1897) p. 184; E. K. Chambers, *The Mediaeval Stage* (Oxford, 1903), i. 208-210 ; H. Munro Chadwick, *The Origin of the English Nation* (Cambridge, 1907), p. 238. Counties in which the custom of Plough Monday is reported to have been observed are Norfolk, Cambridgeshire, Huntingdonshire, Northamptonshire, Lincolnshire, Leicestershire, Nottinghamshire, Derbyshire, Cheshire, and Yorkshire. Thus the custom would seem to have been characteristic of a group of counties in the centre of England. In January 1887, I witnessed the ceremony in the streets of Cambridge. Wooden ploughs of a primitive sort were dragged about by bands of young men who were profusely decked with scarves and ribbons. They ran at a good pace, and beside them ran a companion with a money-box collecting donations. Amongst them I did not observe any woman or man in female attire. Compare *The Folk-lore Journal*, v. (1887) p. 161.

of making the crops grow tall, we may conjecture with some probability that the intention of the dancers on Plough Monday was similar ; the original notion, we may suppose, was that the corn would grow that year just as high as the dancers leaped. If that was so, we need not wonder at the agility displayed on these occasions by the yokels in general and by Bessy in particular. What stronger incentive could they have to exert themselves than the belief that the higher they leaped into the air the higher would sprout the corn-stalks ? In short, the whole ceremony was probably a magical rite intended to procure a good crop. The principle on which it rested was the familiar one of homoeopathic or imitative magic : by mimicking the act of ploughing and the growth of the corn the mummers hoped to ensure the success of the real ploughing, which was soon to take place.

If such was the real meaning of the ritual of Plough Monday, we may the more confidently assume that the Straw-bear who makes his appearance at Whittlesey in Cambridgeshire on the day after Plough Monday represents indeed the corn-spirit. What could be more appropriate than for that beneficent being to manifest himself from house to house the very day after a magical ceremony had been performed to quicken the growth of the corn ?

The Straw-bear a representative of the corn-spirit.

The foregoing interpretation of the rites observed in England on Plough Monday tallies well with the explanation which I have given of the very similar rites annually performed at the end of the Carnival in Thrace.[1] The mock ploughing is probably practised for the same purpose in both cases, and what that purpose is may be safely inferred from the act of sowing and the offering of prayers for abundant crops which accompany and explain the Thracian ceremony. It deserves to be noted that ceremonies of the same sort and closely resembling those of Plough Monday are not confined to the Greek villages of Thrace but are observed also by the Bulgarians of that province at the same time, namely, on the Monday of the last week in Carnival. Thus at Malko-Tirnovsko, in the district of Adrianople, a procession of mummers goes through the streets on that day.

The rites of Plough Monday resemble the rites at the end of the Carnival in Thrace.

Similar rites are performed at the same time by the Bulgarian peasants of Thrace.

---

[1] See above, vol. i. pp. 25 *sqq.*

The principal personages in it bear the names of the *Kuker*
and *Kukerica*. The *Kuker* is a man clad in a goatskin. His
face is blackened with soot and he wears on his head a high
shaggy hat made of an entire skin. Bells jingle at his girdle,
and in his hand he carries a club. The *Kukerica*, who sometimes goes by the name of *Baba*, that is, "Old Woman," is
a man disguised in petticoats with his face blackened. Other
figures in the procession are young men dressed as girls, and
girls dressed as men and wearing masks. Bears are represented by dogs wrapt in bearskins. A king, a judge, and
other officials are personated by other mummers; they
hold a mock court and those whom they condemn receive
a bastinado. Some of the maskers carry clubs; it is their
duty to beat all who fall into their hands and to levy contributions from them. The play and gestures of the *Kuker*
and *Kukerica* are wanton and lascivious : the songs and
cries addressed to the *Kuker* are also very cynical. Towards
evening two of the company are yoked to a plough, and the
Kuker ploughs a few furrows, which he thereupon sows with
corn. After sunset he puts off his disguise, is paid for his
trouble, and carouses with his fellows. The people believe
that the man who plays the part of *Kuker* commits a deadly
sin, and the priests make vain efforts to abolish the custom.
At the village of Kuria, in the district of Losengrad, the
custom is in general the same, but there are some significant
variations. The money collected by the mummers is used
to buy wine, which is distributed among all the villagers at
a banquet in the evening. On this occasion a cake in which
an old coin has been baked is produced by the *Kuker*, broken
into bits, and so divided among all present. If the bit with
the coin in it falls to a farmer, then the crops will be good
that year ; but if it falls to a herdsman, then the cattle will
thrive. Finally, the *Kuker* ploughs a small patch of ground,
"bending his body to right and left in order to indicate
symbolically the ears of corn bending under the weight of
the grain." The others lay hold of the man with whom the
coin was found, bind him by the feet, and drag him over the
land that has just been ploughed.[1]   In these observances the

---

[1] G. Kazarow, "Karnevalbräuche in Bulgarien," *Archiv für Religions·
wissenschaft*, xi. (1908) pp. 407 *sq.*

intention of promoting the fertility of the ground is unmis- The inten-
takable ; the ploughman's imitation of the cornstalks bend- tion of the
rites is
ing under their own weight is a simple case of homoeopathic clearly to
or imitative magic, while the omens drawn from the occupa- fertilise the
ground.
tion of the person who obtains the piece of cake with the
coin in it indicate that the ceremony is designed to quicken
the herds as well as the crops.   We can hardly doubt that
the same serious motive underlies the seemingly wanton
gestures of the principal actors and explains the loose
character of the songs and words which accompany the
ceremony.   Nor is it hard to divine the reason for dragging
over the fresh furrows the man who is lucky enough to get
the coin in the cake.   He is probably looked on as an
embodiment of the corn-spirit, and in that character is compelled to fertilise the ground by bodily contact with the
newly-ploughed earth.

Similar customs are observed at the Carnival not only Similar
by Bulgarian peasants in Thrace but also here and there in customs
are ob-
Bulgaria itself.   In that country the leading personage of the served at
masquerade is the *Baba*, that is, the Old Woman or Mother. the Carnival in
The part is played by a man in woman's clothes ; she, or Bulgaria.
rather he, wears no mask, but in many villages she carries a
spindle with which she spins.   The *Kuker* and the *Kukerica*
also figure in the performance, but they are subordinate to
the Old Woman or Mother.   Their costume varies in
different villages.   Usually they are clad in skins with
a girdle of lime-tree bark and five or six bells fastened to
it ; on their back they wear a hump made up of rags.   But
the principal feature in their attire consists of their masks,
which represent the heads of animals and men in fantastic
combinations, such as the horned head of a man or a bird,
the head of a ram, a bull, and so on.   Much labour is spent
on the manufacture of these masks.   Early in the morning
of Cheese Monday (the Monday of the last week in Carnival)
the mummers go about the village levying contributions.
Towards noon they form a procession and go from house to
house.   In every house they dance a round dance, while
the Old Woman spins.   It is believed that if any householder contrives to carry off the Old Woman and secrete
her, a blessing and prosperity will enter into his dwelling ;

but the maskers defend the Old Woman stoutly against all such attempts of individuals to appropriate her beneficent presence. After the dance the mummers receive gifts of money, eggs, meal, and so on. Towards evening a round dance is danced in the village square, and there the Old Woman yokes the *Kuker* and *Kukerica* to a plough, ploughs with it a small piece of ground, and sows the ground with corn. Next day the performers reassemble, sell the presents they had collected, and with the produce hold a feast in the house of the Old Woman. It is supposed that if strange maskers make their way into a village, fertility will be drawn away to the village from which they have come ; hence the villagers resist an inroad of strange maskers at any price. In general the people believe that the masquerade is performed for the purpose of increasing the luck and fertility of the village.[1]

In these Bulgarian rites, accordingly, we are not left to form conjectures as to the intention with which they are practised ; that intention is plainly avowed, and it is no other than the one which we have inferred for the similar rites observed in Thrace at the same season and in England on Plough Monday. In all these cases it is reasonable to suppose that the real aim of the ceremonial ploughing and sowing of the ground is thereby, on the principles of homoeopathic or imitative magic, to ensure the growth of the corn on all the fields of the community. Perhaps we may go a step further and suggest that in the Bulgarian Old Woman or Mother, who guides the plough and sows the seed, and whose presence is believed to bring a blessing to any household that can contrive to appropriate her, we have the rustic prototype of Demeter, the Corn-Mother, who in the likeness of an Old Woman brought a blessing to the house of Celeus, king of Eleusis, and restored their lost fertility to the fallow Eleusinian fields. And in the pair of mummers, man and woman, who draw the plough, may we not discern the rude originals of Pluto and Persephone ? If that is so, the gods of Greece are not wholly dead ; they still hide their diminished heads in the cottages of the

In all these cases the ceremonial ploughing and sowing are probably charms to ensure the growth of the crops.

---

[1] G. Kazarow, " Karnevalbräuche in Bulgarien," *Archiv für Religionswissenschaft*, xi. (1908) pp. 408 *sq.*

peasantry, to come forth on sunshine holidays and parade, with a simple but expressive pageantry, among a gazing crowd of rustics, at the very moment of the year when their help is most wanted by the husbandman.

Be that as it may, these rites still practised by the peasantry at opposite ends of Europe, no doubt date from an extremely early age in the history of agriculture. They are probably far older than Christianity, older even than those highly developed forms of Greek religion with which ancient writers and artists have made us familiar, but which have been for so many centuries a thing of the past. Thus it happens that, while the fine flower of the religious consciousness in myth, ritual, and art is fleeting and evanescent, its simpler forms are comparatively stable and permanent, being rooted deep in those principles of common minds which bid fair to outlive all the splendid but transient creations of genius. It may be that the elaborate theologies, the solemn rites, the stately temples, which now attract the reverence or the wonder of mankind, are destined themselves to pass away like " all Olympus' faded hierarchy," and that simple folk will still cherish the simple faiths of their nameless and dateless forefathers, will still believe in witches and fairies, in ghosts and hobgoblins, will still mumble the old spells and make the old magic passes, when the muezzin shall have ceased to call the faithful to prayer from the minarets of St. Sophia, and when the worshippers shall gather no more in the long-drawn aisles of Nôtre Dame and under the dome of St. Peter's.

Such rites no doubt date from a remote antiquity

NOTE

AMONG the Garos, an agricultural tribe of Assam, the close of the rice-harvest is celebrated by a festival in which the effigy of a horse figures prominently. The intention of the ceremony is not stated, but possibly it may be to ensure a good rice crop in the following year. If so, the artificial horse of the Garos would be analogous to the October horse of the Romans, as that animal has been explained by W. Mannhardt. For the sake of comparison it may be well to subjoin Major A. Playfair's account of the Garo ceremony :—[1]

Effigy of a horse in a harvest festival of the Garos.

"When the rice harvest has been fully gathered in, the great sacrifice and festival of the year, the *Wangala* or *Guréwata*, takes place. This is the most festive observance of the year, and combines religious sacrifice with much conviviality. It is celebrated by all sections of the tribe except the Duals and some Plains Garos. The cost of the entertainment falls principally on the *nokma* [headman] of the village, who provides a pig to be eaten by his guests, and plenty of liquor. Among the Akawés and Chisaks of the north and north-eastern hills a curious feature of the ceremony is the manufacture of *guré* or 'horses' out of pieces of plantain-stem for the body, and of bamboo for the head and legs. The image of the 'horse' is laid on the floor of the *nokma's* house, and the assembled guests dance and sing around it the whole night long, with the usual intervals for refreshments. Early the next morning, the 'horse' is taken to the nearest river and launched on the water to find its way down stream on the current. For those who possess the necessary paraphernalia, the *guré* takes the shape of a horse's head of large size, made of straw, and covered with cloth. I once saw one in the village of Rongrong, which, when in use, was ornamented with discs of brass on both sides of the face. Its eyes and ears were made of the same metal, and between the ears were fixed a pair of wild goat's horns. To the head were attached a number

Major Playfair's description of the festival.

[1] Major A. Playfair, *The Garos* (London, 1909), pp. 94 *sq.*

337

of bronze bells similar to those hawked about by Bhutia pedlars. The owner, a *laskar*, was unable to tell me whence they came, but said that they were inherited from his wife's mother, and were many generations old.

Dance of a man wearing the mask of a horse's head.

"The manner in which this form of *guré* is used is the following. The head is mounted on a stick, which a man holds before him in such a way that the head comes up to the level of his chest. Two straps pass over his shoulders to relieve his hands of the weight. The body of the 'horse' is then built round his own body with cane and cloth. For a tail, yak's tails are fastened in with his own hair, which, for the occasion, is allowed to hang down instead of being tied up. The performer thus apparelled, commences to dance a shuffling step to the usual music. In front of him dances the priest, who goes through the pantomime of beckoning the animal to come to him. The remaining guests of the *nokma* [headman] form a *queue* behind the 'horse,' and dance after it. When the first man gets tired, another takes his place, and the dancing goes on right through the night. A pleasant part of the performance is the pelting of the *guré* with eggs. A piece of egg-shell was still sticking to the horn of the *guré* which was shown to me.

"Strictly speaking, this festival should last for three days and two nights. When it is over, the *guré* is taken to a stream and the body thrown into the water, the head being preserved for another year. The people who come to see it off, bring rice with them, and a meal by the water's edge closes the proceedings.

"At the *Wangala*, it is the custom to mix flour with water, and for the assembled people to dip their hands into the mixture and make white hand-marks on the posts and walls of the house and on the backs of the guests."

The effigy of the horse at rice-harvest perhaps represents the spirit of the rice.

Can it be that the horse whose effigy is thus made at rice-harvest and thrown into the water, while the head is kept for another year, represents the spirit of the rice? If that were so, the pelting of the head with eggs would be a charm to ensure fertility and the throwing of it into water would be a rain-charm. And on the same theory the horse's head would be comparable to the horse-headed Demeter of Phigalia[1] as well as to the head of the October horse at Rome, which was nailed to a wall, probably to be kept there till next October. If we knew more about the rites of the horse-headed Demeter at Phigalia, we might find that amongst them was a dance of a man or woman who wore the mask of a horse's head and personated the goddess herself, just as, if I am right, the man who dances disguised as a horse at the harvest festival of the Garos, represents the spirit of the rice dancing among the garnered sheaves. The conjecture is to some extent supported by the remains

[1] See above, p. 21.

of the magnificent marble drapery, which once adorned the colossal statue of Demeter or Persephone in the sanctuary of the two goddesses at Lycosura, in Arcadia ; for on that drapery are carved rows of semi-human, semi-bestial figures dancing and playing musical instruments ; the bodies of the figures are those of women, but their heads, paws, and feet are those of animals.   Among the heads set on the figures are those of a horse, a pig, a cat or a hare, and apparently an ass.[1] It is reasonable to suppose that these dancing figures represent a ritual dance which was actually performed in the rites of Demeter and Persephone by masked men or women, who personated the goddesses in their character of beasts.

[1] See my note on Pausanias, viii. 37. 3 (vol. iv. pp. 375 *sqq.*).

INDEX